a handbook for students from overseas
and their advisers

Higher Education
in the United Kingdom
1978-80

published for The British Council
and The Association of Commonwealth Universities
by Longman Group Ltd

Published for The British Council and
The Association of Commonwealth Universities by
Longman Group Ltd, Longman House, Burnt Mill, Harlow, Essex CM20 2JE

Issued every two years
by
The British Council
10 Spring Gardens, London SW1A 2BN
and
The Association of Commonwealth Universities
36 Gordon Square, London WC1H 0PF

First published 1936
Seventeenth revised edition 1978

ISBN 0 582 02116 2

Printed by T. & A. Constable Ltd, Edinburgh

Cover photograph by courtesy of the University of Southampton (Teaching Media Department).
Photographs by courtesy of the University College of North Wales, Bangor, pp 39, 44 and 72;
Queen's University, Belfast, p 30; Robert Gordon's Institute of Technology, Aberdeen, pp 35
and 54; St Andrews University, pp 51 and 61; Trent Polytechnic, Nottingham, p 25.

JM4LZ

FOREWORD

by Frank Thistlethwaite MA, LHD, FRHistS
Vice-Chancellor of the University of East Anglia

Almost as soon as the first universities established themselves in the early Middle Ages students were flocking to them from all over the known civilised world and their teachers moved freely between them across political boundaries as a matter of course. That tradition persists and universities remain the most international of institutions. This is especially true of the universities of the United Kingdom which greatly cherish their international role and their responsibilities as hosts to overseas students. With English increasingly becoming the common language of scholarship and technology, British universities and colleges offer a readily accessible and rich variety of academic disciplines and types of professional education. Indeed the courses listed in this handbook may appear even bewildering in their variety; however, you as an overseas student should be assured that they all lead to degrees, diplomas or certificates which are monitored to common national standards and you need have no concern about the value and international standing of the currency of the particular qualification you will achieve. You should also be able to count on personal teaching and counselling. British universities and colleges still enjoy a favourable ratio of teachers to taught which enables them to maintain not only a certain intensity of teaching but a tradition of personal guidance and concern which can be especially helpful to you students from abroad in adjusting to your life and work in Britain.

CONTENTS

DIRECTORY OF SUBJECTS: MAIN SUBJECT HEADINGS

Accountancy
Acoustics
African Languages and Studies
Agriculture and Forestry
Anaesthetics
Anatomy
Anthropology
Archaeology
Architecture
Art and Design
Arts and/or Science (Joint or Combined)
Arts (General)
Astronomy and Space Science
Aviation, Civil
Bacteriology
Ballet and Modern Dance
Banking
Biochemistry
Biology
Biophysics
Building Science and Technology
Business and Management Studies
Canadian Studies
Cancer Research
Cardiology
Chemistry
Chest Diseases
Chiropody
Commonwealth Studies
Computer Science and Technology
Criminology
Crystallography
Dentistry
Dermatology
Development Studies
Dietetics and Nutrition
Drama and Theatre
Economics
Education
Educational Technology

Engineering
Engineering, Aeronautical
Engineering, Agricultural
Engineering, Automobile
Engineering, Chemical
Engineering, Civil
Engineering, Control
Engineering, Electrical
Engineering, Electronic
Engineering, Marine, and Naval
  Architecture
Engineering, Mechanical
Engineering, Medical
Engineering, Nuclear
Engineering, Production
Engineering, Public Health and
  Municipal
English as a Foreign Language:
  Courses for Teachers
English Language and Literature
Environmental Studies
Ergonomics and Cybernetics
Estate and Farm Management
European Studies
Food Science and Technology
French
Fuel Technology
Genetics
Geography
Geology
Germanic Languages and Studies
Greek and Latin
History
History and Philosophy of Science
Home Economics
Hospital and Health Service
  Administration
Hotel and Institutional Management
Irish, Scottish and Welsh Studies
Italian

Landscape Architecture
Language Studies
Laryngology and Otology
Latin American Studies
Law
Librarianship and Information Science
Mass Media and Communication
  Studies
Materials Science and Technology
Mathematics
Medical/Health Physics
Medical Laboratory Technology
Medicine and Surgery
Medicine, Forensic
Metallurgy
Meteorology
Microbiology
Mining and Mineral Sciences
Museum Studies
Music
Nautical Studies
Neurology
Nursing
Obstetrics and Gynaecology
Occupational Therapy
Oceanography
Operational Research
Ophthalmic and Dispensing Optics
Ophthalmology
Oriental Languages and Studies
Orthopaedics
Orthoptics
Paediatrics
Palaeography
Parasitology
Pathology
Peace and Conflict Studies
Pharmacology
Pharmacy
Philosophy

Photography
Physical Education and Sports Science
Physics
Physiology
Physiotherapy
Political Science
Polymer Science and Technology
Portuguese
Printing and Publishing
Psychological Medicine
Psychology
Public Administration and Finance
Public and Industrial Health
Radiobiology
Radiography
Radiology
Recreation Studies
Religious Studies
Science and Technology
Secretarial Studies
Secretaryship, Chartered and
  Incorporated
Slavonic and other East European
  Languages and Studies
Social Work
Sociology
Soil Science
Spanish
Speech Therapy
Statistics
Surveying
Surveying, Land
Textiles
Town and Country Planning
Transport
Tropical Medicine and Hygiene
United States Studies
Urology and Venereology
Veterinary Medicine and Surgery
Youth Services

SOME STATISTICS

There are at present forty-five universities in Great Britain and Northern Ireland, and in addition to these there are thirty-one polytechnics offering both degree and other advanced courses, mainly in science and technological subjects.

The forty-five universities include the Open University (see also page 27), which is not at present able to enrol students in countries outside the United Kingdom.

There are also many other institutions offering advanced academic courses and preparation for the various professions, both full-time and part-time, including over 600 colleges of further education.

In the universities there are about 280,000 full-time (including sandwich course) students, while about the same number attend full-time and sandwich courses in polytechnics, technical, commercial and art colleges. Of the 114,000 students from overseas in Britain, about 32,000 are in universities, 10,500 in polytechnics, 32,500 in other further education establishments and about 700 in colleges of education, while the rest are undergoing various kinds of professional training elsewhere.

GUIDE TO THIS BOOK

An overseas student who is thinking of coming to Britain for advanced study will need to consider at least four important points before making up his mind:

Are there suitable courses in his subject?
Is he qualified to take a course?
Can he afford it?
Is his English good enough?

In such a short book we cannot provide *all* the information that the student needs to help him answer these questions or give more than the briefest details of individual courses of study. Before a student applies to take a course he should obtain full information about it direct from the university or college concerned; but if he lives in a country in which the British Council has an office (see pages 287–291) he will probably find it helpful to consult its staff before he writes to any academic institution. They will advise him whether his qualifications are likely to be acceptable, and whether he needs to improve his knowledge of English. Most Council offices have prospectuses of the universities, containing details of courses of study, and information about courses in other institutions.

A student who is thinking of taking a course of advanced study at an institution not listed in this handbook is advised in any case to ask the British Council for information about the institution, and about the standing of the qualifications which it offers, before he commits himself to taking the course.

SOMETHING FOR EVERYBODY*

by Harold Perkin, MA (Cantab), FRHistS
Professor of Social History, University of Lancaster

'Wisdom is the principal thing'

About twenty-five centuries ago an unknown sage in the Middle East advised his students:

> Wisdom is the principal thing, therefore get wisdom; and with all thy getting, get understanding. Exalt her, and she shall promote thee; . . . a crown of glory shall she deliver thee. (*Proverbs*, IV. 7–9)

Wisdom is more than knowledge and the ability to argue and experiment. It includes experience of life and the ability to make use of it, to comprehend the world as it is but see what it might become, to grasp reality and yet imagine how it might be changed. It has not always been taught in schools and universities, since they, like all human institutions, tend to ossify and degenerate into routine and precedent; but since the Greek lyceums, the Chinese mandarin schools and the medieval Christian and Muslim universities, they have always aimed at embracing the current wisdom of their age. In the words of the new university charters of the 1960s, their objects are 'to advance knowledge, wisdom and understanding by teaching and research and the example of [their] corporate life'. Higher education is concerned with teaching and research at the highest level, at the frontiers of knowledge; but wisdom, understanding and corporate life link it firmly to the world outside.

Higher education does, or should, provide something for everybody and it does so in two ways. In the first place everybody benefits indirectly from its services; without the specialists increasingly trained in universities, polytechnics and other colleges a civilised social life would be impossible.

* This article is an amended version of the one which appeared in the 1976–78 edition.

Secondly, higher education together with its helpmate further education, which in Britain cannot be separated from it, provides something for everybody wishing to take a specific course, however exalted or humble their chosen subject may be. Together they provide training for technicians as well as technologists, laboratory assistants as well as scientists, mechanics as well as engineers, nurses and radiographers as well as doctors, shorthand-typists as well as administrators, skilled operatives as well as factory managers, and often, in the non-university sector, by the same teachers in the same institutions. The difference is literally one of degree rather than kind; the Department of Education and Science defines 'advanced' education as *courses*, not *colleges*, leading to a degree or near-equivalent qualification, 'non-advanced' as leading to qualifications below that level. Tertiary education, as we should rightly call it, provides something for everybody, including overseas students.

In 1975–76 overseas students constituted 11·7 per cent of full-time university students in Britain. In polytechnics and institutions of further education the proportion was 7·7 per cent of full-time students. Since in very few cases did the fees cover more than a fraction of the cost, Britain is proud to make so large a contribution to international education.

A learning society

Britain, like most Western European countries, is in transition from élitist to mass higher education, from post-secondary education for the few, say 5 per cent or less of the 18-year-old age group, to that for the many, say the 35–40 per cent now usual in the United States or the Soviet Union. In 1900 1·2 per cent entered higher education, between the World Wars 2·7 per cent, in 1960 8·3 per cent, in 1971 15 per cent; by 1981 it will be 19 per cent, even on the reduced 1975 forecast. If we include part-time education, however, Britain has already reached mass post-school education. Well over four million people are taking courses of education outside school. An unknown number of people are taking secretarial, language, computer and other courses in private colleges, or taking correspondence courses with *Adult* commercial or non-profit-making colleges. Others are taking 'adult *education* education', non-vocational courses of all kinds for pleasure – academic (university tutorial classes); artistic (classes in drama); practical (car maintenance) and so on – organised by the university extra-mural departments, the Workers' Educational Association and other voluntary bodies. Much of the further education sector is non-vocational too, *Voca-* especially in the evening institutes, but nearly 2 million part-time students *tional* are taking vocational courses leading to qualifications ranging from *education* degrees to the craft and secretarial examinations of the City and Guilds of London Institute and the Royal Society of Arts. Over half of these are evening students attending only in their spare time, but many are part-time day students, mostly released by their employers for one or more days a week as well as, in some cases, attending classes in the evening. In addition, in 1975–76, there were 26,300 part-time students, mostly postgraduates, studying at universities. This does not include students of the Open University, studying at home by television, radio and correspondence tuition, who in 1977 numbered almost 55,000.

Recurrent and permanent education   The universities, polytechnics and other colleges also provide hundreds of 'refresher' or 'post-experience' courses, from a day to six months, which allow professional people such as doctors, teachers, systems engineers and business managers to update their specialisms, or enable those who wish to do so to start new careers. Many are on 'block release', i.e. paid leave from their employers. Such 'recurrent education' is necessary if society is to keep abreast of rapidly changing knowledge and transfer well-qualified members of it to new areas of knowledge or industry when the need arises. Indeed, we can now speak of 'permanent education', in which everyone who wishes may constantly learn, either to improve or change his career or simply for pleasure. More than one in ten adults take some form of education each year and, since they are not the same every year, Britain can truly claim to be a learning society.

Of full-time students in higher education, including those on 'sandwich courses' spending alternating periods in industry and in college, women constitute about 42 per cent: 32 per cent in universities, 29 per cent in further education and 70 per cent in colleges of education. Students from the manual working class constitute 28 per cent of university entrants, much more than in most Western countries. New home student enrolments compare favourably with most Western European countries, and with our lower wastage and failure rates we are at the top of the league in Western Europe in graduates produced. In the calendar year 1975, British universities awarded 94,374 degrees and diplomas (including 5,909 from the Open University), of which 62,386 were first degrees and 18,338 were higher degrees; in the same year 12,212 CNAA degrees were awarded. By 1971, 8·3 per cent of adult men and 6 per cent of women had degrees or other advanced qualifications (including nursing and professional qualifications). According to a survey by the Organization for Economic Co-operation and Development in 1970, Britain had the highest proportion amongst member countries of qualified scientists and engineers. That these figures were not reflected in our rate of economic growth perhaps illustrates the distinction between knowledge and wisdom.

Degrees awarded

The historical dimension

The oldest universities   The rich diversity of British higher education, and particularly its division between two sectors, the 'autonomous' or 'private' and the 'public' or government sector, is a product of evolution. Our universities and other colleges have grown up to meet the needs of different ages and societies. Oxford and Cambridge were founded in the twelfth and early thirteenth centuries as schools for churchmen, but soon acquired postgraduate faculties of theology, law and medicine, 'technologies' as necessary to the middle ages as the applied sciences to ours. The ancient Scottish universities, St Andrews (1410), Glasgow (1451), Aberdeen (1495) and Edinburgh (1583), were founded for much the same purposes.

Industrial- When the Industrial Revolution began in the late eighteenth century the *ism and the* six universities, with perhaps 2,000 students, were totally inadequate to the *new society* needs of the new society. A whole range of new institutions, colleges and medical schools for the new industrial and professional classes, and *Mechanics'* mechanics' institutes for craftsmen and factory operatives, sprang up. The *institutes* first was Anderson's Institution in Glasgow, founded in 1796 for skilled working men, the second oldest surviving technical institution in Europe. It was followed by the mechanics' institutes in London and Glasgow founded in 1823 by George Birkbeck, a professor at Anderson's Institution, and others in Manchester, Bradford, Leeds, Birmingham and other industrial towns. Many of these, including Anderson's, Manchester and Bradford, were to grow first into technical colleges and in the twentieth century into technological universities.

London The first new university to be founded in over two centuries was *University* University College, London, opened in 1828 by a group of Whigs and Dissenters incensed at the expense, Anglican exclusiveness and traditionalism of Oxford and Cambridge. The Church responded the following year by founding King's College, and the two were subsequently united in the federal University of London, founded in 1836. Both colleges taught modern subjects including medicine, science, engineering and modern languages. The University of London was not a teaching but an examining body, which was able to absorb other London colleges as they were founded and from 1858 to grant external degrees which enabled colleges far from London to serve an apprenticeship for university status.

The civic Apart from Durham University, founded by the Church in 1832 to ward *univer-* off the expected attacks of the newly reformed Parliament, university *sities* colleges were built by successful business men in a number of cities throughout the country between 1851 and 1897. Based on the Scottish and continental model of research-oriented professorships, they became especially famous for science and technology: Manchester for chemistry under Sir Edward Frankland, Sir Henry Roscoe and William H. Perkin, Leeds for leather and textile technology under Henry Procter and the two Beaumonts, Birmingham for mining and oil engineering under Sir Richard Redmayne and Lord Cadman, Sheffield for metallurgy under Viriamu Jones, Henry Sorby and Oliver Arnold, Liverpool for electrical engineering under Sir Oliver Lodge, Bristol for automobile engineering under Professor Morgan, and so on. After a generation or so it became difficult to deny them full university status and the right to grant their own degrees: the federal Victoria University, which united Manchester (1880), Liverpool (1884) and Leeds (1887), separated in 1903; the federal University of Wales (1893), which embraced the colleges of Aberystwyth (1872), Cardiff (1883) and Bangor (1884); the universities of Birmingham (1900), Sheffield (1905) and Bristol (1909). Queen's College, Belfast, was the only government foundation, created as a constituent college along with Cork and Galway of the Queen's University in Ireland in 1849–50 and separated from them as the Queen's University of Belfast in 1908. All the rest were monuments to Victorian civic pride and upper middle-class demand for relevant education. From 1889 they were aided by the state, from 1904 through the University Colleges Committee, which in 1919 became the University Grants Committee.

Reform of Meanwhile, Oxford and Cambridge were forced to reform, partly by the
Oxbridge competition of London and the new provincial universities, mainly by the pressure of public opinion, internal and external, and of Parliament. Royal Commissions in 1850 and 1872 and Acts of Parliament in 1854, 1856, 1871 and 1877 strengthened the universities and the professors against the colleges and fellows, abolished religious tests and opened them up to non-Anglicans. Both universities began to teach modern subjects and to found laboratories.

Technical Technical, commercial and art education for the lower-middle and
education skilled working classes also grew apace. With government grants from the Science and Art Department set up after the Great Exhibition of 1851, technical and art classes and schools were developed and the (Royal) Society of Arts, founded in 1754 to encourage invention and industrial training, became an examining body for arts and crafts. Vocational education was given a further boost by the threat of foreign, especially German and American, competition, which led to the Technical Instruction Act, 1889, under which the new County and County Borough Councils were empowered to aid or establish technical colleges and schools, long before they became responsible for school education in 1902. The first 'polytechnic' was opened in Regent Street, London, in 1882 by Quintin Hogg, a philanthropic merchant, and was soon followed by others, aided by the Technical Education Board of the London County Council. The Manchester mechanics' institute became a technical college in 1883, and in 1905 the faculty of technology of Manchester University. Anderson's Institution became a technical college in 1886 and the Royal Technical College, Glasgow, in 1912. The rich London livery companies were persuaded to set up the City and Guilds of London Institute for the Advancement of Technical Education in 1881 and this took over the examining of a range of craft skills from workshop engineering to

bricklaying. By the early 1900s, 639,000 students a year, 13,000 full-time, were taking courses in local authority establishments.

Training colleges There was a third sector of higher education, the training of non-graduate teachers. This was until recently larger than the full-time advanced sector of further education. It began with the 'normal schools' founded by the voluntary religious bodies to train teachers for the elementary schools and aided by the state from 1833 onwards. By 1900 there were about 5,000 student teachers and by 1922 fifty voluntary and twenty-two local authority training colleges with about 15,000 students.

Between the World Wars Between the World Wars very few new universities were founded. Reading was raised to full university status (1926), Swansea became a constituent college of Wales (1920), university colleges were established at Exeter (1922), and Leicester and Hull (1927), which, along with Nottingham and Southampton, continued to work for London external degrees until after the Second World War. In a time of depression and graduate unemployment student numbers grew slowly and teacher training outside the universities stagnated. Further education nearly doubled, however, and a significant number of full-time advanced students began to emerge. The most important development was the inauguration in 1921 of the National Certificate examinations in technology. These were for awards made by Joint Committees of the Board of Education (later the Ministry and now the Department of Education and Science) and the professional bodies concerned (e.g. the institutions of Mechanical or Electrical Engineering, Chemistry or Naval Architecture), the examinations being set and marked, with the aid of external examiners, by the colleges. They were at two levels and by two modes: Ordinary and Higher National Certificates, usually two years for each, for part-time students, and Ordinary and Higher National Diplomas, usually two years plus three years and often on a 'sandwich course' or 'block release' basis, for full-time students. Ordinary awards grew from 663 in 1923 to 4,070 in 1944 and Higher awards from 168 to 1,405. The Higher awards were 'of near-pass degree standard', and gave exemption from at least part of the examinations for the qualifying professional associations (e.g. AMIMechE, the Associate Membership of the Institution of Mechanical Engineers, equivalent to a degree in engineering). In this way, in addition to the London external degree scheme, an avenue was created to higher education outside the universities.

The National Certificate Scheme

Since the Second World War Since the Second World War the expansion of higher education, both university and non-university, has been spectacular; this is especially true of the 1960s. The number of universities and independent university colleges grew from 25 in 1960 to 45 (including the Open University) by 1969. Full-time university student numbers in Great Britain rose from 113,143 in 1961–62 (plus 3,741 in Northern Ireland) to 251,226 in

1971–72 (plus 7,578). Part of this growth was due to the splitting of universities – Newcastle was separated from Durham in 1963 and Dundee from St Andrews in 1967 – and to the raising of ten Colleges of Advanced Technology, a designation introduced only in 1956, to university status some ten years later. But most of it was real expansion: the experimental University College of North Staffordshire was opened in 1950 (the University of Keele, 1962), the first institution since the 1930s allowed to grant its own degrees from the beginning, and 'the mother of the New Universities'. In the late 1950s and early 1960s, partly to meet student demand but mostly to experiment with new courses and structures ("It was one-third student numbers and two-thirds new ideas," said Lord Murray, then chairman of the University Grants Committee), nine new universities were created by the state: Sussex (opened in 1961); East Anglia and York (1963); Essex, Lancaster, and Warwick (1964); Kent (1965); Stirling (1967); and the New University of Ulster (1968). Some of the latter establishments were the result of the Report of the Robbins Committee. This was set up by the government in 1961 under the chairmanship of Lord Robbins to investigate ways of meeting the expected increase in student demand due to the postwar 'bulge' in the birthrate and the 'trend' to stay on at school to qualify for higher education.

The new universities

The Robbins Report

The Robbins Committee, the first comprehensive enquiry into the whole of higher education in Great Britain, found that besides 118,400 university students and 54,700 in the 153 training colleges in 1962–1963, there were 42,800 full-time advanced students in the further education colleges. A whole new sector of higher education had grown up almost unnoticed. There were 10 Colleges of Advanced Technology (CATs), 8 National Colleges for particular industries and occupations from aeronautics, leather and rubber to the Royal College of Art, 25 Regional Colleges of Technology, 708 Area and local colleges, including colleges of art, of drama and speech training, of commerce and further education, and 7,561 evening institutes. Most of the advanced full-time work was in the CATs and Regional Colleges and the 15 similar Scottish Central Institutions, but over 40 per cent was done in over 300 other major establishments.

The pressure of numbers

The Robbins Committee forecast an increase in demand for student places from the current 216,000 to 390,000 by 1973–74 (a figure which was outstripped by over 50 per cent in the event). It therefore recommended a crash programme of expansion; all the universities to be expanded, seven more new universities founded, the ten CATs to be raised to university status, and other National, Regional and Area colleges to follow them as they expanded their full-time advanced work to the required level. To this end a new body, the Council for National Academic Awards (CNAA), was created out of the National Council for Technological Awards (which had been set up in 1955), and given the task of validating courses and awarding degrees in further education institutions. This was part of the 'Robbins philosophy' of a hierarchy of higher education institutions up which the colleges would climb by their own efforts to university status, as so many had done before them. Its critics called it 'academic drift' and forecast that the aspiring colleges would shed their part-time and non-advanced work in their effort to rise, and so abandon their most important function, the education of the bulk of the technicians and skilled workers, as indeed the CATs were already doing.

The techno-logical univer-sities
The ten CATs attained to university status in April 1965: Aston in Birmingham; Bristol (now the University of Bath); Bradford; Brunel, in London, which moved out to a new site at Uxbridge; Northampton CAT, London, as The City University; Loughborough; Salford; Battersea CAT, which moved to Guildford as the University of Surrey; Chelsea CAT, which elected to become a college of London University; and the Welsh CAT, which is now the University of Wales Institute of Science and Technology. They were joined by the Royal College of Science and Technology, Glasgow, as the University of Strathclyde, and by Heriot-Watt in Edinburgh, a former Scottish Central Institution. These mainly technological universities have expanded into the humanities and social sciences but still maintain their sandwich-course students and close links with industry.

Specialist post-graduate institutions
After the Franks Report on management education in 1963 the government also established the postgraduate London and Manchester Business Schools. Two of the National Colleges were raised to university status: the College of Aeronautics as the postgraduate Cranfield Institute of Technology in 1969, and the postgraduate Royal College of Art, which preferred to remain funded directly by the Department of Education and Science instead of the University Grants Committee, in 1967. The National College of Food Technology at Weybridge has been merged with the University of Reading; the other National Colleges, except for the College of Agricultural Engineering (which is now a constituent of Cranfield), merged with polytechnics.

The binary policy
Then, in 1966, came a complete reversal of the Robbins policy. In a famous speech at Woolwich Mr. Anthony Crosland, Secretary of State for Education and Science, announced what has come to be termed the 'binary policy'. The binary system, the twin sectors of higher education – the 'autonomous' or university, and the 'public' or further education sector – had come into existence to serve two different purposes: the one mainly full-time academic education and the other mainly vocational, including a large element of part-time and non-advanced work. Henceforward, instead of the traditional 'academic drift' of colleges into the university sector, leaving behind their part-time and non-advanced work, the two sectors would enjoy separate but equal development.

*The
polytech-
nics*

The main instrument of this policy was to be the polytechnic, a comprehensive institution in which most of the advanced work, full-time and part-time, in an area was to be concentrated. Under the White Paper *A Plan for Polytechnics and Other Colleges of Higher Education in the Further Education Sector* (Cmnd. 3006, 1966) thirty polytechnics were to be created either singly or by amalgamation from existing Regional and other technical colleges, colleges of commerce and colleges of art. They were all designated between 1969 and 1972: Brighton, Bristol, City of Birmingham, Glamorgan (in Cardiff), Hatfield, Huddersfield, Lanchester (in Coventry and Rugby), Leeds, City of Leicester, Liverpool, Manchester, Newcastle upon Tyne, North Staffordshire (in Stoke-on-Trent and Stafford), Oxford, Plymouth, Portsmouth, Preston, Sheffield, Sunderland, Teesside (in Middlesbrough), Trent (in Nottingham), Wolverhampton, and in the London area Central London, City of London, Kingston-upon-Thames, Middlesex, North London, North East London, South Bank, and Thames. Ulster College was also established as the polytechnic for Northern Ireland. Scotland does not have polytechnics, but the thirteen Central Institutions directly financed by the Scottish Education Department have a similar concentration of full-time advanced work. By 1974–75 the thirty polytechnics in England and Wales had 159,190 students, 82,892 full-time and sandwich-course and 76,298 part-time, of whom 76,820 full-timers and 40,286 part-timers were on degree or advanced courses. They ranged in size from Glamorgan with 2,218 students (1,119 full-time, the others sandwich) to Central London with 12,316 (3,750 full-time, the others sandwich), most having between 3,000 and 7,000. They were therefore as large as most universities.

*Colleges
of educa-
tion*

The Robbins Committee also recommended that the teacher training colleges, which since the McNair Report, 1944, had been attached for academic purposes to university institutes of education and had quadrupled in size, should be further expanded, renamed colleges of education, and financed by the University Grants Committee through the universities. This last the DES and local authorities successfully resisted. The colleges were expanded, more than doubling in size from 55,400 in 1962–63 to 127,600 in 1972–73 (excluding about 18,200 other trainees in universities and further education); but with the declining birthrate and falling demand for teachers they have been reduced in number and size.

Through this historical evolution, then, the present binary – or trinary, if we include the colleges of education – system came into existence. It is a diverse and complex system, confusing to the outside observer and difficult for the student who has to make a choice of course and institution – a choice which this Handbook tries to make easier. But it has one great advantage: it provides something for everybody.

Something for everybody

The present system of higher education in Britain offers a wide choice not only of courses and institutions but of academic structures, social atmospheres and physical environments in which to study.

Types of institution The range of institutions is not restricted to the choice between a university and a public sector college. Both universities and other colleges differ enormously in size, situation, structure, appearance and in every other respect. Oxford and Cambridge are large, collegiate universities with upwards of 10,000 students, their ancient colleges scattered throughout and dominating comparatively small cities. St Andrews and Durham are also old collegiate universities but smaller, with 3,000–4,000 students, and dominating much smaller cities. The main London colleges are medium-sized (1,000–5,000) but mostly on confined urban sites in one of the largest, most crowded but most exciting cities in the world, though Wye and Royal Holloway are in the countryside. The older civic universities are large, unitary organisations with from 6,000 students (Reading or Nottingham) to 10,000 or more (Edinburgh and Manchester) and in crowded, bustling cities, though some are developing new campuses where slums used to stand (Manchester, Leeds, Sheffield). The younger ones are smaller (4,000–6,000) and often on spacious suburban sites (Exeter, Leicester, Southampton). Keele and the 'New Universities' of the 1960s are all small (2,500–4,500) and on newly built campuses in the green fields: some tightly knit complexes (Lancaster, East Anglia, Essex), some with scattered 'pavilions in a park' (Sussex, Warwick, York); some are collegiate (Kent, Lancaster, York), though the colleges are social rather than academic communities, others are unitary but divided into broad 'schools of study' (Sussex, East Anglia, Ulster). The technological universities are much the same size or larger, and some have moved out to new rural campuses (Bath, Brunel, Surrey) while others are redeveloping their old urban sites (Aston, Salford).

Academic structures Academic structures also vary, and while the single-subject honours degree is still the norm in England and Wales, with combined honours available in the humanities, pure sciences and social sciences, Scotland has long had its multi-subject first year. Interesting new combinations and interdisciplinary courses, pioneered by, though not exclusive to, the new universities, are emerging elsewhere: the foundation year on Western civilisation at Keele, the 'contextual' courses at Sussex, the three-subject first year at Lancaster, liberal studies in science at Manchester, and so on. Whether you wish to take a traditional single honours degree at a large, old, prestigious, bustling, metropolitan university, a general honours degree at an experimental, rural, campus university, or a professional qualification at an equally new technological university, urban or rural, you can find what you want in the university sector.

The public   The public sector is still more versatile. In a polytechnic, technical
sector   college, college of commerce, college of art, drama or music, you can train
full-time or part-time for a variety of qualifications such as: a degree; the
Higher National Diploma or Certificate; the Art Teacher's Diploma and
various advanced professional diplomas and certificates; the Ordinary
National Diploma or Certificate; the craft and technical examinations of
the City and Guilds of London Institute; the General Certificate of
Education at Advanced or Ordinary level; or the certificates of the Royal
Society of Arts in shorthand-typing, secretarial work and office practice. In
a college of education you may train to be a graduate (BEd) or certificated
teacher, and at some it is also possible to take general, non-professional
courses: two-year Diplomas in Higher Education and/or degrees in
subjects other than education.

The further education colleges also vary in size and structure. There are
polytechnics like Central London with over 12,000 students, many on
advanced full-time and sandwich courses, small colleges of further
education with few full-time and fewer advanced students, and evening
institutes with none at all. Nearly all are in the centres of towns and cities
within reach of their part-time clientele. The polytechnics and larger
colleges, however, draw their full-time students from a wider field. Their
degree courses, validated by the CNAA, whose boards and subject panels
and external examiners include many university teachers, are based on
modern developments in course design, e.g. polytechnic modular degrees.

Colleges of education also vary in size, character and situation, but for
the most part they are small (under 1,000 students) and, with some
exceptions such as the famous London colleges, tend to be situated in
smaller towns and villages. But the day of the monotechnical institution
for the teaching profession is over and, in order to provide a wider and more
diversified higher education service, colleges are being amalgamated,
merged with polytechnics or closed.

Professional education and industrial training

One of the unique features of British higher education is the close
involvement of voluntary, non-governmental bodies, especially professional and other occupational bodies, in the planning and validation of
Qualifying courses in their fields. There are about 160 qualifying associations in
associa-   Britain, ranging from the medieval Inns of Court for barristers; through
tions   the great nineteenth-century institutions for different kinds of engineer; to
the many modern institutes for business managers, the para-medical
professions, advertising and public relations, hotel management and
catering, and even packaging. Increasingly, they have tended to 'recognise'
certain courses in universities and other colleges as giving exemption from
all or part of their membership examinations. Since students wish to

qualify for such exemption, professional departments have tended to tailor their courses to meet the associations' requirements. In some cases, such as doctors, mining engineers and architects, the state has insisted on such recognised training before registration: under the Medical Registration Act, 1858, for example, the General Medical Council registers only graduates of approved medical schools. In this way, the various professions strongly influence their own training.

Occupa-tional exam-ining bodies   Below degree level, their influence is more institutionalised. The National Certificate scheme is administered by Joint Committees representing the professional body, the Department of Education and Science and the colleges for each profession. The City and Guilds of London Institute represents the accumulated experience of a wide variety of occupations. The Royal Society of Arts is a general professional body representative of many interests. Other examining boards include specialised occupational bodies and regional examining unions which work very closely with local industry and commerce.

Industrial training   By the Industrial Training Act, 1964, the responsibility for training workers devolves upon the industry concerned. An Industrial Training Board was set up for each of twenty-eight major industries, headed by a central Training Council. The Training Boards are all representative of employers, trade unions, educationists and the government, and their functions are to secure an adequate supply of trained workers, to improve the quality of training and to share the cost between firms and nationalised industries. Though concerned chiefly with apprentices and other trainees within industry, they recommend new and improved courses in the local further education colleges and have a profound effect on their work.

Administration and finance

The two sectors of the binary system are administered and financed quite separately. Apart from Northern Ireland where the government funds all institutions of higher education directly, the universities of Britain, with the exception of the Royal College of Art and Cranfield Institute of Technology with their direct grants from the DES, are financed mainly
The University Grants Committee   through a unique British institution, the University Grants Committee. A committee of senior academics and leading business and professional men under a full-time chairman (the only paid member), it advises the government on the universities' needs and distributes the block grant it receives between them as it thinks fit. As a buffer between the universities and direct state control, it is the main safeguard of university autonomy.

In recent years, however, the UGC has become less of a buffer and more of an instrument of government policy. In 1964 it was transferred from the Treasury to the DES which, with the opening of the universities to parliamentary audit in 1968, gained direct access to their accounts. With the large sums now at stake – the recurrent grant has risen from £9 million in 1947–48 to £518·5 million in 1977–78 – the UGC has been forced to increase its supervision of university expenditure, by means of 'memoranda of guidance' recommending certain developments and discouraging others, and by a tight control of new buildings and capacity planning, exercised through a Secretariat of over a hundred officials. At a time of steep inflation, UGC limits on expenditure are forcing the universities to make large economies and to take more students without corresponding increases in staff or facilities.

Further education finance　The further education sector is financed by the Department of Education and Science in England and Wales, the Scottish Education Department and the Northern Ireland government, and – in Britain – mainly through the local authorities (except for the thirteen Central Institutions financed directly by the Scottish Education Department). In England and Wales the voluntary colleges of education and certain other institutions receive direct grants from the DES. Further education in

Further education coordination　England and Wales is coordinated by a system of National and Regional Advisory Councils, representing the DES and other government departments, the various professional and industrial associations, the examining boards, the local authorities and the teachers. They attempt to ensure that courses in each area are adequate without unnecessary duplication. Most local authority income for further education comes in the form of a block grant, but the DES controls expenditure, both recurrent and capital, more formally but in much the same way as the UGC controls the universities.

The governance of institutions

Most universities, apart from Oxford and Cambridge where complete
University governing bodies　academic autonomy exists, are governed by a large Court of governors widely representative of local authorities, professional bodies, trade unions and other lay members together with academic staff and students; a smaller but similarly representative executive Council; and a Senate of professors, elected lecturers and student representatives (or equivalent bodies under different names in the Scottish and some other universities). At lower levels democracy prevails through a series of boards or committees on each of which sit professors, non-professorial staff and,
Student representation　increasingly, student representatives. In 1971 a survey by the Committee of Vice-Chancellors and Principals showed that students were represented as full members or observers on most Courts, Councils, Senates and equivalent bodies in universities for 'unreserved business', and representation was under discussion in all the rest. At lower levels it was normal for students to be represented on joint committees and boards down to the level

of departments, though personal academic matters such as staff appointments and examination results were 'reserved'.

Further education governing bodies

Technical colleges and local authority colleges of education have long had governing bodies on which the local authorities generally had a decisive majority. Now an Act of Parliament of 1968 requires polytechnics and other maintained colleges to have articles of government which specify the functions of the local authority, the governing body, the principal and the academic board. Government policy is for the governing body to be more independent of the local authority and for the academic staff and students to be represented on it. By 1972 most polytechnics had student representatives on the governing body, academic board and most other committees, and other colleges were following the same path.

Teachers and teaching methods

University and other higher education teachers are appointed by committees of their governing bodies which include, in the case of professors, heads of department and other senior posts, external assessors. A three- or four-year probation is usual for junior lecturers in both sectors, after which tenure is effectively until the age of retirement. Staff–student ratios are comparatively low, 1 : 8·9 in universities, 1 : 6·9 in polytechnics, though government policy is to raise them to 1 : 10 by the end of the decade.

Teaching in both sectors is by a combination of lectures and tutorials, seminars, laboratory classes and other small group tuition, though there is a tendency for contact hours to be longer in non-university colleges. New teaching methods are being experimented with in both sectors, including closed circuit television and language laboratories and the emphasis, especially in the universities, is on the student learning for himself rather than being taught.

Research

All university teachers are expected to conduct research, but some universities are more important research centres than others. This can partly be gauged by the proportions of full-time postgraduate students: the average in Britain is about 17 per cent, but Oxford had 24 per cent, London 25 per cent, Manchester 21·6 per cent and Cambridge 20·1 per cent. The polytechnics, however, were created as mainly teaching institutions, though many of their teachers also conduct research. Few in the technical colleges or colleges of education do so.

Research councils

In addition to moneys received for salaries, equipment and materials from the UGC, the DES and the local authorities, research is also financed by the five Research Councils, for Science, Social Science, Medical Research, Agriculture, and the Natural Environment, which come under the DES, advised by the Advisory Board for the Research Councils. They make grants for individual and team- projects and programmes to both university and further education teachers on the merits of each application, and also award studentships, bursaries and fellowships to British citizens at both kinds of institution. The DES also gives postgraduate awards in the humanities and, along with the Schools Council and Social Science Research Council, makes grants for educational research. There are also numerous private foundations, like the National Foundation for Educational Research, the Leverhulme Trust, the Nuffield Foundation and the Rowntree Trust, which support research in universities and other colleges.

Founda-
tions and
trusts

Future trends

The explosive expansion of higher education in the 1960s has slowed down markedly in the 1970s, and the official government forecasts of student numbers in higher education in 1981 have been successively reduced from 835,000 (1970), to 750,000 (1972), and 600,000 (1976) – although even the last figure is higher than the original Robbins Report forecast of 596,000.

Decelerat-
ing growth

The demand for teachers is falling as the birthrate declines, but so is the number of places available: the government plans to reduce the number of initial training places in colleges of education from the present 130,000 to about 60,000–70,000 by 1981. Many colleges of education have been closed and many amalgamated with universities and polytechnics. They will also be involved with the recurrent education of in-service teachers recommended by the James Report (*Teacher Education and Training*, 1972). In this way for the first time the education of teachers will be integrated with that for other professions.

Fewer
teachers
needed

Integration of the two sectors of the binary system will probably increase over the next few years. Already higher salaries at the junior levels in further education and the shortage of posts in university teaching are attracting into the polytechnics and other colleges young men and women who are academically minded and research-oriented. Many students who used to aspire to university are turning to the polytechnics. The government, while resisting suggestions for a single Higher Education Commission to finance both sectors and the pressure from polytechnic staffs and students for university status, is urging co-operation across the binary frontier, in courses, library provision, laboratory facilities and so on. The National Union of Students is pressing for the amalgamation of universities and neighbouring polytechnics in 'polyversities', an ugly word for a comprehensive institution providing higher and further education for both full-time and part-time students. While not endorsing this particular mode, current trends and economic logic suggest a movement towards a

The end of
the binary
system?

more federal structure for universities and other colleges in the same city. If and when this happens, British higher education will provide not only something for everybody, but something under the same umbrella.

Harold Perkin

A lecture in progress at a polytechnic in the Midlands

COURSES AVAILABLE

There is in Britain no formal, national, system for the 'accreditation' of institutions of higher education; and the conferring of degrees – i.e. qualifications with the title of Bachelor, Master or Doctor – is not restricted by law to particular bodies or institutions. Students in other countries who are thinking of studying for a degree offered by an institution or authority in the United Kingdom that is not mentioned anywhere in this handbook (see particularly pages 8 and 267–283) are therefore advised to consult their nearest British Council office before completing any registration formalities.

The demand from qualified applicants for places in universities in Britain, and (though to a lesser extent) in polytechnics, colleges of technology and other institutions of higher education, is often greater than the number of places available. All entry is competitive; each university and college controls the admission of students to its own courses; and possession of the minimum qualifications does not mean that the holder can be sure of finding a place. The position can of course change from year to year, but in September 1977 the competition among qualified applicants for admission to university first degree courses was greatest for courses in: medicine, dentistry and pharmacy; civil engineering; surveying; forestry; veterinary science; accountancy; law; architecture; drama; and fine art. It is most important, therefore, in his own interests, that a student should not leave home before securing a definite promise that a place is available for him in the institution in which he wishes to study. He should also make sure before he leaves that he has the necessary permit for entry into Britain, and that he will have enough money to meet all the fees and other costs that he will incur during his stay in Britain (see pages 50 and 53). Students should bear in mind that the award of a degree or other qualification can never be guaranteed, and that it is therefore unrealistic to sign an agreement which involves an undertaking to obtain a degree in return for financial support during their period of study.

Courses at universities (and Cranfield Institute of Technology and Royal College of Art)
Note – Students who wish to learn more about the individual universities named in this handbook, and about Cranfield Institute of Technology and the Royal College of Art, before deciding to which of them they will send a direct enquiry, may find it useful to consult the *Commonwealth Universities*

Yearbook (see page 265). The Yearbook contains a separate chapter for each of these institutions, and each chapter includes detailed notes on degrees, diplomas, etc.

Universities provide *undergraduate* courses, which normally lead to a first degree, and also offer opportunities for *postgraduate* work, which usually (although not necessarily) involves preparation for a higher degree or diploma. (For Cranfield Institute of Technology and the Royal College of Art, see page 31.)

Attendance at the university institution granting the degree, diploma or certificate is normally required, except for (i) the Open University which is not dealt with in this handbook, and (ii) students who are enrolled at a college (e.g. a college of education) associated with the university awarding the degree. The Open University provides, for 'home-based' students in Britain, tuition by correspondence which is supplemented by closely-linked radio and television broadcasts, residential summer schools, and an extensive counselling and tutorial service operating through a network of local study centres. It is not possible for students to register with the Open University while living in another country; nor is it possible for an overseas student to obtain a degree from any other UK university by following correspondence courses in his own country. (Suitably qualified students who are normally resident in the British Isles may register as external students of the University of London, making their own arrangements for primarily home-based study; *but the University has ceased to register as external students those who are normally resident overseas* and also those who are attending full-time courses in polytechnics or other institutions in the public sector of higher and further education in the British Isles.)

Under-
graduate
courses

The qualifications to which undergraduate courses at universities lead are usually degrees with the title 'Bachelor' – for example, Bachelor of Arts, Bachelor of Medicine, Bachelor of Science – and are often referred to as 'first' degrees. (Most diploma and certificate courses at universities are open only to graduates, or to students with comparable qualifications or experience – see page 31.) However, not all Bachelor's degrees are first degrees; and at five Scottish universities (Aberdeen, Dundee, Edinburgh, Glasgow and St Andrews) the first degree in arts is almost always called Master of Arts. Moreover the title of a degree does not necessarily reflect the field or faculty in which the student has studied; for example, at several universities the Bachelor of Arts is awarded to students in all, or almost all, disciplines – Science, Engineering, etc – as well as in Arts subjects.

Almost all first degree courses involve full-time attendance at the university or college concerned (although for BEd, see pages 37–39).* In Arts or Science subjects the courses generally last three years, although four years' study may be required in some cases (e.g. in modern languages, if the course involves spending a year abroad, and for Honours degrees at Scottish universities, for which the courses are a year longer than those for Ordinary degrees). For first degrees in other disciplines – Engineering, Architecture, Dentistry, Medicine, etc – the courses vary in length from three to six years; and if the usual period of study for a first degree in a particular subject is more than three or four years, the length of the course is indicated under the relevant heading in the Directory of Subjects on pages 73–264.

Examinations are not necessarily held annually. At many universities there are only two major examinations for the BA or BSc – one at the end of the first year and the 'final' examination – but in all subjects both the intervals between examinations and the methods by which students are examined may vary from one university to another. At some universities the students' work may be assessed at regular intervals throughout the course, and the results of these assessments taken into account in determining their final degree classification. In all examinations, however, written work plays a much greater part than oral tests.

First degree courses in Arts and Science are of two main kinds: those in which the student specialises with some intensity in just one or two subjects, and those which allow him to spread his studies over a wider field but less intensively. The degree obtained at the end of a specialised course is usually called a degree with Honours, or in some universities a Special degree (Special degrees are usually awarded with Honours). The term Joint (or Combined) degree, with or without the designation Honours, is sometimes used for degrees with specialisation in two (or, as may occasionally be possible, three) subjects, to distinguish them from single-subject degrees; but it is important always to remember that the same word may denote different types of course at different universities – 'Combined', for example, is in some cases used to describe a quite broadly based course and not a specialised one. However, degrees obtained at the end of the less specialised type of course in Arts or Science subjects are usually called Ordinary or General degrees. In some universities General degrees, too, may be awarded with Honours; and in certain professional subjects, such as Dentistry, Medicine and Veterinary Science, the word Honours is used solely to denote that special merit has been shown in the final degree examinations.

Some universities, particularly the newer ones, offer degree courses that

*Birkbeck College, of the University of London, specialises in providing part-time study facilities for mature students, but it is a condition of admission to its *first* degree courses that students must be engaged in earning their livelihood during the daytime.

do not conform to either of the two most usual patterns described in the previous paragraph (see also pages 70–71). At certain universities many undergraduate courses, especially those in applied science and technological subjects, are four-year 'sandwich' courses in which academic study in the university is combined with training in industry or in an appropriate professional establishment. This combination may be achieved in various ways – for example, in some courses three or four periods of industrial training may be intercalated with periods of full-time university study, while in others students spend a whole year (usually the third) in industry and the remaining three years at the university. Sandwich-course students at universities may be 'industry-sponsored' or 'university-based', in the way described on page 47.

Post-graduate courses
A postgraduate student may carry out independent research under the supervision of a senior member of the university department in which he is working, or may follow a formal course of instruction which involves regular attendance at prescribed lectures, seminars, etc, and perhaps also the preparation of a dissertation or essay on a topic or project of the student's own choosing. Universities can usually provide facilities for supervised research in at least some aspects of the subjects that they teach at undergraduate level, and such facilities are therefore much too wide-ranging to describe in detail in this handbook. However, lists of the formal courses of instruction that universities offer at the postgraduate level are given under the various headings in the Directory of Subjects.

Postgraduate research may lead to a variety of higher degrees, most of which are Master's or Doctor's degrees although some may have the title of Bachelor (e.g. Bachelor of Letters – BLitt – or Bachelor of Philosophy – BPhil). Postgraduate courses of instruction usually lead to Master's (or in some cases Bachelor's) degrees, but a number of them are for postgraduate diplomas or certificates, and some may lead to either a higher degree or a diploma or certificate (depending upon such factors as the qualifications that the candidate already holds; the standards that he achieves; or whether he completes a satisfactory dissertation or project in addition to passing the examinations).

Most Master's (or postgraduate Bachelor's) degrees require a minimum of one or two years' postgraduate study, and universities do not use a uniform nomenclature to distinguish between those taken by course work and those taken by research. Indeed some universities use the same titles – Master of Arts (MA), Master of Science (MSc), etc – for degrees taken by either method. Others may use titles such as MA and MSc for degrees taken by course work, and offer the degree of Master of Philosophy (MPhil) for research work at Master's level. The MPhil may (like the degree of Doctor of Philosophy at a higher level) be taken in different faculties –

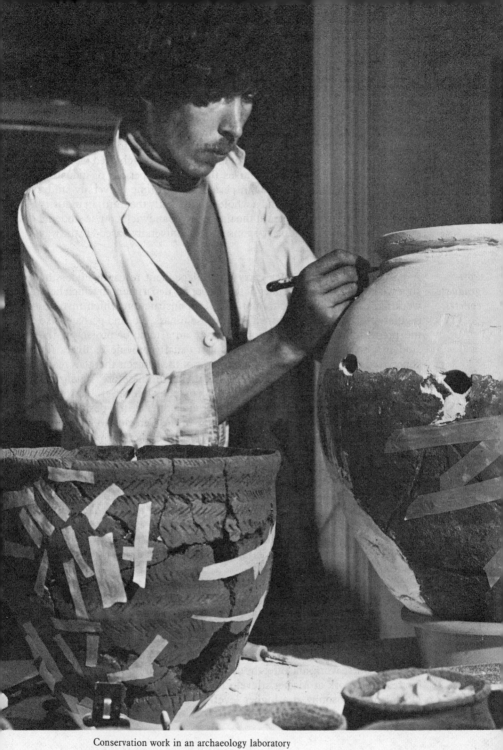

Conservation work in an archaeology laboratory

Science, Engineering, Medicine, etc, as well as Arts – but it is not necessarily a research degree, because in some cases it may, like MA, MSc, etc, be awarded either for research or on successful completion of a formal course.

The whole apparatus of degrees at both undergraduate and postgraduate level is so complex that prospective students *must* refer to the officers or publications of the universities in which they are interested to interpret its relation to their own needs. The Master of Arts provides a good example of the way in which the varied history of the universities in the United Kingdom has resulted in a variety of nomenclature of both first and higher degrees: usually it is awarded only after a prescribed period of postgraduate study, followed by an examination or thesis (or both); but at five Scottish universities (see page 27) it is a first degree in Arts; and at Oxford and Cambridge the holder of a BA of the university may, after a lapse of time, become an MA on payment of a fee and without any further examination.

The degree of Doctor of Philosophy – PhD (DPhil at Oxford, Sussex, Ulster and York) – is awarded after a minimum of two or three years' research and indicates a higher level of attainment than a Master's degree in the same subject. (A few universities will now award a PhD on the basis of published work, but *only* to their own graduates or to members of their own staffs). Other doctorates – of Letters (DLitt), of Science (DSc), etc – are conferred only upon scholars distinguished by outstanding contributions to knowledge, and for many of these 'higher doctorates' candidature is restricted to those who are already graduates of the university concerned.

Most diplomas and certificates (e.g. in Education) are open only to graduates, or to students holding similar qualifications or with substantial practical experience in an appropriate field. Because they usually involve a course of study rather than supervised research, they are included among the courses listed by name in the Directory of Subjects. In certain cases it may be the college of a university (and not the university itself) which awards the diploma or certificate, e.g. Imperial College of Science and Technology (University of London) awards its own diploma (DIC).

Cranfield Institute of Technology and Royal College of Art
Cranfield Institute of Technology and the Royal College of Art are very well-known specialised institutions which have by Royal Charter the power to award their own degrees. Cranfield awards higher degrees (Master's and Doctorates) in various branches of Engineering, Applied Sciences and Management (also a certificate of Membership of the Institute, for courses of three terms' duration); it also offers a first degree and a postgraduate diploma in Agricultural Engineering. The Royal College of Art offers courses at the postgraduate level only and awards Master's, PhD and Higher Doctorate degrees in Art and Design.

University College at Buckingham The University College at Buckingham (Buckingham MK18 1EG) is independent of public finance, being supported by private benefactions and students' fees. The courses, which involve eight 10-week terms of study within two calendar years, lead to a Licence (LUCB); and the Licence in law provides exemption from Part I of the professional examinations referred to on page 188. Tuition fees in 1977 were £1,800 p.a.

Courses outside universities

First degrees The Council for National Academic Awards (CNAA) is a body with authority to award degrees to students who satisfactorily complete courses approved by the Council in non-university institutions (polytechnics, colleges of art, colleges of education, colleges of technology and the Services' colleges) which do not have power to award their own degrees. CNAA degrees are comparable in standard to United Kingdom university degrees and the following first degrees are available: BA, BEd or BSc, unclassified or with appropriate Honours classification, and can be single-subject, multi-disciplinary or inter-disciplinary degrees. They are offered on a full-time, sandwich or part-time basis.

Postgraduate degrees CNAA Postgraduate and research degrees (MA, MSc, MEd, MPhil and PhD) are also awarded. MA, MEd and MSc courses include a formal teaching programme and comprise study in depth of the specialised topic. In a full-time course the student must spend under tuition at least one calendar year, the whole of which may be spent in college or part in industry or commerce and part in college. MPhils and PhDs involve approved supervised programmes of research. Candidates may be sponsored by educational establishments (excluding universities) or by industrial, commercial, or professional research establishments able to meet conditions laid down by the Council. Collaboration between colleges or polytechnics and industrial establishments is encouraged. The usual minimum period of registration for MPhil is 21 months and for PhD 33 months. Higher doctorates, DSc, DLitt and DTech, are granted only to persons ordinarily resident in the United Kingdom.

Diploma courses Diplomas are awarded by the CNAA to students who complete courses which, though postgraduate in time, have different objectives from those of Master's courses and are designed for students with a wide range of academic backgrounds or experience. They are regarded as terminal qualifications in their own right. The normal minimum duration of such a course is 25 weeks of full-time study. The individual contribution by the student is regarded as of major importance and courses may include the completion of an extended essay or approved project. Normal entry requirements are either a first degree, or full or corporate membership of one of the major professional bodies, a Certificate in Education with appropriate experience or substantial experience of employment in an area related to the subject matter of the course.

Certificate courses   The CNAA is also empowered to award a Certificate to students completing approved courses of study at sub-degree level. Such a certificate is regarded as a qualification in its own right and can also mark the completion of a stage in a degree course, e.g. part-time BEd course for non-graduate serving teachers, or give exemption from the first year of an approved degree course. Most of the Certificate courses approved by the Council are in the field of education, leading to a certificate in education.

Post-graduate Certificate in Education   CNAA award this qualification to graduates who have completed a course of initial teacher training. The normal length of this type of course is one academic year of full-time study. On successful completion, candidates are recommended by Council for Qualified Teacher status to the Secretary of State or the appropriate Ministers in Wales and Northern Ireland. Normal entry requirements are a CNAA or United Kingdom university degree or an award recognised as equivalent.

Diploma of Higher Education   The DipHE is a new award validated by the CNAA and some universities to be conferred on students successfully completing a two-year course of study on a full-time basis (or three years part-time), equivalent in standard and often similar in content to that of the first two years of a degree course. The Diploma course will normally be designed to facilitate transfer to a suitable degree programme with two years' credit. It is hoped that the Diploma will also be viewed as a terminal qualification in its own right, thus giving Diplomates the choice of further study on a degree programme, further study leading to a professional qualification, or employment with an acceptable qualification. Entry requirements for such courses are basically the same as those for a degree programme, with additional flexibility to allow entry for students with evidence of appropriate attainment in such fields as art, drama, music, and physical education.

Scottish Central Institutions   The Central Institutions provide most of the advanced full-time courses in Scotland outside the universities and colleges of education. Each Central Institution is managed by an independent governing body and two of them, Robert Gordon's Institute of Technology and Paisley College of Technology, are polytechnic in character. The others are more specialised: i.e. colleges of agriculture, art, music and drama, technology or textiles, and most of the courses offered prepare students for a particular career or group of careers.

Diploma and Associateship courses of degree level are offered by the

Central Institutions and may lead to membership of professional institutions (see below). Degree courses in a wide range of subjects are also offered, most of them validated by the CNAA and a few by universities. Postgraduate facilities for study or research leading to Diploma awards, MA, MSc, MPhil and PhD (CNAA or university validation) and to postgraduate diplomas are also available. A list of full-time, sandwich and part-time courses of higher and further education offered in the Further Education Colleges, in addition to those in the Scottish Central Institutions, is published annually as the *Directory of Day Courses* by the Scottish Education Department. Copies may be obtained from the Scottish Education Department in Edinburgh.

Courses for professional qualifications

Although there is no generally accepted definition the word 'profession' is usually employed in Britain to cover a wider range of occupations than the traditional three 'learned professions' of law, medicine and divinity. One of the distinctive features of the British pattern of higher education is the part played by the professional bodies, i.e. by groups of practitioners of the same occupation who have joined together to promote the interests of the occupation. Such bodies very often conduct examinations (sometimes at different levels) and award qualifications to those seeking to become more qualified in the skills required for the full exercise of the particular occupation. It is, however, only rarely that a professional body itself conducts courses of instruction; courses leading to the qualifications of such bodies are usually provided at other institutions, e.g. colleges of technology or commerce. University or CNAA degrees in a particular subject may exempt the holder from part of the academic requirements laid down by the relevant professional body for admission to a particular level of membership. Terminology and practice vary but it is not unusual for a professional body to have one or more levels of membership with, as a higher qualification, a 'fellowship' which a relatively small number of specially well-qualified members attain.

Details of professional qualifications are given in the Directory of Subjects under the relevant subject headings – see, for example, Business and Management Studies; Law; Social Work, etc. The following notes may also be of assistance.

Applied science and technology There is a wide variety of courses in most branches of engineering and the applied sciences, most of which either lead to membership of a relevant professional body, or to qualifications which allow exemption from some or all of the qualifying examinations prescribed by that body. Such courses include university and CNAA degrees, which have already been mentioned, and the Higher National Diploma (HND) which covers most fields

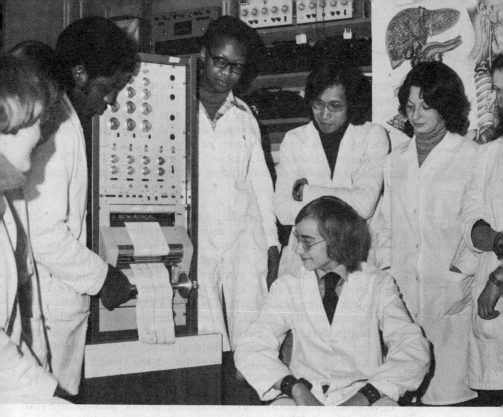

Pharmacy students doing physiological measurements

of technology. The HND is a nationally recognised qualification controlled by joint committees representing the education authorities and the professions concerned. Courses leading to an HND last either two years on a full-time, or three years on a sandwich basis, and nearly all HND courses in engineering and technology are sandwich courses. It is a basic qualification required of high level technicians, and gives exemption from a number of professional examinations, in particular the Part I examination of the Council of Engineering Institutions (CEI). The CEI is composed of a number of the professional institutions, covering the whole field of engineering. Success in the CEI Part I and Part II examinations is accepted by the institutions for entry at the same level as for a graduate. Unlike a degree course however the HND does not give exemption from Part II, which requires a period of further study (usually one year).

Technician and Business Education Councils   The Technician Education Council (TEC) was established by the Secretary of State for Education and Science in 1973, and its awards will eventually replace City and Guilds, OND, HNC and HND awards; only HND awards fall within the province of this handbook. The TEC Higher Diploma is broadly equivalent to the HND and there are at present a few institutions offering full-time or sandwich courses. In this handbook, the courses are given in the sections headed TEC HD courses. The number of such courses is likely to increase over the next few years and applicants should check with the college or polytechnic in which they are interested on whether or not approved courses exist.

The Business Education Council (BEC) was appointed in 1974 and is intended to establish courses leading to Higher Diplomas in business studies.

The arts and architecture   In England, Wales and Northern Ireland most advanced courses in fine art, graphic design, three-dimensional design, and textiles/fashion lead to the BA degree which is awarded by the CNAA. This replaces the National Diploma in Art and Design. As an indication of aptitude and potential, students must normally have completed a full-time foundation course lasting one year and in all a four-year course should be anticipated. One- and two-year courses leading to the CNAA MA degree can be followed at some institutions, though places are very limited and normally only available to holders of the CNAA first degree. Applicants from abroad may in the first instance approach the individual institution for further details but formal application must be made to the Art and Design Admissions Registry, 2 Granada Buildings, Gabriel's Hill, Maidstone, Kent, giving a choice of colleges.

In Scotland four central (art) institutions provide four- or five-year courses leading to Diplomas in drawing and painting, sculpture, design and crafts, and architecture, and are recognised by the Scottish Education Department.

Many colleges of art offer 'vocational' courses for which the entry standard is normally lower than for degree courses. These courses concentrate on practical requirements and contain less history and theory than more advanced courses.

Courses in architecture, leading to the Diploma examinations of the Royal Institute of British Architects, may be taken in many colleges of art and schools of architecture approved by the Institute. The courses are generally five-year sandwich.

Courses in colleges of music and drama vary in length according to the subjects studied and the kind of professional work which the student intends to take up. Details are given in the entries under these headings in the Directory of Subjects.

Medicine   The training required for full medical registration is described in the Directory of Subjects under the heading 'Medicine and Surgery'. Details of advanced specialist training are given elsewhere in the Directory, under such headings as 'Anaesthetics' and 'Cardiology'. Information about the various professions defined as being 'supplementary to medicine' (such as Chiropody and Physiotherapy) is given under the relevant subject heading. For postgraduate study involving clinical responsibility registration with the General Medical Council (GMC) is essential. The GMC will not normally be prepared to grant temporary registration for the first time to any overseas doctor unless he has passed a test of linguistic proficiency and professional knowledge and competence. These tests are held in Britain and are conducted by the Temporary Registration Assessment Board on behalf of the GMC. Details from the Registrar, General Medical Council.

Teaching   In *England and Wales* institutions of teacher training are undergoing a period of transition. The profession is moving towards all-graduate entry; colleges of education are extending their work beyond teacher education and training into other forms of higher education and some of them are amalgamating with polytechnics or colleges of technology. One is now required to have completed a period of professional training before taking up a teaching post in the maintained sector. The courses providing this training are:
Degree courses: Three- or four-year degree courses, incorporating professional training, which lead to a BEd degree at Ordinary or Honours levels. These are either university degrees or courses taken in polytechnic departments of education or other institutions of education and validated by a university or the CNAA.

Some teacher training establishments also offer degrees other than the BEd, which lead to teaching qualifications and some offer degree courses which do *not* lead to teaching qualifications.
Certificate in education courses: These are three-year professional courses below degree level, available at some polytechnic departments of education and colleges of education. The Certificate in Education is being replaced rapidly by the Bachelor of Education degree and is now offered largely in shortage areas of teaching e.g. mathematics and science subjects. The last entry for certificate courses is in 1979. The student studies one or two main subjects intensively together with subjects such as child development and the principles of teaching. Teaching practice in a variety of schools takes place throughout the course. At some colleges suitably qualified students may be invited to transfer to a four-year BEd course.

One- and two-year certificate courses are available at some colleges for mature, well-qualified students. A one-year postgraduate certificate course for graduates is offered by some universities, polytechnic departments and colleges of education.
Diploma of Higher Education: These two-year courses are offered at some teacher training establishments and although the DipHE is intended to be

an award in itself (see page 33) at some institutions students are given the opportunity of going on to a degree course.

Other courses: Some teacher training establishments offer courses for teachers at all levels, from nursery school to secondary school, while others specialise in courses for a particular age-range. Others specialise in the training of teachers of particular subjects such as art, drama, home economics, music, physical education, technical or commercial subjects.

For detailed information about all these courses the *Handbook of Institutions providing Teacher Training* (see page 265) should be consulted as well as the prospectuses of individual institutions.

In *Northern Ireland* three general colleges of education provide three-year initial teacher training courses; BEd courses; one-year post-graduate courses; and in-service courses, all validated by Queen's University, Belfast. Courses may also be taken at Queen's University and at the New University of Ulster, Coleraine.

The training of specialist teachers is concentrated mainly at Ulster College, the Northern Ireland Polytechnic. This institution offers degree and/or certificate (three- and one-year) courses for teachers of the following subjects: art; communication studies; domestic science; heavy crafts, carpentry and joinery; music; physical education; and for teachers of children requiring special care. Londonderry Technical College offers a one-year course of professional training for prospective teachers of commercial subjects.

Further information is available from the Northern Ireland Department of Education.

The system of teacher training in *Scotland* differs in some respects from that in England and Wales. Registration with the General Teaching Council for Scotland is a statutory prerequisite of employment in education authority and grant-aided schools in Scotland. Automatic entitlement to registration is secured by successful completion of a certificate or diploma course of a Scottish college of education which leads to the award of a Teaching Qualification. The departments of education of the Scottish universities do not provide courses of initial teacher training for graduates but Stirling offers courses within the university leading both to a degree of BA and to qualification as a teacher. There are 9 general colleges of education, one of which also offers courses for male teachers of physical education, and one college for female teachers of physical education. The colleges provide one-year courses for graduates and holders of equivalent qualifications leading to the award of a Teaching Qualification in either primary or secondary education. Three-year diploma courses which lead to the award of a Teaching Qualification (Primary Education) are also offered. The colleges (except Craiglockhart College of Education) also offer four-year BEd degrees in conjunction with

A student of education on an observational visit to a local school

a Scottish university or the Council for National Academic Awards. Five-year honours courses are available at Aberdeen and Jordanhill Colleges of Education. Candidates for enrolment to most of these courses must satisfy the required qualifications for university entrance. BEd students in Scotland therefore undertake the study of academic and professional subjects concurrently with teacher training throughout the length of the course.

Further information is available from The Secretary, Scottish Education Department, St Andrew's House, Edinburgh EH1 3DB (for all degree courses) and The Registrar, General Teaching Council for Scotland, 5 Royal Terrace, Edinburgh EH7 5AF (for other qualifications). Details of courses are also listed in the *Memorandum on Entry Requirements to Courses of Teacher Training in Scotland.*

Adult education courses

There are eight *long-term* residential colleges, primarily for students from workers' or other adult educational organisations, which aim to give adults, and especially workers in industry, opportunities for full-time, non-vocational education. Students are mostly over 20 years of age and may have had little or no secondary education of an academic kind before they started work. The usual courses of study last one or two years, though applications for shorter periods are considered. Economic and social studies predominate, but most courses include philosophy, literature and the arts. Details of courses and fees, with the addresses of the colleges, are given on pages 281–283.

There are also forty *short-term* residential colleges which offer courses varying in length from a week-end to three months. These colleges are often aided and in some cases are directly financed by local education authorities; some are sponsored by voluntary organisations, others by universities. The fees vary considerably; a week-end may cost from £7 to £12. Most of the colleges are in the countryside and some are in buildings of historic interest. Their courses deal with such subjects as current affairs, social problems, music, drama, arts and crafts, local history, literature, economics, and science.

The short courses give students from overseas an opportunity of added experience and enjoyment, at week-ends or during vacations, while pursuing full-time studies elsewhere. Details are available from College Wardens (addresses on page 282) or in *Residential Short Courses*, published at 50p, including postage, by the National Institute of Adult Education, 35 Queen Anne Street, London W1M 0BL.

Vacation courses

In Britain there are no regular summer sessions, but summer vacation courses are organised by extra-mural and other departments of some universities, and are open to suitably qualified overseas students and teachers. The British Council also arranges refresher courses for teachers of English in the summer vacation, and advanced courses at other times of the year on various professional subjects for suitably qualified persons, lasting from a fortnight to twelve weeks. These courses are often organised in conjunction with a university, but they do not count towards any degree in Britain. The Association of Commonwealth Universities issues a student information paper listing the published sources of information about summer courses at universities in Britain. Lists of vacation courses at universities and other institutions are published annually by the British Tourist Authority, 64 St James's Street, London SW1A 1NF, and are available direct from that address or from the British Council, Courses Department, 65 Davies Street, London W1Y 2AA.

ADMISSION OF STUDENTS FROM OVERSEAS

Overseas students are eligible to apply for admission to almost all the courses listed in this handbook, provided they have the necessary qualifications. A very few courses are restricted to people already working in a profession or in other ways; where this is the case, it is mentioned in the relevant entry.

Although there are some courses specially designed for students from overseas, most overseas students attend exactly the same courses as United Kingdom students. Those courses that are intended for students from abroad usually have a special emphasis on practical subjects in which there is a demand for advanced training facilities, for example in the economic, social and administrative fields. Such courses are primarily for candidates from developing countries and most are for those of senior graduate or professional level with several years' working experience. Details of these courses may be obtained from British Council offices and British Embassies and High Commissions.

First degree courses

Note – Students wishing to study in Britain at the undergraduate level for just a relatively short period, e.g. one academic year or less, should read the section on 'Occasional' students (page 49).

Univer-
sities

(a) *Entrance requirements.* Each university will want to have from an applicant for admission evidence that his education has qualified him to follow a course leading to a degree, and that he speaks and understands English well. In addition to this 'general' requirement there are at most universities specific 'course' requirements, which may vary from one faculty or department to another and which are intended to ensure that the student's previous studies have included adequate preparation in (and/or indicate sufficient aptitude for) the particular subject or subjects that he wants to study for his degree. At some universities there is a minimum age – usually 17 years but at one or two 18 years – below which no student can be admitted to a degree course; and universities which do not formally prescribe a minimum age for admission may nevertheless normally require entrants to be at least 17 (occasionally 18) years old. (In fact 18 is the age at which a majority of British university students begin their undergraduate studies.)

Each university is responsible for drawing up its own regulations about admission, and both the 'general' requirement and the requirements for admission to a particular kind of course may therefore vary in detail from university to university. At all universities, however, the requirements are expressed mainly in terms of passes in United Kingdom examinations such as those for the General Certificate of Education or the Scottish Certificate of Education. Some of these examinations can be taken overseas (for further information see pages 295–296), but shortage of space makes it impracticable to set out in this handbook each university's requirements in terms of the GCE. A very detailed statement of the GCE passes which will satisfy both the 'general' and (where relevant) the 'course' requirements, together with information about admission on the basis of other UK qualifications such as Ordinary National Diplomas and Certificates, is published annually in the *Compendium of University Entrance Requirements**; and Appendix III of the annual *Commonwealth Universities Yearbook** contains an extended summary of each university's entrance regulations, including any references that they may make to the standing accorded to overseas certificates. However, universities in Britain make no attempt to provide in their formal published regulations comprehensive lists of the overseas qualifications that they may be prepared to consider, and it is usually only from the universities themselves that overseas candidates can obtain definitive and fully up-to-date advice about their eligibility to apply for a place on the particular course that they want to follow.

At Cambridge, Durham, London and Oxford, students must not only be able to satisfy the admission requirements of the university itself but also be accepted by one or other of the colleges, halls, etc, of the university. (At Cambridge candidates may in the first instance consult the Adviser to Overseas Candidates for Admission, University Registry, The Old Schools, Cambridge CB2 1TN, and at Oxford the pamphlet *Admission of Overseas Students* may be obtained from the Adviser to Overseas Students, Oxford Colleges Admissions Office, 58 Banbury Road, Oxford OX2 6PP; however, neither of these Advisers can place students in colleges.) The Joint Matriculation Board of the Universities of Manchester, Liverpool, Leeds, Sheffield and Birmingham lays down the 'general' requirements that must be satisfied before a student can be considered for a place at one of those five universities (full details can be obtained from the Secretary to the Board, Manchester M15 6EU), but each of the five independently prescribes whatever additional 'course' or 'faculty' requirements it considers appropriate. At Brunel, where all undergraduate courses are organised on the 'thin sandwich' pattern, sponsorship by an industrial firm or organisation (preferably in the United Kingdom) is normally a requirement for overseas applicants, particularly in the School of Engineering.

Students seeking admission to one of the constituent institutions of the University of Wales must satisfy the general (matriculation) requirements

*See page 265.

of the university, but each institution prescribes separately the additional 'course' or 'faculty' requirements that must also be satisfied.

The 'general' and 'course' requirements of the universities in Scotland are set out in detail in the *Compendium of Information** published by the Scottish Universities Council on Entrance (Kinburn House, St Andrews, Scotland KY16 9DR).

Students must bear in mind that no qualification of any kind (whether obtained in Britain or in another country) *entitles* its holder to a university place, and that each university makes its own selection of students from among those candidates whose qualifications are acceptable to it. To be eligible for consideration, applicants who are seeking admission on the basis of GCE examinations must normally have, *as a minimum*, passes in either five approved subjects including two at the Advanced level or four approved subjects including three at the Advanced level (although there are several universities that do not conform to this pattern). Students who have taken GCE Ordinary level examinations in or after June 1975 (when a new system of grading GCE Ordinary level results was introduced) may, for university entrance purposes, count as Ordinary level passes only those subjects in which they attain grade A, B or C. Most universities will accept passes in suitable subjects at the principal level in an approved Higher School Certificate examination as corresponding to GCE Advanced level passes, and approved HSC subsidiary level passes, or approved School Certificate passes at credit level or better, as corresponding to GCE Ordinary level passes. A student who holds an International or European Baccalaureate will probably be considered for admission by most universities in the United Kingdom, and applications may in many cases also be considered from overseas students holding certificates awarded by recognised local bodies which would admit them to universities in their own countries. But there are some certificates which, although they would qualify a student to enter a degree course in his own country, would definitely not, by themselves, meet the requirements of any university in the United Kingdom, and no UK university *automatically* accepts evidence of eligibility for admission to another university as satisfying its own entrance requirements. An overseas applicant may therefore be told that he will have to pass a GCE (or equivalent) examination in one or more subjects in order to be eligible for a place, either because his locally obtained qualifications do not fully meet the 'general' requirement for admission to the UK university concerned, or because, although satisfying the 'general' requirement, they do not meet the additional requirements laid down for entry to his chosen course.

It should be noted that, in selecting candidates for the limited number of

*See page 265.

RSV Prince Madog – marine research vessel of the University College of North Wales

places available – see also page 26 – a university pays particular attention to *how well* each applicant has done in his secondary-level school examinations (e.g. in the case of the GCE, to the grades that he has obtained at the Advanced level).

If a student already has a degree from a university in his own country UK universities will normally accept it as qualifying him for admission, provided that it was awarded for studies in a subject relevant to the course that he wants to follow in Britain. In fact it is often better to come to Britain after taking a first degree at a university in one's own country, even if one is going to do another first degree at the British university. Information about the possibility of exemption from some part of the full course of study leading to a first degree being granted to a student who has already studied at an institution of higher education in his own country can be obtained only from the UK university to which the student wishes to apply – see (*b*) below.

It is essential that candidates for admission should have a thorough command of written and spoken English, and candidates whose mother tongue is not English will probably be required to submit evidence that their ability to understand and express themselves in both written and spoken English is sufficient to enable them to take full advantage of university study in Britain (see also page 49).

Before confirming an offer of a place to a student from another country a university may ask for evidence of his ability to support himself financially for the duration of his proposed course (see also pages 50 and 53).

(*b*) *Transfer and 'credit'*. Although it is very occasionally possible, on academic or compassionate grounds, for a student who has begun a degree course at one university in Britain to move to another British university in order to complete the course there, it is rare for students to transfer in this way and there is no national scheme for transfer 'with credit'. In other words there is no *automatic* granting of 'credit' for university studies already completed either in the United Kingdom or elsewhere, and some UK universities will not admit degree students for any period of study shorter than the usual three or four years of the full course for first degrees in arts or science subjects even if they have already studied at a university, although some will allow overseas students who already hold a degree to complete a first degree in arts or science in two years instead of three. Overseas students are strongly recommended to complete a full degree course in Britain.

(*c*) *Method of application* for United Kingdom and overseas applicants. Application for admission to a full-time first degree or first diploma course at a United Kingdom university should be made through the Universities Central Council on Admissions, PO Box 28, Cheltenham, Glos. GL50 1HY. The UCCA handbook *How to Apply for Admission to a University* and an application form may be obtained, free of charge, from the UCCA office after 15 July. Graduate applicants should find out from the UCCA handbook whether a particular university wishes them to apply direct or through the UCCA office. Every candidate submitting an application through UCCA is required to pay a fee of £2.

The opening date for the receipt of applications for admission in October 1979 is 1 September 1978. The last date for receipt of applications is: 15 October 1978 for candidates including Oxford or Cambridge among their entries; or 15 December 1978 for candidates not including Oxford or Cambridge among their entries. Corresponding dates will be announced in respect of entry in October 1980 and subsequent years.

All the United Kingdom universities, except the Open University, participate in the UCCA scheme. Applications for admission to the University College at Buckingham (see below) must be made direct to the College.

Details of the scheme may be obtained from British Council offices throughout the world (see list on pages 287–291). Overseas candidates who are applying from certain countries (see list in UCCA handbook) are advised to submit their applications to UCCA through the recognised agency in London (e.g. the British Council Technical Cooperation Training Department or their own country's High Commission, Embassy, Consulate-General or Students' Office).

The UCCA cannot give academic advice, e.g. about choice of university or course, entrance requirements, scholarships or grants, or an individual candidate's prospects of admission. While this handbook, the *Compendium of University Entrance Requirements** and the *Commonwealth Universities Yearbook** will give intending applicants the basic information they need, a student must in order to obtain up-to-date, full and official information about entrance requirements and courses, write direct to the institutions of his choice at least a year before he hopes to begin his studies, so that he will have decided to which institutions he wishes to seek admission, and obtained the necessary application form, well before the closing date for receipt of applications (see above). For Oxford or Cambridge enquiries should be sent to the college of the student's choice at least eighteen months in advance. In writing to any university or college, it is necessary to give details of qualifications and previous studies and to state what course of study it is desired to follow.

Where a candidate sends to a university or college certificates showing he is qualified to enter a university in his own country, a certified English translation should, if necessary, be sent with them. If the certificate does not state clearly that it would admit the holder to a university in his own country, a letter will be needed which does say this, written by the registrar

*See page 265.

of a university, a government official, or the local British Council representative in his own country, or by an official of his Embassy, Legation or Consulate elsewhere. (Certificates should not be sent to UCCA.)

Buckingham
The minimum entrance requirements of the University College at Buckingham (see page 41) are in general similar to those of the universities. However the College also places weight on interviews and, when appropriate, on its own admission tests (although overseas students may be admitted without interview if the College is satisfied, on other evidence, of their ability to undertake their chosen course). All applications must be made direct, not through the UCCA.

Polytechnics, colleges of technology, etc
The qualifications required for entrance to CNAA degree courses are broadly similar to those for university degree courses (see (*a*) above), and applicants are required to give evidence of their ability to follow a course. The normal minimum entry requirements for HND courses are either five GCE passes including one pass at advanced level or three Ordinary National Certificate passes in appropriate subjects. The procedure for admission to degree or other advanced courses is, however, entirely different from the university procedure: There is no central organisation, equivalent to the UCCA, to deal with applications to polytechnics and other colleges; students must apply to each individual institution. The polytechnics have, however, produced a common application form for all courses other than those in Art and Design, and Education. This form and prospectuses are available direct from each polytechnic. Applications for colleges other than the polytechnics should be addressed to the Principal of the college concerned.

A number of countries have established machinery for placing students in colleges in Britain, through the Ministry of Education or other authority in the country concerned in co-operation with a Students' Office in London. A list of these countries and of the relevant addresses is given on pages 292–295.

Applications should in all cases reach the institution concerned about eighteen months ahead of the date on which the candidate wishes to start his course. This is especially important in the case of a sandwich course.

Students following sandwich courses are either (a) 'industry-based', i.e. employed by a firm which arranges the periods of practical training; or (b) 'college-based', in which case the college itself makes arrangements for training in industry. It is normally difficult for an overseas student to join a course of the former type, because he has first to find a firm willing to sponsor him.

Art
courses

Entry requirements for the CNAA BA Hons Art and Design are as for other degree courses although it is preferred that applicants should have completed a one-year full-time foundation course in Art and Design and have achieved five GCE 'O' level subjects or a combination of 'O' and 'A' level passes. Three of these must be in academic subjects including at least one providing evidence of the applicant's ability to use English.

Applications for places on Art and Design degree courses must be made on Art and Design Admissions Registry forms. Applicants may obtain the form direct from the Registrar, Art and Design Admissions Registry, 2 Granada Buildings, Gabriel's Hill, Maidstone, Kent; all enquiries concerning applications should be made to this address.

Details about other art courses and application procedures should be obtained direct from the institution concerned.

Teacher
training
courses

No minimum age requirement is officially laid down, but candidates applying to colleges and departments of education are normally expected to be at least 18 years of age.

Academic entry requirements to BEd and DipHE courses are normally the same as university degree courses (see page 41). Entry requirements for certificate in education courses are at the discretion of individual institutions and awarding bodies (although the minimum requirements are normally five 'O' level GCE passes) and details should be obtained from individual institutions.

Commonwealth candidates for admission to colleges and departments of education in England and Wales should apply twelve months before the September in which they propose to begin their studies through the education authorities in their own countries. Enquiries from other countries should be addressed to the registrar, Central Register and Clearing House, 3 Crawford Place, London W1H 2BN, except for applicants for the Art Teachers Diploma or Certificate courses. They should apply to the Clearing House for Postgraduate Courses in Art Education, The Manor House, Heather, Leicester LE6 1QP.

Candidates wishing to apply to Scottish colleges should write to the Scottish Education Department, St Andrew's House, Edinburgh EH1 3DB, or the advisory Service on Entry to Teaching, 5 Royal Terrace, Edinburgh EH7 5AS; candidates wishing to apply to Northern Irish colleges (other than the New University of Ulster) should write to the Department of Education, Rathgael House, Balloo Road, Bangor, County Down.

Postgraduate studies

To be considered for admission to a postgraduate course of instruction or to undertake research in a university or polytechnic, etc, an applicant must have at least a first degree from a university in his own or another country, and must know English well. But even if he has these qualifications he is not certain to be admitted, as the institutions accept only a limited number of students for postgraduate study and research.

Only those who are strongly recommended by their own universities and show real promise of scholarly ability are likely to be allowed to undertake *research*. They will normally be expected to carry out independent research under the supervision of the staff of the department in which they are working.

Courses for professional qualifications other than degrees

The qualifications for admission to professional courses described in this Handbook vary according to the type of course, and students should write direct to the institutions of their choice for details (for information on how to apply to polytechnics see above. The warning about sandwich courses applies with equal force in this case). The usual qualifications for entry to a Higher National Diploma course are five passes in the GCE examination, including one at advanced level, or a qualification of similar standard recognised by the college such as an Ordinary National Certificate with high marks.

'Occasional' students

Overseas students often want to attend courses at British universities without qualifying for a degree. The universities vary in their conditions for admitting 'occasional' students during normal term-time. Some universities will not admit them at all, others will only admit graduates, but in general they will admit, for periods of up to a year, a few recommended students who have a good knowledge of English. They will often supply 'occasional' students with certificates of satisfactory attendance. A number of universities in Britain are prepared to consider applications from students who are already attending a university in their own country, and who wish to take a one-year or two-year course in Britain, returning to their own country to take their degrees.

In all cases the number which can be accepted is small. As conditions vary so much from one university to another students should write direct to the university in which they are interested, stating their qualifications, the subjects they wish to study and for how long they would like to stay.

KNOWLEDGE OF ENGLISH

It is essential to have a very good knowledge of the English language before beginning a course of higher education in Britain. A student must be able to follow lectures in English spoken at a pace to which he may not be accustomed, and to take part in discussions with his teachers and fellow students. If a student who has been accepted by a university or college is in any doubt about his ability to meet these requirements, or if an English proficiency test is required by his university or college, he should either arrange to take a course in English before he leaves his own country or, preferably, come to Britain well before his higher studies are due to begin in order to take an intensive course in English. Courses in English of this kind are provided by some of the local education authorities at technical colleges and by private English-language schools recognised by the Department of Education and Science. Advice on suitable courses may be obtained from British Council offices, in Britain and overseas.

MONEY MATTERS

The estimates given below, which relate to conditions early in 1978, are liable to become quickly out of date and prospective students should seek the latest information from the university or college of their choice.

Tuition and other non-residential fees (for fees for residential accommodation, see page 61).

Universities

Precise and fully up-to-date information about tuition fees can be obtained only from the universities themselves and it may not be until some time after the start of one academic year that the fees for the next academic year become known. The figures mentioned in the following paragraphs relate *only* to 1977–78.

At most universities the tuition fee payable by overseas students (for definition, see page 52) who enrolled as full-time students for the academic year 1977–78* was about £650 for those following undergraduate courses and about £850 for those undertaking postgraduate study or research. This fee (sometimes called the 'composition' fee) may or may not include the students' union subscription; and for postgraduates (occasionally also for undergraduates) the fees for one or more of registration, examination and graduation, may be charged separately. In addition, a postgraduate *research* student, or his sponsoring agency, may be required to make a contribution towards the costs of the department in which the research is being undertaken. This contribution (sometimes called a 'bench fee') may be as much as £300–£400 – or even more – for

*Late note: the recommended fees for overseas students for the year 1978–79 are £705 for undergraduates and £925 for postgraduates.

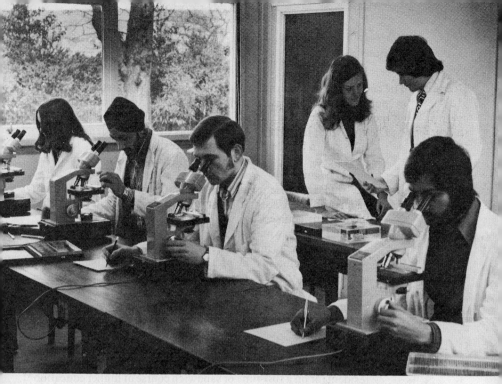

An anatomy class in progress

research in scientific or technological subjects, medicine, etc.; and for some postgraduates the costs of typing and binding their theses may amount to £100 or more.

On some courses extra costs may be incurred for such items as field courses, project work, special instruments or laboratory equipment and materials; and at one or two universities a college/collegiate fee of some £40–£50 p.a. may be payable as well. There may also be additional fees for any student who has to resit an examination or resubmit a thesis, and some minor incidental fees.

Finally, it should be noted that at some institutions there are one or two courses (usually postgraduate) for which considerably higher fees are charged – e.g., in 1977–78, fees of the order of £1,500–£2,000.

Poly-technics, colleges of technology, etc
For students from outside the United Kingdom (see below) the tuition fee for most of the courses in this Handbook is approximately £705 a year. A lower fee may be charged for a few courses not leading to a degree, a Higher National Diploma or other advanced qualification. Details of the cost of a particular course should be obtained from the college concerned.

Definition of an overseas student for fees purposes
The decision as to which students are to be classified as 'overseas students' in connection with the payment of tuition fees and related charges is based on the following criteria:

1. The following should *not* be regarded as overseas students –
   (i) any student who has been ordinarily resident in the UK for at least three years immediately preceding the date his course is, or was, due to begin;
   (ii) any student whose parents (or one of them) have been ordinarily resident in the UK for at least three years immediately preceding the date his course is, or was, due to begin;
   (iii) any student who would have been ordinarily resident in the UK for at least three years immediately preceding the date his course is, or was, due to begin had he or his parents (or one of them) not been employed for the time being outside the UK;
   (iv) any student aged under 21 at the date his course is, or was, due to begin, if he and his parents (or one of them) have been ordinarily resident in the UK for at least one year immediately preceding that date;
   (v) any student who, for at least one year immediately preceding the date his or her course is, or was, due to begin, has been (a) ordinarily resident (or on a full-time or sandwich course of higher education★) in the UK and (b) married to a person who has been ordinarily resident in the UK for at least three years immediately preceding that date; or
   (vi) any student whose parent or spouse is stationed in the UK and is recognised by the Foreign and Commonwealth Office as a member of the staff of a diplomatic mission or as a career consular officer.

2. All other students should be regarded for the purpose of fees as overseas students for the duration of their course.

3. Young overseas students in an establishment of further education are not charged a fee above the standard fee for the course; this provision is applied up to the end of the session in which the student attains the age of 19†. This arrangement for young further education students does not apply to students attending universities.

Notes
(a) A student who has been in the UK either at school or at a course of non-advanced further education† is regarded (in relation to any *subsequent*

★GCE 'O' and 'A' level, and OND courses, are examples of non-advanced further education courses; HND and degree courses are examples of higher further education courses.
†After the end of the session in which such an overseas student attains the age of 19 he is charged the same fees as those paid by all other overseas students.

course) as having been ordinarily resident in the UK during the period of such attendance.

(b) If a student has attended a full-time or sandwich course of *higher* education (higher further education*, college of education or university) in the UK prior to embarking on his present course, his attendance on the earlier course is *not* regarded as ordinary residence and the period of the course is disregarded for the purpose of computing periods of ordinary residence in the UK (e.g. a postgraduate student is not treated as a home student simply because he has spent three years on an undergraduate course in the UK; however, an overseas undergraduate who marries a UK resident may acquire home student status for a postgraduate course – see paragraph 1(v) above).

(c) Residence in the Channel Islands or Isle of Man is treated for this purpose as residence in the United Kingdom of Great Britain and Northern Ireland.

(d) It must be stressed that, although the University Grants Committee and the Department of Education and Science have issued guidance on the classification of students for fees purposes, the final responsibility for determining which students shall be charged at the 'overseas' rate rests with the individual university, local education authority or college concerned.

Other costs

The total cost of study and residence at a university for a student from overseas may vary somewhat from one institution to another and from one part of the country to another. To meet all expenses for a *calendar* year, *except fees* but including maintenance and some travel during vacations, it would be advisable for an overseas student to have about £1,800–£2,100 a year; and to these figures must be added the fees for tuition, examination, etc – see page 50.

The estimate of £1,800–£2,100 a year, which applies only to students who are *not* accompanied by dependants, will allow for an adequate standard of living 'without frills', but does not take account of any non-academic personal interests involving special expenses, nor does it include the cost of travel to and from the student's home country. An indication of the current level of charges for university accommodation is given on page 61.

Throughout the country moderately priced accommodation suitable for married couples is extremely difficult to obtain, especially if the couple are accompanied by a child or children, and any student thinking of bringing his family should take serious note of what is said in the section on

*See Footnote * on page 52.

Failure analysis on an oil drilling bit

accommodation on pages 60–62. It is almost impossible to make a realistic assessment of additional expenses for an overseas student accompanied by dependants. Costs vary widely according to the locality, the type of accommodation required and the ages of any children. Furthermore, a student cannot depend on his wife being able to contribute to the family's income. Even if the immigration regulations permit her to take paid work, a suitable job may not be available locally and it might be difficult for her to arrange adequate care for any young children during working hours. If, after considering these factors, a student wishes to bring his family to Britain he should first seek advice about probable living costs from the university or college at which he will be studying. The following are very general estimates of the *minimum* extra costs that he is likely to incur: if he brings his wife, an extra £1,000–£1,200 (in addition to his own allowance) and he should add at least £350–£450 for each child to his probable annual living expenses. It should be noted that the precise amount will vary widely (for the reasons already stated) and may well be more in some cases.

Although it is very unwise to carry large sums of money while travelling, overseas students arriving in Britain are strongly advised to have with them at least £25 in UK currency to cover their initial expenses, and as these may include the cost of their temporary accommodation, they should have travellers cheques in small denominations of £5 and £10 which they can cash when necessary.

Some universities will not confirm the acceptance of a student from overseas until they have received an adequate written guarantee from a grant-awarding body, a bank, etc, of his ability to support himself financially. 'Caution money' deposited in advance is sometimes required.

The cost of studying at a polytechnic or college of technology is approximately the same for a student from overseas as at a university, though it varies according to the part of the country. It is more expensive to study in the big cities than in a smaller town. A student will probably need at least £1,700–£2,000 a year in addition to his tuition fees.

Before leaving home a student should ensure that he has obtained a permit from the appropriate authority for the foreign exchange he will need for his period of residence in Britain. Private students (i.e. those who are meeting their own costs or are being financed by their parents, relatives, local community or some other agency in their home country) should ensure before they leave home that arrangements have been made for money to be sent to them from home at regular intervals. A student's concentration on his studies may be gravely affected if instalments of money are sent irregularly or in insufficient amounts.

It is advisable when applying for admission to a university to apply also for a place in a hall of residence. The cost of accommodation may be higher than at some lodgings (though this is rarely the case in London), but the extra cost is more than justified by the personal and social advantages. Moreover the difference in costs may prove to be less than it seems, since certain items such as lighting or heating may be charged for as 'extra' in lodgings but not in halls of residence.

Employment In *Britain* employment is inconsistent with student status and, in addition, Commonwealth citizens or foreign nationals seeking work must have permits issued by the Department of Employment. However, *bona-fide* students who have been admitted to Britain for full-time study may, unless their conditions of entry prohibit the taking of employment, work in their free time or vacations providing the approval of the Department of Employment is first obtained. This does not apply to nationals of the European Economic Community (EEC), who may take any employment (except in public service) during their stay, and do not need to seek the approval of the Department of Employment. The wife of a foreign or Commonwealth student is also free to take employment without seeking official approval unless her husband is himself prohibited from doing so, in which case the prohibition will extend to his wife also. Similar arrangements apply in *Northern Ireland* where it is very difficult for a student to get permission even for part-time work. Permission has to be obtained from the Department of Manpower Services, Belfast.

It should, however, be noted that the official university view is that a substantial part, if not all, of the vacations should be occupied in reading and other academic work. It is also becoming increasingly difficult to obtain part-time work in some areas. *Any student who comes to Britain to study must be prepared to devote his whole time to his studies and other university or college activities, and must have sufficient money to be able to do this. It is not possible to 'work one's way through college', i.e. to earn a living while following a full-time course of study; no student should attempt to do so.*

Scholarships

Overseas students wishing to study in the United Kingdom may be eligible for scholarships granted by their own Government, by inter-governmental agencies, or by universities or other educational, industrial and research institutions in the United Kingdom, or by the British Council. In several Commonwealth countries, including those newly independent, many Government scholarships are available which are tenable in the United Kingdom; particulars of these scholarships can be obtained from the appropriate Education Departments.

Information about scholarships can usually be obtained from the Ministry of Education in a student's own country, from the appropriate inter-university organisation, if there is one, or from the Representative of the British Council (see pages 287–289).

The Association of Commonwealth Universities publishes in alternate years a handbook called *Scholarships Guide for Commonwealth Postgraduate Students* (1977–79 edition £3·75, N. America $7.50) which lists awards tenable in one Commonwealth country by graduates from another Commonwealth country. Many of the awards described in it are open to non-Commonwealth graduates as well, but the ACU also issues a supplementary Information Paper listing *Some Awards open to Graduates of Foreign (non-Commonwealth) Universities and tenable at UK Universities* (£1, N. America $3). For prospective undergraduate students the Association has prepared a guide to *Financial Aid for First Degree Study at Commonwealth Universities* (85p, N. America $3), listing awards (most of them for students from developing countries) tenable in a Commonwealth country other than the student's own. All three guides can be obtained from the Association's office, 36 Gordon Square, London WC1H 0PF. Another valuable source of information is the handbook *Study Abroad,* published every two years by Unesco, price £4·20. The *Scholarships Guide* and *Study Abroad* can be consulted in many British Council, university and other reference libraries. Competition for the scholarships listed in such publications is very keen.

The following are among the major scholarship schemes likely to be of interest to students thinking of coming to Britain.

Common-wealth Scholarships and Fellowships Under the Commonwealth Scholarship and Fellowship Plan up to 250 Commonwealth Scholarships are offered annually by the United Kingdom to Commonwealth citizens resident in a Commonwealth country other than Britain itself, usually for university postgraduate study or research, although applications can be considered from candidates for first degrees from countries without undergraduate study facilities in their chosen subject. Commonwealth Scholarships may be awarded in any academic discipline, including Medicine. Candidates *must* apply through the appropriate agency in their *country of normal residence*; a list of these agencies is given in an Appendix to the *Commonwealth Universities Yearbook* (see page 265), or can be obtained from the Commonwealth Scholarship Commission in the United Kingdom at 36 Gordon Square, London WC1H 0PF. Junior members of staff of universities in developing Commonwealth countries may also be eligible for consideration for Commonwealth Academic Staff Scholarships which have conditions similar to those for Commonwealth Scholarships except that nominations for the academic staff awards are normally made by the candidate's vice-chancellor.

Within the framework of the Plan there are also awards at a higher level than the Scholarships: Commonwealth Medical Fellowships and Senior Medical Fellowships; and, for university teachers in subjects other than Medicine, Commonwealth Academic Staff Fellowships (open only to candidates from developing countries of the Commonwealth).

British Council Scholarships
The British Council offers awards at postgraduate level to scholars from many countries for courses of advanced study or research in Britain. These scholarships are normally tenable for one ten-month academic year, or possibly for two academic years, depending on the duration of the approved course of study. Scholars are expected to arrive by the beginning of the autumn term (i.e. in September or October).

British Council Fellowships
These are two- or three-year awards offered by the British Council for postgraduate study or research, not necessarily leading to a higher degree. They are offered in certain European and Latin American countries only.

Enquiries about, and applications for, British Council Scholarships and Fellowships should be made to the Representative of the British Council in the overseas country concerned; the final date for receipt of applications is usually in late October of the year before the awards are due to start. A list of addresses of British Council offices is given on pages 287–292. Where there is no British Council Representative, enquiry should be made at the British Embassy, Legation or local British Consulate.

The British Council, acting through its Representatives abroad, is also able in certain circumstances to assist graduates coming to study in Britain at their own expense or under the sponsorship of some other organisation, by helping them to find suitable places in British academic institutions.

ENTRY TO BRITAIN

Students who are nationals of foreign countries outside the EEC may be admitted to the United Kingdom if they are able to satisfy the Immigration Officer that they have been accepted for a full-time course of study at a university or college of education or further education, an independent school or any *bona fide* private educational institution; that they are able to meet the cost of the course and maintain themselves and any dependants during the course.

If the student is unable so to satisfy the Immigration Officer in all these respects and yet has genuine intentions of studying in the United Kingdom he may be admitted for a short period within the limit of his means to enable him to make suitable arrangements for study.

A foreign student may require a visa and he is advised to approach the nearest British official representative as soon as possible to apply for any requisite visa or to ascertain whether he may be eligible for admission to the United Kingdom for the purpose of study.

A student is not permitted to enter employment which is not associated with his studies except during his vacation or in his free time; in all cases the prior approval of the Department of Employment is necessary.

Students who are nationals of the member states of the EEC are given leave to enter the United Kingdom for an initial period of 6 months and no employment restrictions are imposed. When this period has elapsed a residence permit for up to 12 months may be granted if the student is able to produce evidence of acceptance for a course of full-time study at one of the types of educational institution already named, and of his ability to meet from his own resources the fees, the cost of his maintenance and that of any dependants during the course. EEC students may still take employment without permission while they are permitted to remain in the United Kingdom.

A Commonwealth student will be required by the Immigration Officer at the port of arrival to produce evidence that he has been accepted for a full-time course of study at a university, a college of education or further education, an independent school or any *bona fide* private educational institution. He will also need to show that adequate funds are available to meet the cost of the course and of his own maintenance and that of any dependants.

A passenger who satisfies the Immigration Officer that he has genuine and realistic intentions of studying in the United Kingdom but cannot satisfy the above requirements may be admitted for a short period within the limit of his means.

Before starting out students are strongly advised to apply to their nearest British official representative for an entry certificate. This is not obligatory but an application for one makes it possible to clear up beforehand any doubts about eligibility for admission to Britain. In applying for a certificate the student must be able to show proof that he has been accepted for a full-time course of study; he may also be required to produce evidence of previous academic achievements and proof that adequate financial arrangements have been made on his behalf. A proposal to study only part-time will not justify the issue of an entry certificate on a student basis.

A student is not permitted to enter employment which is not associated with his studies except during his vacation or in his free time; in all cases the prior approval of the Department of Employment is necessary.

STUDENT LIFE IN BRITAIN

The academic year

At most universities the academic year or session is divided into three terms of eight to ten weeks each. The first term usually runs from the beginning of October to the middle of December; the second from mid-January to about the end of March; and the third from towards the end of April to late June or early July. There are, however, special arrangements for 'sandwich course' students (see page 29); and for some courses (or at certain stages of some courses) the periods of attendance required may not conform to the usual three-term pattern. Two universities, Stirling and (for certain courses) The City, follow the American pattern of two 'semesters' a year – September to December (The City: September to February) and February to June/July. The New University of Ulster follows the three-term pattern, but for teaching purposes the year is divided into two semesters (October to January, January to May). The term at polytechnics and other colleges of further education is usually longer than the university term: normally the first term runs from early or mid-September to just before Christmas, the second term from early January to the end of March, and the third term from mid-April to early or mid-July.

Accommodation

Many students in Britain live in rooms such as a 'bed-sitter' (in which the bedroom is also used as a sitting room and may or may not include simple cooking facilities) or in 'lodgings' (which usually means a room with which some meals are provided).

No university is fully residential, but all universities can offer, to some proportion of their students, at least one of two main types of accommodation: halls of residence, in most (although not all) of which some meals are provided; and self-catering halls, houses or flats, in which students must buy and prepare their own food. For each type of accommodation the fees can vary a good deal, even within a single institution, because they may depend upon such factors as: the number of weeks the student can (or wishes to) be accommodated; whether the student has a single room or a shared one; the number of meals provided during the week and/or at week-ends; the location of the hall or house concerned; and the amenities that it offers (e.g. whether heating is included in the fees, whether there are washbasins in each room). It is not, therefore, possible to give, briefly, any precise indication of the fees that were being charged for university accommodation at the time of compilation of this handbook; *and it is in any case essential to obtain full and up-to-date particulars from the universities themselves*, bearing in mind that these fees are kept under regular review and that the charges for the next academic year may not be determined until

A student production of 'Les Jacobites'

the final term of the preceding session. However, it is probably broadly true to say that during 1977–78 the fees being paid by most students who were accommodated for the academic year in a university hall of residence (with some meals provided) were between £450 and £600, while those in self-catering accommodation were usually paying something between £220 and £400 for the accommodation alone.

It is not always easy to obtain a place in university accommodation and it is advisable to apply for such a place at the same time as applying for admission to the university. Most colleges of education are residential, but not many polytechnics or other non-university institutions have halls of residence.

Most institutions of higher education have an accommodation service to help students find a suitable place in which to live. It is advisable to get in touch with this service as soon as possible after acceptance for admission although final arrangements for permanent accommodation probably cannot be made until after arrival in Britain. Some institutions advise overseas students to arrive a week or even two weeks before their course begins, so that preliminary arrangements about accommodation, made from a distance, may be modified if necessary before studies begin. It is important that a student should keep the institution authorities informed of the date on which he proposes to arrive there.

It is very difficult to find suitable accommodation in London and in other large cities, and students who have any choice are well advised to avoid them for this reason. In the larger cities, especially London, the student must be prepared to live at a considerable distance from his place of study.

There is a very serious shortage of accommodation for married couples in Britain. Some universities have no residential accommodation of any kind for married students and at those which do have such accommodation it is available only for very limited numbers. Lodgings which are adequate for the single student are usually not suitable for a married couple because there may be no facilities for the wife to do her own cooking, laundry etc. Furnished flats where children are allowed are particularly difficult to find and many of those that can be found are far too expensive for students. If a student does find such a flat, at a rent he can afford, an agreement usually for not less than 3 months will probably have to be signed. If payment of any cash deposit is also required, students are advised to consult the university lodgings officer before agreeing to make such a payment. The only alternative may be a double room with simple cooking facilities or sharing a kitchen with another couple. *The difficulties are great and some overseas students' wives have said that they wished in the end that they had chosen to stay at home.* An overseas student who does nevertheless decide to bring his family *should travel ahead to Britain* and make arrangements for his wife to follow *only when he has found suitable accommodation.* It is especially important that he should do this if his wife is to be accompanied by a child or children; many owners of furnished flats will not let them to couples who have children with them, and it can therefore be very much more difficult to find accommodation for a family than it would be for a man and wife alone. There might be a delay of weeks before such accommodation is found and the cost of hotel accommodation meanwhile could amount to as much as £8–£10 bed and breakfast a day for each person.

Health and medical treatment
At several universities the registration of overseas students is provisional until they have undergone a medical examination (including an X-ray of the chest) conducted by the university's medical officer on entry. A student who does not pass this examination is not allowed to attend any course. A student should therefore make sure, before leaving his own country, that he is in good health and, in particular, that he is not suffering from tuberculosis or other infectious or contagious disease.

Overseas students residing in this country may receive medical treatment under the National Health Service during their stay. If they are here on a short-term basis this is generally limited to treatment for illness occurring after their arrival in Britain. They may be permitted emergency treatment for illness which began before their arrival here only if treatment cannot be postponed until they return home. The facilities of the National Health Service are free, except for small contributions towards the cost of medicines, spectacles and dental treatment. (In Northern Ireland the provisions of the National Health Service differ in some points of detail from those in the rest of Britain: students at recognised places of study receive general medical and dental services under the National Health Service, but they usually have to pay hospital charges. In Northern Ireland also the families of married students are not eligible for health service benefits.) In order to become eligible for these benefits a student is advised to register with a doctor. At most universities students may register with the university's own medical officer, who is in charge of a student health centre.

Advisers to overseas students
Many British universities and colleges have appointed members of their staff as advisers to overseas students, to give help in solving personal problems and advice about ways in which a student may derive the most benefit from his stay in Britain.

Social life and recreation
There are many students' societies and clubs, organised by the students themselves, at institutions of higher education in Britain. They are usually affiliated to a students' council or union which is the centre of social life and which organises dances and other social events. Sports and other out-of-class activities are regarded as valuable parts of a student's education and many universities hold a special 'freshers' conference to introduce new students to student life and societies.

In order to help overseas students to meet local residents, organisations such as the churches, Rotary clubs, overseas students' friendship committees and many others invite them to social functions where they can meet British people. There are also numbers of voluntary societies which include social and cultural activities for overseas students in their programmes. The Victoria League, the Royal Overseas League and the Royal Commonwealth Society offer special facilities for students from the Commonwealth, as do the Current Affairs Unit of the English Speaking Union (for students from the Commonwealth and the USA) and the Commonwealth Students' Children's Society. The Young Men's and Women's Christian Associations and the International House Association also provide facilities for students. Rotary International, Round Table and Inner Wheel entertain overseas students at their functions and in homes of members. Returned Volunteer Action is able to offer home hospitality and a chance for overseas students to experience family life in Britain. The Women's Corona Society takes an interest in the wives and families of overseas students, as does the British Council Wives' Association.

British Council services

The British Council offers certain facilities to overseas students who are registered at recognised institutions of higher education or who are engaged on approved courses of training, and who intend to return to their homes after the completion of their courses of study.

British Council couriers will meet at the air terminal students who apply either to their college, their sponsoring authorities, or to the Arrivals Section of the British Council. The British Council will also assist students after their arrival to find suitable accommodation or will introduce them to other advisory bodies.

Any student from overseas may ask the British Council, in Britain or abroad, for general practical advice on life in Britain. The Council produces a useful handbook for overseas students, *How to live in Britain*, which is published by Longman Group Ltd, and can be ordered from booksellers or from the local office of the Council, at the price of 25p.

The British Council Students' Centre at 11 Portland Place, London W1N 4EJ, is part of the Overseas Students' Services Department of the British Council. The Centre offers to Council-sponsored and other full-time overseas students, mainly in the London area, an introduction to British life to assist them to integrate as rapidly as possible with the local institutions and activities in the areas where they are resident or studying.

To this end, the Centre organises:

a programme of visits, in and around London, to British institutions (public, professional, commercial and industrial) and to places of wider interest in other parts of the British Isles for *overseas student members*;

an educational, cultural and social programme of lectures, English language classes, theatre, cinema, music recitals, discussions, folk music and dances. These activities, which take place at the Centre every evening in term-time and on a reduced scale in the holidays, are usually free and are for *British and overseas members*.

The Centre building has reading, games and television rooms, a self-service restaurant and a bar. Other services provided include counselling on personal problems and introductions to other British social and cultural organisations.

Membership of the Centre (normally for a maximum of three years) is open to all overseas and British men and women over 18 who are taking a full-time course (at all levels) of study or research in Britain or are on appropriate study attachments. Their wives and husbands are also eligible.

Full details of all the Centre's activities appear in the British Council Visits and Programme Sheets published at the beginning of each term; a more detailed programme of evening activities is published weekly.

ACU services for students

The Association provides students with factual information about universities in Britain and in the other countries of the Commonwealth in three ways: through the Awards Information Service of the ACU, which publishes about 600 pages of scholarship information in three guides (see page 266), and through other publications such as the *Commonwealth Universities Yearbook* (see page 265); by offering a (free) Personal Information Service for any student who wishes to visit, telephone or write to the ACU Office at 36 Gordon Square, London WC1H 0PF (student information papers available without charge include *Postgraduate Study at Universities in Britain, First Degree Courses at Universities in Britain,* and *Summer Courses at Universities in Britain*); and by maintaining a reference library which is open to visitors during office hours and contains UK and other Commonwealth university calendars and prospectuses, guides to courses and scholarships, etc.

For graduates with excellent qualifications who are interested in applying for academic posts at universities in certain Commonwealth countries (notably, but not solely, Australia, New Zealand, Hong Kong and Malaysia), the Association can provide through its Appointments Service information about any current vacancies of which the service has been notified. It can also offer some general guidance on sources of information about academic vacancies in some of those Commonwealth countries which do not normally use the Association's own appointments service.

In addition to publishing information about scholarships awarded by many different bodies the Association helps to administer several scholarship schemes for students, including the Commonwealth Scholarship and Fellowship Plan (for which it provides the British national agency – see page 57) and the awards offered by the Marshall Aid Commemoration Commission to United States graduates for study in Britain.

Directory of Subjects
and Facilities for Study

DIRECTORY OF SUBJECTS AND FACILITIES FOR STUDY

The information in this Directory was as up-to-date as possible at the time of compilation, but the courses that universities and colleges offer are subject to continual change, and *it is essential for a student to obtain direct from the Secretary or Registrar of the institution concerned* the latest available information about the courses he wishes to follow (for addresses, see pages 267–283). This is especially true of teacher training establishments which are currently undergoing institutional reorganisation as well as curriculum changes. A student who wishes to do such a course is strongly advised to consult the annual *Handbook of Institutions Providing both Teacher Training and Other Full-Time Advanced Courses* (see page 265) and then contact colleges to check the details given there. He should also try to seek advice from the nearest British Council office.

Students are reminded that the mention of particular facilities for study does not imply that places will be available for all applicants who can satisfy the entrance requirements (see pages 41–49).

Notes to the Directory

This Directory contains summarised information under some 150 main subject headings about facilities for *full-time* study or research at institutions of higher education in the United Kingdom. The Directory covers all universities (except the Open University, for which see page 27), and all other institutions of higher education that offer full-time courses; but, with a few exceptions (e.g. Birkbeck College, University of London – see page 28), institutions offering courses solely or mainly for part-time students are not mentioned.

In general, only 'advanced' courses are included, i.e. courses for which prospective entrants must have reached *at least* General Certificate of Education Advanced level standard in one or more subjects (see also page 41). For entry to any first degree course, *two* or more Advanced level passes (or a qualification which the university or college will accept in place of two Advanced levels) are essential.

To facilitate reference to the Directory there is a list of main subject headings on pages 6–7 and, at the end of the book, a detailed index to subjects and branches of subjects, which readers are advised to consult before turning to the Directory itself.

Order of institutions **Information about university institutions is distinguished from that about non-university institutions (e.g. polytechnics and other colleges) by a dividing line.** In general the courses listed above the line are given wholly or mainly in the university institutions themselves; courses given wholly or mainly in non-university institutions come after the line, even if they lead to a qualification awarded (or 'validated') by a university.

Where references are made to facilities for study at the universities of London and Wales, the names of the constituent institutions of each university providing them are also given, and mention is made of any college diplomas or certificates; similarly 'Institute of Science and Technology' after the name of the University of Manchester means that the study facilities concerned are provided by the University of Manchester Institute of Science and Technology, which constitutes that university's faculty of technology.

Types of course   With a very few exceptions, **only full-time and sandwich courses are included** in this Handbook, and courses that are only available as part-time courses are not mentioned. In polytechnics, colleges of technology, etc, where there are many part-time courses, a full-time course is generally defined as being one in which the student spends at least fifteen day-time hours a week in college, attending lectures or doing organised practical work. Courses shorter than two months have normally been excluded as being unlikely to interest students not already in the United Kingdom.

At universities, polytechnics, and colleges of technology the term 'sandwich course' means that periods of industrial training (normally totalling at least one year) are integrated with periods of academic study at the university or college, although the way in which this is done may vary from one institution to another.

Overseas students wishing to attend sandwich courses should note that it is usually difficult to make the necessary arrangements for them in industry and they may find that they cannot be accepted for the course of their choice (see page 47).

Length of degree courses   The duration of first degree courses is shown in this Directory only when they usually last longer than three or four years, or when they are sandwich courses (for a fuller note on the duration of first degree courses, see pages 27 and 28). The duration of the postgraduate courses listed is indicated in the Directory itself, where references to a 'year' (1 yr, 2 yrs, etc) normally mean an *academic* year, i.e. about 9 or 10 months (courses lasting one or more full years usually being described as '12 months', '24 months', etc).

Special-isation   In the sections on first degree courses at universities, the phrase 'degrees with specialisation in' usually means that the university awards a degree with Honours, or a Special degree, *in* that subject, *either alone or in combination with* one or, more rarely, two other principal subjects (see also page 28). It should however be particularly noted that the structure of courses leading to Honours degrees may vary quite considerably from one university to another – at Keele, for example, most undergraduate students must attend a 'foundation year' after which they study two principal subjects for three further years to Honours level; while at some of the other newer universities students 'major' or otherwise specialise to Honours level in a particular discipline, but do not normally begin this specialisation until the second year, and both second-year and third-year studies usually involve courses in fields other than the major one. To find out exactly how much specialisation is possible in a particular subject at a particular university, *it is therefore essential to consult the relevant prospectuses.*

Because of the very large number of subject combinations which may be offered for 'Joint' or 'Combined' Honours degrees it has not been possible to list them all in the Directory, although where a subject can be studied for an Honours, or Special, degree *only* in combination with another principal subject that fact is normally mentioned. However a complete index to university courses leading to graduation in two principal subjects is included in the *Compendium of University Entrance Requirements**, and each university's chapter in the *Commonwealth Universities Yearbook** shows what combinations can be offered at that university. Many polytechnics and colleges now offer degree courses in which subjects can be combined in a number of ways: one main subject chosen together with a number of subsidiary subjects; Joint Honours degrees; modular degrees offering a wide and flexible choice of subject modules. These are listed in the *Arts* and *Science* sections, pages 90 and 241, although reference is sometimes made to them under relevant subject headings.

DipHE courses	Details of courses leading to the DipHE award are listed on pages 90 and 241, with the exception of those which form part of teacher training courses. These are placed in the section beginning on page 278.
Postgraduate courses	The words 'postgraduate courses' are used in this Directory to mean formal courses of instruction leading to a higher degree or diploma, etc (as distinct from facilities for postgraduate research); see also pages 29–31.
Research facilities	References to 'research facilities' mean that facilities may be provided for graduate students to undertake individual research, under supervision, in at least some aspect of the subject indicated, normally for the preparation of a dissertation or thesis leading to a higher degree (e.g. PhD). A university or college which provides first degree courses in a particular subject usually also has some research facilities in that subject, but it is impossible within the scope of this Handbook to give details of all the research facilities that may be made available at every institution. However

*See page 265.

Rowing is one of the many sports enjoyed by students

where there is a special centre or institute, etc (as distinct from a department or school), offering research facilities in a given field, or where the facilities available in a particular subject are restricted to, or especially noteworthy in, one or two specified branches of that subject, mention is made of them in the Directory. Research in polytechnics for CNAA MPhil and PhD degrees is carried on in a wide range of subjects, some of which are indicated in the Directory. Anyone who has a specific research interest should contact the polytechnics directly.

Abbrevia- The abbreviations used in this Directory are explained on pages 296–298.
tions Usual titles, such as 'polytechnic', 'college of technology' and 'college of education', are abbreviated throughout to P, CT and CE respectively; 'college of art and design' is given as 'C Art and Design'; less usual titles, such as 'Academy of Art', are given in full. The full names may in all cases easily be found by reference to the relevant address list on pages 270–282.

Accountancy

First degrees Degrees with specialisation in *Accountancy/Accounting* awarded by the following universities: Aston in Birmingham (Finance and Accounting for BSc in Managerial and Administrative Studies), Birmingham (BCom), Bradford (special subject for degree in Business Studies), Bristol (with Economics), Dundee (with Economics, for MA or LLB*), Edinburgh (with Economics, also for BSc (Social Science) and – with Business Studies – BCom), Exeter (with Law, for BA in Accountancy Studies), Glasgow (BAcc Ordinary or Honours, also with Law or Economics for BAcc Honours or with Law for LLB Honours*), Heriot-Watt (with Finance or Computer Science), Hull (special subject for BSc(Econ)), Kent at Canterbury, Lancaster (Accounting and Finance, Management Sciences (Financial Control), or Economics and Financial Control), Leeds (with Data Processing), London (with Finance, at London School of Economics), Loughborough U of Technology (for BSc in Economics, also Accounting and Financial Management for BSc and DIS, 4 yrs S), Manchester (with Business Finance or Computer Science), Newcastle upon Tyne (with Economics), Reading (with Economics), Salford (Finance and Accounting, also Accountancy and Process Engineering), Sheffield (with Financial Management), Southampton, Stirling (alone or with Business Law and Economics, Computing Science, Management Science or Mathematics), Strathclyde, New U of Ulster (Economics with Accounting), Wales (with Financial Administration at Bangor University College, for BScEcon at Cardiff University College and Institute of Science and Technology) and Warwick (with Financial Analysis). Accountancy/Accounting may also be included in the curriculum for first degrees (usually in Commerce, Economics, Law* or Arts) both at these universities and at the following: Aberdeen (also certificate, 1 yr, in Accountancy Studies), Bath (4 yrs S), Belfast, Brunel, Liverpool, Manchester (Institute of Science and Technology, BSc in Management Sciences), Nottingham and Wales (Aberystwyth University College).

The Accounting Education Consultative Board, representing the six principal accountancy bodies and all participating universities and (see below) colleges in Great Britain and Ireland, approves by reference to their course content certain degrees of professional relevance with the result that graduates from such courses receive certain examination exemptions from the professional bodies. Full details may be obtained from the Secretary to the Board, 11 Copthall Avenue, London EC2P 2BJ.

The independent University College at Buckingham (see page 32) awards a licence in the School of Accounting and Financial Management.

Postgraduate courses Courses (1 yr and for MA or MSc, unless otherwise indicated) at the following universities and Cranfield IT.

Accountancy/Accounting, Birmingham (MSocSc, 12 months), Glasgow (MAcc normally 2 years, also diploma 12 months), Heriot-Watt (diploma), Kent at Canterbury, Stirling (certificate, conversion course), Strathclyde (diploma) and Wales (Cardiff University College, for College diploma).

Accounting and Business Finance, Manchester (MA(Econ)).

Accounting and Finance, Lancaster and London (London School of Economics).

Accounting and Financial Management, Sheffield.

Finance, The City (1 yr full-time or 2 yrs part-time).

Finance and Investment, Exeter.

Finance and Management Accounting, Cranfield IT (for MBA in Management).

Financial Economics, Wales (Bangor University College, 1 or 2 yrs, also diploma 12 months).

Financial Management, Bradford (1 or 2 yrs, for diploma in Management and Administration, or MBA).

*It should be noted that the degree in Law of a Scottish University is based on Scots Law.

Financial Managerial Controls, Southampton (diploma 9 months, MSc (Social Sciences) 12 months).

Financial Studies, Heriot-Watt (diploma) and Strathclyde (MSc and diploma).

Management Accounting, Bradford (1 or 2 yrs, for diploma in Management and Administration, or MBA, Operational Research option).

Research facilities   At the universities of Birmingham, Bradford, Dundee, Edinburgh, Glasgow, Heriot-Watt, Kent at Canterbury, Lancaster (including International Centre for Research in Accounting), London (London School of Economics), Manchester, Reading, Sheffield, Southampton, Strathclyde and Wales (Cardiff University College).

First degrees   CNAA degrees in *Accountancy* (4 yrs S unless otherwise indicated) are offered at the following polytechnics. Birmingham P (3 yrs). Glasgow CT (3 yrs). Leeds P. Liverpool P (3 yrs). P of North London (4 yrs). Portsmouth P. Ulster C, Northern Ireland P (3 yrs).

Accountancy Studies, Huddersfield P (3 yrs).

Accountancy, Preston P (3 yrs). City of London P, also as subject in modular degree (3 yrs).

Accounting and Finance, Bristol P (3 yrs). Kingston P (3 yrs). Manchester P (3 yrs). Middlesex P (3 yrs). Trent P.

Finance with Accounting, North East London P (4 yrs).

HND Courses   In *Accounting* (2 yrs). Aberdeen CC. Ayr TC. Bell CT. Dundee CT. Falkirk CT. Glasgow CT. Kirkcaldy TC. Napier CC and T (4 yrs S). North Worcestershire C (3 yrs S). Perth TC. Scottish C of Textiles.

Many colleges offer *Accountancy/Accounting* as an optional subject in the HND courses in *Business Studies*.

Professional courses   The main professional Accountancy bodies in the United Kingdom are: The Institutes of Chartered Accountants in England and Wales (and of Scotland and Ireland); the Association of Certified Accountants and the Institute of Cost and Management Accountants; the Chartered Institute of Public Finance and Accountancy. It is not possible to become a member of these bodies solely by following courses; each one has practical experience requirements which can be satisfied only by a period of practical training in an approved work situation.

Membership of the Institutes of Chartered Accountants can be achieved only by serving as a student under training contract with a Member of the Institute *in the United Kingdom*, whilst undertaking courses of study for the Institute's examinations. These vary in length according to individual requirements.

Approved practical experience and examinations for both the Association of Certified Accountants and the Institute of Cost and Management Accountants may be undertaken in Britain or in certain centres overseas.

Details of the specific qualifications and terms of training required for membership should be obtained from the Secretary of each body. Full-time or sandwich courses (minimum 2 yrs) leading to the Final examinations of the Association of Certified Accountants and/or the Institute of Cost and Management Accountants are held at a number of polytechnics and colleges. Lists of these institutions are also available from the professional bodies.

Acoustics

First degrees University of Southampton awards a BSc in *Acoustical Engineering,* and University of Surrey a BSc in *Physics with Musical Acoustics.* Degree courses in Physics, Music and Architecture/Building may include some study of *Acoustics.*

Postgraduate courses Courses (1 yr and for MSc, unless otherwise indicated) at the following universities:

Acoustic and Vibration Technology, London (Imperial and Chelsea Colleges, joint course for MSc and/or College diplomas, 1 yr full-time or 2 yrs part-time).

Applied Accoustics, London (Chelsea College, MSc and/or College diploma, 1 yr full-time or 2 yrs part-time).

Audiology, Manchester (MEd or diploma, also MSc in Clinical Audiology), Salford (modular course) and Southampton (MSc 12 months, also certificate, 6 months, in Medical Audiology).

Engineering Acoustics, Noise and Vibration, Nottingham (12 months full-time or 2 yrs part-time).

Noise and Building Acoustics, Bristol (option for MSc in Advanced Functional Design Techniques for Buildings, 12 months full-time or 3 yrs – modular course – part-time).

Sonar and Signal Processing, Loughborough U of Technology.

Sound and Vibration Studies (options in Engineering Acoustics, Operational Acoustics, Industrial Noise and Vibration Control, or Structural Dynamics), Southampton (diploma 9 months, MSc 12 months).

Underwater Acoustics and Sonar, Birmingham (option in Electronic and Electrical Systems course).

Research facilities At the following universities: Birmingham, Bradford, Bristol, Edinburgh, Essex, Heriot-Watt, London (Chelsea and Imperial Colleges), Loughborough U of Technology (Centre for Transport Engineering Practice), Manchester (including Institute of Science and Technology), Newcastle upon Tyne, Nottingham, Salford, Sheffield, Southampton (Institute of Sound and Vibration Research) and Warwick (Noise and Vibration).

African Languages and Studies

First degrees Degrees with specialisation awarded by the universities of Birmingham (African Studies with another subject, also African and Medieval History, or BSocSc in School of African Studies) and London (School of Oriental and African Studies – see below). Less specialised study may be included in first degree courses at the universities of Aberdeen (Modern History of Tropical Africa – at Honours level only), Edinburgh (African History), Kent at Canterbury (English with African and Caribbean Studies – African languages are *not* taught, also – entry in alternate yrs, next in October 1979 – French with African and Caribbean Studies), Reading (African Government and Politics), Sheffield (Modern African Literature), Sussex (BA in School of African and Asian Studies with major in one of various subjects – African languages are *not* taught) and York (Swahili in BA courses in Language).

School of Oriental and African Studies (University of London): BA Honours in an African Language (Amharic or Hausa or Swahili) and History or Law or Linguistics or Social Anthropology; in Bantu Languages; and in History (History with special reference to Africa) or African History and Social Anthropology. Also School diploma (normally 3 yrs) in certain African Languages.

Postgraduate   Courses (1 yr and for MA, unless otherwise indicated) at the following universities:
courses   *African Studies*, Birmingham (diploma, also – 12 months – MA or MSocSc), Edinburgh
                 (diploma, also MSc 12 months, MLitt or MPhil 2 yrs), London (School of Oriental and
                 African Studies, in an African Language (Hausa or Swahili) or in Area Studies – see also
                 below) and Sussex.
             Modern African Literature (since 1945), Sheffield.
             Politics and Government of Africa, London (London School of Economics, for MSc in Politics).
             Southern African Studies, York (12 months).
                 School of Oriental and African Studies (University of London) may provide teaching in the
                 following languages for students in other disciplines preparing for research in the field:
             Bantu – Bemba, Kongo, Ndebele, Nyanja, Shona, Swahili, Swazi, Tonga, Xhosa, Zulu.
             West African – Efik, Fula, Grebo, Hausa, Igbo, Ijaw, Krio, Mandinka, Mende, Nupe, Temne,
                 Tiv, Yoruba.
             North and North East African – Acholi, Amharic, Berber, Galla, Gurage, Harari, Somali, Tigre,
                 Tigrinya.

Research   At the universities of Aberdeen (African Studies Group), Birmingham (Centre of West African
facilities Studies), Cambridge (Centre of African Studies), Edinburgh (Centre of African Studies),
              London (London School of Economics, School of Oriental and African Studies), Oxford (in
              some 20 centres throughout the university), Sussex (including Institute of Development
              Studies) and York (Centre for Southern African Studies). School of Oriental and African
              Studies (University of London): in language and literature in many African fields, in Phonetics
              and Linguistics, and in fields of History, Law, Anthropology, Economics, Politics and
              Geography.

Agriculture and Forestry

*See also Engineering, Agricultural; Estate and Farm Management; Soil Science; and Veterinary
Medicine and Surgery*

Agricultural Economics and Marketing

First degrees   Degrees with specialisation in *Agricultural Economics* awarded by the universities of Aberdeen,
              Exeter (with Economics), Glasgow, London (Wye College), Manchester (BA(Econ)), Newcastle
              upon Tyne (also Agricultural and Food Marketing), Nottingham, Reading and Wales
              (Aberystwyth and – Agriculture with Agricultural Economics – Bangor University Colleges).

Postgraduate   Courses (normally 1 yr, and for master's degree, unless otherwise indicated) at the following
courses   universities:
             Agricultural Economics, Aberdeen, Belfast (Farm Business Economics), Glasgow (1 or 2 yrs),
                 Leeds, London (Wye College, 1 or 2 yrs), Manchester, Newcastle upon Tyne (1 or 2 yrs),
                 Oxford, Reading (diploma, also – 12 months – MSc including options in Agricultural
                 Policy, Agricultural Finance, and Population, Resources and World Trade) and Wales
                 (Aberystwyth University College, MSc or diploma).
             Agricultural Policy and Europe's Rural Problems and *Capital and Finance in Contemporary
                 European Farming*, Reading (Graduate School of Contemporary European Studies –
                 MA 1 yr, MPhil 2 yrs).
             Marketing, Newcastle upon Tyne (Agricultural Marketing, 1 or 2 yrs), Reading (Food and
                 Horticultural Marketing options for MSc in Agricultural Economics), Strathclyde
                 (Food and Agricultural Marketing, diploma) and Wales (Aberystwyth University
                 College).

Research facilities At most of the universities named in the paragraphs above and (Agricultural Economics) Bradford.

Agricultural Sciences (including Animal Husbandry)

First degrees Degrees in *Agriculture/Agricultural Science* are awarded by the universities of Aberdeen, Belfast, Edinburgh, Leeds, London (Wye College), Newcastle upon Tyne (also Agricultural and Environmental Science), Nottingham, Oxford (Agricultural and Forest Sciences), Reading and Wales (Aberystwyth and Bangor University Colleges). In addition degrees with specialisation in particular branches of agricultural science are awarded as follows:

Agricultural Bacteriology, Belfast.

Agricultural Biochemistry/Biochemistry, Newcastle upon Tyne, Nottingham (Applied), Reading (Physiology and Biochemistry of Farm Animals) and Wales (Aberystwyth and – Soil Science and Biochemistry – Bangor University Colleges).

Agricultural Botany, Belfast, Glasgow, Leeds, Nottingham, Reading and Wales (Aberystwyth and Bangor University Colleges).

Agricultural Chemistry, Belfast, Glasgow, Leeds and London (Wye College), also Brunel (Medicinal, Agricultural and Environmental Chemistry, 4 yrs S).

Agricultural Microbiology, Nottingham.

Agricultural Zoology, Belfast, Glasgow, Leeds, Newcastle upon Tyne, Nottingham and Wales (Aberystwyth University College).

Agronomy, Nottingham.

Animal Science(s) (see also 'Biology'), Aberdeen, Glasgow (Animal Developmental Biology, also – tuition at university and Hannah Research Institute – Animal Nutrition), Leeds (Animal Physiology and Nutrition), London (Wye College), Nottingham (Applied Animal Physiology, Animal Production) and Reading (Physiology and Biochemistry of Farm Animals).

Applied Biology (see also 'Biology'), Wales (Bangor University College).

Economic Entomology or *Genetics* or *Nutrition*, Nottingham.

Plant Science(s), Aberdeen, Belfast (Mycology and Plant Pathology), London (Wye College), Newcastle upon Tyne and Nottingham (Plant Pathology, Physiology and Breeding of Crop Plants, Plant Cell Physiology and Genetics).

Soil Science, Aberdeen, Newcastle upon Tyne, Nottingham, Reading and Wales (Bangor University College, with Biochemistry).

Some study of agricultural subjects is included in undergraduate Botany and Chemistry courses at Imperial College, London; and the Edinburgh School of Agriculture also provides Scottish Diploma courses in Agriculture (5 terms) and Dairying (2 yrs), and short courses.

Postgraduate courses Courses (normally 1 yr, and for master's degree, unless otherwise indicated) at the following universities and Cranfield IT:

Agricultural Architecture, Manchester.

Agricultural Building, Reading (MSc 9 or 12 months, MAgrEng 23 months).

Agricultural Extension, Reading (diploma 9 months, MSc 9 or 12 months).

Agricultural Management, Reading (9 or 12 months).

Agricultural Science, Wales (Aberystwyth and Bangor University Colleges, diploma, 1 or 2 yrs).

Animal Breeding, Edinburgh (diploma, also MSc 12 months).

Animal Nutrition, Aberdeen, Belfast, Newcastle upon Tyne (1 or 2 yrs) and Wales (Bangor University College, MSc or diploma).

Animal Parasitology, Wales (Bangor University College, MSc or diploma).

Animal Production, Aberdeen and Reading.

Applied Biology, Cambridge.

Applied Entomology, London (Imperial College, MSc and/or DIC) and Newcastle upon Tyne
(1 or 2 yrs).
Applied Plant Sciences, London (Wye College, 1 or 2 yrs).
Crop Physiology, Reading (12 months).
Crop Production, Aberdeen.
Equine Studies, Wales (Aberystwyth University College).
Improvement and Renovation of Grassland, Wales (Aberystwyth University College, 2 yrs).
Nematology, London (Imperial College, MSc and/or DIC).
Pedology and Soil Survey, Reading (12 months).
Physiology and Biochemistry of Farm Animals, Reading.
Physiology and Ecology of Grasses and Grasslands, Belfast.
Plant Breeding, Cambridge and Wales (Aberystwyth University College, 2 yrs).
Poultry Science, Reading.
Ruminant Health and Production, Wales (Aberystwyth University College, 2 yrs).
Rural Science, Edinburgh (diploma).
Soil Chemistry, Reading (12 months).
Soil Science, Aberdeen, Newcastle upon Tyne (1 or 2 yrs), Oxford (diploma), Reading (2 yrs) and
Wales (Aberystwyth University College, diploma).
Technology and Management of Pesticide Application, Cranfield IT.
Technology of Crop Protection, Reading (12 months).
Tropical Agricultural Development, Reading (MSc 12 months, MAgrSc 23 months).
Tropical Animal Health and Production, Edinburgh (MSc or diploma, 12 months).

Research   At universities named above, also Bradford and Bristol, and at Cranfield IT. Bradford: Project
facilities   Planning Centre for Developing Countries. Bristol: Agricultural and Horticultural Research
Station, Long Ashton, Somerset (limited number of students, mainly for studies in Fruit
Growing) and Veterinary Research Station, Langford, Somerset (Animal Husbandry).
Cambridge: various Research Institutes. Cranfield IT: Ecological Physics (Airborne Pests –
Dispersion and Management). Glasgow: West of Scotland Agricultural College, Auchincruive,
and Hannah Research Institute, Ayr. London: Imperial and Wye Colleges and (see below)
Rothamsted Experimental and East Malling Research Stations. Newcastle upon Tyne:
University Agricultural Experimental Station, Cockle Park, Northumberland; also Close
House Field Station (Agricultural Zoology). Oxford: Wytham Estate and University Field
Station, Wytham. Reading: National College of Food Technology, Weybridge (within Faculty
of Agriculture and Food); National Institute for Research in Dairying attached to the
University; and, associated with it, Grassland Research Institute, ARC Institute for Research on
Animal Diseases (Compton), River Laboratory of Freshwater Biology Association, ARC
Radiobiological Laboratory (Wantage) and ARC Weed Research Organisation (Oxford).

Rothamsted Experimental Station, Harpenden: departments for Bee Research, Biochemistry,
Botany, Chemistry, Entomology, Insecticides and Fungicides, Nematology, Pedology, Plant
Pathology, Physics, Soil Microbiology and Statistics in relation to Agriculture. East Malling
Research Station: fundamental and applied investigations in Hardy Fruit Culture in the field
and laboratory – a very few postgraduate students with first-class academic record, and,
preferably, some years' research experience, may be accepted in the following sections:
Pomology, Statistics, Plant Physiology, Biochemistry, Plant Pathology, Entomology and Plant
Protective Chemistry.

Forestry

First degrees   Degrees in *Forestry* awarded by the universities of Aberdeen (BSc(For)), Edinburgh (BSc in Ecological Science with Honours in Forestry, also 2-yr diploma course in School of Agriculture), Oxford (BA in Agricultural and Forest Sciences) and Wales (Bangor University College – also first degree course in *Wood Science*).

Postgraduate   Courses (1 yr) at the following universities:
courses   *Forestry*, Wales (Bangor University College, diploma).
                  Forestry and its relation to Land Management, Oxford (MSc).
                  Resource Management, Edinburgh (diploma 9 months, MSc 12 months).
                  Wood Science, Wales (Bangor University College, diploma).

Research   At the universities named in the paragraphs above.
facilities

Horticulture

First degrees   Degrees in *Horticulture* awarded by the following universities: Bath (4 yrs S), London (Wye College), Nottingham, Reading (also Horticultural Botany) and Strathclyde; at Edinburgh, School of Agriculture provides Scottish diploma course.

Postgraduate   Courses (for MSc) at the following universities:
courses   *Horticultural Economics and Management*, Reading (option in Agricultural Economics course, 12 months).
                  Horticulture, Bath (12 months).
                  Landscape Ecology, Design and Maintenance, London (Wye College, 1 yr).

Research   At the universities providing first degree courses, also at Bristol, Dundee (Scottish Horticultural
facilities   Research Institute) and St. Andrews. (For Bristol and London, see also under 'Agricultural Sciences' above.)

HND courses   (3 yrs S). Edinburgh School of Agriculture. Harper Adams AgC, also *Agricultural Marketing and Business Administration*, and *Poultry*. Lancashire CAg. North of Scotland CAg. Royal AgC (men). Seale-Hayne AgC, also *Natural Resources* and *Rural Economy*. Shuttleworth AgC. Welsh AgC. West of Scotland AgC, also *Dairy Technology*. Writtle AgC, also *Commercial Horticulture* and *Amenity Horticulture*. *Landscape and Horticultural Technology*, Askham Bryan C of Horticulture (in conjunction with Leeds P).
                  Poultry, Loughry CAg and Food Technology.

Post-diploma   (1 yr unless otherwise indicated):
courses   *Advanced Farm Management*, Royal AgC.
                  Agricultural Marketing and Business Administration, Harper Adams AgC.
                  Crop Protection, Harper Adams AgC.
                  Farm Management, Seale-Hayne AgC.
                  Farm Organisation and Management, North of Scotland CAg.
                  Horticulture, Writtle AgC.
                  Marketing, option in *Food and Agricultural Marketing*, West of Scotland AgC (U of Strathclyde diploma, 9 months).
                  Pig Technology, Harper Adams AgC.
                  Work Organisation and Planning, Seale-Hayne AgC (1 term).

Anaesthetics

First degrees   Degree courses in Medicine (for list of awarding universities, see page 198) include the study of *Anaesthetics.*

Postgraduate courses   No full-time courses at universities, but short courses or part-time courses of varying lengths for Primary and/or Final FFARCS are provided by several of the universities named below. Further information is given in 'Summary of Postgraduate Diplomas and Courses in Medicine' – see page 266.

Research facilities   At the universities of Belfast, Birmingham, Cambridge, Dundee, Edinburgh, Glasgow, Leeds, Liverpool, London (most of the Medical Schools), Manchester, Newcastle upon Tyne, Nottingham, Oxford, Salford (Postgraduate Medical Institute), Sheffield, Southampton and Wales.

Postgraduate courses   The diploma in Anaesthetics is awarded by the Examining Board in England of the Royal College of Physicians of London and the Royal College of Surgeons of England.

The Faculty of Anaesthetists of the Royal College of Surgeons of England confers a Fellowship (FFA) by examination. For advice on training (including 3-week courses), apply to the Postgraduate Adviser. For courses for Primary FFA see 'Anatomy'. Particulars of both examinations may be obtained from the Secretary of the Examining Board in England.

Anatomy

First degrees   Degrees with specialisation in *Anatomy* awarded by the universities of Aberdeen, Belfast, Birmingham (Anatomical Studies), Bristol, Cambridge, Edinburgh, Glasgow, London, Newcastle upon Tyne, St Andrews and Sheffield (Human Biology and Anatomy); also – but open only to students already enrolled in the course for a degree in medicine or dentistry (see also page 198) – Dundee, Leeds, Manchester, Nottingham and Wales (Cardiff University College). At Oxford, Anatomy may be included in courses for first degrees in Science. Anatomy is also included in courses for first degrees in Medicine (see page 198).

Postgraduate courses   Revision courses (full-time) in the basic medical sciences, including Anatomy (suitable for one or more of: Primary FRCS, Primary FFA, Primary FDS, MRCOG Part I), are organised by the Edinburgh Postgraduate Board for Medicine (16 weeks) and the University of London Institute of Basic Medical Sciences (including 12 weeks for Primary FRCS, 8 weeks for Primary FDS). Similar courses, but on a part-time/day-release basis, are offered by several universities; further information is given in 'Summary of Postgraduate Diplomas and Courses in Medicine' – see page 266.

Research facilities   At the universities of Aberdeen, Belfast, Birmingham, Bristol, Cambridge, Dundee, Glasgow, Leicester, Liverpool, London (British Postgraduate Medical Federation, University College and various Medical Schools), Manchester, Newcastle upon Tyne, Nottingham, St Andrews, Sheffield, Southampton and Wales (Cardiff University College).

Anthropology

First degrees Degrees with specialisation awarded by the following universities:
Anthropology, Cambridge, Durham (alone or with Archaeology, Geography, Psychology or Sociology) and London (University College, alone or with Geography or Linguistics).
Social Anthropology, Belfast, Cambridge, Edinburgh (alone or with Linguistics or Sociology), Hull (with Sociology), Keele (with another principal subject), Kent at Canterbury, London (alone or with Economics at London School of Economics, alone or with one of certain other subjects at School of Oriental and African Studies, and with Ancient History or Economics at University College), Manchester, Stirling (with Sociology), Sussex (Schools of African and Asian Studies and of Social Sciences) and New U of Ulster (with Sociology).
Less specialised study of Anthropology/Social Anthropology may be included in courses leading to first degrees at most of these universities (Hull: also with particular reference to South East Asia) and at Aberdeen, East Anglia, Newcastle upon Tyne, Oxford, Reading and Wales (Swansea University College).

Postgraduate courses Courses (1 yr and for diploma, unless otherwise indicated) at the following universities:
Anthropology, Durham (1 yr, 2 yrs in certain cases).
Biological Anthropology, Durham (MSc).
Ethnology or *Human Biology,* Oxford.
Material Culture, London (University College, 2 yrs).
Physical Anthropology, Cambridge (certificate) and London (University College, 2 yrs).
Social Anthropology, Belfast (also Social Anthropology (Ethnomusicology), MA or diploma), Birmingham (with other subjects for MSocSc, 12 months), Cambridge (certificate), Edinburgh, Kent at Canterbury, London (London School of Economics and University College, 2 yrs), Manchester (for MA(Econ) or diploma), Oxford and Sussex (MA).

Research facilities At the universities of Belfast, Birmingham, Cambridge, Durham, Edinburgh, Kent at Canterbury (Centre for Research in the Social Sciences), London (London School of Economics, School of Oriental and African Studies, University College), Manchester, Newcastle upon Tyne, Oxford (Pitt Rivers Museum), Sussex and Wales (Swansea University College).

First degree Huddersfield P, *Human Ecology* (4 yrs S).

Archaeology

First degrees Degrees with specialisation in *Archaeology* awarded by the universities of Belfast, Birmingham (Ancient History and Archaeology, alone or with another subject), Bristol (for Joint Honours, also Ancient Mediterranean Studies), Cambridge, Durham (alone or with Anthropology or Latin), Edinburgh (alone or with Ancient History or Sociology), Exeter (with History or Geography), Glasgow (alone or with another subject), Lancaster (with Latin, Ancient History, Italian Studies or Medieval Studies), Leeds (with one of certain other subjects), Leicester (Archaeological Studies – Archaeology with another subject and a third – minor – subject), Liverpool (Archaeology of the Eastern Mediterranean, also Archaeology with Ancient and Medieval History or Medieval History), London (including Conservation of Archaeological Materials at Institute of Archaeology, also Classical Archaeology with Classics or Greek at Bedford and King's Colleges, Archaeology of South or South East Asia or Archaeology and

Geography or History at School of Oriental and African Studies, Medieval Archaeology or Classics and Classical Archaeology at University College), Manchester (with Ancient History), Newcastle upon Tyne (alone or with Ancient History), Nottingham (with Latin or History or Ancient History or Geography), Reading (alone or with another subject), Sheffield (Prehistory and Archaeology), Southampton and Wales (Cardiff University College, also – with History, Welsh History, Classical Studies or Sociology – Bangor University College). Bradford awards a BTech (4 yrs S) in *Archaeological Sciences* and Surrey a BSc in *Physics with Archaeometry*. Less specialised study of Archaeology may be included in first degree courses at most of these universities and at St Andrews.

Some study of *Egyptology* (see also page 215) may be included in first degree courses (usually in Oriental Studies) at Birmingham (for Honours in Ancient History and Archaeology), Cambridge, Durham, Liverpool, London (University College, for Honours in History, Anthropology or Hebrew), Oxford and Wales (Swansea University College).

Postgraduate courses Courses (1 yr and for master's degree, unless otherwise indicated) at the following universities:
Aegean and Anatolian Prehistory, Bristol.
Ancient History and Classical Archaeology, Liverpool (BPhil 1 or 2 yrs).
Anglo-Saxon Archaeology, London (Birkbeck College, diploma, normally 2 yrs).
Archaeological Method and Technique, Birmingham.
Archaeology, London (Institute of Archaeology).
Archaeology of Ancient Egypt, London (University College, 2 yrs).
Archaeology of Classical Greece, Newcastle upon Tyne (2 yrs).
Archaeology of Medieval England, Reading (Graduate Centre for Medieval Studies, option for MA, 12 months, or MPhil, 24 months).
Archaeology of the Roman Empire, Newcastle upon Tyne (2 yrs).
British Archaeology, Durham (Romano-British or Anglo-Saxon Studies, or Prehistoric European Archaeology).
Chinese Archaeology, London (School of Oriental and African Studies, diploma, normally 2 yrs).
Classical Archaeology, Cambridge (diploma), London (University College, diploma, normally 2 yrs) and Oxford (diploma 1 yr, BPhil 2 yrs).
Dark Age and Saxon Archaeology of the British Isles, Reading (Graduate Centre for Medieval Studies, option for MA, 12 months, or MPhil, 24 months).
Egyptology, London (University College, diploma, normally 2 yrs).
European Archaeology, Oxford (diploma 1 yr, BPhil 2 yrs).
Human Environment, London (Institute of Archaeology).
Indian Archaeology or *Islamic Archaeology*, London (School of Oriental and African Studies, diplomas, normally 2 yrs).
Latin-American Archaeology, London (Institute of Archaeology, 1 or 2 yrs).
Minoan-Mycenaean and Early Greek Archaeology, London (Bedford College, minimum 1 yr, normally 2 yrs).
Prehistoric and Roman Britain in its European Context, Newcastle upon Tyne (2 yrs).
Prehistoric Archaeology, Cambridge (certificate), Liverpool (BPhil), London (Institute of Archaeology, 1 or 2 yrs) and Oxford (diploma 1 yr, BPhil 2 yrs).
Prehistory and Archaeology, Sheffield.
Roman and Early Byzantine Archaeology, Newcastle upon Tyne (2 yrs).
Roman Archaeology, London (Institute of Archaeology, 1 or 2 yrs).
Scientific Methods in Archaeology, Bradford (diploma 9 months, MA 12 months).
South East Asian Archaeology, London (School of Oriental and African Studies, diploma, normally 2 yrs).
Western Asian Archaeology, London (Institute of Archaeology, MA 2 yrs, diploma 3 yrs).
Western European Archaeology – The British Isles in the Anglo-Saxon Period, London (University College, diploma, normally 2 yrs).

Research facilities At most of the universities named above, and (Prehistoric Archaeology) at East Anglia (Centre of East Anglian Studies). Cambridge: Museums of Classical Archaeology and of Archaeology and Ethnology. London: Institute of Archaeology, School of Oriental and African Studies (Chinese, India, Islamic or Western Asian), and Birkbeck (Anglo-Saxon) and University Colleges. Oxford: Institute of Archaeology, Ashmolean Museum of Art and Archaeology, Research Laboratory for Archaeology and the History of Art. Wales: Bangor and Cardiff and – Egyptology – Swansea University Colleges.

Dorset IHE, certificate *Practical Archaeology* (2 yrs, in conjunction with U of Southampton).

Architecture

See also Building Science and Technology, Landscape Architecture, and Town and Country Planning

First degrees Degrees in *Architecture* awarded by the following universities (5 yrs unless otherwise indicated): Bath (BSc 4 yrs, plus 2 yrs for BArch), Belfast (BSc 4 yrs, including 1 yr spent outside the university), Bristol (BA, 3 yrs), Cambridge (BA, Architecture Tripos, 3 yrs), Dundee (BSc 3 yrs, followed by 1 yr's professional training, then BArch 2 yrs), Edinburgh (MA Honours), Glasgow (BArch, 3 yrs), Heriot-Watt (BArch, 5 yrs including 1 yr spent outside the university), Liverpool (BA 3 yrs, then 2 yrs for BArch), London (University College – BSc, 3 yrs, in Architecture, Planning, Building and Environmental Studies), Manchester (BA 3 yrs, plus 1 yr's practical experience, then BArch 2 yrs), Newcastle upon Tyne (BA in Architectural Studies 3 yrs, then BArch 2 yrs), Nottingham (BA in Architecture and Environmental Design 3 yrs, 1 yr in an office, then BArch 2 yrs), Sheffield (BA 3 yrs), Strathclyde (BSc in Architectural Studies 4 yrs, then BArch 1 yr) and Wales (BSc/BArch at Institute of Science and Technology). Aston in Birmingham awards a BSc in *Architectural Studies* taken with another subject, and Leeds a BSc in *Architectural Engineering. History of Architecture* may also be included in first degree courses at· East Anglia (History of Art and Architecture in School of Fine Arts and Music), Essex (in Honours course in Art History and Theory, School of Comparative Studies) and Reading (including BA in History of Art and Architecture).

Postgraduate courses Courses (1 yr, and for MA or MSc, unless otherwise indicated) at the following universities (for BArch, see above):

Advanced Architectural Studies, Belfast (diploma, 2 yrs) and London (University College, option in MSc in Architecture).

Advanced Art-Historical Studies, East Anglia.

Advanced Functional Design Techniques for Buildings, Bristol (12 months full-time or 3 yrs – modular course – part-time).

Agricultural Architecture, Manchester.

Architectural Conservation, Newcastle upon Tyne.

Architectural Criticism or *Architectural Theory from Vitruvius to le Corbusier* or *the Architect and Building Trades in History,* Manchester.

Architecture (normally 2 yrs), Belfast, Bristol (diploma, following BA), Cambridge (diploma, following BA), Edinburgh (diploma), Glasgow (diploma), Heriot-Watt (diploma, also MArch 9 months full-time plus 12 months non-residential study), Liverpool (MArch), London (University College, also College diploma), Newcastle upon Tyne and Sheffield (also diploma).

Conservation Studies, York (diploma).

Environmental Conservation, Heriot-Watt (diploma or – 9 months full-time plus 12 months non-residential study – MSc).

History and Theory of Architecture, Essex (School of Comparative Studies, 12 months).

History of Architecture and *Housing,* Newcastle upon Tyne (MPhil, each 2 yrs).

Housing and Urban Revitalisation, York (diploma).

Industrial Architecture, Manchester.

Liturgy and Architecture, Birmingham (Institute for the Study of Worship and Religious Architecture, diploma).

Methods and Techniques of Research, Recording and Documentation or *North American Architecture* (from colonial times to the present day) or *Principles of Preservation and Conservation of Historic Buildings* or *Regional Domestic Architecture and Building* or *Theory of Architectural Design Method,* Manchester.

Urban Architectural Design, Newcastle upon Tyne (MPhil, 2 yrs).

Western Architecture 1750–1950, Manchester.

Research facilities	At most of the universities named above (London: also, in History of European Art and Architecture, at Courtauld Institute of Art; York: Institute of Advanced Architectural Studies).

First degrees	CNAA degrees (except where otherwise indicated) are offered at the following polytechnics and colleges (3 yrs). Birmingham P. Brighton P, *Architectural Design.* Canterbury C Art. P of Central London. Duncan of Jordanstone C Art, BSc degree in conjunction with U of Dundee followed by BArch (Hons) (2 yrs). Edinburgh C Art (BArch Heriot-Watt U). Glasgow S Art (BA, Glasgow U). Kingston P. Leeds P (also 4 yrs and 5 yrs S). Leicester P. Liverpool P, *Architectural Studies.* Manchester P (4 yrs S). P of North London. North East London P. Oxford P, *Architectural Studies.* Portsmouth P. Robert Gordon's IT (4 yrs). P of the South Bank. Thames P.

Professional courses	Courses of study for the diploma examinations of the Royal Institute of British Architects may be followed at many schools approved by the Institute for this purpose. Courses normally last five years, with a break, usually between the third and fourth years, for practical training. All candidates must have two years' practical experience before taking the Examination in Professional Practice and Practical Experience. This is necessary before they can qualify for corporate membership of the RIBA.

The schools of architecture of the following colleges are recognised for exemption from the Institute's Part I and Final Part II Examinations:

Aberdeen: Robert Gordon's IT. Birmingham P. Brighton P. Canterbury C Art. Dundee: Duncan of Jordanstone C Art and U of Dundee. Edinburgh C Art. Glasgow S Art. Hull CHE. Leeds P. Leicester P. Liverpool P. London: Architectural Association School of Architecture; P of Central London; Kingston P; P of North London; P of the South Bank; Thames P. Manchester P. Oxford P. Portsmouth P.

Students who successfully complete courses at the schools of architecture of the following colleges are exempted from Part I of the RIBA examinations: Gloucestershire C Art. Huddersfield P. North East London P. Plymouth P.

The schools of architecture of the following colleges prepare students to take RIBA Part II examinations externally: Gloucestershire C Art. Huddersfield P. North East London P. Plymouth P.

Art and Design

See also Printing and Textiles

Most university courses in Art are concerned wholly or largely with history, theory or criticism, but many include practical classes.

First degrees Degrees with specialisation awarded by the following universities:

Art/Fine Art, Edinburgh (5 yrs or, with Sculpture as special subject, 6 yrs – curriculum partly theoretical (taken at the university) and partly practical (taken at Edinburgh C Art)), Exeter (with English, French, Italian or Spanish, in association with Exeter C Art), Leeds, London (Slade School of Fine Art at University College), Newcastle upon Tyne (partly practical, partly theoretical, with specialisation in Painting, Sculpture or Design), Oxford, Reading and Wales (Aberystwyth University College).

Creative Design, Loughborough U of Technology (3 yrs or, with certificate in Education, 4 yrs).

History of Art/Fine Art, Aberdeen, Bristol (History of European Art with another subject), Cambridge, East Anglia, Edinburgh, Essex (Art History and Theory in School of Comparative Studies – no practical classes), Glasgow (Combined Honours), Leeds (with one of certain other subjects), Leicester (Art History Studies – History of Art with one of certain other subjects plus a third – minor – subject), London (History of European Art at Courtauld Institute of Art, History of Art at University and Westfield Colleges, also – part-time – at Birkbeck College), Manchester, Nottingham (with English or History), Reading (also History of Art and Architecture), St Andrews (with one of certain other subjects), Sussex (Schools of Cultural and Community or English and American or European Studies) and Warwick.

Typography and Graphic Communication, Reading.

At some of the universities providing courses with specialisation in Art or Art History alone, the subject may also be offered with another principal subject for a Joint (or Combined) Honours degree; and less specialised study of Art or History of Art may be included in first degree courses at most of them, and at Birmingham, Hull, Kent at Canterbury (Art History and Theory), Lancaster (Art and Environment – minor course or, with Geography, as major course), Southampton, Stirling and Wales (Swansea University College).

Also *Art Teacher's* certificate course (1 yr, open to non-graduates) at London (Institute of Education).

Postgraduate courses Courses leading to MFA (2 yrs) at the universities of Newcastle upon Tyne and Reading (Painting or Sculpture). Other postgraduate courses (1 yr and for MA, unless otherwise indicated) at the following universities:

Advanced Art-Historical Studies, East Anglia.

Aesthetics and Theory of Art, Essex (12 months).

Art Gallery and Museum Studies, Manchester (diploma).

Conservation of Paintings, London (Courtauld Institute of Art, Institute certificate, 2 yrs).

English Literature and Fine Art, Birmingham.

Fine Art, London (Slade School of Fine Art at University College, 2 yrs for higher diploma – advanced courses include Drawing, Sculpture, Painting, Etching and Engraving, Design, Architecture, Stage and Decorative Painting, also History of Art and of Architecture).

History of Art, Essex (History and Theory of Nineteenth- and Twentieth-Century Art or of Renaissance and Baroque Art, or Pre-Columbian and Colonial Art in Central and South America, each 12 months), Glasgow (diploma 2 yrs), London (History of Art, Courtauld Institute of Art and University and Westfield Colleges), Oxford (diploma) and Sussex.

History of Dress, London (Courtauld Institute of Art, 2 yrs).
Medieval Studies, St Andrews (diploma 1 yr, MLitt 2 yrs) and York (12 months).
Modern English Literature (concerned with the literary response to the Visual Arts 1850–1920), Reading (11 months).
Visual Art, Wales (Aberystwyth University College).
Royal College of Art: courses for master's degree (normally 2 yrs and for MA or MDes, unless otherwise indicated) include the following: Automotive Design (MDes or diploma); Ceramics; Design Research; Environmental Design; Fashion; Furniture Design (3 yrs); General Studies; Glass; Graphic Design (3 yrs); Graphic Information; Illustration (3 yrs); Industrial Design (3 yrs); Painting (3 yrs); Sculpture (3 yrs); Silversmithing and Jewellery (3 yrs).
Diploma/certificate courses (1 yr) for *Art Teachers* at universities of Leeds (diploma in Art Education for in-service teachers), London (Institute of Education, diploma in Art Education, also Graduate Certificate in Education with reference to Art and Design) and Reading (postgraduate certificate in Education with Art Method).

Research facilities   At most of the universities which offer first degree courses (London: also in Islamic and Chinese Art at School of Oriental and African Studies and in Character and History of the Classical Tradition at Warburg Institute), and at Royal College of Art. Oxford: research laboratory for Archaeology and the History of Art.

First degrees   CNAA degree courses (3 yrs) are available in the following schools in the areas of study indicated:

Fine art   *Painting and Sculpture*
Bath Academy of Art. Birmingham P. Brighton P. Bristol P. Camberwell S Arts and Crafts. Canterbury C Art. Central S Art and Design. Chelsea S Art. Exeter C Art and Design. Falmouth S Art. Gloucestershire C Art and Design. Goldsmiths' C S Art. Gwent CHE. Hull CHE. Kingston P. Lanchester P. Leeds P. Leicester P. Liverpool P. Loughborough C Art and Design. Maidstone C Art. Manchester P. Middlesex P. Newcastle upon Tyne P. North East London P. North Staffordshire P. Norwich S Art. Portsmouth P. Preston P. Ravensbourne C Art and Design. St Martin's S Art. Sheffield P. South Glamorgan IHE. Stourbridge C Art. Sunderland P. Trent P. Ulster C, Northern Ireland P. West Surrey C Art. Wimbledon S Art. Winchester S Art. Wolverhampton P.

Graphic design   Bath Academy of Art. Birmingham P. Brighton P. Bristol P. Camberwell S Arts and Crafts. Canterbury C Art. Central S Art and Design. Chelsea S Art. Exeter C Art and Design. Gwent CHE. Hull CHE. Kingston P. Lanchester P. Leeds P. Leicester P. Liverpool P. London C of Printing. Maidstone C Art. Manchester P. Middlesex P (option in *Scientific and Technical Illustration*, or *Information and Editorial Design*) (also 4 yrs S). Newcastle upon Tyne P. North Staffordshire P (*Multidisciplinary Graphic and 3-D Design* course). Norwich S Art. Preston P (4 yrs S). Ravensbourne C Art and Design. St Martin's S Art. Ulster C, Northern Ireland P. Wolverhampton P.

Three-dimensional design   *Ceramics*, Bath Academy of Art. Bristol P. Camberwell S Arts and Crafts. Central S Art and Design. Falmouth S Art. Leicester P. Loughborough C Art and Design. Middlesex P. Ravensbourne C Art and Design. West Surrey C Art and Design. Ulster C, Northern Ireland P. Wolverhampton P.
Furniture, Birmingham P. Bristol P. Buckinghamshire CHE. Kingston P. Leeds P. Leicester P. Loughborough C Art and Design. Middlesex P. Ravensbourne C Art and Design. Trent P. Ulster C, Northern Ireland P.

Glass, Stourbridge C Art.

Industrial Design (Engineering), Birmingham P. Central S Art and Design. Lanchester P (4 yrs S). Leeds P. Leicester P. Manchester P. Napier CC and T. Newcastle upon Tyne P (4 yrs S). Sheffield P. Teesside P.

Interior Design, Birmingham P. Brighton P. Buckinghamshire CHE. Kingston P. Leeds P. Leicester P. Manchester P. Middlesex P (4 yrs S). Teesside P. Trent P (4 yrs S). Ulster C, Northern Ireland P.

Silversmithing and Jewellery, Birmingham P. Buckinghamshire CHE (*Silvermetal*). Central S Art and Design (*Jewellery*). Leicester P (*Silversmithing*). Loughborough C Art and Design. Middlesex P. Sheffield P. Ulster C, Northern Ireland P.

Theatre, Birmingham P. Central S Art and Design. Trent P. Wimbledon S Art.

Wood-Metal-Ceramics-Plastics. Brighton P. Manchester P (*Wood-Metal-Ceramics*). Newcastle upon Tyne (*Wood-Metal-Ceramics*, 4 yrs S). Ravensbourne C Art and Design. Wolverhampton P (*Wood-Metal-Ceramics*).

Textiles and fashion

Couture Fashion, Leicester P.

Embroidery, Birmingham P. Goldsmiths' C S Art and Design. Manchester P. Ulster C, Northern Ireland P.

Fashion, Birmingham P. Brighton P (4 yrs S). Bristol P. Gloucestershire C Art and Design. Kingston P. Leicester P. Liverpool P. Manchester P. Middlesex P. Newcastle upon Tyne P (4 yrs S). Preston P (4 yrs S). Ravensbourne C Art and Design. St Martin's S Art (also *Fashion/Textiles* 4 yrs S). Trent P. Ulster C, Northern Ireland P.

Footwear Design, Leicester P.

Knitwear Design, Trent P (4 yrs S).

Textile Design, Brighton P (4 yrs S). Leicester P. Trent P.

Woven and Printed Textiles, Birmingham P. Camberwell S Arts and Crafts. Central S Art and Design. Falmouth S Art. Leicester P. Liverpool P. Loughborough C Art and Design. Manchester P. Middlesex P. Ulster C, Northern Ireland P. West Surrey C Art and Design. Winchester S Art.

Other courses

Art Therapy, postgraduate diploma Hertfordshire C Art and Design (1 yr).

Expressive Arts, Brighton P (3 yrs).

History of Art in the Modern Period, Leicester P (3 yrs).

History of Art, Design and Film, Sheffield P.

History of Design, Manchester P.

History of Modern Art and Design, Newcastle upon Type P (3 yrs).

Scottish diploma courses

Four Central Institutions in Scotland offer diploma courses of degree equivalence in *Art*. (Drawing and Painting: Design and Crafts). Other options are given below (4-yr courses unless otherwise stated). Robert Gordon's IT S Art, *Ceramics with Sculpture* or *Sculpture with Ceramics*. Duncan of Jordanstone C Art, *Graphic Design, Textile Design, Embroidery, Illustration and Print-making, Ceramics, Product Design and Silversmithing and Jewellery* and *Interior Design*. Edinburgh C Art, *Ceramics, Fashion Design, Furniture Design, Glass Design, Graphic Design, Interior Design, Jewellery, Mural, Silversmithing and Allied Crafts, Stained Glass, Printed Textiles, Woven Textiles and Tapestry*. Glasgow S Art, *Sculpture* (5 yrs), *Ceramics, Embroidery and Weaving, Furniture, Graphic Design, Printmaking, Product Design, Interior Design, Mural Decoration, Mosaics, Stained Glass, Textile Design, Silversmithing and Jewellery*.

Postgraduate courses

(i) CNAA degrees (1 yr, also 2 yrs for *Industrial Engineering, Interior Design* and *Ceramics*). Birmingham P, *Fine Art (Painting and Sculpture), Graphic Design, Industrial Design, Textiles/Fashion* and also CNAA postgraduate diploma in *History of Art and Design*.

Buckinghamshire CHE, *Furniture Design and Technology* (1 yr).

Central S Art and Design, *Graphic Design, Industrial Design (Engineering), Textile/Fashion.*

Chelsea S Art, *Fine Art (Painting, Sculpture, Autographic Printmaking).*

Leicester P, *Graphic Design, Industrial Design (Engineering), Interior Design, Textiles/Fashion* (4 terms).

Manchester P, *Fine Art (Sculpture), Graphic Design, Industrial Design (Engineering), Textiles/Fashion.*

North Staffordshire P, *Design (Ceramics)* (2 yrs S).

(ii) Post-diploma courses in Scotland (1 yr).

Duncan of Jordanstone C Art, *Drawing and Painting, Design and Crafts, Sculpture.*

Edinburgh C Art, *Design, Painting, Sculpture.*

Glasgow S Art, *Art.*

Robert Gordon's IT, *Art.*

(iii) Other courses.

Brighton P, *Specialist Printmaking* (1 yr).

Buckinghamshire CHE, diploma in *Furniture Production and Management* (3 yrs).

Goldsmiths' C, Advanced Diploma in *Art and Design (Painting), Sculpture, Textiles/Fashion, Graphic Design* or *Ceramics* (1 yr).

Middlesex P, *Engineering Design Methods* (3 months).

P of North London, *Interior Decoration and Design* (4 yrs).

Scottish C of Textiles, *Design* (1 yr).

Swansea C Art, diplomas in *Architectural Glass, Graphic Design,* and *Technical and Pictorial Illustration* (3 yrs).

Teesside P, *Interior Design* (3 yrs), and Diploma of Clothing Institute, Part I (2 yrs).

Trent P, *Architectural Ceramics, Furniture Design* (3 yrs), and courses leading to Graduateship of the Institute of British Decorators and Interior Designers (3 yrs).

Wimbledon S Art, *Graphic Design* (3 yrs), *Wardrobe* (2 yrs) and *Graphics* (1 yr).

College diplomas and certificates
(These are vocational courses as described on page 36.)

Birmingham P, *Ceramics* (3 yrs).

Blackpool CT and Art, advanced diploma in *Technical Illustration* (3 yrs S).

Brighton P, *Fashion/Textiles.*

Byam Shaw S of Drawing and Painting, *Fine Art* (2 yrs and 3 yrs) and post-diploma certificate (1 yr).

Cambridgeshire C Arts and T, LSIAD courses in *Graphic Design (Typography, Illustration)* (3 yrs).

Canterbury C Art, *Graphic Design, Dress and Textiles* (3 yrs).

Cardiff C Art, *Interior Design, Integrated Design (2-dimensional), Industrial Design* (all 3 yrs).

City of London P, *Silversmithing/Engraving/Jewellery* (4 yrs).

Croydon C Art, diploma in *Fine Art, Graphic Design, Fashion, Textiles, Theatre, 3-dimensional Design* (3 yrs).

Dundee CT, *Textiles* (3 yrs).

Ealing TC, *Integrated Design* (3 yrs).

Gateshead CT, *Conservation of Painting* (2 yrs).

Glasgow C Building and Printing, *Design and Decoration (Interior Design)* (4 yrs).

Gloucestershire C Art and Design, LSIAD *Graphic Design* (3 yrs), *Graphic Design, Technical Illustration* (3–4 yrs), BDS Advanced Diploma *Display* (4 yrs), *Retail Fashion and Display* (4 yrs).

Goldsmiths' C, *Fine Art, Art and Design (Graphics)* (both 1 yr).

Harrow S Art *Studio Pottery* (2 yrs), *Illustration, Fashion Design, Information Graphics* (3 yrs).

Huddersfield P, *Graphic and Advertising Design* (2 yrs), and course leading to Associateship of

Textile Design Institute (3 yrs).

Hull CHE, *Graphic Design, Textile Design and Surface Decoration* (3 yrs).

Leicester P, *Shoe Design* (3 yrs), and Associateship of Textile Design Institute (3 yrs).

London C of Fashion and Clothing Technology, *Clothing Management* (4 yrs S), certificate in *Fashion Writing* (1 yr).

London C of Furniture, *Furniture Design and Construction* (2 yrs S), *Furnishing and Interior Design* (option in *Play Equipment* and *Equipment for the Disabled*) (2 yrs S).

Loughborough C Art and Design, *Graphic Design, Fashion* (both 3 yrs).

Middlesex P, *Jewellery and Ceramics* (3 yrs).

Napier CC and T, *Interior Design* (4 yrs).

Nene C, *Fashion* (3 yrs), *Graphic Design, 3-dimensional Design* (both 3 yrs).

North East London P, *Fashion/Textile Design* (3 yrs).

Preston P, *Ceramics* (3 yrs).

Reigate S Art, Surrey diploma courses in *Graphic Design, Textile Design, Fine Art (Painting, Sculptured Media), Interior and Exhibition Design, Calligraphy, Heraldry* and *Illumination* (3 yrs), also leading to possible Licentiateship of the Society of Industrial Artists and Designers and the Society of Designer Craftsmen.

St Martin's S Art, Advanced Studies in *Painting, Sculpture, Graphic Design, Fashion, Textiles* (1 yr).

Salford CT, *Graphic/Advertising Design, 3-dimensional Design, Dress and Fashion Design* (all 2–3 yrs).

Scottish C Textiles, Honours Associateship (4 yrs) and diploma (3 yrs) in *Textile Design.*

Southampton C Art, *Fine Art/Environmental Design Studies* (2 yrs).

Trent P, *Graphic Design* (3 yrs).

Ulster C, Northern Ireland P, *Fashion* (3 yrs).

Willesden CT, *Interior Design* (2 yrs).

Art teaching The colleges and polytechnics listed below provide courses leading to the Art Teacher's Diploma or Certificate for students who already have recognised advanced qualifications in art. All the courses are 1 yr unless otherwise indicated. Birmingham P, also MA *Art Education,* diploma *Curriculum Studies in Art and Design.* Brighton P, also Advanced Diploma in *Art Education,* supplementary courses in *Art Education* including one for overseas teachers, and opportunities for higher degrees and research. Bristol P, also MPhil *Art Education* (2 yrs), diploma *Research in Art Education.* Goldsmiths' C. Leeds P. Leicester P, also opportunities for research. Liverpool P. Manchester P. Middlesex P. South Glamorgan IHE, also MEd *Art Education,* also Advanced Diplomas in *Art Education,* and *Curriculum Development in Art Education.*

In addition to the above, Rolle C and Bretton Hall C provide 1 yr courses for non-graduates who wish to teach Art and who have successfully completed 2 yrs study at a School or College of Art.

Courses of general teacher training with an art and craft bias may be followed in many colleges of education and other teacher training establishments (see page 124).

Arts and/or Science (Joint or Combined)

See also page 28

First degrees As well as providing courses leading to first degrees with Honours (or Special degrees) in *single* arts or science subjects, and also (at most universities) courses leading to General or Ordinary degrees involving the less specialised study of *several* arts or science subjects (see below, and under 'Science and Technology'), many universities offer courses leading to Joint (or Combined) Honours degrees (usually BA or BSc) which involve specialisation in *two* (occasionally three) arts and/or science subjects. The pairs of subjects available for Joint (or Combined) degrees are too numerous to include in this handbook, but full lists are given in the *Compendium of University Entrance Requirements* and the *Commonwealth Universities Yearbook* (see page 265).

Arts (General)

First degrees   As well as providing courses leading to first degrees with Honours (or Special degrees) in a *single* arts subject, or Joint (or Combined) Honours degrees in *two* arts subjects (see above), many universities also offer less specialised degree courses which involved the study of *several* arts subjects. It is not possible to include in this handbook details of the varying structures and titles of these less specialised degrees but summarised information is set out in one of the Tables in the annual *Compendium of University Entrance Requirements* (see page 265). These degrees are usually called either 'General' or 'Ordinary' degrees, and at some universities General degrees may be awarded with Honours – see also page 28.

First degrees   CNAA degrees (3 yrs unless otherwise indicated).
Arts, Cambridgeshire C Arts and T.
Combined Arts, Leicester P.
Combined Studies, Nene C.
Cultural Studies, Portsmouth P.
English and History, Newcastle upon Tyne P (also *History of Modern Art and Design*).
Humanities, Bristol P. Bolton IT. Bournemouth CT. Dorset IHE. Ealing TC. Hatfield P. Huddersfield P. Manchester P (*Humanities/Social Studies*). Middlesex P. P of North London (also *Geography* and *History*). Plymouth P. C of St Mark and St John (in association with Plymouth P). Teesside P (*History, Literature, Politics and Languages*). Thames P. Trent P. P of Wales. Wolverhampton P (3–4 yrs, also *Modern Languages with Political Studies*).
Modern Arts, Kingston P (*English, History, French*; also 4 yrs; also *Languages, Economics and Politics*, 4 yrs).
Modern Studies, Lanchester P. Sheffield City P. North Staffordshire P.
   For courses leading to Joint (or Combined) CNAA Honours degrees in science subjects see 'Science (General)'.
   BA and BSc modular degrees (CNAA) are offered at the following polytechnics (see below). Students choose a pattern of modules that relate either to a single subject and thus to a specialised degree or to a combination of modules that constitute a broader education. Initially the students take three or four basic courses and subsequently select advanced modules (usually related to the basic courses) chosen from the subject areas mentioned below.
City of London P, *Modular Degree Scheme* (3 yrs) incorporates the following main subject areas: Accountancy, Biology, Chemistry, Computing, Economics, French, Geography, Geology, Law, Mathematics, Metallurgy, Physics, Politics, Psychology, Secretarial Studies, Sociology, Statistics.
Oxford P. *Modular Degree Course* (3–4 yrs) offers the following fields: Anthropology, Art and Design, Biology, Combined Science, English, Environmental Biology, French Language and Contemporary Studies, French Literature, Food and Nutrition, Geography, Geology, Geology and Environment, German Language and Contemporary Studies, German Literature, History,

History of Art, Human Biology, Mathematical and Computer Studies, Movement Studies, Music, Physical Sciences, Psychology.

A number of teacher training establishments now offer BA combined or general studies degrees which do *not* lead to teaching qualifications. Details of these are given in the *Handbook of Institutions providing . . . Teacher Training*

DipHE courses

(2 yrs). The following institutions offer DipHE programmes as a self-contained programme of study or as a coherent programme possibly leading to a degree programme. The courses include subjects in the Humanities and the Sciences. The number of colleges and polytechnics offering DipHE programmes is likely to increase.

Avery Hill C. Bath CHE. Bingley C. Bradford C. Brighton P. Buckinghamshire CHE. Bulmershe CHE. City of London P. City of Manchester CHE. Crewe and Alsager CHE. Gwent CHE. Huddersfield P. Ilkley C. King Alfred's C. La Sainte Union CE. Leicester P. Manchester P. Middlesex P. Newman C. North East London P. Oxford P. Padgate CHE. C Ripon and York St John. West London IHE. Wolverhampton P.

Astronomy and Space Science

First degrees

Degrees with specialisation awarded by the following universities:
Aeronautics and Astronautics (various options), Southampton.
Astronomy, Glasgow, Leicester (Mathematics with Astronomy), London (University College, alone or with Physics), Newcastle upon Tyne (with Astrophysics) and St Andrews.
Astrophysics, Edinburgh, Leeds (Physics with Astrophysics), Leicester (Physics with Astrophysics), London (Queen Elizabeth College – Astrophysics with Mathematics and Physics, or Physics and Astrophysics – and Queen Mary College), Newcastle upon Tyne (with Astronomy) and Wales (Aberystwyth University College, Planetary and Space Physics).

Less specialised study of Astronomy may be included in first degree courses at Belfast, Birmingham, Edinburgh, Glasgow, Keele, Leicester, London (Queen Mary College), Sheffield, Sussex and Wales (Cardiff University College); and of Astrophysics at Cambridge (for Part III of Mathematical Tripos) and Leeds (Physics with Astrophysics).

Postgraduate courses

Courses (1 yr and for MSc, unless otherwise indicated) at the following universities:
Astronomy, Manchester (diploma) and Sussex.
Astrophysics, Cosmology and General Relativity, Wales (Cardiff University College).
Experimental Space Physics, Leicester.
Geophysics and Planetary Physics, Newcastle upon Tyne.
Physics of the Atmosphere, Wales (Aberystwyth University College).
Physics of the Earth's Environment, Exeter (12 months).
Radio-Astronomy, Manchester (MSc or diploma).

Research facilities

At the following universities: Birmingham (Space Research), Bristol, Cambridge (Institute of Astronomy, Radio Astronomy Observatory), Edinburgh, Glasgow, Heriot-Watt (Satellite Radiometry, Solar Physics), Kent at Canterbury, Leicester, London (Imperial and University Colleges, also – Astrophysics – Queen Elizabeth and Queen Mary Colleges; University Observatory), Manchester (Astronomy and Radio-Astronomy, radio telescope at Jodrell Bank), Newcastle upon Tyne (Astrophysics and Cosmology; small Observatory at Close House), Oxford (Astrophysics, Atmospheric Physics, University Observatory), St Andrews, Sheffield (Radio-Astronomy), Southampton, Sussex (Theoretical and Observational Astronomy; Astronomy Centre; collaboration with Royal Greenwich Observatory, Herstmonceux) and Wales (Cardiff University College, Astrophysics).

Aviation, Civil

See also Engineering, Aeronautical

Postgraduate courses Cranfield IT awards an MSc (1 or 2 yrs) in Air Transport Engineering including *Air Transport Operations*.

Professional courses Unless exempted by means of previous and extensive flying experience, candidates for the Commercial Pilot's Licence (Aeroplanes) and Instrument Rating, CLP/IR, or the Commercial Pilot's Licence (Helicopters), CPL(H), must attend a course of flying and ground training approved by the Civil Aviation Authority. Full details of the entry requirements are contained in Civil Aviation Authority publication CAP 54, obtainable from CAA, Printing and Publication Services, 37 Gratton Road, Cheltenham, Gloucester, GL50 2BN.

The schools offering approved professional pilot training courses are listed below. Courses start every 2–3 months and last a minimum of 13 months for the CPL/IR and 9 months for the CPL(H). Most schools offer pre-course training in English language for students from overseas. The minimum educational qualifications for entry to training are 5 passes at GCE 'O' level, or equivalent, including passes in English language, Mathematics and a recognised Science subject. Entrants also have to pass a medical examination to professional pilot standards.

Air Service Training, Perth Aerodrome, Perth. CPL/IR Courses

Bristow Helicopters Ltd, Redhill Aerodrome, Surrey. CPL(H) Courses

College of Air Training, Hamble, Southampton. CPL/IR Courses

Oxford Air Training School, Carlisle Airport, Carlisle, Cumbria. CPL/IR Courses

Oxford Air Training School, Oxford Airport, Kidlington, Oxford. CPL/IR and CPL/H Courses

Bacteriology

See also Microbiology

First degrees Degrees with specialisation awarded by the following universities: *Bacteriology*, Birmingham, Edinburgh, Manchester (with Virology) and Newcastle upon Tyne; *Immunology*, Glasgow, London (Chelsea College, with Biochemistry, Microbiology or Physiology) and Strathclyde (Biochemistry with Immunology); *Virology*, Manchester (with Bacteriology) and Warwick (with Microbiology). Less specialised study of Bacteriology may also be included in first degree courses (in some cases only in the Faculty of Medicine) at these universities and at the following: Aberdeen, Belfast, Bristol, Cambridge, Dundee, Glasgow, London, Nottingham, Oxford, Reading, Sheffield, Southampton, Surrey, Wales (Aberystwyth, Bangor and Swansea University Colleges) and York.

Postgraduate courses Courses (1 yr and for MSc, unless otherwise indicated) at the following universities:
Bacteriology, London (School of Hygiene and Tropical Medicine, diploma) and Manchester (diploma).
Bacteriology and Virology, Manchester (1–2 yrs full-time, 2 yrs part-time).
Immunobiology, Aberdeen.
Immunology, Birmingham.
Virology, Reading (12 months).

Research facilities At the universities of Aberdeen, Birmingham, Bristol, Cambridge, Dundee, Edinburgh, Glasgow (including Immunology, Virology), London (St Bartholomew's, St Mary's and St Thomas's Hospital Medical Schools, and Chelsea College), Manchester, Newcastle upon Tyne, Reading (Virology), Sheffield (Medical Microbiology), Southampton, Surrey and Warwick (Virus research).

Ballet and Modern Dance

First degrees University of Birmingham awards a BA Special Honours in *Music, Drama and Dance.*

Professional and teacher training courses Benesh Institute of Choreology, diploma course for Repetiteurs, Teachers, Professional Dancers/Dance Students (Benesh Notation) (16 months).

Guildford S Acting and Drama, Classical Ballet and Related Arts diploma (3 yrs), teacher training course in Ballet and Modern Dance (3 yrs with 1 yr at East Sussex CE).

Laban Centre for Movement and Dance at Goldsmiths' C, courses leading to qualification as Dancer, Choreographer, Notator (Laban System) or Movement Expert (2 yrs for certificate, 3 yrs for diploma). Courses for intending teachers of Movement and Modern Educational Dance (2 yrs plus 1 yr). Courses for qualified teachers in Movement Study and Modern Educational Dance (1 yr).

London C Dance and Drama, teacher training course (3 yrs followed by 1 yr at Dartford CE).

London S Contemporary Dance, professional course (3 yrs and 1 yr – Martha Graham technique).

Royal Academy of Dancing, diploma in teaching of Classical Ballet and related subjects (3 yrs), teaching course for professional dancers (6 months).

Rambert S Ballet, professional course (3 yrs).

Royal Ballet S, professional course (2–3 yrs), teacher training course (3 yrs). Many institutions of education offer options in Movement and Dance in Certificate in education and BEd courses. Some of the colleges listed as offering physical education courses on page 223 are in this category. For full details of these courses the *Handbook of Institutions providing both Teacher Training and other Full-Time Advanced Courses* should be consulted.

Banking

First degrees Degrees with specialisation awarded by the following universities: *Banking and Finance,* Loughborough U of Technology (3 yrs, or – BSc and DIS – 4 yrs S) and Wales (Institute of Science and Technology, for BScEcon); *Banking and International Finance,* The City (3 yrs, or 4 yrs S); *Banking, Insurance and Finance,* Wales (Bangor University College). Some study of Banking may also be included in degree courses in Commerce and/or Economics at the universities of Birmingham, Hull, Liverpool, London (London School of Economics), Reading (Money and Banking, option for BA Honours in Economics or Economics and Accounting) and Stirling.

Research facilities At the following universities: The City, Loughborough U of Technology and Wales (Bangor University College and Institute of Science and Technology).

Professional courses Opportunities to specialise in *Banking* are available within the framework of other courses at Dorset IHE.

The examinations of the Institute of Bankers are available to staff currently employed by banks recognised by the Institute, from which details may be obtained.

Biochemistry

First degrees   Degrees with specialisation awarded by the following universities:

Applied Biochemistry, Brunel (4 yrs S).

Biochemical Engineering, see 'Engineering, Chemical'.

Biochemistry, Aberdeen, Aston in Birmingham (with another subject), Bath (4 yrs S), Belfast, Birmingham, Bristol, Cambridge, Dundee (also BMSc – see page 198), East Anglia (Honours in School of Biological Sciences with specialisation in group of subjects relevant to Biochemistry), Edinburgh, Glasgow, Heriot-Watt, Hull, Kent at Canterbury, Lancaster, Leeds, Leicester (Chemistry with Biochemistry, also Honours in Biology with specialisation in group of subjects relevant to Biochemistry), Liverpool, London (at Bedford, Chelsea, Imperial, King's, Queen Elizabeth, Royal Holloway and University Colleges, also – with Genetics – Queen Mary College, and – with Biology, Botany, Chemistry or Zoology – Westfield College), Manchester (including Institute of Science and Technology), Newcastle upon Tyne, Nottingham (with Botany, Chemistry, Genetics or Zoology), Oxford, Reading (with Physiology, integrated course), St Andrews, Salford, Sheffield (BSc and – see page 198 – BMedSci), Southampton (with Physiology, integrated course), Stirling, Strathclyde, Surrey (3 yrs, or 4 yrs S), Sussex (major subject in Schools of Biological or Molecular Sciences), Wales (Aberystwyth, Bangor, Cardiff and Swansea University Colleges), Warwick and York.

Biological Chemistry, Essex, Kent at Canterbury, London (Queen Mary College) and New U of Ulster.

Brewing, Heriot-Watt (3 yrs or, with Biochemistry or Microbiology, 4 yrs).

Medical Biochemistry, Birmingham, Leeds (Biochemistry in relation to Medicine, for students who have successfully completed second MB ChB examination), London (Royal Holloway College), Manchester (Institute of Science and Technology, Biochemistry with Clinical Biochemistry), Nottingham (only for students who have completed Part I of BMedSci course), Surrey (4 yrs S, also 3 yrs) and Wales (Cardiff University College, only for medical students who have completed pre-clinical part of MB BCh).

Pathobiology, Reading.

Toxicology, Bradford (Nutrition and Toxicology for BTech in Applied Biology, 4 yrs S) and Surrey (Biochemistry (Toxicology), 3 yrs, or 4 yrs S).

At some of the universities offering degrees with specialisation in this subject alone, Biochemistry may also be studied with another principal subject for a Joint (or Combined) Honours degree; and at many universities less specialised study of Biochemistry may be included in first degree courses.

Postgraduate courses   Courses (1 yr and for master's degree, unless otherwise indicated) at the following universities:

Biochemical Engineering, see 'Engineering, Chemical'.

Biochemical Pharmacology, Southampton.

Biochemistry, Cambridge, London (1 yr full-time or 2 yrs part-time for MSc or College diploma at Chelsea College, 1 or 2 yrs at University College, also 1 yr for diploma in General Biochemistry at St Bartholomew's Hospital Medical College, open to graduates or equivalent or those who have passed 2nd MB), Wales (Aberystwyth University College) and York (12 months).

Biochemistry of Reproduction, Strathclyde.

Brewing, Heriot-Watt (diploma).

Brewing Science, Birmingham.

Chemical Microbiology, Cambridge (certificate of postgraduate study).

Clinical Biochemistry, Birmingham (2 yrs – next entry 1978, and in alternate yrs thereafter), Newcastle upon Tyne and Surrey (full-time study for 3 separate terms in 2 calendar yrs alternating with collaborative study in an approved clinical laboratory).

Plant Biochemistry, Cambridge (certificate of postgraduate study).
Steroid Endocrinology, Leeds (12 months).
Toxicology, Surrey (12 months).

Research facilities   At most universities (at Keele postgraduate certificate in Education may be taken concurrently with research for PhD). Aberdeen: also at Institute of Marine Biochemistry of Natural Environment Research Council. Aston in Birmingham: including Biodeterioration Information Centre. East Anglia: also at ARC Food Research Institute which has been recognised by the university for purposes of postgraduate studies. London: Bedford, Chelsea, Imperial, King's, Queen Elizabeth, Queen Mary, Royal Holloway and University Colleges, and various Medical Schools. Oxford: including Nuclear Magnetic Resonance Section of SRC Oxford Enzyme Group. Surrey: including Wolfson Bioanalytical Centre. Sussex: including ARC Units of Nitrogen Fixation and of Invertebrate Chemistry and Physiology.

First degrees   CNAA degrees (usually *Applied Biology,* 4 yrs S) which provide opportunities for specialisation in *Biochemistry* are offered at the following. Bristol P, *Applied Biological Science.* Glasgow CT (3 and 4 yrs). Hatfield P. Huddersfield P. Lanchester P. Liverpool P. Luton CHE, *Science* (3 yrs). Manchester P, *Biological Sciences* (3 and 4 yrs). North East London P. Portsmouth P, *Biomolecular Science* (3 yrs). Thames P (also 3 yrs). Trent P.

Research facilities   Lanchester P. Huddersfield P. North East London P.

Professional courses   Students may follow full-time courses in Biochemistry leading to membership of the Institute of Biology at the following colleges: North East Surrey CT. Manchester P. Paisley CT. Trent P. Courses in Biochemistry can be studied both at Part I and Part II level at some of these colleges whilst at others Biochemistry is available as a special subject at Part I level only. Enquiries about the courses should be made to the head of the department at the college concerned. Part-time courses are also available and a list of full-time and part-time courses may be obtained from the Institute of Biology.
The Royal College of Physicians, The Royal Institute of Chemistry, the Royal College of Pathologists and the Association of Clinical Biochemists award a joint qualification Mastership in *Clinical Biochemistry.* Details may be obtained from the Royal Institute of Chemistry. Membership of the Royal College of Pathologists is available in *Chemical Pathology* (see 'Pathology').

Biology

See also Agriculture and Forestry, Microbiology, and Radiobiology

First degrees   Degrees with specialisation in *Botany* and/or *Zoology* awarded by the following universities: Aberdeen, Belfast, Birmingham (Honours in School of Biological Sciences with specialisation in groups of relevant subjects), Bristol, Cambridge, Dundee, Durham, East Anglia (Honours in School of Biological Sciences with specialisation in group of relevant subjects), Edinburgh, Exeter, Glasgow, Hull, Lancaster (major in Biological Sciences allowing specialisation in various branches), Leeds, Leicester (Honours in Biology with specialisation in group of relevant subjects), Liverpool, London (Bedford, Chelsea, Imperial, King's, Queen Elizabeth, Queen Mary, Royal Holloway, University and Westfield Colleges, also Goldsmiths' College),

Manchester, Newcastle upon Tyne, Nottingham, Oxford, Reading, St Andrews, Sheffield, Southampton and Wales (Aberystwyth, Bangor, Cardiff and Swansea University Colleges).

Other first degrees with specialisation awarded as follows:

Animal and Plant Biology, Sheffield.

Animal and Plant Ecology, Loughborough U of Technology.

Animal Biology, East Anglia and London (Queen Elizabeth College).

Animal Physiology, East Anglia and Stirling.

Applied Biology, Bath (4 yrs S), Bradford (4 yrs S), Brunel (4 yrs S), Cambridge, London (Chelsea College), Salford (4 yrs S) and Wales (Institute of Science and Technology, 3 yrs, or 4 yrs S).

Applied Zoology, Reading and Wales (Bangor University College).

Biology/Biological Sciences, Aberdeen, Aston in Birmingham, Birmingham, Dundee, Durham, East Anglia, Essex, Exeter, Keele (with another principal subject, but Biology alone possible in final yr), Kent at Canterbury, Lancaster, Leicester, London (Bedford, Birkbeck (part-time), Chelsea, King's, Queen Elizabeth, Queen Mary, University and Westfield Colleges), Manchester, Salford, Southampton, Stirling, Strathclyde, Sussex, New U of Ulster, Wales (Aberystwyth University College), Warwick and York.

Cell Biology, Glasgow, London (King's – Cell and Molecular Biology – and Queen Elizabeth Colleges), Manchester (Genetics and Cell Biology), Sheffield (Biochemistry and Cell Biology), Wales (Aberystwyth University College, Cell and Immunobiology) and York (Cell Biology and Biochemistry).

Developmental Biology, Aberdeen, East Anglia, Glasgow (Animal Developmental Biology) and Wales (Aberystwyth University College).

Ecology, East Anglia, Edinburgh, Lancaster, Leicester, London (Royal Holloway College), Stirling, New U of Ulster and York.

Environmental Biology, see 'Environmental Studies'.

Human Biology, Aston in Birmingham (Biology of Man and his Environment), London (Chelsea College, 3 yrs, or 4 yrs S), Loughborough U of Technology, Salford (Human Movement Studies with Physiology), Sheffield (with Anatomy), Surrey (3 yrs, or 4 yrs S) and York (Human and Environmental Biology).

Human Sciences, London (University College), Oxford and Sussex (major subject in School of Cultural and Community Studies).

Marine Biology, Heriot-Watt, Liverpool, London (Marine and Freshwater Biology at Westfield College), Stirling (Marine and Freshwater Biology) and Wales (Bangor University College – with another subject, also Zoology with Marine Zoology or Botany with Marine Botany – and Swansea University College).

Medical Biology (for students who have completed pre-clinical studies in Medicine), Aberdeen.

Medical Cell Biology, Liverpool (with Biochemistry).

Molecular Biology, Edinburgh, Glasgow and London (King's College, Cell and Molecular Biology).

Neurobiology, Sussex.

Pathobiology, Reading.

Physiology of Organisms, York.

Plant Biology, East Anglia, Hull, London (Queen Elizabeth College), Newcastle upon Tyne, Sheffield (Animal and Plant Biology) and Wales (Bangor University College).

Plant Physiology, Sheffield (with Biochemistry) and Stirling.

Plant Protection, Bradford (for BTech in Applied Biology, 4 yrs S).

Plant Science and Genetics, Sheffield.

Resource Management, Edinburgh and New U of Ulster (History of Resource Management).

Wild Life and Fisheries Management, Edinburgh.

At many of these universities Biology/Biological Sciences, or Botany or Zoology, may also be studied with another principal subject for a Joint (or Combined) Honours degree; and less specialised study may be included in first degree courses at almost all universities. Marine and Freshwater Biology or Ecology is usually included in courses for degrees in Biology/Biological Sciences or Zoology.

Postgraduate courses　Courses (1 yr and for master's degree, unless otherwise indicated) at the following universities:

Applied Biology, Cambridge.

Applied Entomology (*Temperate and Tropical*), London (Imperial College, MSc and/or DIC).

Applied Hydrobiology, London (Chelsea College) and Wales (Institute of Science and Technology).

Applied Parasitology, Liverpool.

Aquaculture and *Aquatic Pathobiology*, Stirling (both in alternate yrs, next 1978–79).

Biological Anthropology, Durham.

Biological Chemical Engineering, Birmingham.

Biology, Edinburgh (diploma).

Biology and Biological Education, York (2 yrs).

Biology of Water Management, Aston in Birmingham.

Computation in the Life Sciences, York (12 months).

Conservation, London (University College, MSc or College diploma).

Conservation and Utilisation of Plant Genetic Resources, Birmingham.

Developmental Biology, Aberdeen.

Ecology, Aberdeen, Durham and Wales (Bangor University College).

Environmental Resources, Salford.

Human Biology, Loughborough U of Technology (MSc or associateship) and Oxford (diploma).

Immunobiology, Aberdeen.

Marine Biology, Wales (Bangor University College).

Molecular Enzymology, Warwick.

Nematology, London (Imperial College, MSc and/or DIC).

Neurobiology, London (Chelsea College).

Plant Breeding, Cambridge.

Plant Pathology, Exeter.

Plant Taxonomy, Reading (12 months).

Reproductive Biology, Manchester (normally 1 yr).

Resource Management, Edinburgh (diploma 9 months, MSc 12 months).

Science Education (see also under 'Education'), Keele.

Steroid Endocrinology, Leeds (12 months).

Underwater Science and Technology, Salford (modular course, 1 yr full-time or 2 yrs part-time).

Vertebrate Palaeontology, London (University College).

Weed Biology, Brunel.

Research facilities　At most universities and (including Ecological Physics: Insect and Bird Migration, Aerobiology) Cranfield IT; at Keele postgraduate certificate in Education may be taken concurrently with research for PhD. East Anglia: also at ARC Food Research Institute and John Innes Institute, which are recognised by the university for purposes of postgraduate studies. Reading: also at associated institutions – Grassland Research Institute, River Laboratory of Freshwater Biology Association, Royal Botanic Gardens (Kew) and ARC Weed Research Organisation (Oxford). Sussex: field station in Ashdown Forest.

　Marine Biology stations, or similar facilities (as indicated) at Aberdeen (Marine Laboratory of Department of Agriculture and Fisheries for Scotland, recognised by the university for purposes of postgraduate studies), Belfast (Portaferry, Co. Down), East Anglia (Fisheries Laboratory of Ministry of Agriculture, Fisheries and Food, at Lowestoft, recognised by the university for purposes of postgraduate studies), Glasgow (University Marine Biological station, Millport, also Freshwater Biology station on Loch Lomond), Leeds (Robin Hood's Bay), Liverpool (Port

Erin, Isle of Man), Newcastle upon Tyne (Dove Marine Laboratory, Cullercoats), St Andrews (Gatty Marine Laboratory), Stirling (Scottish Marine Biological Association Laboratory, Oban), New U of Ulster (Freshwater Biology Laboratory, Lough Neagh) and Wales (Bangor University College – Natural Environment Research Council Unit of Marine Invertebrate Biology, also Marine Science Laboratory, Menai Bridge – and Swansea University College and Institute of Science and Technology).

First degrees   CNAA degrees (unless otherwise stated) in *Applied Biology* are offered at the following (normally 4 yrs S). Bristol P, *Applied Biological Science.* City of London P, *Biology* (modular degree scheme, 3 or 4 yrs). East Sussex CHE, *Human Movement and Human Biology* (3 yrs). Glasgow CT (3 or 4 yrs). Hatfield P. Lanchester P. Liverpool P. Manchester P, *Biological Sciences* (3 yrs). Napier CC and T, *Biological Sciences* (3 yrs). North East London P (modular degree scheme). Oxford P, *Environmental Biology* and *Human Biology* (both part of modular 3 yr degree). Paisley CT, *Biology* (3 or 4 yrs). Plymouth P, *Biological Sciences* (3 yrs), *Fishery Science* (4 yrs S). Portsmouth P, *Biology* (options in *Plant Science* and *Zoology* 3 yrs). Thames P. Trent P. Wolverhampton P, *Biological Sciences* (3 yrs).

HND Courses   In *Applied Biology* (2 yrs unless otherwise indicated). Bell CT (3 yrs S). Brighton TC. Bristol P, option in *Animal* and *Crop Biology* or *Food Science* and *Microbiology*. Dundee CT (3 yrs S). Leicester P. Manchester P (also 3 yrs). Napier CC and T (3 yrs S). North East London P. North East Surrey CT (also 3 yrs S). Paisley CT (3 yrs S). Plymouth P. Seale-Hayne Ag C. Sheffield P. P of the South Bank. South Glamorgan IHE, option in *Food Science* (3 yrs S). Sunderland P (3 yrs S). Trent P, option in *Microbiology* (3 yrs S). Ulster C, Northern Ireland P. Wolverhampton P.

Research facilities   At most polytechnics mentioned above.

Professional courses   Information on courses where students can study for the examinations of the Institute of Biology (MIBiol) can be obtained from the Institute.

Biophysics

See also Radiobiology

First degrees   Degrees with specialisation in *Biophysics* awarded by the universities of Aberdeen, East Anglia (Honours in School of Biological Sciences with specialisation in a group of relevant subjects), Leeds, London (King's – Biology/Physics – and Queen Elizabeth Colleges), Sussex and York.

Postgraduate courses   Courses (for MSc unless otherwise indicated) at the following universities:
Bioengineering and Biophysics in Medicine, Dundee (12 months).
Biophysics and Bioengineering, London (2 yrs full-time or 3 yrs part-time at Chelsea College).
Biophysics and Medical Physics, Manchester (for MSc or diploma in Physics).
Medical Biophysics, London (1 yr intercollegiate course at Guy's, Middlesex and St Mary's Hospital Medical Schools).
Radiation Biophysics, Dundee (1 yr or 21 months).
Also special introductory course in Biophysics at London (King's College).

Research facilities At the following universities: Cambridge, Dundee, East Anglia, Edinburgh, Leeds (aspects of Biology involving Structure of Macromolecules of biological interest), London (Chelsea, Imperial, King's, Queen Elizabeth and University Colleges, and Institute of Cancer Research), Loughborough U of Technology, Manchester, St Andrews, Sussex and York; and at Cranfield IT – Ecological Physics: Biophysics of Natural Flight and Migration.

First degrees CNAA degree in *Biophysical Science* at North East London P (4 yrs S).

Research facilities P of Central London.

Building Science and Technology
See also Engineering, Civil; and Surveying

First degrees Degrees with specialisation in *Building* awarded by the following universities: Aston in Birmingham (including option in Building Economics and Measurements), Bath (Building Engineering, 4 yrs S, or Structural Engineering, 3 yrs or 4 yrs S), Brunel (Building Technology, 4 yrs S), The City (Environmental Engineering (Buildings), 4 yrs S), Heriot-Watt (also Building Economics and Quantity Surveying, each 4 yrs or 5 yrs S), Liverpool (Building Engineering), London (University College – Architecture, Planning, Building and Environmental Studies), Loughborough U of Technology (Environmental Engineering, 4 yrs S), Manchester (Institute of Science and Technology, Building Technology), Reading (Building Construction and Management or Building Surveying) and Salford (also Building Surveying, or Quantity Surveying and Construction Economics, each 4 yrs S).

Postgraduate courses Courses (1 yr and for master's degree, unless otherwise indicated) at the following universities and Cranfield IT:

Advanced Functional Design Techniques for Buildings, Bristol (12 months full-time or 3 yrs – modular course – part-time).

Building Economics and Management, London (University College, option in MSc in Architecture).

Building Maintenance Management, Reading (12 months).

Building Science, Sheffield (diploma) and Strathclyde (1 yr full-time or 2 yrs part-time).

Building Science and Environmental Design, Newcastle upon Tyne (2 yrs).

Building Services Engineering, Brunel (12 months) and Manchester (Institute of Science and Technology, MSc or diploma).

Construction, Loughborough U of Technology (MSc or associateship).

Construction Management, Brunel (12 months), Heriot-Watt (modular course, 12 months full-time or up to 36 months part-time) and Reading (12 months).

Construction Management and Economics, Aston in Birmingham (12 months).

Engineering Design, Loughborough U of Technology (MTech or associateship, 1 yr full-time or 3 yrs part-time).

Environmental Aspects of Building Design, Manchester.

Environmental Design and Engineering, London (University College, option in MSc in Architecture).

Environmental Engineering, Cranfield IT (1 or 2 yrs).

Industrialised Building, Newcastle upon Tyne (2 yrs).

Methods and Techniques of Research, Recording and Documentation or *Principles of Preservation and Conservation of Historic Buildings* or *Regional Domestic Architecture and Building,* Manchester.

Structural Dynamics, Cranfield IT (1 or 2 yrs).
Structures, Manchester (for diploma for Advanced Studies in Engineering, also MSc in Structural Engineering).
Techniques of Building Repair and Conservation, Manchester.

Research facilities At the universities named above (London: also Imperial College), and at Wales (Institute of Science and Technology). Glasgow: Building Services Research Unit. Loughborough U of Technology: Engineering Design Centre.

First degrees CNAA degrees in *Building* are offered at the following (4 yrs S unless otherwise indicated). Brighton P. P of Central London. Lanchester P. Leeds P. Newcastle upon Tyne P. P of the South Bank (also in *Building Economics*). Trent P. Sheffield P (*Construction*).

HND courses (3 yrs S unless otherwise indicated). Bell CT. Bristol P. Bolton IT. Chelmer IHE (2½ yrs S). Dundee CT. Glasgow C Building and Printing. Guildford County CT (*Building and Surveying*, also *Structural Engineering*, 2 yrs). Hammersmith and West London C (also 2 yrs). Hertfordshire C of Building. Huddersfield P. Leeds P (2 yrs). Leicester P. Liverpool P (*Building Administration*). Medway and Maidstone CT (2 yrs). Napier CC and T. Newcastle upon Tyne P. North East Surrey CT (also *Structural Engineering* option). North Gloucestershire TC (2 yrs). Oxford P. Preston P. Sheffield P. P of the South Bank. Southampton CT (with *Quantity Surveying* and *Structural Engineering*). Trent P. Ulster C, Northern Ireland P (options in *Architectural Technology* and *Construction Management*). P of Wales. Willesden CT (2 yrs, also *Building-Structural Engineering*). Wolverhampton P.

College diplomas *Building*, Liverpool P (post-HND, 1 yr). P of Wales (1 yr).
Building Economics and Management, Preston P (post-HND, 1 yr).
Building Management, Chelmer IHE (1 yr).
Building Services Engineering, Newcastle upon Tyne P (2 yrs S). Sheffield P (3 yrs S).
Construction Management, Ulster C, Northern Ireland P (1 yr).
Construction Management and Economics, Sheffield P (6 months), Guildford County CT (2 terms).
Design and Decoration, Glasgow C Building and Printing (4 yrs).

Postgraduate courses Glasgow C Building and Printing, *Construction* (30 weeks).
P of Central London, course for candidates for managerial posts in the building industry (2 yrs S).
Trent P, MSc *Building Economics* (2 yrs) and Diploma *Building Services* (1 yr).

Research facilities Brighton P. Leeds P. Portsmouth P. P of Wales. Wolverhampton P.

Professional qualifications Bolton IT, professional course for non-technical graduates (1 yr). Preston P, Corporate Membership of the Institute of Building (1 yr), Associate Membership of the Institute of Building.
The HND exempts from the whole of the Licentiate Examination of the Institute of Building (IOB) and, with appropriate experience, qualifies for Licentiate Membership (LIOB). The HND also exempts from the Final Examination Part I; the Final Examination Part II then has to be passed. Degrees in Building, acceptable to the Institute, confer exemption from the Final Examination Part I and Part II of the IOB.
The Professional Interview (Final Examination Part III) can be taken after appropriate experience and leads to admission to the Member class of the Institute of Building (MIOB).

Further details and a comprehensive list of building courses may be obtained from the Institute.

Holders of degrees and diplomas of the following institutions are granted complete exemption from the examinations in *Building Surveying* of the Royal Institution of Chartered Surveyors but have to pass the Test of Professional Competence: Glasgow C Building and Printing. Leicester P. Liverpool P. Thames P.

Business and Management Studies

See also Estate and Farm Management; Operational Research; and Secretarial Studies

First degrees Degrees with specialisation awarded by the following universities:

Administration, Aston in Birmingham (Managerial and Administrative Studies, 4 yrs S), The City (Chemical and Administrative Sciences, 3 yrs, or 4 yrs S), Dundee (Administrative Studies), Salford (Business and Administration) and Strathclyde.

Business Administration, Aston in Birmingham (with another subject), Bath (4 yrs S), Belfast (major subject for BSSc), Loughborough U of Technology (with a modern language) and Wales (Institute of Science and Technology).

Business Economics, see under 'Economics'.

Business Law or *Business Organisation,* Heriot-Watt.

Business Studies, Bradford, The City, Edinburgh (with Accounting for MA, with Law for LLB★), Newcastle upon Tyne (Chemical Engineering and Business Studies), Salford (Business and Administration, 3 yrs, also Business Operation and Control or Chemistry and Business Studies, each 4 yrs S), Sheffield (also BEng with Business Studies), Stirling, Strathclyde (Technology and Business Studies) and Wales (Aberystwyth University College, with Physics or Chemistry, also Economics and Business).

Commerce (BCom), Birmingham, Edinburgh and Liverpool.

Decision Theory, Manchester (for BA(Econ)).

Finance/Financial Control, see under 'Accountancy'.

Industrial Economics, Wales (Institute of Science and Technology, 3 yrs, or 4 yrs S).

Industrial Relations, Kent at Canterbury (certain aspects: economics, law, politics and government, or sociology), Salford (Organisational Analysis and Industrial Relations), Strathclyde (with another principal subject) and Wales (Cardiff University College).

Management Science(s), Aston in Birmingham (Managerial and Administrative Studies, 4 yrs S), Bradford (Industrial Technology and Management, 4 yrs S, also special subject for BSc Honours in Business Studies), Brunel (Engineering and Management Systems, or Management with Materials Technology or Polymer Technology, also Metallurgy with Management, all 4 yrs S), The City (Systems and Management), Kent at Canterbury (alone or with Computing or Mathematics), Lancaster (Management Sciences (Economics) or (Financial Control) or (Marketing) or (Operational Research), also Management Studies (Marketing) with French), Leeds (Management Studies with one of certain other subjects), London (London School of Economics, also, at Queen Elizabeth College, Food and Management Science, or Mathematics or Physics or Chemistry and Management Studies), Loughborough U of Technology (Management Sciences, also Management with Chemical Engineering or Chemistry, each 3 yrs for BSc or 4 yrs S for BSc and DIS, and – 4 yrs S for BTech – Management with Metallurgical or Production Engineering), Manchester (Institute of Science and Technology, alone or with Mathematics, also Management and Chemical Sciences, and

★It should be noted that the degree in Law of a Scottish university is based on Scots Law.

Textile Economics and Management), Sheffield (Mechanical and Management Sciences), Stirling (for degree in Business Studies, also Management Science and Technology Studies, alone or with one of certain other subjects), Wales (Management Studies, Cardiff and Swansea University Colleges) and Warwick.

Marketing (see also 'Agriculture and Forestry'), Aston in Birmingham (for BSc in Managerial and Administrative Studies), Lancaster (see 'Management Science(s)', above) and Strathclyde.

Operations Management, Bradford (4 yrs S).

Organisational Studies, Aston in Birmingham (Human and Organisational Studies for BSc in Managerial and Administrative Studies), Lancaster (Organisation Studies, alone or with Psychology) and Salford (Organisational Analysis and Industrial Relations).

Personnel Administration, Strathclyde (with another principal subject).

Courses in which Business/Management subjects may be combined with Engineering/Technological subjects are also listed under the various 'Engineering' headings.

Less specialised study of various aspects of Business and Management Studies may be included in first degree courses (often in Economics or Engineering) at Birmingham (Industrial Relations, Marketing), Bradford (Industrial Relations, Marketing), Brunel (Mathematics with Management Applications, 4 yrs S), Cambridge (Principles of Industrial Management), The City (Industrial Relations), Durham (with Engineering Science or Geography), Hull (Business Economics, Economics of Industry), Lancaster (Industrial Relations, Marketing Systems), Leeds (Industrial Relations), Liverpool (Engineering Science and Industrial Management), London (London School of Economics, also Imperial and – with Chemistry – Royal Holloway Colleges), Nottingham (Industrial Relations, Insurance Studies, Marketing), Reading (Business Finance, Industrial Economics and – in Agricultural Economics course – Business Management), Salford (Industrial or Transport Administration), Stirling (Business Law, Industrial Science, Management Economics), Surrey (certain science or technological subjects taken with Business Economics), Sussex (Applied Sciences with Management Science), Wales (Industrial and Commercial Law, also in certain Chemistry and Physics courses, at Aberystwyth University College, in Banking, Insurance and Finance course at Bangor University College, Management Studies at Cardiff University College, and in Industrial Chemistry and Chemistry courses at Institute of Science and Technology) and Warwick (Business Studies with one of certain other subjects).

Trade Union Studies may be included in first degree courses at many universities; at London, London School of Economics offers 1-yr course, primarily for persons taking up responsible work in trade union organisations, although other qualified applicants considered.

Postgraduate courses   Courses (normally 1 yr and for MA or MSc, unless otherwise indicated) at the following universities and at Cranfield IT and Royal College of Art:

Administrative Sciences, The City.

Airline Management, Cranfield IT.

Arts Administration, The City (diploma, 12 months).

Business Administration, Aston in Birmingham (diploma 6 months, MSc 12 months), Bath, Belfast (diploma 1 yr, MBA 1–2 yrs), Bradford (MBA, minimum 12 months), Cranfield IT (MBA in various management fields – see separate entries), Edinburgh (diploma), Liverpool (MBA, 1–2 yrs), Manchester (Manchester Business School, diploma 1 yr, MBA 2 yrs) and Strathclyde (MBA, 1 yr full-time or 3 yrs part-time).

Business Analysis, Lancaster.

Business Economics, Surrey (for MSc in Economics).

Business Planning, Salford (MSc in Management).

Business Studies, Edinburgh, Liverpool (diploma, 1 or 2 yrs for approved graduates or those with other approved qualifications/experience), London (London Graduate School of Business Studies), Sheffield (diploma or MA) and Warwick (with Management).

Business Systems, Cranfield IT.

Business Systems Analysis and Design, The City.

Commerce, Birmingham (diploma, for graduates in science, engineering, arts and law) and Liverpool (MCom).

Construction Management, see 'Building Science and Technology'.

Decision Analysis, Bath.

Decision Theory, Manchester (MA(Econ) or diploma).

Design and Management Studies for Industry, Wales (Swansea University College).

Design Management Studies, Royal College of Art (2 yrs).

Economic and Corporate Planning, Bradford (for diploma in Management and Administration, or MBA, 1 or 2 yrs).

Finance/Financial Management, etc, see under 'Accountancy'.

Food and Management Science, London (Queen Elizabeth College).

Industrial Administration, Aston in Birmingham (diploma 6 months, MSc 12 months) and Wales (Cardiff University College, diploma).

Industrial Education, see under 'Education'.

Industrial Management, Birmingham (with Engineering Production) and Loughborough U of Technology (MSc or associateship).

Industrial Relations, Bath, Glasgow, London (London School of Economics, also Industrial Relations and Personnel Management, for MSc in Management Studies), Oxford (for MSc in Social Research and Social Policy, 2 yrs), Salford (MSc in Management), Strathclyde, Wales (Cardiff University College, MScEcon) and Warwick.

Industry and Development, Surrey (for MSc in Economics or in Quantitative Business Methods, minimum 12 months).

International Business, Bradford (for diploma in Management and Administration, or MBA, 1 or 2 yrs).

International Business Legal Studies, Exeter (LLM).

International Business Management, Cranfield IT (for MBA in Management).

International Trade and Investment, Surrey (for MSc in Economics, minimum 12 months).

Labour Studies, Sussex.

Management, Bradford (diploma in Management and Administration, or MBA, 1 or 2 yrs), Cranfield IT (MBA, for honours graduates or professional accountants, etc, with several yrs' professional experience), Heriot-Watt (diploma), Salford, Wales (Management and Technology, Institute of Science and Technology) and Warwick (with Business Studies).

Management Accounting/Accountancy, see under 'Accountancy'.

Management Education and Organisational Change, Manchester (Institute of Science and Technology, MSc or diploma).

Management Science(s), Cranfield IT (Management Science and Operational Research option for MSc in Industrial Engineering and Administration, 1 or 2 yrs), Kent at Canterbury, Leeds, London (Imperial College, MSc and/or DIC), Manchester (Institute of Science and Technology, MSc or diploma, 2 yrs) and Warwick (Management Science and Operational Research).

Management Studies, Bradford (diploma in Management and Administration, or MBA, 1 or 2 yrs), Durham, Heriot-Watt (12 months, following diploma in Management), Leeds (with reference to Developing Countries, 12 months), Manchester (Manchester Business School, diploma 1 yr, MBA 2 yrs), Oxford (BPhil, 2 yrs), Salford and Wales (Cardiff University College, MScEcon).

Manpower Studies, London (Birkbeck College, 1 yr full-time or 2 yrs part-time) and Manchester (Institute of Science and Technology, MSc or diploma).

Marketing (see also 'Agriculture and Forestry'), Bath (Industrial Marketing), Bradford (Marketing Management, for diploma in Management and Administration, or MBA, 1 or

2 yrs), Lancaster (Marketing/Marketing Education/Market Research), Manchester (Institute of Science and Technology, MSc or diploma, 15 months), Salford (Marketing Management, for MSc in Management) Strathclyde (Marketing/International Marketing, MSc or diploma) and Warwick (Marketing Management).

Marketing and Logistics and *Operations Management,* Cranfield IT (for MBA in Management).

Organisational Psychology, Lancaster (diploma, also MA 12 months).

Organisation Analysis and Development, Bath.

Organisation Studies, Leeds.

Personnel and Employment Relations, Cranfield IT (for MBA in Management).

Personnel Management, Aston in Birmingham (diploma 1 yr, MSc 15 months), Bradford (for diploma in Management and Administration, or MBA, 1 or 2 yrs), London (London School of Economics, diploma 1 yr – see also 'Management Studies' above), Oxford (for MSc in Social Research and Social Policy, 2 yrs), Salford (Personnel Administration for MSc in Management), Strathclyde (diploma) and Wales (Cardiff University College, diploma or MScEcon, also as specialisation in Management and Technology course at Institute of Science and Technology).

Production Management, Bradford (for diploma in Management and Administration, or MBA, 1 or 2 yrs), Brunel (Production, MTech) and Strathclyde.

Quantitative Business Methods, Surrey (for engineers and scientists, minimum 12 months).

Systems in Management, Lancaster.

Technological Economics, Stirling (12 months).

Trade and Development, Lancaster.

Short (post-experience) courses for business and industrial executives, etc, at the following universities: Aston in Birmingham, Bath, Birmingham, Bradford, The City, Durham, Lancaster, Liverpool (including post-experience Marketing course), London (Imperial College), Manchester (Manchester Business School), Oxford (Centre for Management Studies), Salford, Sheffield, Strathclyde (Strathclyde Business School) and Warwick, and at Scottish Business School (Universities of Edinburgh, Glasgow and Strathclyde); London Graduate School of Business Studies offers own Senior Executive and Executive Development programmes; and Cranfield IT offers Management Development, Senior Management and Young Managers' programmes, also numerous short courses in various management techniques and services.

Research facilities　At most of the universities named above and at Scottish Business School (Universities of Edinburgh, Glasgow and Strathclyde) and Cranfield IT. Brunel: Henley Administrative Staff College. The City: Graduate Business Centre. Lancaster: including Centre for Development of Management Teachers and Trainers. London: Imperial College, London School of Economics and London Graduate School of Business Studies, also – various aspects of Marketing of Horticultural Produce – Wye College. Manchester: Manchester Business School (Faculty of Business Administration of the university), also Centre for Business Research; research degrees include MBSc. Oxford: also Centre for Management Studies, Kennington. Strathclyde: Strathclyde Business School. Sussex: Institute of Manpower Studies. Warwick: Centre for Industrial Economic and Business Research.

First degrees　CNAA Degrees in *Business studies* are offered at the following (4 yrs S unless otherwise indicated):

Birmingham P. Brighton P. Bristol P. P of Central London. City of London P, also *Business Law* (3 yrs). Dundee CT (also 4½ yrs S). Ealing CHE. Glasgow CT. Hatfield P. Huddersfield P, also *Marketing (Engineering)* and *Textile Marketing.* Hull CHE. Kingston P, also *Chemistry with Business Administration* (4 yrs). Lanchester P, also *Business Law* (3 yrs). Leeds P. Leicester P. Liverpool P. Manchester P. Middlesex P, with option in *Industrial Relations,* also *European*

Business Administration, Mathematics for Business. Napier CC and T, also *Science* or *Technology with Industrial Studies.* Newcastle upon Tyne P. North East London P. North Staffordshire P, options in *Finance, Marketing* and *Transport.* Oxford P. Paisley CT, *Business Economics* (with *Marketing*). Plymouth P. Portsmouth P. Preston P. Robert Gordon's IT. Sheffield P, also *Industrial Studies, Engineering with Business Studies.* P of the South Bank. Sunderland P. Teesside P, options in *Finance, Industrial Relations, Marketing.* Thames P, also *International Marketing.* Trent P. Ulster C, Northern Ireland P. P of Wales. Wolverhampton P.

HND courses Courses for the HND in *Business Studies* (2 yrs or 3 yrs S) are available at many polytechnics and colleges; details of courses in England and Wales are given in *A Compendium of Advanced Courses in Colleges of Further and Higher Education,* and for those in Scotland in *Further Education in Scotland: Directory of Day* Courses (see page 264). Specialisation in a wide variety of subjects (including Accounting, Advertising, Business Administration, Computer Studies, Languages, Law, Marketing, Personnel Management, Statistics, and Tourism) is provided by most polytechnics and colleges.

Postgraduate degree courses (1 yr unless otherwise indicated).
Business Administration, Thames P (2 yrs).
Business Law, City of London P.
Education Management, Sheffield P.
Management Information Systems, Sheffield P (18 months).
Management Studies, Administrative Staff C (1½–2 yrs, in association with Brunel U). P of Central London (18 months, specialisation in *Manpower Studies*).
Organisation Development, Sheffield P.

Postgraduate and post-experience courses *Diploma in Management Studies* (DMS) (1 yr unless otherwise indicated). Bristol P. P of Central London. Derby C Art T (6 months). Dundee CT. Glasgow CT. Hatfield P (8 months). Kingston P. Leeds P. Leicester P. Luton CHE (options in *Local Government, Management in Education, Manufacturing* and *Recreational Management*). Napier CC and T. P of North London (specialisation in *Recreation Management*). North Staffordshire P. North East London P (option in *Local Government, Human Resources, Manufacturing* and *Marketing*). Plymouth P (6 months). Portsmouth P. Preston P. Sheffield P. Slough CHE. Sunderland P. Teesside P (options in *European Management* and *Leisure Management*). P of Wales.

Other postgraduate diploma courses (1 yr unless otherwise indicated).
Administration Studies, Leeds P.
Administration of the Arts, P of Central London.
Business Administration/Management, London Graduate S Business Studies. Manchester Business S. Middlesex P. Newcastle upon Tyne P. Oxford P (certificate course). Robert Gordon's IT. Seale-Hayne AgC (in association with Plymouth P). Trent P. Ulster C, Northern Ireland P. P of Wales (*Professional Administration*).
Commerce, Dundee CT. North Staffordshire P (*International Commerce*).
Education Management, Bristol P.
European Management, Leeds P.
Fisheries Management, Grimsby CT.
Foreign Language for Business, Birmingham P (3 yrs).
Industrial Administration/Management, Bell CT. Glasgow CT. Napier CC and T. Scottish C Textiles. Thames P. P of Wales.
Management Services, Sunderland P.
Purchasing and Supply, P of North London.
Secretarial, Business and Management Studies, Bristol P.
Shipping Management, Plymouth P (6 months).
Work Study, P of the South Bank.

Marketing
Postgraduate courses (1 yr unless otherwise indicated.
Bristol P. Buckinghamshire CHE, *Export Marketing* (2 yrs). P of Central London, diploma *Overseas Marketing for Language Graduates*. Harper Adams AgC, *Agricultural Marketing and Business Administration*. Kingston P. Liverpool P. Napier CC and T, *European Marketing and Languages*. Newcastle upon Tyne P. North East London P, *Marketing Management*, also *International Marketing Management* (2 yrs). North Staffordshire P, also *International Marketing*. Scottish C Textiles, *European Marketing with Languages*. Salford CT, *Textile Marketing*. P of Wales, *Analytical Marketing*. Watford CT, *Advertising Administration* (6 months).

Other courses
Cornwall TC, *Marketing* included in *Management* course for overseas students. C for the Distributive Trades, diploma *Marketing and Advertising* for overseas students. Hammersmith and West London C, *Business Studies* including *Export Marketing* (3 yrs). Huddersfield P, *Marketing Studies*. Redditch CFE, diploma (2 yrs).

Some of the above courses offer exemption from the examinations of the Institute of Marketing. For full details, one should contact the Institute.

Personnel Management Diploma courses (1 yr unless otherwise indicated).
Bell CT. Bristol P. Dundee CC. Cornwall TC, as part of *Management* course for overseas students. Farnborough CT. Glasgow CT. Gwent CHE. Hammersmith and West London C. Kingston P. Kirkcaldy TC. Leeds P (15 months), also certificate course. Manchester P, also certificate course. Middlesex P (4 terms). Napier CC and T. Robert Gordon's IT. Scottish C Textiles. Sheffield P, diploma *Human Resources Management*. Slough CHE (15 months). Teesside P. P of Wales.

Some of the above courses lead to exemption from the examinations of the Institute of Personnel Management. For full details, one should write to the Institute.

Other courses
Chelmer IHE, diploma *Building Management* (1 yr). City of London P, *Business Studies with English* for overseas students (6 months). C of the Distributive Trades, *Retail Management* (6 months). Cooperative C, diploma *Cooperative Development* (1 yr), certificate *Cooperative Management and Administration* (1 yr). Cordwainer's TC, diploma *Production Management* (*Footwear*) (3 yrs). Cornwall TC, courses in *Management* and related studies for overseas students (1 yr). Dorset IHE, diploma *Tourism Studies* for overseas students (1 yr). Dundee CT, *Commerce* (3 yrs S). Glasgow Central CC, certificate *Distributive Management* (2 yrs). Glasgow CT, diploma *Commerce* (3 yrs S). Hammersmith and West London C, diploma *Business Studies*, also with special reference to modern languages (both 3 yrs). Kirkcaldy TC, diploma *Industrial Administration for Graduate Secretaries* (1 yr). Leeds P, diploma *Modern Languages and Business Studies* (2 yrs). London C Fashion, *Clothing Management* (4 yrs S). Middlesex P, diploma *Industrial Relations and Trade Union Studies* (1 yr). Napier CC and T, diploma *Commerce* (3 yrs). North East Wales IHE, certificate *Management Services* (3 months). P of North London, diplomas *Economic Development, Labour Studies, Purchasing and Supply* (1 yr). Portsmouth P, *Engineering with Business Studies* (4 yrs). Robert Gordon's IT, diploma *Commerce* (3 yrs). Warley CT, *Industrial Training for Graduates* (3–4 months). Wolverhampton P, *Languages for Business* (2 yrs).

Canadian Studies

First degrees May be included in first degree courses at the universities of Birmingham (options within Special Honours course in American Studies, also course option in Evolution of Political Institutions and Processes in Canada in certain BSocSc courses) and Edinburgh (major component in degree in Social Sciences or secondary major component in Faculty of Arts).

Postgraduate courses Courses at University of Edinburgh for MPhil or MLitt (2 yrs) in *North American Studies (Canada and/or USA)*.

Research facilities At the universities of Birmingham, Edinburgh (Centre of Canadian Studies) and London (Institute of Commonwealth Studies).

Cancer Research

Research facilities At most of the universities which award degrees in Medicine (see page 198) (London: King's College, Middlesex and University College Hospital Medical Schools and Institute of Cancer Research), also at Bradford (Chemotherapy) and Brunel (Radiosensitisation, Biochemistry of Cell Injury), and at Royal Beatson Memorial Hospital, Glasgow. University of London Institute of Cancer Research (Royal Marsden Hospital) is concerned with all aspects of research into causation and treatment of cancer, training of research workers and advanced clinical teaching.

Cardiology

First degrees Degree courses in Medicine (for list of awarding universities, see page 198) include *Cardiology*.

Postgraduate courses Courses (full-time) for physicians in training as cardiologists and for general physicians at University of London Cardiothoracic Institute.

Research facilities At the universities of Belfast, Birmingham, Cambridge, Dundee, Edinburgh, Glasgow, Leeds, London (Guy's, King's College, St George's and University College Hospital Medical Schools, and Cardiothoracic Institute), Manchester, Newcastle upon Tyne, Nottingham, Oxford, St Andrews, Sheffield and Southampton.

Chemistry

See also Biochemistry; and Engineering, Chemical

First degrees Degrees with specialisation in *Chemistry* awarded by all universities except Brunel. Aston in Birmingham, Bath and Bradford: 3 yrs, or 4 yrs S. Keele: with another principal subject, but Chemistry alone possible in final yr. London: at Bedford, Birkbeck (part-time), Chelsea, Imperial, King's, Queen Elizabeth, Queen Mary, Royal Holloway, University and Westfield Colleges, also – with another subject – Goldsmiths' College). Loughborough U of Technology: 3 yrs, or 4 yrs S. Manchester: University and Institute of Science and Technology. Sheffield: BSc or – see page 198 – BMedSci. Surrey: 3 yrs, or 4 yrs S. Sussex: major subject in School of Molecular Sciences, including degree taken mainly by research and thesis following 2 terms' basic course work. Wales: Aberystwyth, Bangor, Cardiff and Swansea University Colleges and Institute of Science and Technology. Warwick: also Molecular Sciences.

First degrees with specialisation in various branches of Chemistry also awarded as follows:

Applied Chemistry, Brunel (alone or with German, each 4 yrs S), Kent at Canterbury (with Control Engineering), Salford (4 yrs S) and Strathclyde.

Chemical Physics, see 'Physics'.

Chemistry of Natural Resources, Brunel (4 yrs S).

Colour Chemistry, Belfast (Polymer and Colour Science for BSc in Industrial Chemistry), Bradford (Colour Chemistry and Colour Technology, 4 yrs S) and Leeds.

Colouring Matters, Manchester (Institute of Science and Technology).

Environmental Chemistry, Edinburgh and London (Wye College).

Geochemistry, Leicester (Chemistry with Geochemistry), Liverpool and Reading.

Industrial Chemistry, Belfast, Brunel (4 yrs S), The City (4 yrs S) and Wales (4 yrs S, at Institute of Science and Technology).

Mathematical Chemistry, Essex.

Medicinal, Agricultural and Environmental Chemistry, Brunel (4 yrs S).

Medicinal and Pharmaceutical Chemistry, Loughborough U of Technology (3 yrs, or – BSc and DIS – 4 yrs S).

Medicinal Chemistry, London (University College).

Polymer Chemistry, see 'Polymer Science and Technology'.

Textile and Colour Chemistry, Manchester (Institute of Science and Technology).

Theoretical Chemistry, Sussex (major subject in School of Molecular Sciences).

At many universities Chemistry may also be studied with another principal subject for a Joint (or Combined) Honours degree (Surrey also offers a unified course in Physical Science – see under 'Physics'). At most universities less specialised study of Chemistry may be included in courses leading to first degrees.

Postgraduate courses   Courses (normally 1 yr and for master's degree, unless otherwise indicated) at the following universities:

Adhesion Science and Technology, The City (1 yr full-time or 2 yrs part-time).

Analytical Chemistry, Aberdeen, Birmingham (also Water Technology option), Bristol, London (Chelsea College, 1 yr full-time or 2 yrs part-time), Loughborough U of Technology (Analytical Chemistry and Instrumentation, MSc or associateship, 1 yr full-time or 3 yrs part-time) and Salford.

Applied Heterocyclic Chemistry, Salford (modular course – candidates must complete six 'modules' and write a dissertation on a research project over 1 or 2 yrs).

Applied Organic Chemistry, Birmingham.

Chemical Education, see 'Education'.

Chemical Microbiology, see 'Microbiology'.

Chemical Physics, see 'Physics'.

Chemical Spectroscopy, East Anglia.

Chemistry, Cambridge (certificate of postgraduate study), Glasgow (MAppSci, 1 or 2 yrs full-time or 2 or 3 yrs part-time) and York (12 months).

Chemistry (Polymer Science), Manchester (MSc or diploma).

Colour Chemistry, Leeds (minimum 12 months).

Coordination Chemistry, East Anglia.

Electrochemical Technology, The City.

Electrochemistry, Newcastle upon Tyne.

Fibre Science and Technology, Leeds (1 or 2 yrs).

Geochemistry, see 'Geology'.

Heterocyclic Chemistry, East Anglia.

Instrumental Methods of Analysis, Southampton (diploma 9 months, MSc 12 months) and Strathclyde (MSc or diploma).

Marine Pollution Chemistry, Liverpool (diploma, 6 months).

Medicinal Chemistry, Loughborough U of Technology (MSc or associateship, 1 yr full-time or 3 yrs part-time).

Methods, Design and Techniques of Organic Synthesis, Strathclyde.

Microbiological Chemistry, Newcastle upon Tyne.

Mineral Chemistry, Birmingham.

Molecular Enzymology, Warwick.

Nuclear and Radiation Chemistry, Salford.

Organometallic Chemistry, Sussex.

Petrochemicals and Hydrocarbon Chemistry, Manchester (Institute of Science and Technology, MSc or diploma).

Photochemistry, Southampton.

Physical Organic Chemistry, East Anglia.

Science Education (see also under 'Education'), Keele.

Silicate Chemistry, Aberdeen.

Soil Chemistry, Reading (12 months).

Solid State Chemistry, Wales (Aberystwyth University College).

Surface Chemistry and Colloids, Bristol and Strathclyde (Applied Surface and Colloid Chemistry).

Research facilities

At all universities (Keele and Leicester: postgraduate certificate in Education may be taken concurrently with research for PhD), and at Scottish Universities Research and Reactor Centre, East Kilbride. Surrey: including Wolfson Bioanalytical Centre. Warwick: British Universities National Mass Spectrometry Research Facility.

First degrees

CNAA degrees in *Applied Chemistry* or *Chemistry* are offered at the following polytechnics and colleges (4 yrs S unless otherwise indicated). Brighton P (also 3 yrs). City of London P (part of modular degree). Hatfield P. Huddersfield P. Kingston P, also with *German* or *Business Administration.* Lanchester P. Leicester P (3 yrs). Liverpool P. Newcastle upon Tyne P. P of North London (also 3 yrs). Paisley CT, *Chemistry* (4 yrs). Portsmouth P. Robert Gordon's IT (also 3 yrs). Sheffield P. P of the South Bank, *Chemical and Polymer Technology.* Thames P (also 3 yrs). Trent P. P of Wales (2 yrs).

CNAA degrees in Combined Studies (3 yrs) with specialisation in *Chemistry* are offered at some polytechnics (see 'Science (General)').

HND courses

(3 yrs S unless otherwise indicated), Falkirk CT. Glasgow CT. Grimsby CT, *Applied Chemistry* (*Food Science*). Halton CFE. Huddersfield P. Kingston P (2 yrs). Leicester P (2 yrs). Manchester P (2 yrs). Napier CC and T (3 yrs S). Newcastle upon Tyne (2 yrs). North East London P (2 yrs). North East Wales IHE. North Staffordshire P (2 yrs). Preston P. St. Helens CT (2 yrs). Sheffield P. P of the South Bank, options in *Polymer Chemistry* or *Metal Finishing* (2 yrs) and *Analytical Chemistry* (2 yrs). Teesside P (2 yrs). Trent P, *Applied Chemistry – Dyeing and Surface Chemistry.* Ulster C, Northern Ireland P, *Applied Chemistry* (*Industrial Science*) (3 yrs S). P of Wales.

Postgraduate courses

Advanced Studies in Chemistry, North East Wales IHE (1 yr).

Organic Macromolecules, P of North London (1 yr).

Polymer and Adhesion Science, Leicester P (1 yr).

Technology and Economics of Chemical Processes, Oxford P diploma or MSc (1 yr).

Research facilities

Available at all polytechnics mentioned above.

Chest Diseases
(including Tuberculosis)

First degrees   Degree courses in Medicine (for list of awarding universities, see page 198) include *Chest Diseases/Tuberculosis.*

Postgraduate   Diploma course (6 months) in *Tuberculosis and Chest Diseases* at University of Wales (Welsh
courses   National School of Medicine). Information about short courses at University of London Cardiothoracic Institute and elsewhere is given in 'Summary of Postgraduate Diplomas and Courses in Medicine' – see page 266.

Research   At the universities of Belfast, Birmingham, Cambridge, Dundee, Edinburgh, Glasgow, Leeds,
facilities Liverpool, London (King's and University College Hospital Medical Schools, and Cardiothoracic Institute), Manchester, Newcastle upon Tyne, Nottingham, Oxford, Southampton and Wales (Welsh National School of Medicine).

Chiropody
No university courses.

Professional   The recognised qualifying body in chiropody is the Society of Chiropodists, whose designatory
courses   letters are MChS (Member) and FChS (Fellow). The Council for Professions Supplementary to Medicine maintains a State Register of chiropodists, and has approved for purposes of State Registration the courses (3 yrs) given at the eight schools of chiropody recognised by the Society. Full information may be obtained from the Society.

Commonwealth Studies
See also Canadian Studies

First degrees   Degree courses including *Commonwealth Studies* at the universities of Cambridge (Commonwealth History), Exeter (American and Commonwealth Arts with English), Kent at Canterbury (English with African and Caribbean Studies, also – entry in alternate yrs, next entry October 1979 – French with African and Caribbean Studies) and Oxford (in Honour Schools of Modern History and of Philosophy, Politics and Economics).

Postgraduate   Courses (1 yr and for master's degree, unless otherwise indicated) at the following universities:
courses   *Area Studies (the Commonwealth)*, London (Institute of Commonwealth Studies).
Commonwealth and American History, Oxford (BPhil, 2 yrs).
Commonwealth History, London (Birkbeck College, 1 yr full-time or 2 yrs part-time) and Sheffield.

Research   At the universities of Cambridge, Edinburgh, London (Institute of Commonwealth Studies –
facilities centre of research in the social sciences and history relating to the Commonwealth and its member countries – also King's College), Manchester (Department of Administrative Studies for Overseas Visiting Fellows) and Oxford (Institute of Commonwealth Studies, Rhodes House).

Computer Science and Technology

See also Engineering, Control; Engineering, Electronic; and Mathematics

First degrees Degrees with specialisation awarded by the following universities:

Computation/Computational Science, Dundee (with Mathematics), Hull, Leeds, Liverpool (Computational and Statistical Science), Manchester (Institute of Science and Technology), St Andrews and Salford (Computational Mathematics and Statistics).

Computer Engineering/Technology, Birmingham (Electronic and Computer Engineering), The City, Essex (also Computer and Communication Engineering), Heriot-Watt, Hull, Loughborough U of Technology (Electronic, Computer and Systems Engineering, 3 yrs or 4 yrs S), Manchester and Wales (Swansea University College).

Computer Science, Aston in Birmingham (with another subject), Bath (with Mathematical Studies, 3 yrs or 4 yrs S), Belfast, Birmingham (with Mathematics), Bradford (4 yrs S), Bristol (with Mathematics), Brunel (also Computer and Social Sciences, both 4 yrs S), Cambridge (as 1-yr course in third yr, or 2-yr course after Honours in another Tripos), The City (3 yrs or 4 yrs S), Edinburgh, Exeter, Heriot-Watt, Keele (with another principal subject but Computer Science alone possible in final yr, also for BSc in Integrated Physical Sciences), Kent at Canterbury, Liverpool, London (University and Westfield Colleges, also with Physics at Queen Elizabeth College, with one of certain other subjects at Queen Mary College, and with Statistics or Mathematics or Physics or Chemistry at Royal Holloway College), Manchester, Reading, Salford (with Economics or Geography or Mathematics or Physics), Strathclyde, Sussex, Wales (Aberystwyth and – with another subject – Swansea University Colleges), Warwick and York (with Mathematics or Physics).

Computer Studies, Hull (with Chemistry or Mathematics or Physics or Physics Studies), Kent at Canterbury (Computers and Cybernetics), Lancaster and Loughborough U of Technology (3 yrs, or – BSc and DIS – 4 yrs S).

Computer Systems, Essex, London (King's College, Computer Systems and Electronics), Salford (Electronic Computer Systems) and Wales (Cardiff University College).

Computing, Bradford (with Data Processing, 4 yrs S), Durham (with Electronics), Exeter (with Mathematics), Kent at Canterbury (with Management Science or Mathematics or Physics, also Computing, Operational Research and Statistics), Leeds (Operational Research with Computing) and London (London School of Economics).

Computing Science, Aberdeen, Aston in Birmingham (from 1978 or 1979, 3 yrs or 4 yrs S), Essex, Glasgow, London (Imperial College), Newcastle upon Tyne, Sheffield (with Applied Mathematics), Stirling and Surrey (Mathematics or Physical Science with Computing Science, 4 yrs S).

Computing Studies, East Anglia.

Data Processing, Bradford (with Computing, 4 yrs S), Leeds and Loughborough U of Technology (3 yrs, or – BSc and DIS – 4 yrs S).

Data Processing Systems, The City (3 yrs, or 4 yrs S).

Numerical Analysis, Brunel (with Computer Science, 4 yrs S), Lancaster (with Statistics) and Salford (with Mathematics and Statistics, 4 yrs S).

Systems and Information Management, Brunel (4 yrs S).

At a number of the universities offering degrees with specialisation in this subject alone, Computer Science or Computing, etc, may also be studied with another principal subject for a Joint (or Combined) Honours degree; and less specialised courses in Computer Science may be included in first degree courses (usually in Mathematics or Science) at many universities. Numerical Analysis may also be included in first degree courses at Aberdeen (also Numerical Science), Leicester, Liverpool (Numerical Mathematics for Combined Studies degree) and Reading.

Postgraduate courses   Courses (1 yr and for master's degree unless otherwise indicated) at the following universities and Cranfield IT:

Applied Numerical Analysis and Optimisation, Edinburgh.

Business Systems Analysis and Design, The City.

Cognitive Studies and Computing Studies, Sussex.

Computation, Manchester (Institute of Science and Technology, MSc or diploma).

Computational and Statistical Methodology in the Analysis of Large-Scale Data, Hull (12 months).

Computational Mathematics, Leeds (minimum 12 months).

Computational Methods and Fluid Mechanics, Salford.

Computational Science, Leeds (minimum 12 months).

Computation in the Life Sciences, York (12 months).

Computer Applications in Psychology, Belfast.

Computer Management, London (University College, diploma).

Computer Management Studies, London (Birkbeck College, 12 months, diploma).

Computer Science, Birmingham, Bradford (MSc or diploma), Cambridge (diploma), Edinburgh (diploma), Essex (Computer Studies, 12 months), Lancaster, London (Queen Mary and Westfield Colleges, also – 1 yr full-time or 2 yrs part-time for MSc or diploma – Birkbeck College, and – at those three Colleges with Imperial and University Colleges – intercollegiate MSc course), Manchester (MSc or diploma), Strathclyde and Wales (Aberystwyth, Bangor and Cardiff University Colleges, diploma or MSc).

Computer Science and Applications, Aston in Birmingham and Belfast (MSc 12 months, diploma 1 academic yr).

Computer Simulation, Salford.

Computer Systems and Cybernetics, Kent at Canterbury (MSc 12 months, diploma 9 months).

Computing Mathematics, Wales (Cardiff University College).

Computing Science, Glasgow (diploma, 1 yr full-time or 2 yrs part-time), London (Imperial College, for MSc and/or DIC) and Newcastle upon Tyne.

Computing Software and Systems Design, Newcastle upon Tyne.

Control/Computer Systems Engineering, Surrey (MSc minimum 12 months, diploma 1 academic yr).

Digital Electronics: Computers, Communications and Instrumentation, London (Chelsea College, 1 yr full-time or 2 yrs part-time).

Industrial Applied Mathematics, Hull and Sheffield jointly.

Mathematical Computation, Essex (12 months).

Mathematics of Modern Control Systems, Loughborough U of Technology (MSc or associateship, 1 yr full-time or 2 or 3 yrs part-time).

Non-numerical Applications of Computer Science, St Andrews.

Numerical Analysis, Bath (MSc or diploma, 12 months full-time or 2 yrs part-time), Brunel (1 yr full-time or $2\frac{1}{2}$ yrs part-time), Lancaster (Numerical and Statistical Mathematics), Liverpool, London (Imperial College, MSc and/or DIC), Oxford (for MSc in Mathematics) and Sussex (for MSc in Mathematics).

Numerical Analysis and Approximation Theory, Kent at Canterbury (diploma 9 months, MSc 12 months).

Numerical Analysis and Computing, Cranfield IT (1 or 2 yrs, for MSc in Applicable Mathematics) and Manchester (MSc or diploma).

Numerical Analysis and Electronic Computation, Liverpool.

Numerical Analysis and Programming, Dundee (1 yr–21 months).

Numerical Computation, Newcastle upon Tyne.

Operational Research with Computing, Leeds (minimum 12 months).

Optimisation and Computing, Loughborough U of Technology (MSc or associateship).

Small Computer Systems, Cranfield IT (1 or 2 yrs).

Systems Analysis, The City (diploma) and London (London School of Economics, School diploma).

Theory and Applications of Computation, Loughborough U of Technology (MSc or associateship, 1 yr full-time or 2 or 3 yrs part-time).

Theory of Programming Languages and Computation, Oxford (for MSc in Mathematics).

Research facilities   At most universities (Keele: postgraduate certificate in Education may be taken concurrently with research for PhD). London: Birkbeck, Imperial, Queen Elizabeth, Queen Mary, Royal Holloway, University and Westfield Colleges. Computer/Computing laboratories – or units (u) or centres (c) – at Aberdeen, Aston in Birmingham, Belfast (c), Birmingham, Bradford, Bristol (c), Brunel (u), Durham, East Anglia (c), Edinburgh (u), Essex, Heriot-Watt (c), Keele (c), Kent at Canterbury, Lancaster, Liverpool, Loughborough U of Technology (c), Manchester (c, u), Newcastle upon Tyne, Oxford, Reading (c), St Andrews, Salford, Sheffield, Southampton, Surrey (u), Sussex (c), New U of Ulster, Wales (Bangor (c), Cardiff (c) and Swansea (c) University Colleges), Warwick (u) and York.

First degrees   CNAA degrees in *Computer Science* are offered at the following polytechnics and colleges (4 yrs S unless otherwise indicated). Brighton P. City of London P (as part of modular degree). Hatfield P. Kingston P. Lanchester P (also *Computer and Control Systems,* 3 yrs). Leicester P. North Staffordshire P (also *Information Systems*). Portsmouth P. Sheffield P. Thames P (also *Mathematics, Statistics and Computing,* 3 yrs). Ulster C, Northern Ireland P (*Data Processing*). P of Wales (also 2 yrs). Wolverhampton P.

Applied Statistics and Computing, Liverpool P.

Computers in Business, Huddersfield P (4 yrs S).

Computer Technology, Teesside P (also part of modular degree in *Mathematical and Computer Sciences*).

Computing with Operational Research, Paisley CT (also 3 yrs).

Mathematics and Computing, P of North London (also *Statistics and Computing*). P of the South Bank.

Mathematics and Computer Science, P of Wales (4 yrs).

Operational Research with Computing, Leeds P.

Systems Analysis, Bristol P.

HND courses   In *Computer Studies* or *Data Processing* (2 yrs unless otherwise indicated). Aberdeen CC. Bell CT. Birmingham P (3 yrs S). Brighton P. Bristol P (in conjunction with Seale-Hayne AgC). P of Central London. Derby C Art and T (3 yrs S). Dundee CC. Falkirk CT. Glasgow CT (also *Data Processing*). Hatfield P (3 yrs S). Huddersfield P (3 yrs S). Kirkcaldy CT. Lanchester P. Leeds P (3 yrs S). Leicester P. Liverpool P. Londonderry CT. Manchester P. Medway and Maidstone CT. Mid-Essex TC. Napier CC and T (3 yrs S, also *Data Processing,* 2 yrs). North East London P. North East Wales IHE. North Gloucestershire TC (3 yrs S). North Staffordshire P. North Worcestershire C (3 yrs S). Norwich City C (3 yrs S). Oldham CT (3 yrs S). Oxford P. Plymouth P. Portsmouth P. Preston P (3 yrs S). Scottish C of Textiles. Sheffield P (3 yrs S). Slough CT (3 yrs S). P of the South Bank. Southampton CT. Sunderland P (3 yrs S). Teesside P. Thames P. Trent P (3 yrs S). Ulster C, Northern Ireland P. P of Wales. West Glamorgan IHE (3 yrs S).

Mathematics, Statistics and Computing (normally 2 yrs). Blackburn CT. Bristol P. Hatfield P (3 yrs). Lanchester P. Leeds P (3 yrs S). Leicester P. Letchworth CT. Liverpool P. Manchester P (3 yrs S). North East London P. North Gloucestershire CT (3 yrs S). P of North London. North Staffordshire P. Oxford P (3 yrs S). Portsmouth P. Sheffield P (3 yrs S). Teesside P. Thames P. Ulster C, Northern Ireland P. P of Wales.

Postgraduate *courses*	*Applications of Computing*, P of North London MSc. *Computer Science*, North Staffordshire P MSc (2 yrs S). P of the South Bank diploma. Teesside P MSc. *Computer Studies* or *Computing*, Leicester P diploma, MSc (1 yr). Teesside P advanced diploma. *Operational Research and Computer Techniques*, Southampton CT. *Systems Analysis*, Aberdeen CC (with *Design*). Napier CC and T (with *Design*). Richmond upon Thames C.
Other courses	A number of colleges offer courses which prepare candidates for the Part I and Part II examinations of the British Computer Society. For full details, one should contact the Society.
Research *facilities*	P of Central London. Hatfield P. Kingston P. Leeds P. Leicester P. P of North London. North Staffordshire P. Portsmouth P. Sheffield P. Teeside P. P of Wales. Wolverhampton P.

Criminology

First degrees	Degree courses (usually in Law) including some study of *Criminology* at the following universities: Aberdeen*, Bath (Sociology course), Birmingham (also in School of Social Administration courses, for BSocSc), Edinburgh*, Exeter (also in Sociology, Social Administration and Social Policy courses), Keele, Leeds (also in Sociology course), London (BSc(Econ) and Sociology courses), Manchester, Newcastle upon Tyne, Nottingham (also in Social Administration course), Oxford, Reading (also in Sociology course), Sheffield, Southampton, Wales (Cardiff University College) and Warwick.
Postgraduate *courses*	Courses (1 yr and for master's degree, unless otherwise indicated) at the universities of Cambridge, Edinburgh (diploma), Hull (BPhil/MA), Keele, London (London School of Economics and University College), Sheffield (also Socio-Legal Studies) and Wales (Cardiff University College).
Research *facilities*	At the universities of Bath, Birmingham, Cambridge, Edinburgh, Exeter, Hull, Oxford, Sheffield, Southampton and Wales (Cardiff University College).

*It should be noted that the degree in Law of a Scottish university is based on Scots Law.

Crystallography

First degrees   At many universities some study of *Crystallography* may be included in degree courses in Science and/or Applied Science (Cambridge, *Crystalline State* in Natural Sciences Tripos; London, at Birkbeck, Imperial and Queen Mary Colleges; Manchester, in Chemistry and Geology courses; Wales, at Cardiff and Swansea University Colleges).

Postgraduate   Courses (for MSc) at the universities of London (Birkbeck College – 1 yr full-time or 2 yrs
courses   part-time – and University College) and Newcastle upon Tyne.

Research   At the following universities: Aberdeen, Belfast, Birmingham, Bradford, Bristol, Cambridge,
facilities   Durham, Edinburgh, Glasgow, London (Birkbeck, Imperial, King's and University Colleges), Manchester (University and Institute of Science and Technology), Newcastle upon Tyne, Nottingham, Sussex, Wales (Cardiff University College) and Warwick; also – X-ray Crystallography – Dundee, Essex, Lancaster, Surrey, New U of Ulster and York; and – Chemical Crystallography – Oxford and Salford.

Dentistry

Qualifying   First degrees in *Dentistry* – BDS (Leeds: BChD) – are granted by the universities of Belfast,
degrees and   Birmingham, Bristol, Dundee, Edinburgh, Glasgow, Leeds, Liverpool, London (Guy's, King's,
diplomas   London, Royal Dental and University College Hospital Dental Schools), Manchester, Newcastle upon Tyne, Sheffield and Wales (Welsh National School of Medicine). The period of study is generally about 4 or 5 yrs, depending on qualifications at entry. At Dundee students may intercalate 1 yr's additional study for BMSc (see also page 198), and at some of the other universities dental students may intercalate 1 or 2 yrs' additional study for a BSc in one of various science subjects (Anatomy, Physiology, etc).

Diplomas in Dental Surgery (LDS; course of at least 4 yrs) are awarded by the University of Bristol (no students admitted solely to read for LDS, but may be awarded on results of final BDS Section II examination), and by the Royal College of Surgeons of England, the Royal College of Surgeons of Edinburgh, and the Royal College of Physicians and Surgeons of Glasgow.

On graduating or on passing the diploma examination candidates may apply for admission to the Dentists' register and if accepted may then practise dentistry in all its branches.

Higher   The degree of Master of Dental Surgery (MDS) is awarded by all universities granting a first
qualifications   degree, except Leeds and Wales, each of which awards a degree of Master of Dental Science (Leeds, MDSc; Wales, MScD), and Birmingham and Edinburgh. However, in general, only Bristol, Dundee, Leeds, Liverpool, Manchester, Newcastle upon Tyne and Wales permit graduates of other approved universities to become candidates for these degrees (Liverpool, only graduates registrable with the General Dental Council; Manchester, also non-graduate dentists who are registrable with the General Dental Council); and such candidates must normally (i) be Bachelors of Dental Surgery of 1–3 yrs' standing and (ii) undertake advanced study or research for at least 2 yrs in the university (Dundee, 1 yr or equivalent preceded by at least 2 yrs' appropriate professional experience; Leeds, at least 12 months).

At many of the universities offering first degree courses, suitably qualified graduates of other universities may undertake research in Dentistry for higher degrees (usually PhD – London, Institute of Dental Surgery, MPhil and PhD); but the degrees of DDS (Birmingham, Edinburgh and Manchester), DDSc (Dundee, Glasgow, Leeds and Newcastle upon Tyne) and DChD (Wales) are, in general, open only to graduates of the awarding university or to those who have been staff members for a specified number of years.

Full-time postgraduate courses (1 yr and for diploma, unless otherwise indicated) open to candidates with recognised qualification in Dentistry are offered by the following universities:

Children's Dentistry (Paedodontics) and *Conservation Dentistry*, London (Institute of Dental Surgery and Royal Dental Hospital School of Dental Surgery, MSc).

Dental Health, Birmingham.

Dental Radiology, London (King's College Hospital Dental School, MSc).

Dental Surgery, London (Institute of Dental Surgery, 1-yr and – with Royal College of Surgeons – 8-week courses suitable for Final FDS (see below), also 8-week revision courses suitable for Primary FDS at Institute of Basic Medical Sciences).

Experimental Oral Pathology, London (London Hospital Medical College, MSc).

Oral Pathology, London (Institute of Dental Surgery, MSc).

Orthodontics, Glasgow (suitable for DDO – see below) and London (Institute of Dental Surgery and Royal Dental Hospital School of Dental Surgery, MSc).

Periodontology, London (Guy's Hospital Medical School, Institute of Dental Surgery, Royal Dental Hospital School of Dental Surgery and University College Hospital Medical School, MSc).

Prosthetic Dentistry, London (Guy's Hospital Medical School and Institute of Dental Surgery, MSc).

Public/Public Health Dentistry, Dundee and London (London Hospital Medical College, Dental Public Health, for MSc, also Institute of Dental Surgery with other London Dental Schools for DDPH – see below).

The Royal Colleges of Surgeons of England and of Edinburgh and the Royal College of Physicians and Surgeons of Glasgow each grant a Fellowship in Dental Surgery (FDS). In addition the Royal College of Surgeons of England awards a Diploma in Orthodontics (DOrth) and a Diploma in Dental Health (DDPH); and the Royal College of Physicians and Surgeons of Glasgow a Diploma in Dental Orthopaedics (DDO).

Dermatology

See also Urology and Venereology

First degrees Degree courses in Medicine (for list of awarding universities, see page 198) include some study of *Dermatology*.

Postgraduate courses Diploma course (1 yr) at University of London Institute of Dermatology. Information about short/part-time courses is given in 'Summary of Postgraduate Diplomas and Courses in Medicine' – see page 266.

Research facilities At the universities of Dundee and London (Guy's Hospital Medical School and Institute of Dermatology).

Development Studies

First degrees Degree courses at the following universities may include *Development Studies*: Birmingham (BSocSc – special programme in School of Joint Honours), East Anglia (BA Honours in School of Development Studies), Kent at Canterbury (Sociology and Social Anthropology, or

Economics, or Economic and Social History), London (London School of Economics, International Trade and Development for BSc(Econ)), Reading (part of BSc courses in Agricultural Economics, Land Management, Quantity Surveying), Sussex (School of African and Asian Studies), Wales (Planning Studies at Swansea University College, also part of BA course in Town Planning at Institute of Science and Technology) and Warwick (for students taking Economics). Swansea University College (University of Wales) awards a College diploma (2 yrs) in *Social Development and Social Administration* (for overseas candidates with some social work experience).

Postgraduate courses Courses (1 yr and for master's degree, unless otherwise indicated) at the following universities:

Applied Social Studies, Surrey (diploma, 12 months) and Wales (Swansea University College, College diploma for overseas candidates with some social work experience).

Community Development (diplomas), Edinburgh (for graduates or holders of equivalent qualifications), London (with Extension Work, 1 term at Institute of Education for senior administrators, advisers and trainees, also, at Queen Elizabeth College, Food Resources related to Community Development) and Manchester (for graduates or other suitably qualified persons, also MEd in Adult Education and Community Development).

Co-operative Development Overseas, Loughborough U of Technology (diploma).

Design and Planning Education, London (University College, diploma, 2 yrs).

Development Administration (diplomas), Birmingham (only for overseas candidates who are graduates or established public servants) and Manchester.

Development Economics, East Anglia, Strathclyde (2 yrs) and Sussex.

Development Planning, London (University College, diploma).

Development Policy (diplomas), Glasgow and Wales (Swansea University College).

Development Studies, Bath, Cambridge (options in Economic Policy and Planning, Sociology and Politics of Development, Land Policy and the Environment, also course on Development with similar options for diploma or certificate), Durham (Development Studies (Britain and Overseas)), Manchester and Sussex (2 yrs, with Institute of Development Studies).

Economic Development, Glasgow (12 months or 24 months), Leeds, Leicester, Manchester (1 or 2 yrs, diploma) and Oxford (diploma).

Environmental Planning for Developing Countries, Nottingham (2 yrs).

Industry and Development, Surrey (for MSc in Economics or in Quantitative Business Methods, minimum 12 months).

Integrated Land Resources Survey, Reading (2 yrs).

Management Studies with reference to Developing Countries, Leeds (12 months).

National Development and Project Planning, Bradford (12 months).

Planning Studies (Developing Countries), Edinburgh (diploma).

Rural Social Development, Reading (MA 11 months, diploma 9 months).

Social Planning in Developing Countries, London (London School of Economics, MSc and School diploma).

Social Policy, Wales (Swansea University College, diploma for overseas candidates in senior positions in social service, and preferably with graduate training in social science).

Technology and Development, London (Imperial College, MSc and/or DIC).

Tropical Agricultural Development, Reading (MSc 12 months, MAgrSc 2 yrs).

Urban Studies, Salford.

Urban Studies (Developing Countries), London (University College, College diploma).

Aspects of Development Studies may also be included in higher degree courses at Birmingham (for MSocSc, 12 months), Glasgow (MPhil in Economics), Reading (MSc courses in Agricultural Economics and Agricultural Engineering) and Sussex (MA courses in African Studies, Comparative Politics, Social Anthropology and Sociological Studies).

University of Bradford (Project Planning Centre for Developing Countries) provides post-experience courses (3 months) in project planning in various aspects of development (industry, agriculture, finance, tourism, social services etc.).

Research facilities At the universities of Bath (Sociology of Developing Countries), Bradford (Project Planning Centre for Developing Countries), Cambridge (Overseas Studies Committee), East Anglia (School of Development Studies), Edinburgh, Glasgow, Manchester (including Centre for Overseas Educational Development), Reading (Agricultural Extension and Rural Development Centre), Salford, Sussex (Institute of Development Studies) and Wales (Swansea University College – Centre for Development Studies).

Post-HND course P of North London, diploma in *Economic Development* (1 yr).

Dietetics and Nutrition

See also Agriculture and Forestry (Agricultural Sciences); and Food Science and Technology

First degrees Degrees with specialisation in *Nutrition* awarded by the universities of Bradford (Nutrition and Toxicology for BTech in Applied Biology, 4 yrs S), London (Queen Elizabeth College), Nottingham (Animal and Human) and Surrey (4 yrs S, with optional specialisation in *Dietetics*). Dietetics and Nutrition also included in course for BSc in Physiology and Biochemistry at Southampton.

Postgraduate courses Courses (1 yr unless otherwise indicated) at the following universities:
Dietetics, London (Queen Elizabeth College, diploma).
Human Nutrition, London (School of Hygiene and Tropical Medicine, MSc minimum 15 months, School diploma 1 yr).
Nutrition, Cambridge (diploma) and London (Queen Elizabeth College, MSc or College diploma).

Research facilities At universities of London (Queen Elizabeth College and School of Hygiene and Tropical Medicine) and Surrey.

First degrees *Catering Science and Applied Nutrition,* Huddersfield P (4 yrs S).
Dietetics, Leeds P (4 yrs S), Queen's C (4 yrs S), Queen Margaret C (4 yrs).
Nutrition and Dietetics, Robert Gordon's IT (3 yrs).

Professional courses Degree courses of the following institutes are recognised by the British Dietetic Association and for State Registration by the Council for Professions Supplementary to Medicine: London University (plus the postgraduate diploma in *Dietetics*) and Surrey University (see above the line); Leeds P and Robert Gordon's IT (if followed by 1 yr's approved practical training).

Diploma courses Recognised diploma courses are also provided by the following colleges. They vary in length from 18 months to 4 yrs according to the student's qualifications.
Cardiff C Food Technology and Commerce (3–4 yrs). Leeds P (18 months and 3 yrs). Manchester P (2 yrs S). P of North London (18 months). Queen's C (18 months). Queen Margaret C (4 yrs). Robert Gordon's IT (4 yrs). South Glamorgan IHE (3 yrs).

Drama and Theatre

First degrees Degrees with specialisation in *Drama* awarded by the following universities: Birmingham (Drama and Theatre Arts), Bristol, Exeter, Glasgow (with another subject), Hull, Kent at Canterbury (with another subject), London (Drama/Theatre Studies with English at Royal Holloway College, Drama with one of certain other subjects at Westfield College in collaboration with Central School of Speech and Drama), Loughborough U of Technology, Manchester, Wales (with another subject at Aberystwyth University College, with English or Welsh at Bangor University College, and with English at Swansea University College) and Warwick (Theatre Studies with English or French or Italian). Universities offering degrees with specialisation in this subject alone also provide courses in which Drama/Theatre Studies may be taken with one of certain other subjects for a Joint (or Combined) Honours degree; and less specialised study of Drama may be included in courses for first degrees awarded by most of the universities named above, and Lancaster (Theatre Studies).

Diplomas/certificates (see also 'Postgraduate courses', below): (*a*) general – University of Glasgow certificate course (3 yrs) in Dramatic Studies, for full-time students of Royal Scottish Academy of Music and Drama; (*b*) for teachers – see under 'Education'. Stage Design included in courses for University of London diploma in Fine Art (see 'Art and Design').

Postgraduate Courses (1 yr and for MA, unless otherwise indicated) at the following universities (see also
courses under 'Education'):

Drama, Bristol (certificate), Essex (scheme in Literature, School of Comparative Studies, 12 months) and Manchester (diploma).

Drama and Theatre Arts, Leeds.

Dramatic Studies, Glasgow (diploma, 2 yrs).

Elizabethan and Shakespearian Drama, Newcastle upon Tyne (MA 1 yr, MPhil 2 yrs).

English Theatre Studies, Lancaster.

French Classical Drama and Theatre History, Bristol.

French Theatre Studies, Lancaster.

Modern French Literature: Poetry, Novel and Drama, Hull (BPhil/MA).

Spanish and Latin American Studies (*Hispanic Drama*), Newcastle upon Tyne.

Theatre Studies, Wales (Cardiff University College, for College diploma).

Stage Design may be offered for University of London higher diploma in Fine Art (see 'Art and Design').

Research At most of the universities named in the paragraphs above.
facilities

CNAA degree Bingley C, *Performing Arts* (3 yrs). Brighton P, *Expressive Arts* (3 yrs). Dartington C Arts,
courses Theatre (4 yrs).

Courses in Birmingham S of Speech Training and Dramatic Art, Acting course (3 yrs).
acting, Bristol Old Vic Theatre S, Acting (2 or 3 yrs), postgraduate course (1 yr). (Only a small number of
direction and places available.)
stage British Theatre Association, course for Teachers and Producers of Amateur Drama (10 weeks).
management Central S Speech and Drama, diploma Acting (3 yrs), Technical course (2 yrs).
Coventry TC, Drama and Speech Training (1 or 2 yrs).
Croydon C Art and Design, Lighting Design (3 yrs).
Drama Centre London Ltd, Acting (3 yrs), Directing (3 yrs), Professional Instructors' course (2 yrs).
East 15 Acting S, Acting (3 yrs), Directing (3 yrs).

Edinburgh C Speech and Drama, diploma Acting (including Production and Stage Management) (3 yrs).

Guildford S Acting and Drama, Performers' course ($2\frac{1}{4}$ yrs), diploma Musical Theatre ($2\frac{1}{2}$ yrs), Stage Management (1 yr).

Guildhall S Music and Drama, Performers' course (3 yrs), certificate Stage Management (2 yrs), postgraduate course Speech and Voice (1 yr).

London Academy of Music and Dramatic Art, Acting (3 yrs), Stage Management (2 yrs), postgraduate course for overseas students with a degree or recognised training (1 yr).

Manchester P, diploma Theatre (3 yrs).

Mountview Theatre S, preparatory Acting course (1 yr), Acting (3 yrs), postgraduate Acting (1 yr), Management and Design course (2 yrs).

Northern C Speech and Drama, professional course (3 yrs), Technical Theatre course (3 yrs), supplementary course in Drama (1 yr).

Queen Margaret C, diploma Drama and the Spoken Word (3 yrs).

Royal Academy of Dramatic Art, Acting course leading to RADA Diploma or U of London diploma in Drama (7 terms), Specialist diploma (4 terms), Stage Management (4 terms).

Rose Bruford Training C Speech and Drama, diploma course (3 yrs) in Community Theatre and Technical Theatre, degree preparation course (2 yrs), advanced course (1 yr).

Royal Scottish Academy of Music and Drama, diploma Dramatic Art (Performers) (3 yrs), diploma Speech and Drama (3 yrs), Technical course (1 yr).

Webber-Douglas Academy of Dramatic Art, Acting (8 terms), postgraduate course (1 yr).

Welsh C Music and Drama, diploma courses (3 yrs), advanced certificate course (1 yr), Technical Theatre course for graduates and teachers of Drama (1 yr).

Courses in theatre design

First degree courses are listed under Art and Design on page 87. All the following courses require candidates to have completed at least one year's Foundation or Pre-degree course.

Bristol Old Vic Theatre S, Technical/Production course for Directors and Designers (1–2 yrs).

Croydon C Art and Design, Technical course (including Stage Management and Design) (2 yrs).

Royal Academy of Dramatic Art, courses in Scene Painting and Design, Stage Carpentry and Property Making (2–4 terms).

English National Opera, postgraduate course (1 yr).

Teacher Training courses

Birmingham P, postgraduate certificate in education Drama Teachers (1 yr).

Bretton Hall CE, certificate in education (3 yrs), BEd (3 and 4 yrs, Leeds U), postgraduate Drama course (1 yr).

Central S Speech and Drama, course leading to U of London certificate in education English and Drama (3 yrs), Advanced certificate Drama in Education for qualified teachers (1 yr), BEd in Drama, Voice and English (jointly with P of Central London, 3 yrs).

Chelmer IHE, Drama Board certificate Drama in Education (2 yrs S).

City of Manchester CHE, specialist course Speech and Drama (1 yr).

Dartington C Arts, course for specialist teachers of Dance and Drama (2 yrs) followed by 1 yr at Rolle C.

Guildford S Acting and Drama, 3 yr course followed by 1 yr at East Sussex CHE.

Manchester P, postgraduate certificate Drama (1 yr).

Northern C Speech and Drama, course for Speech and Drama diploma (4 yrs).

Rose Bruford Training C Speech and Drama, diploma course (3 yrs).

Royal Scottish Academy of Music and Drama, diploma Speech and Drama (3 yrs) followed by 1 yr at an institution of education.

St Luke's C, BEd (3 and 4 yrs) and certificate in education with main subject in Drama (3 yrs).

South Glamorgan IHE, specialist course in Drama and Music (1 yr).

Welsh C Music and Drama, college course (2 yrs) followed by 1 yr at South Glamorgan IHE.

Economics

See also Agriculture; Business and Management Studies; and Development Studies

First degrees

Degrees with specialisation in *Economics* awarded by all universities. Aston in Birmingham: special subject for degrees in Behavioural Science and in Managerial and Administrative Studies, 4 yrs S. Bradford and Brunel: 4 yrs S. The City: 3 yrs, or 4 yrs S. Keele: only with another principal subject. London: at London School of Economics, and Queen Mary and University Colleges, also – with another subject – School of Oriental and African Studies. Oxford: with Philosophy and/or Politics or with Modern History or Engineering Science. Surrey: jointly with Mathematics, or combined in interdisciplinary course with Sociology and Statistics, 3 yrs or 4 yrs S. Sussex: as major subject in Schools of African and Asian Studies, European Studies, and Social Sciences. Wales: Aberystwyth, Bangor, Cardiff and Swansea University Colleges and Institute of Science and Technology.

First degrees with specialisation in *Economic/Economic and Social History* awarded by the following universities (for Social History, see also under 'History'): Aberdeen, Belfast, Birmingham (also History and Social Science), Bristol (Economic and Social History, or Economic History with Economics), Durham, East Anglia, Edinburgh (with Accounting or Economics or Geography or Politics, also Sociology and Social and Economic History), Exeter, Glasgow, Hull, Kent at Canterbury, Lancaster (with Economics), Leeds, Leicester, Liverpool, London (at London School of Economics, also with Public Administration at Bedford College, with Modern History and Politics at Royal Holloway College and with Economics at University College), Loughborough U of Technology (also Economic and Technological History), Manchester, Newcastle upon Tyne (with Economics), Nottingham, Reading (option in History course), Sheffield, Southampton (with Economics or Politics), Strathclyde, Sussex, Wales (Swansea and – with Economics – Aberystwyth University Colleges), Warwick and York.

Other branches/aspects of Economic Studies in which students may specialise for a first degree:

Applied Economics, Loughborough U of Technology (for BSc in Economics).

Business Economics, Southampton, Surrey (with one or two of certain other subjects, 4 yrs S) and Wales (Institute of Science and Technology).

Econometrics, Birmingham, Hull, Kent at Canterbury, London (London School of Economics, special subject for BSc(Econ)), Loughborough U of Technology (for BSc in Economics), Manchester (with Social Statistics for BA(Econ)) and Newcastle upon Tyne (with Economics).

Economic Statistics, Glasgow (with Political Economy) and York (Social and Economic Statistics with Economics or Politics or Sociology).

Industrial Economics, Nottingham and Wales (3 yrs, or 4 yrs S, at Institute of Science and Technology).

International Studies (with Economics, Economic History or Politics), Warwick.

Land Economy, see under 'Estate and Farm Management'.

Management Studies (Economics), Lancaster.

Mathematical Economics, Birmingham (BSocSc) and Essex (School of Mathematical Studies).

Quantitative Economics, Kent at Canterbury and Lancaster (with Economics).

Technological Economics, Stirling (Economics, a science, and Industrial Science).

Textile Economics and Management, Manchester (Institute of Science and Technology).

Many of the universities offering degrees with specialisation in Economics alone also provide courses in which Economics (and in some cases Economic/Economic and Social History) may be studied with another principal subject for a Joint (or Combined) Honours degree. *Engineering and Economics* may be studied together at Birmingham (Mechanical or Production Engineering, 3 yrs for Joint Honours BSc, 4 yrs for Double Honours BSc & BCom), Bradford (Chemical Engineering with Management Economics, 4 yrs S), Brunel (Engineering, Social and European Studies), Dundee (Civil, Electrical or Mechanical Engineering), Loughborough U of

Technology, Oxford (Engineering Science), Strathclyde (Technology and Business Studies), Surrey (Chemical or Mechanical Engineering with Business Economics, 4 yrs S), Sussex (Applied Sciences with Social Sciences) and Warwick. Reading awards a degree in *Food Science and Food Economics.*

Less specialised study of Economics and of Economic History may also be included in first degree courses in arts or social studies (or, for Economic History, in Economics degree courses) at many universities.

The independent University College at Buckingham (see page 32) awards a licence in the Schools of Economics and of Law, Economics and Politics.

Postgraduate Courses (normally 1 yr and for master's degree, unless otherwise indicated) at the following
courses universities:
Analysis of Economic Policy and Planning, Sussex.
The Atlantic Economy, Exeter.
Business Economics, Surrey (for MSc in Quantitative Business Methods, minimum 12 months).
Contemporary European Economics, etc, Reading (MA 1 yr, MPhil 2 yrs, in Graduate School of Contemporary European Studies).
Contemporary European Studies, Sussex.
Econometrics, Birmingham (12 months), Manchester and – with a selected branch of Economic Theory – Wales (Swansea University College, 1–2 yrs).
Econometrics and Mathematical Economics, London (London School of Economics).
Econometrics and Statistics, Surrey (for MSc in Economics or in Quantitative Business Methods, minimum 12 months).
Economic and Social History, Birmingham (12 months) and Exeter.
Economic and Social Statistics, Exeter (diploma).
Economic History, Leeds, London (London School of Economics), Manchester, Sheffield, Wales (Swansea University College, diploma) and York (12 months).
Economic Policy and Planning, Cambridge (option in Development Studies course).
Economics, Birmingham (12 months), Brunel (1 yr full-time or 2 yrs part-time), Cambridge (MPhil and diploma), East Anglia (MA or diploma), Essex (MA 12 months, also diploma), Glasgow (12 months), Kent at Canterbury, London (London School of Economics, Birkbeck – 1 yr full-time or 2 yrs part-time – and Queen Mary Colleges, School of Oriental and African Studies), Manchester, Oxford (BPhil, 2 yrs), Stirling, Surrey (12 months), New U of Ulster, Wales (Cardiff University College), Warwick (12 months) and York (12 months, with special reference to one of: Public Finance, International Economics, Economics of Human Resources, Health Economics).
Economics and Corporate Planning, Bradford (for diploma in Management and Administration, or MBA, 1 or 2 yrs).
Economics and Econometrics, Southampton (including Operational Research, for diploma or MSc (Social Sciences)).
Economics of Education, London (Institute of Education).
Economics of Finance, Sheffield.
Economics of Financial Intermediation, Surrey (for MSc in Economics, minimum 12 months).
Economics of Industry, Sussex.
Economics of Natural Resources, Aberdeen (12 months).
Economics of Public Policy, Leicester and London (University College).
Economic Statistics, Leeds, Manchester (Economic and Social Statistics, diploma) and York (12 months).
European Economic Studies, Exeter.
Finance/Financial Studies, see 'Accountancy'.
Forecasting and Financial Analysis, Surrey (for MSc in Economics or in Quantitative Business Methods, minimum 12 months).

The Growth of the Welfare State, East Anglia.

Industrial Economics, Lancaster.

International Trade and Investment, Surrey (for MSc in Economics, minimum 12 months).

Labour Economics, Leeds.

Mathematical Economics, Birmingham (12 months) and Surrey (for MSc in Economics, minimum 12 months).

National Development and Project Planning, Bradford (12 months).

National Economic Planning, Birmingham (diploma 1 yr, MSoc Sc 12 months or 24 months).

Public and Industrial Economics, Newcastle upon Tyne.

Public Sector Economics, Salford.

Quantitative Business Methods, Surrey (for engineers and scientists, MSc minimum 12 months and maximum 24 months, diploma 1 academic yr).

Quantitative Economics, Bristol (1 or 2 yrs).

Regional Economics and Planning, Lancaster.

Shipping Economics and Policy, Wales (Institute of Science and Technology, option for MSc in Management and Technology).

Technological Economics, Stirling (12 months, for graduates with experience in a science-based industry or scientific departments of public service).

Trade and Development, Lancaster.

Trade Growth and Development, Wales (Cardiff University College).

Transport Economics, see 'Transport'.

Urban and Regional Economics, Wales (Cardiff University College).

USSR and East Europe, London (School of Slavonic and East European Studies).

Research facilities At almost all universities (London, colleges named above). Bradford: Project Planning Centre for Developing Countries. Hull: Centre for South-East Asian Studies. Kent at Canterbury: Centre for Research in the Social Sciences. Leicester: Public Sector Economics Research Centre. Reading: Graduate School of Contemporary European Studies. Sussex: Institute of Development Studies, Institute of Manpower Studies, Centre for Contemporary European Studies. Wales (Bangor University College): Institute of Economic Research, Institute of European Finance. York: Institute of Social and Economic Research.

First degrees CNAA degrees in *Economics* are offered at the following polytechnics and colleges (3 yrs unless otherwise indicated): Birmingham P. City of London P. Ealing TC. Kingston P, also *Languages, Economics and Politics* (4 yrs). Leeds P, *Economics and Public Policy*. Lanchester P. Leicester P. Manchester P. Middlesex P, with *Geography*. Newcastle upon Tyne P, also *Modern Languages and Economic Studies* (4 yrs). North East London P. North Staffordshire P. Paisley CT, *Land Economics* (4 yrs S). Portsmouth P, option in *Economic History*, also *Economics and Geography*. Roehampton IHE, *Business Economics*. Sheffield P, *Urban Land Economics* (4 yrs S). Sunderland P, *Social Science* (*Economics*). Trent P. Wolverhampton P.

Postgraduate course P of North London, diploma in *Economic Development* (1 yr).

Research facilities Birmingham P. Kingston P. Leeds P. Portsmouth P. Thames P.

Education

See also Educational Technology; English as a Foreign Language: Courses for Teachers; and Physical Education and Sports Science

First degrees   Degrees in *Education – BEd –* are awarded by the following universities: Aberdeen, Belfast, Birmingham, Bristol, Cambridge, Dundee, Durham, East Anglia, Edinburgh, Exeter, Glasgow, Hull, Keele, Lancaster, Leeds, Leicester, Liverpool, London, Loughborough U of Technology, Manchester, Newcastle upon Tyne, Nottingham, Oxford, Sheffield, Southampton, Strathclyde, Sussex, Wales and Warwick. With certain exceptions, the BEd is normally open *only* to students at colleges associated with the university (usually with the university's Institute or School of Education). BEd candidates study at least one, sometimes two, principal subjects in addition to Education itself and a wide range of such subjects is available at most colleges (see also page 37); fuller information is given in the *Handbook of Institutions providing both Teacher Training and Other Full-Time Advanced Courses* – see page 265).

Exeter also awards a BEd in Advanced Studies (1 yr full-time plus 1 yr part-time) for qualified teachers with normally not less than 3 yrs' teaching experience, in one of: Counselling, Curriculum, Language in Education, Remedial and Special Education, Sociology of Education.

Courses in Education which lead to, or may be combined with study for, other first degrees such as BA or BSc are available at the following universities: Aston in Birmingham (Education with another subject, 3 yrs or with professional training yr, 4 yrs), Bath (concurrent degree and certificate courses in one of several different subjects with Education), Brunel (Mathematical Studies or Physics with Education, 4 yrs S), Cambridge (4 yrs – 2 yrs for Education Tripos following 2-yr course in another subject, leading to degree and certificate), Hull (Education with one of certain other subjects for degree plus certificate, 4 yrs), Keele (training leading to a qualification in Education may be incorporated within 4-yr degree courses, also Education as principal subject in conjunction with a science subject), Lancaster (Educational Studies, 3 yrs, also combined with certain other subjects, 3 or 4 yrs), Liverpool (Mathematics and Education, for degree plus certificate), London (Chelsea College, 4 yrs), Loughborough U of Technology (4 yrs S, for degree plus certificate – Education taken with one of certain other subjects throughout the course, or combined with one or two other subjects during final 2 yrs), Manchester (Education and Audiology, 4 yrs, for degree in Combined Studies which is recognised for status as qualified teacher and qualified teacher of the deaf, also – Institute of Science and Technology – Mathematics and Education), Salford (Applied Physics or Chemistry or Mathematics or Science with Education, 4 yrs S), Southampton (Mathematics with Education, 4 yrs), Stirling (Education with one of various school subjects, $3\frac{1}{2}$ yrs for General degree with university diploma, $4\frac{1}{2}$ yrs for Honours degree with university diploma or Double Honours degree, each conferring professional qualification to teach in secondary schools), Surrey (for degree in Human Biology, 4 yrs, 3rd yr being spent in educational training college, also – 3 yrs or, with professional training yr, 4 yrs – Chemistry or Physical Science with Science Education), New U of Ulster (3 yrs for degree with Education as principal subject, or 4 yrs for Honours degree in another subject or subjects, or in Education taken with one or two other subjects, plus professional teaching qualification), Wales (Honours in Education at Aberystwyth, Bangor – Educational Studies – and Cardiff University Colleges), Warwick (Mathematics or Philosophy and Education, Education and Psychology, also course in Sociology and Education which is concerned with sociology of education, not with teaching) and York (BA in Language (English) plus teaching certificate). Education may also be included in first degree courses in arts at Aberdeen and Glasgow (1-yr courses for MA Ordinary) and York (subsidiary subject in arts, sciences or social sciences).

Postgraduate Full-time courses leading to *MEd* (usually 1 or 2 yrs and in various topics or options) are offered
courses for by the universities of Aberdeen, Bath (also part-time), Birmingham, Bristol, Dundee,
higher degrees Edinburgh, Exeter, Glasgow (1 yr full-time plus 1 yr part-time, or 3 yrs part-time), Hull, Leeds
(for diplomas/ (also part-time), Leicester (1 yr full-time or 2 yrs part-time), Liverpool, London (in Science
certificates, Education at Chelsea and King's Colleges), Manchester, Newcastle upon Tyne (1 yr full-time or
see below) 2 yrs part-time for good Honours graduates or equivalent, otherwise 1 yr part-time plus 1 yr
full-time, or 3 yrs part-time – regulations under review), Nottingham (1 yr full-time or 2 yrs
part-time, for good Honours graduates or equivalent with at least 2 yrs' experience in Education,
also – for suitably experienced graduates – 1 yr part-time plus 1 yr full-time, or 3 yrs part-time),
Sheffield (for graduate teachers of 2 yrs' experience) and Wales (Aberystwyth, Bangor, Cardiff
and Swansea University Colleges). (Courses leading to MEd, but part-time only, are also
provided by Belfast, Brunel, Warwick and Stirling; and at Durham, also Bath, Birmingham,
Bristol, Hull, Liverpool, Manchester, Newcastle upon Tyne and Wales, the MEd may be taken
as a research degree.)

Full-time courses leading to other higher degrees in *Education* (usually 1 yr and for MA or
MSc) are offered by the universities of Aston in Birmingham (Educational Studies),
Birmingham (BPhil(Ed), 1 yr full-time plus 6 months part-time), Bradford (1 yr full-time plus at
least 12 months part-time), Durham, Edinburgh (Educational Studies, 12 months), Hull
(BPhil), Keele (1 yr full-time or 2 yrs part-time), Lancaster (1 yr full-time or 2 or 3 yrs part-time),
Leeds, Leicester (Educational Studies, 1 yr full-time or 2 yrs part-time), London (Institute of
Education and King's College, MA 12 months, MPhil 2 yrs), Oxford (Educational Studies),
Reading (MA(Education) with wide choice of options and MSc (Science & Education), each 12
months full-time or 36 months part-time, also – with another option – for MA or MPhil in
Graduate School of Contemporary European Studies), Sussex, New U of Ulster and York
(Educational Studies, 12 months).

Full-time courses for master's (or BPhil) degrees in various branches/aspects of Education are
offered by the following universities (at Manchester not all of the courses mentioned are
necessarily available every year):

Administration and Organisation of Education, London (Institute of Education).

Adult Education and Community Development and *Aesthetic Education,* Manchester.

Agricultural Extension, Reading (diploma 9 months, MSc 9 or 12 months).

Audiology, Manchester and Southampton (12 months).

Biological Education, Southampton and – Biology and Biological Education – York (2 yrs).

Chemical Education, East Anglia, Reading (12 months full-time or 36 months part-time),
Southampton and York (Chemistry and Chemical Education, 24 months).

Child Development or *Child Development with Clinical Studies,* London (Institute of
Education).

Comparative Education, London (Institute of Education, 1 yr full-time or 2 yrs part-time).

Continuing Education, New U of Ulster (Institute of Continuing Education).

Curriculum Studies, London (Institute of Education), Manchester (Curriculum Development),
Southampton and Sussex (Curriculum Development and Educational Technology).

Developmental and Educational Psychology, Belfast.

Developmental Psychology, Sussex (2 yrs).

Dyslexia, Wales (Bangor University College).

Economics of Education, London (Institute of Education).

Educational Planning and Development in Developing Countries, London (Institute of
Education).

Educational Psychology, Aberdeen, Birmingham, Edinburgh (12 months), Exeter (for candidates
with degree in Psychology and some teaching experience), Glasgow (Educational
Psychology and Child Guidance, 1 or 2 yrs for MAppSci), London (University College, 1
or 2 yrs), Manchester (also Educational Psychology (Child Guidance), for suitably
qualified and experienced graduate teachers), Newcastle upon Tyne (normally 2 yrs),

Sheffield (not less than 1 yr normally for qualified experienced teachers), Southampton (1 yr, also 4-yr integrated scheme, both restricted intake), Strathclyde, Sussex (2 yrs) and Wales (Swansea University College).

Educational Research and Innovation, Southampton.

Educational Sciences, Manchester.

Education of Maladjusted Children and *Education of the Deaf*, Manchester and Newcastle upon Tyne).

Foreign Language Learning, Manchester.

Geographical Education, Southampton (12 months).

Geography in Education, London (Institute of Education, 1 yr).

Health Education, London (Chelsea College, 1 yr full-time or 2 yrs part-time).

Higher Education, Manchester (1 yr).

History of Education, Leicester, London (Institute of Education) and Manchester (History of English Education).

Industrial Education and Training, Manchester.

Mathematics and Education, Reading (for MSc (Science&Education), 12 months full-time or 36 months part-time).

Mathematics and Mathematical Education, York (2 yrs).

Mathematics Education, Keele (Mathematics Education and/or Science Education), London (Chelsea College) and Southampton.

Music Education, London (Institute of Education, 1 yr full-time or 2 yrs part-time).

Organisation and Planning of Education, Manchester.

Pastoral Guidance and Counselling, Wales (Swansea University College).

Philosophy of Education, Leicester, London (Institute of Education) and Manchester.

Physics and Education, Reading (for MSc (Science&Education), 12 months full-time or 36 months part-time).

Physics and Physics Education, York (1 or 2 yrs).

Physics Education, Southampton.

Primary Education, Manchester.

Psychology of Education, Leicester and London (Institute of Education, 12 months full-time or 21 months part-time, also with Clinical Studies).

Religious Education, Lancaster (1 yr full-time or 2 yrs part-time).

Rights in Education, London (Institute of Education, 1 yr full-time or 2 yrs part-time).

Rural Social Development, Reading (diploma 9 months, MA 11 months).

Science Education, Keele (see 'Mathematics Education' above), London (King's College) and Manchester.

Social and Community Education, Wales (Swansea University College).

Social Science Research in Education, Keele.

Sociology of Education, London (Institute of Education) and Manchester.

Sociology of Education and Mass Communication, Leicester.

Special Education, Wales (Swansea University College).

Teacher Education, Manchester.

Urban Education, London (Institute of Education – 1 yr full-time or 2 yrs part-time – and King's College).

Youth Studies, Manchester.

Research facilities   In various branches of Education, for master's degrees and/or PhD, at most of the universities named above and (especially in Institute for Educational Technology) at Surrey. Edinburgh: Centre for Research in the Educational Sciences. Exeter: Teaching Services Centre. Lancaster: Centre for Educational Research and Development; Institute for Research and Development in Post-Compulsory Education. London: Institute of Education; Centre for Science Education at Chelsea College. Loughborough U of Technology: Centre for the Advancement of Mathematical Education in Technology. Manchester: including Centres for Overseas Educational Development and for Youth Studies, and Hester Adrian Centre for the Study of Learning Processes in the Mentally Handicapped. Reading: including Agricultural Extension and Rural Development Centre. Sussex: including Reginald M. Phillips Research Unit for the Deaf and Other Handicaps. Wales: Aberystwyth, Bangor, Cardiff and Swansea University Colleges. Warwick: History, Philosophy and Psychology of Education, especially in Education Centre. York: facilities of Language Teaching Centre available to graduates taking graduate certificate of Education who intend to teach modern languages.

Diplomas and certificates Postgraduate courses (1 yr) leading to diploma or certificate in *Education,* mainly for intending secondary school teachers*, are offered at the following universities: Aberdeen, Bath, Belfast, Birmingham, Bristol, Brunel (primarily for graduates in mathematics, technology and social or physical sciences), Cambridge, Dundee, Durham, Edinburgh, Exeter, Glasgow, Hull, Keele (mainly for graduates in mathematics, sciences, social science, geography, history or modern languages – may be taken concurrently with research in certain science subjects for PhD), Leeds, Leicester (may be taken concurrently with research in Chemistry for PhD), Liverpool, London (King's College and Institute of Education, also – for graduates in science and mathematics – Chelsea College), Manchester, Newcastle upon Tyne, Nottingham, Oxford, Reading, Sheffield, Southampton, Sussex, Wales (at Aberystwyth, Bangor, Cardiff and Swansea University Colleges) and York; New U of Ulster provides 3-yr certificate course in Education (not postgraduate), with provision for transfer to Honours degree course (see above).

Other university diploma/certificate courses (1 yr and for diploma, unless otherwise indicated – many, although not all, of these courses are normally intended for qualified and/or experienced teachers):

Adolescent Development, London (Institute of Education) and Wales (Swansea University College).

Adult Education (see also 'Community Development' and 'Continuing Education'), Edinburgh (for graduates or holders of equivalent qualifications), Glasgow (postgraduate), Leeds, Liverpool, Manchester (1 yr full-time or 3 yrs part-time) and Nottingham (postgraduate, for holders of an approved university diploma or certificate in Education, or equivalent, who wish to prepare for teaching or administrative work in Adult Education).

Agricultural Extension, Reading.

Applied Child Psychology, Stirling (2 yrs postgraduate).

Applied Educational Studies, York (for qualified teachers with at least 5 yrs' experience).

Art Education, see under Art and Design.

Audiology, Manchester (for qualified and experienced teachers of the deaf, speech therapists, etc) and Southampton (Medical Audiology, certificate, 6 months).

Bilingual Education, Wales (Aberystwyth University College, College certificate, mainly for graduates).

Careers Guidance, Strathclyde.

Child Development, London (Institute of Education) and Newcastle upon Tyne (Development and Education of Young Children, for diploma in Advanced Educational Studies).

Children's Literature, Sheffield.

Community Development, Edinburgh (for graduates or holders of equivalent qualifications) and Manchester.

Community Education, Nottingham (option for diploma in Education, for experienced teachers and college of education lecturers) and Wales (Social and Community Education, Swansea University College).

*It should be noted that the diploma in Education in the Scottish Universities is *not* a recognised teaching qualification, though it is normally taken concurrently with a teacher training course in a college of education.

Community Education and the Nursery School, Sheffield.

Continuing Education, New U of Ulster (Institute of Continuing Education).

Curricular Studies, Keele (diploma of Advanced Study in Education with special reference to Curriculum Development).

Design and Planning Education, London (University College, 2 yrs).

Drama in Education, Durham, Keele (for diploma of Advanced Study in Education), Newcastle upon Tyne and New U of Ulster (for diploma in Advanced Studies in Education).

Education, Bristol (for those with at least 3 yrs' experience as qualified teachers), Cambridge (by thesis, open only to holders of Cambridge certificate in Education), Hull (postgraduate), Keele (Advanced Study in Education), Leeds (Educational Studies, primarily for overseas teachers with, normally, at least 5 yrs' approved teaching experience, also certificate or graduate certificate), Leicester (Educational Studies, for qualified teachers with at least 3 yrs' experience), Liverpool (Advanced Study of Education, for those with approved initial qualification in Education and appropriate professional experience), London (Institute of Education and King's College, also Institute associateship), Manchester (Advanced Study in Education, 1 yr full-time or 2 yrs part-time), Newcastle upon Tyne (Advanced Educational Studies, with choice of emphasis and subject, see also 'Education for Overseas Teachers'), Nottingham (for experienced teachers and college of education lecturers), Oxford (special diploma in Educational Studies), Reading (Advanced Educational Studies), Southampton (Advanced Educational Studies), New U of Ulster (Advanced Studies in Education) and Wales (Educational Studies, certificate, mainly for graduates, Aberystwyth University College).

Educational Administration, Leeds, Reading (option in diploma in Advanced Educational Studies) and New U of Ulster (for diploma in Advanced Studies in Education).

Educational Broadcasting, York (for experienced teachers, 1 term full-time plus 2 terms part-time).

Educational Psychology, Glasgow (postgraduate, 1 or 2 yrs).

Education for a Multi-Cultural Society, Sheffield.

Education for/of Overseas Teachers (for Teaching of English as a Foreign Language, see page 154), Birmingham (course for Commonwealth Teachers), Bristol (1 or 2 yrs, for teachers or intending teachers in training colleges overseas), Leeds (see 'Education', above), Leicester (for diploma in Educational Studies), London (Institute of Education courses include Education in Developing Countries), Manchester (diploma or certificate, also certificate for Teaching Technical Subjects Overseas), Newcastle upon Tyne (courses – for diploma in Educational Studies – in Primary and Junior/Secondary Education in overseas countries, and the Education of Handicapped Children in overseas countries), Nottingham and Oxford (Further Educational Studies for senior educators from overseas).

Education of Backward Children, Leeds (for qualified teachers with, normally, at least 5 yrs' approved teaching experience, also certificate or graduate certificate).

Education of Young Children, Durham (for superintendents, heads, etc, of nursery schools, and college lecturers preparing students to teach in such schools) and Newcastle upon Tyne (Development and Education of Young Children, for diploma in Advanced Educational Studies).

Education/Teaching of the Deaf, Birmingham (Teaching of Hearing – Impaired Children), London (Institute of Education, Advanced Study of the Education of Deaf Children), Manchester (Advanced Study in Education of the Deaf, also certificate for Teachers of the Deaf) and Newcastle upon Tyne (for diploma in Advanced Educational Studies).

Education/Teaching of Handicapped/Physically Handicapped Children (see also 'Teaching of . . .', below), Birmingham (Teachers of Visually Handicapped Children), London (Institute of Education), Manchester, Newcastle upon Tyne (see 'Education for/of Overseas Teachers') and Sheffield (Education of Children with Learning Difficulties).

Education/Teaching of Maladjusted Children, Birmingham (for diploma in Special Education), Keele (diploma of Advanced Study in Education with special reference to Deprivation and Maladjustment), Leeds (for qualified teachers with, normally, at least 5 yrs' approved teaching experience, also certificate or graduate certificate), London (Institute of Education), Manchester, Newcastle upon Tyne (for diploma in Advanced Educational Studies) and Wales (Cardiff University College, for College diploma).

English Language Teaching, Exeter (for those with at least 3 yrs' experience as qualified teachers); for *Teaching of English as a Foreign Language/Overseas,* see page 154.

Environmental Education, Reading (option in diploma in Advanced Educational Studies).

Environmental Studies, Sheffield and New U of Ulster (Cultural and Environmental Studies, for diploma in Advanced Studies in Education).

European Studies, Sheffield.

Extension Work, see entries for 'Adult Education', 'Agricultural Extension' and 'Community Development', above.

Further Education, Nottingham (for experienced teachers and college of education lecturers).

General Studies for the 16–19 age range, Keele (for diploma of Advanced Study in Education).

Guidance and Counselling in Education, Aston in Birmingham (Counselling in Educational Settings), Keele (diploma of Advanced Study in Education with special reference to Counselling), Manchester, Newcastle upon Tyne (Counselling, for diploma in Advanced Educational Studies), Reading, New U of Ulster (for diploma in Advanced Studies in Education) and Wales (Pastoral Care, Guidance and Counselling, Swansea University College).

Health Education, Leeds (for qualified teachers with, normally, at least 5 yrs' teaching experience and appropriate qualifications in e.g. Biology, and suitably qualified and experienced members of national or local health services).

Human Relations in Education, Nottingham (option for diploma in Education, for experienced teachers and college of education lecturers).

Industrial Education and Training, Manchester (1 yr full-time or 2 yrs part-time or 3 terms full-time separated by 2 terms of supervised study).

Language and Learning, Nottingham (option for diploma in Education, for experienced teachers and college of education lecturers).

Language in Education (Education with special reference to the role of), London (Institute of Education).

Learning Difficulties, Nottingham (option for diploma in Education, for experienced teachers and college of education lecturers).

Mathematics Education, Keele (diploma of Advanced Study in Education with special reference to Secondary School Mathematics or Primary School Mathematics), Sheffield (Mathematical Education) and New U of Ulster (Mathematics with Education, also for diploma in Advanced Studies in Education) – for Durham and London, see 'Science Education'.

Middle Years of Schooling, Sheffield.

Music in Education, Exeter (for qualified teachers with, normally, at least 3 yrs' approved teaching experience) and Keele (for diploma of Advanced Study in Education).

Music Teacher's, London (Institute of Education, certificate).

Pastoral Care, Guidance and Counselling, Wales (Swansea University College).

Philosophy of Education, Leicester (Philosophy and History of Education), London (Institute of Education) and New U of Ulster (for diploma in Advanced Studies in Education).

Primary Education, Durham, Keele (diploma of Advanced Study in Education, with special reference to First Schools (age range 4+ to 9 – see also 'Mathematics Education'), Leeds (for qualified teachers with, normally, at least 5 yrs' approved teaching experience), Newcastle upon Tyne (see 'Education for/of Overseas Teachers', above) and Wales (Cardiff University College, Education in the Junior School).

Psychology and Sociology of Education (see also 'Sociology of Education'), Bradford (postgraduate) and Leicester (Sociology and Psychology of Education, for qualified teachers and social workers with at least 5 yrs' relevant experience).

Psychology of Childhood, Birmingham.

Psychology of Reading, Dundee.

Religious Education, Edinburgh (Christian Education, postgraduate), London (Institute of Education) and Nottingham (for experienced teachers or college of education lecturers).

Remedial Education, Wales (Bangor University College).

Residential Education, Newcastle upon Tyne (for diploma in Advanced Educational Studies).

Rural Social Development, Reading.

School Libraries and Resource Centres (see also 'Teacher Librarians'), Keele (for diploma of Advanced Study in Education).

School Organisation and Management, Sheffield (for teachers with at least 3 yrs' experience).

Science Education (see also 'Mathematics Education'), Durham (Science and Mathematics in Education, for holders of degree or approved qualification in science or mathematics), London (Science and Mathematics Education, diploma for overseas students, Chelsea College), Reading (option in diploma in Advanced Educational Studies) and New U of Ulster (for diploma in Advanced Studies in Education, also Chemistry with Education and Physics with Education).

Secondary Education, Keele (see 'Mathematics Education'), Leeds (for qualified teachers with, normally, at least 5 yrs' approved teaching experience) and Newcastle upon Tyne (see 'Education for/of Overseas Teachers', above).

Social and Community Education, Wales (Swansea University College).

Special Education, Birmingham, Liverpool (for those with approved initial qualification in Education and at least 3 yrs' approved professional experience), New U of Ulster (for diploma in Advanced Studies in Education) and Wales (Swansea University College).

Teacher Librarians (see also 'School Libraries'), London (Institute of Education, 1 yr full-time or 2 yrs part-time).

Teaching of Blind or Partially Sighted Children, Birmingham (for diploma in Special Education).

Teaching of Educationally Subnormal Children, Birmingham (for diploma in Special Education), London (Institute of Education) and Southampton (Education of Educationally Subnormal Children, for diploma in Advanced Educational Studies).

Teaching of Reading, Nottingham (option for diploma in Education, for experienced teachers and college of education lecturers) and Sheffield.

Teaching of Social Studies, Sheffield.

Teaching of World Studies, Keele (for diploma of Advanced Study in Education).

Teaching Studies, New U of Ulster (for diploma in Advanced Studies in Education).

Vocational Guidance, Reading (postgraduate certificate).

Youth and Community Work, Sheffield (for teachers with at least 3 yrs' experience).

Teacher training courses

Teacher training combined with study for a degree is available not only at universities (see *First degrees* above the line) but also at a large number of teacher training establishments. Three-year courses leading to a certificate are also offered at most of these colleges, some of which also provide one-year training courses for graduates. These colleges are listed on pages 278–281 where the type of course offered by each college is indicated.

Courses with specialist subjects in the degree and certificate courses and Specialist Courses are listed below. These are not comprehensive lists and the annual *Handbook of Institutions providing both Teacher Training and other Full-Time Advanced Courses* should be consulted for fuller information. It also contains details of shortened one- or two-year courses for older students with suitable previous education and experience which are provided by the majority of colleges. A number of establishments of education now offer degrees which do not lead to teaching qualifications and these are also listed in it.

Courses for teachers of art, dancing, drama and speech training, and music, some of which are given in colleges not wholly concerned with teacher training, are included in the entries for those subjects elsewhere in the Directory: see pages 89, 93, 120 and 204 respectively.

First degree courses other than BEd	Huddersfield P. C. of St Hild and St Bede. Sunderland P. These courses include the study of Education and lead to teaching qualifications.
Arts and crafts, handicraft, technical subjects (specialist courses in brackets)	Aberdeen CE. Avery Hill C (*Craft and Technical Studies*). Bingley C. Bristol P. Callendar Park CE. City of Liverpool CHE (*Workshop Craft and Design*). Craigie CE. Craiglockhart CE. Crewe and Alsager CHE. (*Design and Technology*). De La Salle CE (*Design and Technology*). Dundee CE. Eaton Hall CE (*Design and Craft*). Goldsmiths' C. Gwent CHE (*Craft, Design and Technology*) Hamilton CE. Jordanhill CE. King Alfred's C. Leeds P (*Craft and Technical Studies*). Middlesex P Resource Centre for Performing Arts (*Craft and Design*). Newcastle upon Tyne P (*Design and Craft*). Normal CE. Notre Dame CE. Ripon and York St John (*Design and Technical Studies*). C of St Mark and St John. Sheffield P (*Technology, Crafts and Design*). Shoreditch C (*Handicraft cert, postgraduate cert Design Technology, Craft and Design* for middle schools). Trinity C. Ulster C, Northern Ireland P (diploma *Craft Teachers*). Wolverhampton P (*Wood and Metalwork*).
Commerce/ Business Studies (specialist courses in brackets)	Aberdeen CE. Bristol P. Crewe and Alsager CHE (*Commerce Instructors*, 1 yr). Gwent CHE (*Business Studies* conversion course). Hull CHE. Jordanhill CE. Moray House CE. North East Wales IHE (*Commercial/Business Studies*). Roehampton IHE. Sunderland P. West Glamorgan IHE. Wolverhampton P (*Commerical subjects*).
Home Economics (specialist courses in brackets)	Aberdeen CE. Bath CHE. College of All Saints. Dundee CE. F L Calder CE. Gloucestershire IHE. Ilkley C. Jordanhill CE. Leeds P (*Home Economics*, 1 yr) Leicester P. Madeley CE. Manchester P. Newcastle upon Tyne P (*Home Economics*, 3 yrs). Normal CE. Roehampton IHE. Sheffield P. P of the South Bank (postgraduate *Home Economics*, 2 yr). Trent P. Trinity and All Saints C. Ulster C, Northern Ireland P (diploma *Home Economics*, 3 yrs). Worcester CE.
Physical Education	See Physical Education and Sports Science, page 223.
Rural Studies	Bath CHE (*Rural and Environmental Sciences*). Bingley C. Bishop Grosseteste C. Buckinghamshire CHE. Eaton Hall CE. Hertfordshire CHE. Leeds P. North Worcestershire C. Preston P. Ripon and York St John CHE. Rolle C (included in *Biology* course). Trinity C. Worcester CE.
Science	Science (chemistry, physics and biology), Mathematics and English are offered at most teacher training establishments.

Technical subjects (in Further Education) The following colleges provide one-year courses of teacher training for students with qualifications in technical or commercial subjects who intend to teach in technical colleges and other further education establishments:
Bolton CE (Technical). Garnett College. Huddersfield P. Jordanhill CE. Wolverhampton P Faculty of Education.

First degrees Hertfordshire CHE, BA *English with Education,* and *History with Education* (both 3 yrs). Huddersfield P, BSc *Science and Education* (4 yrs). Roehampton IHE, BH *Education* (3 yrs). Sunderland P, BSc *Education and Physical Sciences* (4 yrs), BA *Education and Mathematics* (4 yrs). West Sussex IHE, BA *History with Education* (3 yrs).

Other courses Brighton P, supplementary courses for teachers from overseas. Dundee CE, diploma in *Advanced Studies in Education.* Edge Hill CHE, MA *Reading Studies* (1 yr). Leicester P, diploma *Educational Studies* (1 yr, also postgraduate). North East London P, MSc *Educational Psychology* (1 yr). Roehampton IHE, MA *Curriculum Studies* (1 yr). Sheffield P, MSc *Education Management* (1 yr, also diploma). Thurrock TC, diploma *Play Leadership* (1 yr). West London IHE, MA *Curriculum Studies (Primary or Special Education)* (1 yr).

In addition to the advanced courses in education offered by universities and by Institutes of Education (see above), several colleges of education offer advanced courses for experienced qualified teachers. Details are given in *Programme of One Year Courses and One Term Courses for Qualified Teachers,* issued annually by the Department of Education and Science. There are also various courses designed especially for teachers from overseas.

Courses for teachers of the handicapped Three-year courses for the training of teachers of mentally handicapped children are available at several teacher training establishments. Information on these courses and courses for all handicapped children can be obtained from the Department of Education and Science. One-year diploma courses for the training of teachers of mentally handicapped adults are offered at several teacher training establishments. A list of colleges and further information can be obtained from the Central Council for Education and Training in Social Work.

Courses for teachers of the blind
A trained teacher who has had appropriate experience can apply for any suitable vacancy in a school for the blind. No special further training prior to appointment is required, but within three years of taking up a post in a school for the blind a teacher is required by the DES to take the Diploma Examination (External) of the College of Teachers of the Blind. Regulations and Syllabus of this examination can be obtained from the Hon. Registrar, CTB, Royal School for the Blind, Church Road North, Wavertree, Liverpool L15 6TQ.

Courses for teachers of the deaf
Moray House CE (Scottish Centre for the Education of the Deaf), diploma in the *Education of Deaf and Partially Deaf Children* (1 yr) for qualified teachers. P of North London, course for social workers with the deaf who hold a basic professional social work qualification. Oxford P course leading to the University of Oxford Certificate in Education of Deaf and Partially Hearing Children (1 yr), for qualified teachers and students completing their college course. 1-yr courses also at West London IHE and Hertfordshire CHE. Further information may be obtained from the Royal National Institute for the Deaf.

Educational Technology

First degrees Included in first degree courses at University of Surrey (Chemistry or Physical Science with Science Education, 3 yrs, or 4 yrs including 3rd yr at Berkshire CE) and New University of Ulster (Education).

Postgraduate courses Courses (1 yr, unless otherwise indicated) at the following universities: Birmingham (BPhil(Ed), 1 yr full-time plus 6 months part-time, also diploma), Brunel (included in MEd course), Glasgow (MEd), London (Institute of Education, Theory and Practice of Audio Visual Aids, diploma), Sussex (Curriculum Development and Educational Technology, MA), Wales (Aberystwyth University College, advanced diploma, also Aspects of Educational Technology, Curriculum Development and Management of Learning Resources in MEd course) and York (Educational Broadcasting, diploma, for experienced teachers, 1 term full-time plus 2 terms part-time). May also be included in courses for postgraduate diplomas/certificates in Education.

Research facilities At the following universities: Birmingham, Glasgow, Lancaster, London (Institute of Education and – Centre for Science Education – Chelsea College), Loughborough U of Technology (Centre for the Advancement of Mathematical Education in Technology), Surrey (Institute for Educational Technology), Sussex (Centre for Educational Technology, Reginald M. Phillips Research Unit for the Deaf and Other Handicaps), Wales (Aberystwyth University College, also College of Librarianship, Wales) and York (Audio-Visual Centre, Language Teaching Centre).

All courses are for postgraduate students and qualified teachers.

First degrees North East Wales Institute (Cartrefle College), BEd for serving teachers (2 yrs).

Diplomas and certificates Dorset IHE, diploma in *Advanced Educational Studies* (1 yr). Dundee CE, diploma (1 yr). Jordanhill CE, diploma (6 terms). Middlesex P, advanced diploma *Film and TV in Education* (1 yr). National Audio-Visual Aids Centre, diploma (1 yr), certificate *Production Techniques* (3 months). Plymouth P, CNAA diploma (1 yr), college diploma (1 term).

Postgraduate degree course Brighton P, MA *Curriculum Development and Educational Technology* (1 yr).

The British Council provides a number of training courses each year in audio-visual media and educational broadcasting (radio and television). The courses deal with the applications of communications media to educational problems; they are practical in-service courses of short duration (3–6 months).
Audio-Visual Media in Non-Formal Education (14 weeks).
Radio Production in Non-Formal Education (14 weeks).
Television Production in Formal and Non-Formal Education (30 weeks).
Radio Production in Formal Education (15 weeks).
Audio-Visual Media Production in Formal Education (15 weeks).
Television Scriptwriting for Formal and Non-Formal Education (15 weeks).
The Role of Broadcasting and Audio-Visual Media in Education, a course for teacher-trainers } (alternate years,
Utilisation and Evaluation of Educational Broadcasting } 15 weeks).
Entry to these courses is restricted to educationalists and broadcasters with experience, and with a good knowledge of English, who have been nominated by ministries and broadcasting

authorities. Applications should be made through the nearest British Council office, Embassy or High Commission, from which further information on courses and financial assistance may also be obtained. Students already in the United Kingdom may apply direct to Education and Science Division, The British Council, Tavistock House, Tavistock Square, London WC1 9LL.

A number of short courses in educational technology and audio-visual aids are arranged by education departments and colleges of education. Details can be obtained from the Council for Educational Technology, the National Committee for Audio-Visual Aids in Education and the British Council.

Engineering
(General Engineering/Engineering Science)

First degrees   In addition to the first degree courses in various branches of Engineering which are listed under the other 'Engineering' headings, universities provide the following courses which involve the study of Engineering either without specialisation in particular branches of the subject or with specialisation in an area not directly related to any one of the headings on pages 135–154:

Applied Sciences with Management Science or *with Social Sciences*, Sussex.

Classical Studies and Engineering, Reading.

Education and Engineering, Loughborough U of Technology.

Energy Engineering, Leeds (Fuel and Energy Engineering) and London (Queen Mary College).

Energy Studies, Sheffield and Wales (Swansea and – with Mechanical Engineering – Cardiff University Colleges).

Energy Technology, Aston in Birmingham.

Engineering (principles, practice, management and applications of), Surrey (4 yrs S).

Engineering and/with Business Studies, Sheffield, Strathclyde (Technology and Business Studies) and Warwick.

Engineering and Computer Science, Warwick.

Engineering/Engineering Science and Economics, see under 'Economics'.

Engineering and Environmental Sciences, Warwick.

Engineering and French or *Engineering and German*, Bath (each 4 yrs S).

Engineering and Management Systems, Brunel (4 yrs S).

Engineering Science and Management, Durham.

Engineering and Social Sciences, Newcastle upon Tyne.

Engineering Science (see also under Civil, Electrical and Mechanical Engineering), Aberdeen, Durham, Exeter, Liverpool (with Industrial Management), Loughborough U of Technology (Engineering Science and Technology, 3 yrs, or 4 yrs S) and Reading.

Engineering, Social and European Studies, Brunel (4 yrs S).

Environmental Engineering, see 'Environmental Studies'.

Management Science and Technology Studies (alone or with one of certain other subjects), Stirling.

Materials and Engineering Sciences, Warwick.

Offshore Engineering, Heriot-Watt (specialisation after first 2 yrs of course in one of: Building, Civil, Chemical, Electrical and Electronic or Mechanical Engineering).

Systems Engineering, Bath (3 yrs, or 4 yrs S).

Postgraduate courses   See under separate headings below.

The Council of Engineering Institutions, which was set up to establish common standards for the profession and for the qualification of 'Chartered Engineer', conducts a joint examination for its constituent members (listed on page 284). A British university or CNAA degree in engineering may carry exemption from this examination. A student who obtains an HND will be exempted from Part 1 of the CEI examination but will be required to take Part 2 after further study. Most colleges which offer HND courses in engineering also provide facilities for Part 2.

First degrees CNAA degrees in *Engineering* are offered at the following polytechnics and colleges (4 yrs S unless otherwise indicated):
Farnborough CT. Kingston P. Lanchester P (3–4 yrs). Middlesex P. Oxford P (3 yrs). Paisley CT (with *Marketing*). Portsmouth P (with *Business Studies*). Royal Military C Science (3 yrs). Sheffield P. Thames P (3 yrs). Ulster C, Northern Ireland P.
Engineering Science, Sunderland P (3 yrs).
Engineering Technology, Manchester P. Robert Gordon's IT (3 yrs).
Technology with Industrial Studies, Napier CC and T.

HND courses Bell CT. Buckinghamshire CHE. Dundee CT. Falkirk CT. Glasgow CT. Hull CT. Ipswich Civic C. Kirkcaldy TC. Napier CC and T. Paisley CT. Robert Gordon's IT.

Engineering, Aeronautical
(including Air Transport)

First degrees Degrees with specialisation awarded by the following universities:
Aeronautical Engineering, Bath (3 yrs, or 4 yrs S), Belfast, Bristol, Cambridge, The City (3 yrs or, for students sponsored by British firms, 4 yrs S), Glasgow, London (Queen Mary College), Loughborough U of Technology (4 yrs S), Manchester and Salford (4 yrs S, also Aeronautical Engineering Science, 3 yrs).
Aeronautics, London (Imperial College) and Southampton (Mathematics with Aeronautics).
Aeronautics and Astronautics, Southampton (3 yrs or – for students selected jointly by the university and aircraft firms – 5 yrs S).
Air Transport Engineering, The City (4 yrs S for students sponsored by British firms).

Postgraduate courses Courses (normally 1 yr and for MSc, unless otherwise indicated) at the following universities and Cranfield IT:
Aerodynamics and Flight Dynamics, Cranfield IT (1 or 2 yrs).
Aeronautics, London (Imperial College, Aeronautics, Fluid and Structural Mechanics, MSc and/or DIC) and Southampton (diploma 9 months, MSc 12 months).
Aircraft Design, Cranfield IT (1 or 2 yrs, with options in Air Transport Design and Development, Flight Testing and Development, Structural Design or Systems and Engineering).
Aircraft Propulsion, Cranfield IT (1 or 2 yrs for MSc in Thermal Power, with options in Gas Turbine Technology and Design or Rocket Technology).
Airline Management, Cranfield IT.
Air Transport, Cranfield IT (1 or 2 yrs, with options in Engineering or Operations).
Aviation Electronics, Cranfield IT (1 or 2 yrs).
Flight Control, Cranfield IT (1 or 2 yrs, for MSc in Control Systems).
Fluid Mechanics, see under 'Engineering, Mechanical' and 'Mathematics'.

High Temperature Gas Dynamics and *Rotorcraft and V/STOL Aircraft*, Southampton (options in MSc/diploma course in Aeronautics).

Structural and Aerospace Dynamics, Cranfield IT (1 or 2 yrs) and Southampton (option in MSc/diploma course in Sound and Vibration Studies).

Research facilities   At most of the universities named in the paragraphs above (Loughborough U of Technology: Centre of Transport Engineering Practice), and at Cranfield IT.

First degrees   CNAA degrees in *Aeronautical Engineering* (4 yrs S) are offered at the following: Hatfield P. Kingston P.

HND courses   *Mechanical Engineering* courses with an *aeronautical* bias or option (3 yrs S): Bristol P. Farnborough TC. Hatfield P. Hull CT. North East Wales IHE. Stockport CT.

College diplomas   Hatfield P, polytechnic diploma in *Aeronautical and Mechanical Engineering* (1 yr S after HND). Chelsea College of Aeronautical and Automobile Engineering (2½ yrs). Southall CT, *Air Transport Engineering* (6 months).

Research facilities   Hatfield P.

Engineering, Agricultural

First degrees   Degrees in *Agricultural Engineering* awarded by University of Newcastle upon Tyne (also Agricultural Mechanisation) and by Cranfield IT (National College of Agricultural Engineering, Silsoe); less specialised study included in courses for first degrees in Agriculture at universities of Nottingham and Reading.

Postgraduate courses   Courses (1 yr and for MSc, unless otherwise indicated) at the following universities and Cranfield IT:

Agricultural Engineering, Cranfield IT (National College of Agricultural Engineering, Silsoe, 1 or 2 yrs, options in Agricultural Machinery Engineering, Agricultural Mechanisation, Soil and Water Engineering, Land Resource Management, Tropical Crop Storage and Primary Processing, also diploma in similar options), Newcastle upon Tyne (1 or 2 yrs) and Reading (MSc 9 or 12 months, MAgrEng 2 yrs, with options in Agricultural Mechanisation, Agricultural Building).

Technology and Management of Pesticide Application, Cranfield IT.

Research facilities   At the universities of Newcastle upon Tyne (including Nafferton Farm, Stocksfield, Northumberland) and Reading, and at Cranfield IT (National College of Agricultural Engineering, Silsoe).

HND course   *Agricultural Engineering*, Harper Adams AgC (3 yrs S).

Postgraduate course   *Advanced Agricultural Engineering* (1 yr), West of Scotland AgC.

Engineering, Automobile

See also Transport

First degrees Loughborough U of Technology awards a BTech (4 yrs S) in *Automotive Engineering* and University of Salford a BSc in *Vehicle Engineering Science.*

Postgraduate courses Courses (for MSc, unless otherwise indicated) in:
Automobile Engineering, Cranfield IT (1 or 2 yrs, with options in Engines and Transmissions, Vehicle Dynamics and Chassis Design or Vehicle Structures and Body Design, also 10-week modular courses in each of these options).
Automotive Design, Royal College of Art (MDes or diploma, 2 yrs).
Environmental and Energy Aspects of Automotive Engineering Design and Operation, U of Southampton (12 months).

Research facilities At Cranfield IT, Loughborough U of Technology (including Centre of Transport Engineering Practice) and Royal College of Art (Automotive Design).

First degree Hatfield P, *Mechanical Engineering* with *Vehicle Engineering* option (4 yrs S).

HND courses *Mechanical Engineering* with *Automobile* bias (3 yrs S) at: Bolton IT. North Worcestershire C. Oxford P.

Postgraduate courses Lanchester P, CNAA MSc in *Diesel Engine Technology*, also *Turbine Technology* (both 1 yr). Royal Military C Science, CNAA MSc in *Military Vehicle Technology* (overseas applicants in government service are eligible as well as military personnel).

College diplomas Bolton IT (2 yrs), also higher diploma in *Automotive Engineering* (3 yrs S). Chelsea C Aeronautical and Automobile Engineering, diploma (2½ yrs), also diploma *Automobile Engineering and Administration* (3 yrs). Gateshead TC, *Motor Vehicle* diploma (2 yrs S and 1 yr). Napier CC and T, diploma (3 yrs S). North Worcestershire C, diploma (3 yrs S). Waltham Forest C, diploma (1 yr). Willesden CT (3 yrs S).

Engineering, Chemical

See also Fuel Technology

First degrees Degrees with specialisation awarded by the following universities:
Biochemical Engineering, Reading (4 yrs S, at National College of Food Technology), London (University College) and Wales (Swansea University College).
Chemical Engineering, Aston in Birmingham (3 yrs, or 4 yrs S), Bath (3 yrs, or 4 yrs S), Belfast, Birmingham, Bradford (4 yrs S, alone or with Management Economics), Cambridge (2 yrs following course in Natural Sciences or Engineering), Edinburgh, Exeter (also Environmental Chemical Engineering), Heriot-Watt, Leeds, London (Imperial and University Colleges), Loughborough U of Technology (alone or with Management, each 3 yrs, or – for BSc and DIS – 4 yrs S), Manchester (Institute of Science and Technology), Newcastle upon Tyne (alone or with Business Studies), Nottingham, Salford (4 yrs S, also Accountancy and Process Engineering, 3 yrs), Sheffield (with Fuel Technology), Strathclyde, Surrey (4 yrs or, exempt yr in industry, 3 yrs, also with Business Economics 4 yrs) and Wales (Swansea University College, alone or with Microbiology).
Petroleum Engineering, London (Imperial College).

Postgraduate courses Courses (normally 1 yr and for master's degree, unless otherwise indicated) at the following universities:

Advanced Chemical Engineering, London (Imperial College, MSc and/or DIC), Loughborough U of Technology (MSc and associateship, 1 yr full-time or 3 yrs part-time), Manchester (Institute of Science and Technology, MSc or diploma) and Newcastle upon Tyne (diploma).

Biochemical Engineering, London (University College, MSc or College diploma) and Wales (Swansea University College).

Biological Chemical Engineering, Birmingham.

Chemical Engineering, Aston in Birmingham (diploma), Bath, Bradford, Cambridge (certificate of postgraduate study or of advanced study), London (University College, diploma), Newcastle upon Tyne (Chemical Engineering Science), Salford, Sheffield (diploma or MSc), Surrey (diploma for graduate chemists, physicists or engineers) and Wales (Swansea University College, MSc and diploma).

Chemical Reaction Engineering and Applied Catalysis, Bath.

Food Process Engineering, Reading (option in MSc course in Food Technology at National College of Food Technology, 12 months).

Fuel and Energy Engineering, Leeds (diploma, 1, 2 or 3 yrs).

Petroleum Engineering, Exeter (Petroleum Resources Engineering), Heriot-Watt and London (Imperial College, MSc and/or DIC).

Petroleum Geology, London (Imperial College, MSc and/or DIC).

Plant and Process Design, Strathclyde.

Plant Engineering in the Process Industries, Loughborough U of Technology (MSc or associateship).

Process Analysis and Development, Aston in Birmingham.

Research facilities At most of the universities named above, also at Scottish Universities Research and Reactor Centre, East Kilbride.

First degrees CNAA degrees in *Chemical Engineering* are offered at the following polytechnics (4 yrs S): North East London P. P of the South Bank, *Chemical Engineering*, also *Chemical and Polymer Technology*. Teesside P, option in *Process Chemistry, Metals Extraction, Process Analysis, Biochemical Engineering*. P of Wales.

HND courses Birkenhead CT (3 yrs S). Huddersfield P (2 yrs). P of the South Bank (2 yrs). Southampton CT (2 yrs). Teesside P, also *Biochemical Engineering* (2 yrs). Ulster C, Northern Ireland P (3 yrs S). P of Wales (2 yrs).

Post-HND courses and college diplomas (1 yr post-HND unless otherwise indicated): Birkenhead CT (also 4 yrs S). Huddersfield P. P of the South Bank. Southampton CT. Teesside P.

Postgraduate course Oxford P, CNAA MSc *Technology and Economics of Chemical Processes* (1 yr).

Research facilities North East London P. P of the South Bank. Teesside P. P of Wales.

Engineering, Civil

First degrees Degrees in Engineering involving the study of subjects relevant to *Civil Engineering* may be awarded by the following universities: Aberdeen, Aston in Birmingham (3 yrs, or 4 yrs S, also – with another subject – Water Resources (Engineering)), Belfast, Birmingham, Bradford (4 yrs S), Bristol, Cambridge, The City (3 yrs, or 4 or $4\frac{1}{2}$ yrs S for students sponsored by British firms), Dundee (also Civil Engineering and Economics), Durham, Edinburgh, Exeter, Glasgow, Heriot-Watt (also Structural Engineering, and Civil Engineering for Gas Engineers), Lancaster (3 yrs, or 4 yrs S – final-yr Engineering students may specialise in branches that span the conventional divisions), Leeds (also Architectural Engineering, and Civil Engineering with Computational Science or French or Management Studies or Operational Research), Leicester, Liverpool, London (Imperial, King's and Queen Mary Colleges and – Civil, Structural and Environmental Engineering – University College), Loughborough U of Technology (3 yrs, or 4 yrs S), Manchester (University and – Civil or Civil and Structural Engineering – Institute of Science and Technology), Newcastle upon Tyne (also Civil and Environmental Engineering), Nottingham, Oxford, Salford (3 yrs, or 4 yrs S), Sheffield, Southampton (3 yrs, or 5 yrs S), Strathclyde, Surrey (4 yrs or, exempt industrial training yr, 3 yrs), Sussex (Structural Engineering), Wales (at Cardiff University College – Civil and Structural, at Swansea University College – also Civil Engineering and Environmental Studies, and at Institute of Science and Technology – 3 yrs, or 4 yrs S) and Warwick (3 yrs, or 4 or 5 yrs S).

Students following these courses may normally concentrate to a greater or lesser extent on Civil Engineering subjects, although usually not until after the first, or sometimes the second, yr. However the structure of the courses varies considerably from one university to another, and at several universities the course is a broadly-based one in Engineering Science, allowing some specialisation in Civil Engineering during the final yr only. (See also 'Engineering', page 134).

Postgraduate courses Courses (normally 1 yr and for master's degree, unless otherwise indicated) at the following universities and Cranfield IT:

Advanced Structural Engineering, Southampton (diploma 9 months or MSc 12 months or in 3 parts over 33 months for diploma or 36 months for MSc).

Bridge Engineering, Surrey (MSc minimum 12 months, diploma 1 academic yr).

Civil Engineering, Dundee (diploma, also MSc – 12 months – in Civil Engineering in Hot Climates), Edinburgh (diploma), London (King's College) and Sheffield (Civil and Structural Engineering).

Civil Engineering Hydraulics, London (Imperial College, MSc and/or DIC) and Strathclyde (diploma 1 yr, MSc 1 or 2 yrs).

Civil Engineering (Structures), The City (14 months full-time or 2–3 yrs part-time).

Concrete Structures, London (Imperial College, MSc and/or DIC).

Construction, Loughborough U of Technology (MSc or associateship).

Construction Engineering, Leeds (12 months).

Construction Management, Reading (12 months).

Desalination Technology, Glasgow.

Engineering Geology, see 'Geology'.

Engineering Hydrology, Newcastle upon Tyne.

Engineering Mechanics, Wales (Swansea University College).

Engineering Science (Science and Applications of Electric Plasmas, and Two-Phase Flow), Oxford.

Engineering Seismology, London (Imperial College, DIC).

Fire Engineering, Edinburgh (MSc or diploma).

Fluid Mechanics, Wales (Swansea University College).

Foundation Engineering, Birmingham.

Geomechanics, Wales (Swansea University College).

Highway Engineering, see 'Transport'.

Hydrogeology, London (University College, MSc or College diploma).

Hydrology, Newcastle upon Tyne (diploma).

Irrigation Engineering, Southampton (diploma 9 months, MSc 12 months).

Maritime Civil Engineering, Liverpool (diploma) and Manchester (MSc or diploma).

Materials and Construction Management, Birmingham.

Offshore Structures, Cranfield IT (1 or 2 yrs).

Reservoir Engineering, Newcastle upon Tyne.

River Engineering, Birmingham.

Rock Mechanics and Excavation Engineering, Newcastle upon Tyne.

Soil and Rock Mechanics, Wales (Swansea University College, 1 or 2 yrs).

Soil Mechanics, London (Imperial College, MSc and/or DIC).

Soil Mechanics and Foundation Engineering, Newcastle upon Tyne.

Structural Design, Cranfield IT (1 or 2 yrs) and Newcastle upon Tyne (certificate).

Structural Dynamics, Cranfield IT (1 or 2 yrs).

Structural Engineering, Dundee (diploma), Manchester (Institute of Science and Technology, MSc or diploma), Sheffield (Civil and Structural Engineering), Strathclyde (diploma 1 yr, MSc 1 or 2 yrs) and Surrey (MSc minimum 12 months, diploma 1 academic yr).

Structural Mechanics, Wales (Swansea University College).

Structural Steel Design, London (Imperial College, MSc and/or DIC).

Theory and Technology of Solid Mechanics, Cranfield IT (1 or 2 yrs).

Timber Structures and Technology, London (Imperial College, MSc and/or DIC).

Traffic/Transport Engineering, see 'Transport'.

Urban Science, Birmingham.

Water Resources, Newcastle upon Tyne.

Water Resources Technology (including options in Engineering Hydrology, Water Engineering), Birmingham.

Research facilities
At almost all those universities which offer first degree courses and at Cranfield IT. Leeds, Newcastle upon Tyne and Salford: Centres for Transport Studies.

First degrees
CNAA degrees in *Civil Engineering* are offered at the following (4 yrs S unless otherwise indicated): Bolton IT. Brighton P (3 yrs). P of Central London (also 3 yrs). Dundee CT. Hatfield P (also 3 yrs). Kingston P. Lanchester P. Liverpool P. Middlesex P. North East London P. Oxford P. Paisley CT. Plymouth P. Portsmouth P (also 3 yrs). Royal Military C of Science (3 yrs). Sheffield P. Sunderland P. Teesside P. Thames P. Trent P. Ulster C, Northern Ireland P. P of Wales.

HND courses
(3 yrs S unless otherwise indicated): Birmingham P, also *Construction Management.* Bolton IT. Glasgow CT. Hatfield P (2½ yrs S). Kingston P. Leeds P. Liverpool P. Napier CC and T. North East London P. North East Surrey CT, *Structural Engineering* as part of HND *Building* (entry also in January). Oxford P. Portsmouth P, also *Engineering Geology* (3 yrs). Sheffield P. P of the South Bank. Stockport CT. Teesside P. Thames P. Trent P. P of Wales. Wolverhampton P.

College diplomas
Buckinghamshire CHE, diplomas in *Advanced Timber Technology* (3 yrs), *Timber Studies* (1 yr), *Timber Studies for Graduates and Executives* (1 yr).

Postgraduate courses
P of Central London, MSc *Transportation Planning and Management* (1 yr).

Research   Brighton P. Kingston P. Lanchester P. Leeds P. North East London P. North Staffordshire P.
facilities   Portsmouth P. Plymouth P. P of the South Bank. Sheffield P. Sunderland P. Thames P. P of
                Wales. Wolverhampton P.

Professional Most colleges with advanced courses provide where necessary additional courses leading to Part
courses   2 of the examination of the Council of Engineering Institutions (see page 135).

Engineering, Control

See also Computer Science; and Engineering, Electronic

First degrees Degrees with specialisation awarded by the following universities: Aston in Birmingham (with
                 another subject), Birmingham (Electronic and Control Engineering), Bradford (Electronic and
                 Control Systems Engineering, or Chemistry and Control Engineering, each 4 yrs S), The City
                 (Control, Instrumentation and Systems Engineering, 3 yrs, or 4 yrs S), Hull, Kent at Canterbury
                 (Applied Chemistry with Control Engineering), Leeds, Loughborough U of Technology
                 (Electronic, Computer and Systems Engineering, 3 yrs or – for BSc and DIS – 4 yrs S), Reading
                 (Cybernetics and Control Engineering), Sheffield (Control Systems), Sussex and Warwick
                 (diverges from Engineering Science course during 3rd yr). Less specialised study of Control
                 Engineering included in courses for degrees in Engineering (usually Electrical) at Bradford
                 (Industrial Technology and Management course), Brunel, Nottingham, Reading (for degrees in
                 Electrical Engineering, Engineering Science, Classical Studies and Engineering), Salford,
                 Southampton and Wales (Bangor, Cardiff and Swansea University Colleges).

Postgraduate Courses (1 yr and for master's degree, unless otherwise indicated) at the following universities
courses   and Cranfield IT:
                Applied Science (various options), Dundee (diploma).
                Control/Computer Systems Engineering, Surrey (MSc minimum 12 months, diploma 1 academic
                    yr).
                Control Engineering, Aston in Birmingham (Control Engineering and Digital Electronic
                    Systems option for MSc in Electrical Engineering), Bradford (options in Chemical,
                    Electrical or Mechanical Engineering), Cambridge (Control Engineering and Opera-
                    tional Research), Cranfield IT (1 or 2 yrs, several options), Loughborough U of
                    Technology (Power and Control or Electronics and Control – options in Electrical
                    Engineering course) and Sheffield (MEng or diploma, also short courses).
                Control Systems, Cranfield IT (1 or 2 yrs, including Flight, Industrial and Electrical Control,
                    option for MSc in Control Engineering) and London (Imperial College, MSc and/or
                    DIC).
                Control Theory, Cranfield IT (1 or 2 yrs, option for MSc in Control Engineering) and Warwick.
                Cybernetics and Instrument Technology, Reading (12 months).
                Digital Techniques, Heriot-Watt (MSc or diploma, 1 yr full-time or 2 yrs part-time).
                Electrical and Electronic Engineering (Microprocessors), Newcastle upon Tyne.
                Electrical Engineering, Loughborough U of Technology (MSc or associateship, options in
                    Instrumentation or Electronic Circuits).
                Electrical Power and Control, Nottingham (1 yr full-time or 2 yrs part-time).
                Electrical Power and Machines, Heriot-Watt (MSc or diploma, 1 yr full-time or 2 yrs part-time).
                Electrical Power System Analysis and Control, Manchester (Institute of Science and Tech-
                    nology, for MSc or diploma in Power Systems Engineering).
                Electronic and Electrical Systems (Control option), Birmingham.
                Electronic Control Engineering, Salford.

Electronic Instrumentation, Aston in Birmingham (option for MSc in Electrical Engineering) and Wales (Swansea University College).

Engineering Control, jointly at Sussex, Wales (Bangor University College, MSc or diploma) and Warwick (Inter-University Institute of Engineering Control).

Industrial Systems Engineering, Wales (Swansea University College).

Instrument Design and Application, Manchester (University and Institute of Science and Technology, MSc or diploma).

Instrument Technology, Loughborough U of Technology.

Manufacturing Technology, Cranfield IT (1 or 2 yrs, options in Fluidic Systems or Numerical Control).

Mathematics of Modern Control Systems, Loughborough U of Technology (MSc or associateship, 1 yr full-time or 2 or 3 yrs part-time).

Microelectronics, Edinburgh (diploma).

Systems Engineering, The City.

Theory and Practice of Automatic Control, Manchester (Institute of Science and Technology, MSc or diploma).

Research facilities At most of the universities named in the paragraphs above, at Essex (Digital and Stochastic Control), and at Cranfield IT. Manchester (Institute of Science and Technology): Control Systems Centre. Warwick: Control Theory Centre.

First degrees CNAA degrees are offered at the following polytechnics (4 yrs S unless otherwise indicated).

Communication Engineering, Plymouth P.

Control Engineering, Sheffield P.

Electronic Engineering with final year option in *Instrumentation and Control,* Leicester P.

Engineering Systems and Control, Huddersfield P.

Instrumentation and Control Engineering, P of Central London (3 yrs).

Instrumentation and Systems Engineering, Teesside P.

HND courses (3 yrs S) Gwent CHE, *Mechanical Engineering* with *Systems and Control* bias. Leicester P, *Electronic Engineering* with final year option in *Control Technology.*

Measurement and Control, Hatfield, P. Huddersfield P. Lanchester P. Richmond upon Thames C (options in *Medical Electronics* and *Electrical Machines*). Teesside P. Ulster C, Northern Ireland P. P of Wales.

College diploma *Measurement and Control,* Hatfield P (1 yr).

Research facilities P of Central London. Bolton IT. Huddersfield P. Liverpool P. Teesside P.

Engineering, Electrical

See also Engineering, Electronic

First degrees Degrees in Engineering involving the study of subjects relevant to *Electrical Engineering* may be awarded by the following universities: Aberdeen, Aston in Birmingham (3 yrs, or 4 yrs S), Bath (3 yrs, or 4 yrs S), Belfast, Birmingham, Bradford (4 yrs S), Bristol, Brunel (4 yrs S – applicants should normally be sponsored by UK firm or organisation), Cambridge, The City (also Mechanical Engineering with Electrical Engineering, each 3 yrs, or 4 or 4½ yrs S for students sponsored by British firms), Dundee (also Electrical Engineering and Economics),

Durham, Edinburgh, Exeter, Glasgow, Heriot-Watt, Lancaster (3 yrs, or 4 yrs S – final-yr Engineering students may specialise in branches that span the conventional divisions), Leeds, Leicester, Liverpool, London (Imperial, King's, Queen Mary and University Colleges), Loughborough U of Technology (3 yrs, or 4 yrs S), Manchester (University and Institute of Science and Technology), Newcastle upon Tyne (also Electrical Engineering and Computing Science), Nottingham, Oxford, Reading, Salford (4 yrs S, also Electrical Engineering Science, 3 yrs), Sheffield, Southampton (3 yrs, or 5 yrs S), Strathclyde, Surrey (4 yrs or, exempt industrial training yr, 3 yrs), Sussex (also Electrical and Mechanical Engineering), Wales (at Cardiff University College, at Bangor University College – Electrical Engineering (including Power Electronics), at Swansea University College – also Electro-Mechanical Engineering, and at Institute of Science and Technology – 3 yrs, or 4 yrs S) and Warwick (3 yrs, or 4 or 5 yrs S).

Students following these courses may normally concentrate to a greater or lesser extent on Electrical – in some cases Electrical and Electronic – Engineering subjects, although usually not until after the first, or sometimes the second, yr. However the structure of the courses varies considerably from one university to another, and at several universities the course is a broadly-based one in Engineering Science, allowing some specialisation in Electrical Engineering during the final yr only. (See also 'Engineering', page 134).

Postgraduate courses Courses (1 yr and for MSc, unless otherwise indicated) at the following universities and Cranfield IT:

Communication Systems, Aston in Birmingham (option for MSc in Electrical Engineering).

Electrical Engineering (various options), Aston in Birmingham (diploma 6 months, MSc 12 months), Bradford (Electrical and Electronic, MSc or diploma), Brunel (Electrical Engineering and Electronics, jointly with Manchester (Institute of Science and Technology)), Dundee (diploma), Loughborough U of Technology (MSc or associateship), Nottingham (1 yr full-time or 2 yrs part-time) and Salford (diploma for Advanced Studies, 10 weeks full-time and 10-week project in industry or university).

Electrical Engineering Control, Cranfield IT (1 or 2 yrs, for MSc in Control Systems).

Electrical Machines, Aston in Birmingham (option for MSc in Electrical Engineering).

Electrical Machines and Power Systems, London (Imperial and Queen Mary Colleges, joint course for MSc and/or College diplomas).

Electrical Power Engineering, Heriot-Watt (MSc or diploma, 1 yr full-time or 2 yrs part-time) and Newcastle upon Tyne (diploma or certificate).

Electrical Power Systems, Bradford (diploma).

Electric Power Engineering, Strathclyde.

Electric Power Systems, Belfast.

Electroheat and Industrial Process Heating, Loughborough U of Technology.

Electronic and Electrical Systems, Birmingham.

Fire Engineering, Edinburgh (MSc or diploma).

Materials in Electrical Engineering, London (Imperial College, DIC).

Power Systems Engineering, Manchester (Institute of Science and Technology, MSc or diploma, Electrical Power Systems Analysis and Control or High Voltage Insulation Engineering or Electrical Transmission and Distribution Technology or Switchgear Technology) and Wales (Swansea University College).

Power System Technology, Bradford (for MSc in Electrical and Electronic Engineering) and Salford.

Pulse and Digital Systems, Aston in Birmingham (option for MSc in Electrical Engineering).

Systems Engineering, London (Queen Mary College, MSc or College diploma).

Research facilities At almost all those universities which offer first degree courses and at Cranfield IT, also Scottish Universities Research and Reactor Centre, East Kilbride.

First degrees   CNAA degrees in *Electrical Engineering* are offered at the following polytechnics and colleges (4 yrs S unless otherwise indicated). Brighton P (also 3 yrs and 3 yrs S). P of Central London (also 3 yrs). Liverpool P. Manchester P. North East London P. North Staffordshire P, also *Electro-Mechanical Engineering*. Paisley CT. Portsmouth P (also 3 yrs). Royal Military C of Science (*Instrumentation and Communication*). P of the South Bank, options in *Power, Electronics*, and *Illuminating Engineering*. Trent P. P of Wales.

Electrical and Electronic Engineering (4 yrs S unless otherwise indicated). Brighton P (also 3 yrs). Dundee CT (also 3 yrs S). Hatfield P. Huddersfield P. Kingston P. Lanchester P. Middlesex P. Newcastle upon Tyne P. North Staffordshire P. Portsmouth P (3 yrs). Preston P. Robert Gordon's IT. Royal Military C of Science. Sunderland P (3 yrs). Thames P.
Communication Engineering, Leeds P (4 yrs S).

HND courses   *Electrical and Electronic Engineering* (3 yrs S). Bell CT. Birmingham P. Bristol P. Cambridgeshire C Arts and T. Chelmer IHE. Derby C Art and T. Dundee CT. Glasgow CT. Gwent CHE, *Electrical Engineering*. Hatfield P. Huddersfield P. Kingston P. Kirkcaldy TC. Lanchester P. Leeds P. Leicester P. Letchworth CT. Liverpool P. Manchester P. Medway and Maidstone CT. Middlesex P. Napier CC and T. Newcastle upon Tyne P. North East London P. North East Wales IHE. Norwich City C. Oldham CT, also with *Radio and Television* bias. Plymouth P. Portsmouth P. Preston P. Robert Gordon's IT. Sheffield P. P of the South Bank. South East London C. Southall CT. Swindon College, *Electrical Engineering* option in *Mechanical Engineering* course. Trent P. Ulster C, Northern Ireland P. P of Wales.

College diplomas   (1 yr after HND unless otherwise indicated) Derby C Art and T (4 yrs S). Manchester P. Oldham CT. Plymouth P. Southall CT. P of Wales, polytechnic Associateship (1 yr).

Research facilities   Available at most polytechnics.

Professional courses   Most colleges with advanced courses provide, where necessary, additional courses leading to Part 2 of the examination of the Council of Engineering institutions (see page 135).

Engineering, Electronic
(including Radio and Television Engineering and Telecommunications)

See also Computer Science; and Engineering, Control

First degrees   Degrees with specialisation awarded by the following universities:
Biomedical Electronics, Salford.
Communication(s), Bradford (European Industrial Studies – French with Communications, 4 yrs S including 1 yr abroad), Salford (Electronic Communication) and Sheffield (Electronic Engineering (Communications option)).
Communication(s) Engineering, Birmingham (Electronic and Communication Engineering), Bradford (4 yrs S), Essex (Computer and Communication Engineering), Hull (Electronic and Communication Engineering) and Kent at Canterbury.
Electro-Mechanical Engineering, Wales (Swansea University College).
Electronic and Electrical/Electrical and Electronic Engineering, Bath (3 yrs or 4 yrs S), Belfast, Birmingham, Bradford, The City (4 yrs S), Dundee (Electrical Engineering and

Electronics), Heriot-Watt, Lancaster, Leeds, London (King's and Queen Mary Colleges), Loughborough U of Technology (3 yrs or 4 yrs S), Manchester (University and Institute of Science and Technology), Newcastle upon Tyne, Strathclyde, Surrey and Wales (Bangor – Electrical Engineering including Power Electronics – and Cardiff and Swansea University Colleges and – 3 yrs, or 4 yrs S – Institute of Science and Technology).

Electronic Engineering, Birmingham (Electronic and Computer or Communication or Control Engineering), Bradford (Electronic and Control Systems Engineering, 4 yrs S), Bristol, Brunel, The City (3 yrs, also Mechanical Engineering with Electronic Engineering, 3 yrs or 4 yrs S), Essex (School of Physical Sciences), Glasgow (Electronics and Electrical Engineering), Hull (Electronic and either Communication or Systems Engineering), Leeds (with Physics), Liverpool, London (with Computer Science or Physics at Queen Mary College, alone or with Computer Science at University College), Loughborough U of Technology (with Physics, also Electronic, Computer and Systems Engineering, 3 yrs or 4 yrs S), Manchester (with Physics), Nottingham, Sheffield, Southampton, Sussex, Wales (alone or with Mathematics or Physics or Physical Oceanography at Bangor University College, with Physics at Swansea University College) and Warwick (Engineering Science (Electronic)).

Electronics (see also 'Physics'), Bradford (Physical Electronics, 4 yrs S), Brunel (with Physics, 4 yrs S), The City (with Physics), Dundee, Edinburgh (with Physics, also Computer Science), Exeter (Physics with Solid State Electronics), Glasgow (with Electrical Engineering), Hull (Mathematics and Electronic Systems), Keele (with another principal subject, but Electronics alone possible in final yr, also for BSc in Integrated Physical Sciences), Kent at Canterbury, Lancaster (Applied Physics and Electronics), Leicester (Physics with Electronics), Liverpool, London (Chelsea and University Colleges, also Computer Science and Electronics at King's College and Physics or Computer Science and Electronics at Queen Mary College), Manchester (Institute of Science and Technology), Reading (Physics and Electronics), Salford, Southampton (alone or with Chemistry, Physics or Mathematics), Sussex, Wales (Institute of Science and Technology, 3 yrs or 4 yrs S, also – Electrical Engineering (including Power Electronics) – Bangor University College) and Warwick (Physical Electronics).

Telecommunication Engineering, Essex (School of Physical Sciences).

Less specialised study of *Electronics* may be included in Science or Engineering courses at almost all universities. Courses in the basic principles of *Radio Engineering/Technology* are provided by most universities in their departments of Physics and/or Electrical Engineering; and most Electrical Engineering courses include *Telecommunications*.

Postgraduate courses
Courses (normally 1 yr and for master's degree, unless otherwise indicated) at the following universities and Cranfield IT:

Applied Electronics, Aberdeen and Newcastle upon Tyne (diploma or certificate).

Aviation Electronics, Cranfield IT (1 or 2 yrs, for MSc in Electronics).

Communication Engineering, London (Imperial College, MSc and/or DIC) and Manchester (Institute of Science and Technology, MSc or diploma).

Control Engineering and Digital Electronic Systems, Aston in Birmingham (option for MSc in Electrical Engineering).

Digital Communication Systems, Loughborough U of Technology (MSc or associateship).

Digital Electronics, Manchester (Institute of Science and Technology, MSc or diploma).

Digital Electronics and Communication Engineering, Bradford (for MSc in Electrical and Electronic Engineering).

Digital Electronics: Computers, Communications and Instrumentation, London (Chelsea College, 1 yr full-time or 2 yrs part-time).

Digital Techniques, Heriot-Watt (MSc or diploma, 1 yr full-time or 2 yrs part-time).

Electroheat and Industrial Process Heating, Loughborough U of Technology (MSc or associateship).

Electronic and Communication Engineering, Bradford (diploma).

Electronic and Electrical Systems (Radar and Radiocommunications options), Birmingham.

Electronic Control Engineering, Salford.

Electronic Design, Cranfield IT (1 or 2 yrs).

Electronic Engineering (various options), Bradford (Electrical and Electronic, MSc or diploma), Hull (diploma) and Newcastle upon Tyne (Electrical and Electronic Engineering (Microprocessors)).

Electronic Instrumentation, Aston in Birmingham (option for MSc in Electrical Engineering) and Wales (Swansea University College).

Electronic Materials and Devices, Wales (Bangor University College, also diploma).

Electronic Physics, Wales (Aberystwyth University College).

Electronics, Belfast, Brunel (Electrical Engineering and Electronics, various options, jointly with Manchester (Institute of Science and Technology)), Cranfield IT (1 or 2 yrs), Dundee, Kent at Canterbury (MSc 12 months, diploma 9 months), London (Chelsea and King's Colleges), Southampton (diploma 9 months, MSc 12 months, or in 3 parts over 33 months for diploma or 36 months for MSc) and Wales (Institute of Science and Technology, diploma or MSc, 12 months).

Electronic Science of Materials, Salford.

Microelectronics, Edinburgh (diploma).

Microwave Communications Engineering, Leeds and Sheffield (joint course, also at Sheffield short courses).

Microwave Engineering, London (University College, College diploma).

Microwaves and Modern Optics, London (University College).

Opto-electronics, Belfast, The City (12 months) and Essex.

Power Electronics, Bradford, jointly with Loughborough U of Technology.

Power Electronics and Systems, Manchester (Institute of Science and Technology, MSc or diploma).

Power Electronics Engineering, Loughborough U of Technology (MSc or associateship, jointly with Bradford).

Quantum Electronics, Essex (12 months).

Semiconductor Physics and Technology, Brunel (1 yr full-time or $2\frac{1}{2}$ yrs part-time).

Solid-State Electronics, Birmingham, Bradford (for MSc in Electrical and Electronic Engineering), Liverpool and Manchester (Institute of Science and Technology, MSc or diploma).

Telecommunications Technology, Aston in Birmingham (diploma, 6 months).

Telecommunication Systems, Essex.

Research facilities   At the following universities (Electronic Engineering/Electronics): Bath, Birmingham, Bradford (Electronic Engineering), Bristol, Brunel Dundee, Durham (Electronics), Essex, Glasgow, Heriot-Watt, Hull, Kent at Canterbury, Lancaster, Leeds (Electronic Engineering), Leicester, Liverpool, London, Loughborough U of Technology, Manchester (University and Institute of Science and Technology), Newcastle upon Tyne, Nottingham, Reading, Salford, Sheffield, Southampton (Electronics), Strathclyde, Surrey, Sussex, Wales (Aberystwyth, Bangor, Cardiff and Swansea University Colleges, and Institute of Science and Technology) and Warwick; and at Cranfield IT.

First degrees   CNAA degrees in *Electronic Engineering* are offered at the following (4 yrs S unless otherwise indicated). Bolton IT (3 yrs). Brighton P (also 3 yrs). Leicester P. Middlesex P. Napier CC and T, *Communication and Electronic Engineering*. Newcastle upon Tyne P, *Physical Electronics*. P of

North London, *Electronic and Communications Engineering* (3 yrs). North Staffordshire P. Paisley CT (4 yrs). Plymouth P, *Communication Engineering.*

HND courses Napier CC and T, *Applied Physics with Electronics* (3 yrs). For HNDs in *Electrical and Electronic Engineering* see page 144. Many colleges offer HNDs with an *Electronic* or *Power* bias.

Diplomas and Bolton IT, Associateship (1 yr) and higher diploma (2 yrs). Coventry TC, *Telecommunications*
certificates *Engineering Technicians* diploma (3 yrs S). Plymouth P, *Marine Electronics* (26 weeks).

Postgraduate P of North London, MSc *Physical Basis of Electronics* (1 yr).
courses

Research Available at most polytechnics mentioned above.
facilities
Professional Most colleges with advanced courses provide where necessary additional courses leading to Part
examinations 2 of the examination of the Council of Engineering institutions (see page 135).

Engineering, Marine, and Naval Architecture

First degrees Degrees with specialisation awarded by the following universities:
Marine Engineering, Newcastle upon Tyne, also, at Surrey, option for degree in Mechanical Engineering (4 yrs S).
Maritime Studies (*Maritime Technology,* with specialisation in Ship Science or Offshore Studies), Wales (Institute of Science and Technology, 3 yrs, or 4 yrs S).
Naval Architecture, Strathclyde.
Naval Architecture and Ocean Engineering, Glasgow and London (University College).
Naval Architecture and Shipbuilding, Newcastle upon Tyne.
Offshore Engineering, Heriot-Watt (specialisation after first 2 yrs of course in one of: Building, Civil, Chemical, Electrical and Electronic, or Mechanical Engineering).
Offshore Studies, Wales – see above.
Ship Science, Southampton and – see above – Wales.

Postgraduate Courses (1 yr and for MSc, unless otherwise indicated) at the following universities and
courses Cranfield IT:
Electronic and Electrical Systems (*Underwater Acoustics and Sonar* option), Birmingham.
Marine Engineering, Newcastle upon Tyne (MSc or diploma).
Marine Oilfield Engineering, Leeds (12 months).
Marine Technology, Newcastle upon Tyne (MSc or diploma) and Strathclyde.
Maritime Civil Engineering, Liverpool (diploma) and Manchester (MSc or diploma).
Naval Architecture, London (University College, College diploma and MSc in Ocean Engineering (Naval Architecture or Mechanical Engineering)) and Newcastle upon Tyne (certificate).
Offshore Structures, Cranfield IT (1 or 2 yrs).
Ship Production Technology, Strathclyde (1 or 2 yrs).
Underwater Science and Technology, Salford (modular course, 1 yr full-time or 2 yrs part-time).

Research At most of the universities named in the paragraphs above (Heriot-Watt: Offshore Engineering
facilities and Underwater Technology), and at Cranfield IT.

First degree Liverpool P, *Mechanical Engineering* with *Marine* Option (4 yrs S).

HND courses Hull CT, *Mechanical engineering* with specialist option in *Marine Engineering* (3 yrs S). Southampton CT, *Marine Engineering* (3 yrs S) also *Naval Architecture* (3 yrs). Ulster C, Northern Ireland P, *Shipbuilding Technology* (3 yrs S).

Post-HND   Southampton CT, college Associateship in *Naval Architecture and Marine Engineering* (1 yr).
course

College   Liverpool P. *Marine Engineering* (3 months). Robert Gordon's IT, diploma in *Offshore*
diplomas   *Engineering* (1 yr). Southampton CT, college diploma in *Yacht and Boatyard Management*, also in *Yacht and Boat Design* (both 3 yrs S). Sunderland P, college diploma in *Naval Architecture* (3 yrs).

Research   Liverpool P. Portsmouth P. Sunderland P.
facilities

Engineering, Mechanical

See also Engineering, Automobile

First degrees Degrees in Engineering involving the study of subjects relevant to *Mechanical Engineering* may be awarded by the following universities: Aberdeen, Aston in Birmingham (3 yrs, or 4 yrs S – may also be taken with one of a number of other subjects, including Business Administration or Computer Science or Education), Bath (also Thermal Power Engineering, each 3 yrs, or 4 yrs S), Belfast, Birmingham (also Mechanical Engineering and Economics, 3 yrs for Joint Honours BSc or 4 yrs for Double Honours BSc & BCom), Bradford (4 yrs S), Bristol, Brunel (Mechanical or Mechanical/Production Engineering, 4 yrs S – applicants should normally be sponsored by UK firm or organisation), Cambridge, The City (also Mechanical/Materials Engineering or Mechanical Engineering with Electrical or Electronic Engineering, each 3 yrs, or 4 or 4½ yrs S for students sponsored by British firms), Dundee (also Mechanical Engineering and Economics), Durham, Edinburgh, Exeter, Glasgow, Heriot-Watt, Lancaster (3 yrs, or 4 yrs S – final-yr Engineering students may specialise in branches that span the conventional divisions), Leeds, Leicester, Liverpool, London (Imperial, King's, Queen Mary and University Colleges), Loughborough U of Technology (4 yrs S), Manchester (University and Institute of Science and Technology), Newcastle upon Tyne, Nottingham, Oxford, Reading, Salford (4 yrs S, also Mechanical Engineering Science, 3 yrs), Sheffield (also Mechanical and Management Sciences), Southampton (3 yrs, or 5 yrs S, also Acoustical Engineering), Strathclyde, Surrey (4 yrs or, exempt industrial training yr, 3 yrs, also – 4 yrs S – Mechanical Engineering with Business Economics), Sussex (also Electrical and Mechanical Engineering), Wales (at Cardiff University College – Mechanical Engineering and Energy Studies, at Swansea University College – also Electro-Mechanical Engineering, and at Institute of Science and Technology – 3 yrs, or 4 yrs S) and Warwick (3 yrs, or 4 or 5 yrs S).

Students following these courses may normally concentrate to a greater or lesser extent on Mechanical Engineering subjects, although usually not until after the first, or sometimes the second, yr. However the structure of the courses varies considerably from one university to another, and at several universities the course is a broadly-based one in Engineering Science, allowing some specialisation in Mechanical Engineering during the final yr only. (See also 'Engineering', page 134).

Postgraduate Courses (normally 1 yr and for master's degree, unless otherwise indicated) at the following
courses universities and Cranfield IT:

Acoustic and Vibration Technology, London (Imperial and Chelsea Colleges, joint course for MSc and/or College diplomas).

Advanced Functional Design Techniques for Buildings, Bristol (options in Thermal Dynamics and Aerodynamics of Buildings and in Noise and Building Acoustics, 12 months full-time or 3 yrs – modular course – part-time).

Applied Dynamics, Edinburgh (diploma).

Applied Dynamics and Mechanical Vibrations, Surrey (MSc minimum 12 months, diploma 1 academic yr).

Applied Mechanics, London (Imperial College, MSc and/or DIC) and Sheffield (diploma).

Biomechanics, Surrey (MSc minimum 12 months, diploma 1 academic yr).

Desalination Technology, Glasgow.

Design and Management for Industry, Wales (Swansea University College).

Design of Production Machines and Systems, Cranfield IT (1 or 2 yrs).

Engineering Acoustics, Noise and Vibration, Nottingham.

Engineering Design, Salford.

Engineering Thermodynamics (options include Combustion or Heat Transfer), Cranfield IT (1 or 2 yrs).

Exploitation of Materials, Leeds (12 months).

Fire Engineering, Edinburgh (MSc or diploma).

Fluid Mechanics, Bristol, Manchester (Applied Mathematics and Fluid Mechanics for MSc, Mechanics of Fluids for diploma) and Salford (Computational Methods and Fluid Mechanics).

Fluid Power (System Design or Technology), Bath.

Heat Transfer Engineering, London (Imperial College, MSc and/or DIC).

Internal Combustion, London (King's College, for MSc or College diploma).

Internal Combustion Engineering, Bath.

Machines and Vehicles, Wales (Swansea University College).

Manufacturing Technology, The City (1 yr full-time or 2 yrs part-time) and Cranfield IT (1 or 2 yrs).

Mechanical Engineering, Dundee (various options, for diploma), Manchester (Institute of Science and Technology, MSc or diploma), Newcastle upon Tyne, Sheffield and Strathclyde (several options).

Mechanical Engineering Design, Aston in Birmingham.

Mechanics and Materials, The City (1 yr full-time or 2 yrs part-time).

Mechanics, Measurement and Control of Fluids, Surrey (MSc minimum 12 months, diploma 1 academic yr).

Mechanics of Rotating Machinery, Cranfield IT (1 or 2 yrs).

Mechanics of Solids, Aston in Birmingham and Cranfield IT (1 or 2 yrs).

Plant Engineering and Terotechnology, Aston in Birmingham (12 months).

Power Plants and Related Studies (several options), Liverpool (MEng).

Refrigeration and Air Conditioning, London (King's College).

Sound and Vibration Studies (options include Industrial Noise and Vibration Control), Southampton (diploma 9 months, MSc 12 months).

Structural and Aerospace Dynamics, Cranfield IT (1 or 2 yrs).

Systems Engineering, London (Queen Mary College, MSc or College diploma) and Wales (Institute of Science and Technology, option for MSc in Management and Technology).

System Test Technology, Wales (Institute of Science and Technology).

Terotechnology, Manchester (University and Institute of Science and Technology, MSc or diploma).

Theoretical and Applied Mechanics, Manchester (Institute of Science and Technology, MSc or diploma).
Thermal Power (options in Gas Turbine or Rocket Engine Technology), Cranfield IT (1 or 2 yrs).
Thermal Power Engineering, London (Imperial College, MSc and/or DIC).
Thermodynamics and Fluid Mechanics, The City (1 yr full-time or 2 yrs part-time).
Thermodynamics and Related Studies, Birmingham.
Tribology, Leeds (12 months) and Wales (Swansea University College).
   Cranfield IT also offers 10-week modular and other short courses in various aspects of Mechanical Engineering and Manufacturing Technology.

Research facilities   At all those universities which offer first degree courses, at Essex (Fluid Mechanics Research Institute), and at Cranfield IT. Leeds: Industrial Unit of Tribology. Salford: Industrial Centre for Design and Manufacturing Engineering. Strathclyde: facilities in Mechanical Engineering Design at Institute of Advanced Machine Tool and Control Technology (Ministry of Technology). Wales (Institute of Science and Technology): Dynamic Analysis Group.

First degrees   CNAA degrees in *Mechanical Engineering* are offered at the following polytechnics and colleges (4 yrs S unless otherwise indicated). Brighton P (3 yrs). P of Central London (3 yrs). Dundee CT (also 4½ yrs S). Hatfield P, also options in *Production and Vehicle Engineering.* Huddersfield P. Kingston P. Lanchester P. Liverpool P. Manchester P. Middlesex P. Newcastle upon Tyne P. North East London P. North Staffordshire P (4½ yrs S), also *Electromechanical Engineering.* Paisley CT. Plymouth P. Portsmouth P (3 yrs). Preston P Royal Military C of Science (3 yrs). P of the South Bank, *Environmental Engineering* (also 2 yrs) and *Manufacturing Technology* (2 yrs). Sunderland P (3 yrs). Teeside P. Thames P. Trent P. P of Wales, *Plant* option. Wolverhampton P.

HND courses   (3 yrs S unless otherwise indicated) Birmingham P. Bolton IT. Bournemouth CT. Bristol P. Buckinghamshire CHE. P of Central London. Cornwall TC, with *Introductory Management Studies.* Croydon C Design and Technology. Derby C Art and Technology. Dorset IHE. Farnborough TC, *Aeronautical* option. Glasgow CT. Grimsby CT, *Refrigeration Engineering.* Gwent CHE. Hatfield P, *Aeronautical* option. Huddersfield P. Hull CT. Ipswich Civic C. Kingston P. Leeds P. Leicester P (3 yrs). Letchworth CT. Liverpool P. Luton CT. Manchester P, with *Production Engineering.* Medway and Maidstone CT. Middlesex P. Napier CC and T. Newcastle upon Tyne P. North East London P. North East Wales IHE. North Gloucestershire CT. North Staffordshire P. North Worcestershire C. Oldham CT. Oxford P. Paisley CT. Plymouth P. Portsmouth P. Preston P, with *Production Engineering* (4 yrs S), also *Mechanical/Industrial Engineering.* Richmond upon Thames C. St Helens TC, also *Mechanical Engineering for the Glass Industry.* Sheffield P. Slough CT. P of the South Bank. South East London TC. Southall CT. Stockport CT. Sunderland P. Swindon C, with *Electrical and Electronic,* and *Production.* Teesside P. Trent P. Twickenham TC. Ulster C, Northern Ireland P. P of Wales. Warley CT (entry in January). Wolverhampton P, option in *Production Engineering.*

College diplomas   (1 yr after HND unless otherwise indicated) Bolton IT (also 4 yrs S). Derby C Art and T, diploma jointly with Trent P (4 yrs S). Manchester P. Middlesex P. North Staffordshire P. Oldham CT. P of the South Bank, *Environmental Engineering* (2 yrs S) and diploma in *Refrigeration* (1 yr). Trent P. Willesden CT, diploma *Refrigeration* (3 yrs). Wolverhampton P.

Postgraduate courses   Lanchester P, MSc *Turbine Technology* (1 yr). Liverpool P, MSc *Mechanisms and Machines* (1 yr). Middlesex P, diploma *Heat Exchanger Technology* (1 yr). P of the South Bank, diploma *Environmental Engineering and Design* (1 yr), *Refrigeration* (1 yr).

Research facilities Available at the polytechnics mentioned above.

Professional courses Most colleges with advanced courses provide where necessary additional courses leading to Part 2 of the examination of the Council of Engineering Institutions (see page 135).

Engineering, Medical

See also Medical/Health Physics

First degrees University of Salford awards degrees in *Biomedical Electronics* and in Mechanical Engineering Science with specialisation in *Medical Engineering*, and University of Sussex a degree in *Electronics with Medical Instrumentation*. May also be included in first degree courses at the following universities: Manchester (Institute of Science and Technology, Medical Engineering option in Mechanical Engineering course), London (Imperial College, final-yr Engineering undergraduates can take part in certain Biomechanics Unit projects) and Surrey (Mechanical Engineering course – 4 yrs or, exempt industrial training yr, 3 yrs – provides facilities for projects related to Biomedical Engineering).

Postgraduate courses Courses (1 yr and for MSc, unless otherwise indicated) at the following universities:
Applications of Engineering in Medicine and Biology, London (Imperial College, DIC).
Bioengineering, Strathclyde (1 or 2 yrs).
Bioengineering and Biophysics in Medicine, Dundee (12 months).
Biomechanics, Surrey (MSc minimum 12 months, diploma 1 academic yr).
Bio-medical Engineering, Newcastle upon Tyne.
Biophysics and Bioengineering, London (Chelsea College, 2 yrs full-time or 3 yrs part-time).
Medical Electronics, London (St Bartholomew's Hospital Medical College).
Medical Engineering option in Mechanical Engineering courses at Manchester (Institute of Science and Technology).

Research facilities At the universities of Aberdeen, Birmingham, Glasgow, Liverpool (joint Faculty of Medicine/Faculty of Engineering Unit), London (Chelsea and Imperial Colleges and – Biomedical Engineering – King's College Hospital Medical School), Manchester (Institute of Science and Technology), Oxford (including Orthopaedic Engineering Centre), Salford, Southampton, Strathclyde (Bioengineering Unit; facilities available to Unit students include National Centre for Training and Education in Prosthetics), Surrey (Biomechanics), Sussex (Biomedical Engineering) and Warwick (Bioengineering).

Diploma courses Glasgow CT, diploma in *Prosthetics and Orthotics* (3 yrs S) (the diploma is awarded by the Scottish Technical Education Council). Lanchester P, *Electrical and Electronic Engineering* with *Biomedical Electronics* option (4 yrs S). Paddington TC, certificate of *Prosthetist* or *Orthotist* (4 yrs) (10 weeks of each year in college, last year spent in clinical work). Certification is arranged in conjunction with the examinations of the British Institute of Surgical Technicians.

Research facilities North Staffordshire P.

Engineering, Nuclear

First degrees Degrees with specialisation in *Nuclear Engineering* awarded by universities of London (Queen Mary College, also Nuclear Reactor Science and Technology, and Energy Engineering) and Manchester. First degree courses may include some study of Nuclear Engineering at the universities of Glasgow (additional subject for BSc in Engineering), Liverpool (option for final-yr BEng students) and Nottingham.

Postgraduate Courses (1 yr and for MSc, unless otherwise indicated) at the following universities:
courses *Nuclear Engineering*, Liverpool (option in MEng course in Power Plants and Related Studies).
Nuclear Power, Dundee (included in Mechanical Engineering diploma courses) and London (Imperial College, MSc and/or DIC).
Nuclear Reactor Science and Engineering, London (Imperial and Queen Mary Colleges, joint course for MSc or College diplomas).
Nuclear Technology, Surrey (MSc minimum 12 months, diploma 9 months).
Physics and Technology of Nuclear Reactors, Birmingham.

Research At the following universities: Aston in Birmingham, Bath (Centre for Nuclear Studies),
facilities Birmingham, Liverpool, London (Imperial and Queen Mary Colleges), Manchester, Nottingham, Oxford, Southampton and Strathclyde; also at Scottish Universities Research and Reactor Centre, East Kilbride. Manchester and Liverpool: (joint) Universities Research Reactor.

First degrees CNAA degrees in *Mechanical Engineering* are offered at Middlesex P with option in *Nuclear Power*.

Postgraduate P of the South Bank, MSc *Applied Nuclear Physics* (1 yr).
courses

Engineering, Production
(including Machine Tool Technology)
See also Operational Research

First degrees Degrees with specialisation awarded by the following universities:
Design and Manufacture, Loughborough U of Technology (3 yrs, or – for BSc and DIS – 4 yrs S).
Engineering Manufacture and Management, Manchester (Institute of Science and Technology).
Industrial Engineering, Belfast.
Manufacturing Management with Technology, Brunel (4 yrs S).
Manufacturing Systems Engineering, Bradford (alone or with Psychology, 4 yrs S).
Production Engineering/Engineering Production, Aston in Birmingham (3 yrs, or 4 yrs S), Bath (3 yrs, or 4 yrs S), Birmingham (also with Economics, 3 yrs for Joint Honours BSc, 4 yrs for Double Honours BSc & BCom), The City (3 yrs, or 4 yrs S), Loughborough U of Technology (with Management, 4 yrs S), Nottingham, Strathclyde (with Management, also in Technology and Business Studies course) and Wales (Institute of Science and Technology, 3 yrs, or 4 yrs S).
Production Technology (with Production Management or Mechanical Engineering), Brunel (4 yrs S, applicants should normally be sponsored by UK firm or organisation).
Production Engineering may also be offered as a subject for first degrees in Engineering

(usually Mechanical) at Bath, Bradford (also in Industrial Technology and Management course), Glasgow (Production Management), Heriot-Watt and Salford.

Some study of *Machine Tool Technology* included in first degree courses in Engineering at Belfast and Nottingham (Mechanical Engineering).

Postgraduate courses   Courses (1 yr and for master's degree, unless otherwise indicated) at the following universities and Cranfield IT:

Design of Production Machines and Systems, Cranfield IT (1 or 2 yrs).

Design of Production Systems, Loughborough U of Technology (MSc or associateship, also constitutes 1st yr of 3-yr PhD programme in Total Technology).

Engineering Design, Loughborough U of Technology (MTech or associateship).

Engineering Management, Wales (Swansea University College).

Engineering Production, Aston in Birmingham (certificate, 3 months, in Principles of Production Engineering), Birmingham (with Management Studies, also short courses), Newcastle upon Tyne (diploma or certificate) and Strathclyde (diploma).

Food Process Engineering, Reading (option for MSc in Food Technology at National College of Food Technology, 12 months).

Industrial Engineering, Belfast (12 months).

Industrial Engineering and Administration, Cranfield IT (1 or 2 yrs, options include Industrial Engineering or Production Control).

Machine Tool Technology, Birmingham.

Machine Tool Technology and Design, Manchester (Institute of Science and Technology, MSc or diploma).

Manufacturing Technology, Cranfield IT (with options in Machine Tool Design, Numerical Control, Optical Production Technology or Precision Engineering, 1 or 2 yrs).

Production, Brunel.

Production Management and Manufacturing Technology, Strathclyde (1 or 2 yrs).

Production Technology and Management, Aston in Birmingham.

Quality and Reliability Engineering, Birmingham.

Systems Engineering, Wales (Institute of Science and Technology, option for MSc in Management and Technology).

Work Design and Ergonomics, Birmingham.

Research facilities   At most of the universities named above (Manchester, Institute of Science and Technology) and at Cranfield IT. Birmingham: Institute of Engineering Production. Loughborough U of Technology: Centre for Industrial Studies; Engineering Design Centre. Salford: Industrial Centre for Design and Manufacturing Engineering. Strathclyde: Institute of Advanced Machine Tool and Control Technology (Ministry of Technology).

First degrees   CNAA degrees in *Production Engineering* are offered at the following polytechnics and colleges (4 yrs S).

Engineering Product Design, P of the South Bank.

Industrial Engineering, Dundee CT. Hatfield P.

Industrial Design and Technology, Napier CC and T.

Manufacturing Engineering, Liverpool P.

Manufacturing Technology, P of the South Bank (2 yrs).

Mechanical and Production Engineering, Birmingham P. Brighton P. Sheffield P.

HND courses   In *Mechanical and Production Engineering* or *Mechanical Engineering* with *Production* option (indicated by (P)) (3 yrs S). Birmingham P. Bolton IT (P). Farnborough CT (P). Hatfield P. Kingston P (P). Lanchester P. Medway and Maidstone CT. North East London P. North

Worcestershire C (P). Preston P. Salford CT, *Product Design.* Sheffield P. South East London C. Southall TC (P). Southampton CT. Swindon College (P). Trent P. Ulster C, Northern Ireland P. Warley CT (entry in January). Willesden CT (4 yrs S).

Postgraduate and post-diploma courses (1 yr after HND unless otherwise indicated): Birmingham P (4 yrs S or 1 yr). Medway and Maidstone CT, College associateship (1 yr). Colchester IHE, diploma (3 months). P of the South Bank, advanced diploma in *Work Study* (1 yr). Trent P (1 yr).

College diploma Willesden CT (4 yrs S).

Research facilities Birmingham P. Brighton P. Huddersfield P. Lanchester P. Leicester P. Liverpool P. Manchester P. Plymouth P. Sheffield P. P of the South Bank. Trent P. Polytechnic of Wales.

Professional courses Most colleges with advanced courses provide where necessary additional courses leading to Part 2 of the examination of the Council of Engineering Institutions (see page 135).

Engineering, Public Health and Municipal

First degrees BSc(Eng) in *Civil and Municipal Engineering* awarded by University of London (courses at University College) and BSc in *Environmental Health* by universities of Aston in Birmingham (4 yrs S) and Strathclyde. Some study of Public Health/Municipal Engineering included in many Civil Engineering courses.

Postgraduate courses Courses in *Public Health Engineering* (1 yr, unless otherwise indicated) at the universities of Dundee (for diploma in Civil Engineering), London (Imperial College, MSc and/or DIC), Newcastle upon Tyne (MSc, diploma or certificate) and Strathclyde (diploma 1 yr, MSc 1 or 2 yrs).

Research facilities At most of the universities and colleges named above, and at Salford.

English as a Foreign Language: Courses for Teachers

For English Language and Literature, see page 156; see also Education, and Language Studies

Postgraduate courses Courses (1 yr and for diploma, unless otherwise indicated) at the following universities (some of these courses may be open to non-graduates with suitable qualifications and/or experience):

Applied Linguistics, Edinburgh (for graduates with at least 3 yrs' experience in teaching of English as a second language or teaching of other languages, also MLitt, 2 yrs) and Essex (MA, for qualified and experienced graduate teachers of foreign languages in Britain or of English as a foreign language overseas).

Applied Linguistics, Phonetics and the Teaching of English, Essex (for graduates or equivalent with at least 3 yrs' appropriate professional experience, also 10-week certificate course in Applied Linguistics and the Teaching of English for teachers, or intending teachers, who are not native English speakers but have reached a high standard of proficiency in English).

Bilingual Education, Wales (Aberystwyth University College, College certificate, mainly for graduates).

English and Education, London (Institute of Education, MPhil, 2 yrs).

English as a Second Language, Leeds (postgraduate, principally for British graduates – includes some professional training in teaching although graduates with teaching experience may also take the course).

English as a Second or Foreign Language, Wales (Bangor University College, for graduates with teaching experience, diploma or MA).

English Language and Literature for Overseas Students (including intending teachers of English), Exeter (see under 'English Language and Literature', page 156).

English Language Teaching, Exeter (testamur – for which all candidates register initially – and diploma – transfer to which depends on satisfactory performance in 1st term's work – in Education (English Language Teaching), for qualified teachers with, normally, at least 3 yrs' approved teaching experience).

General and Applied Linguistics, Reading (for experienced or qualified graduate teachers of English from overseas).

Linguistics for English Language Teaching, Lancaster (MA).

Teaching of English as a Foreign Language, Leicester (certificate course for English language teachers from French-speaking Africa), London (Institute of Education, primarily for graduates, though non-graduates with good professional qualifications may be admitted, also graduate certificate in Education with special reference to the Teaching of English as a Foreign Language, for which overseas candidates should preferably have had several yrs' teaching experience and for which candidates' mother tongue should normally be English) and Wales (Institute of Science and Technology, also option within MEd – joint course with Cardiff University College).

Teaching of English Overseas, Leeds (certificate or diploma, for administrative officers and teachers from overseas with, normally, suitable school-teaching or other approved experience) and Manchester (for British and foreign graduates and teachers).

Diploma and certificate courses

Birmingham P, courses may be arranged for teachers from overseas (1 term or 1 yr). Moray House CE, diploma in the Teaching of English as a Second Language for trained teachers; (i) introductory and intermediate stages in primary and secondary schools; (ii) at senior stages (1 yr). Postgraduate diploma in Linguistics and English Language teaching (1 yr).

London: Ealing CHE, diploma in English Studies for foreign students with provision of practical study for teachers.

Courses leading to the Royal Society of Arts certificate in the Teaching of English as a Second or Foreign Language (Adults) are available at Birmingham P, Preston P and 33 colleges and Schools of English. (For British graduates and qualified teachers and for teachers of English from overseas, 1 yr.) Further details are available from the RSA and from *Academic Courses in Great Britain* (see page 265).

English Language and Literature

See also Language Studies; for Courses for Teachers of English as a Foreign Language, see page 154

First degrees Degrees with specialisation involving the study of both *English Language* and *English Literature* awarded by the following universities: Aberdeen, Belfast, Birmingham, Bristol, Cambridge, Dundee, Durham, East Anglia (Honours in School of English and American Studies with specialisation in English Literature, also in Comparative Literature including English and/or American Literature with European Literature), Edinburgh, Exeter (also English Medieval Studies), Glasgow, Hull, Keele (only with another principal subject), Lancaster, Leeds, Leicester, Liverpool, London (Bedford, Birkbeck (part-time), King's, Queen Mary, Royal Holloway, University and Westfield Colleges, also Goldsmiths' College), Loughborough U of Technology (English Studies), Manchester, Newcastle upon Tyne, Nottingham, Oxford, Reading, St Andrews, Sheffield, Southampton, Stirling, Strathclyde, New U of Ulster, Wales (Aberystwyth, Bangor, Cardiff, Swansea and St David's University Colleges, and – Modern English Studies – Institute of Science and Technology) and York (either predominantly literary course, or English Language as area of specialisation, with Linguistics and another language, for degree in Language).

Degrees with specialisation entirely or mainly in *English Language* awarded by the following universities: Cambridge (Anglo-Saxon, Norse and Celtic Tripos), Durham (English Language and Medieval Literature), Leeds (English Language and (Medieval) Literature), Newcastle upon Tyne and Sheffield (for York, see above). Degrees with specialisation entirely or mainly in *English Literature* awarded by the following universities: Cambridge, Essex (School of Comparative Studies), Exeter, Kent at Canterbury (also Renaissance Studies), Leeds, Newcastle upon Tyne, Sheffield and Sussex (in Schools of African and Asian, English and American, Cultural and Community, and European Studies). (For East Anglia and York, see above). At Aberdeen students may under certain circumstances specialise in either Language or Literature in final stage of English course.

At many of the universities named above, English, or English Language, or English Literature, may also be studied with another principal subject for a Joint (or Combined) Honours degree; and the curricula for first degrees in arts may include less specialised study of English.

The independent University College at Buckingham (see page 32) awards a licence in the School of History, Politics and English Literature.

English Studies for Overseas Students (see also under 'Postgraduate courses', below) – courses especially intended for overseas students:

Applied Linguistics and the Teaching of English, Essex (certificate, 10 weeks – see page 155).

English as a Foreign Language, Edinburgh (1 yr, for those whose native language is not English, as part of MA or BCom course) and London (London School of Economics, for those whose native tongue is not English, also special course in Phonetics of English for Foreign Students at University College).

English Language and Literature for Overseas Students, Exeter (1 yr, for testamur, for students of English from foreign countries – or for intending teachers of English – who must *at the least* be qualified for admission to universities in their own countries; students currently attending courses – preferably specialising in English – at European universities may be admitted to courses for 1 or 2 terms; in addition special English Literature courses provided for American students spending 1 yr in the university to follow courses in other departments).

English Studies, Nottingham (certificate, 2 terms, intended for students who are reading English as a degree subject in their own country).

Postgraduate Courses (1 yr and for MA, unless otherwise indicated) at the following universities:
courses *Anglo-Irish Literature*, Leeds and New U of Ulster.
Anglo-Irish Studies, Belfast.
Bibliography and Textual Criticism, Leeds.
Comparative Literary Studies, Manchester and St Andrews (diploma 1 yr, MLitt 2 yrs).
Comparative Literature, Sussex and Warwick.
Dialectology, Leeds.
Drama, see 'Drama and Theatre'.
Early Modern English Language 1500–1800, Lancaster.
Eighteenth Century English Literature, London (Queen Mary College).
Eighteenth Century English Studies, Lancaster.
English, Glasgow (MPhil, 2 yrs), Wales (Aberystwyth and – MA or diploma – Bangor University Colleges) and York (12 months).
English and American Literature, Kent at Canterbury.
English and American Literature of the Twentieth Century, Newcastle upon Tyne.
English History and Literature, East Anglia.
English History and Literature 1880–1920, Sheffield.
English Language, New U of Ulster.
English Language and General Linguistics, Newcastle upon Tyne (MA 1 yr, MPhil 2 yrs).
English Language and Literature after 1525, London (Queen Mary College – either 1660–1790 or 1880 to present day).
English Language and Literature before 1525, London (University College).
English Language and Medieval Literature, Durham and Leeds.
English Literature, East Anglia, Leeds, Liverpool (BPhil, 1 or 2 yrs), Manchester, Sussex, Wales (Bangor University College) and Warwick.
English Literature and Fine Art, Birmingham.
English Literature and its Background (*1830–75*), Leicester.
English Literature before 1525, London (Queen Mary College).
English Studies, Edinburgh (English Literature or English Language or Medieval English Studies – diploma 1 yr, MLitt 2 yrs), Leeds (diploma) and Oxford (BPhil, 2 yrs, various options in Modern and Medieval English Studies).
Folk Life Studies, Leeds (MA or diploma).
General and Comparative Literature of 2 or 3 languages, Oxford (BPhil, 2 yrs).
Literature and Cultural Change in the Twentieth Century, Lancaster (1 yr full-time or 2 yrs part-time).
Medieval English Language or *Literature*, Sheffield.
Medieval English Literature, Bristol, Newcastle upon Tyne (MA 1 yr, MPhil 2 yrs) and Wales (Cardiff University College).
Medieval Literature and History, Birmingham (1 or 2 yrs).
Medieval Studies, Aberdeen (including Old and Middle English, for MLitt), Leeds, Manchester (MA or diploma), St Andrews (diploma 1 yr, MLitt 2 yrs) and York (12 months).
Middle English and Medieval French, Lancaster.
Middle English Literature, Reading (11 months full-time or 22 months part-time).
Modern African Literature, Sheffield.
Modern English, Leeds.
Modern English and American Literature, Leicester.
Modern English Literature, Reading (11 months full-time or 22 months part-time) and Wales (Cardiff University College).
Nineteenth Century Literature and *Renaissance Literature*, New U of Ulster.
Shakespeare Studies, Birmingham.
Sociology of Literature and *Theory and Practice of Literary Translation*, Essex (School of Comparative Studies, each 12 months).

Twentieth Century English Literature, London (Queen Mary College).
Victorian Literature, Hull (BPhil).
Victorian Studies, Keele (2 yrs) and Leicester.

ENGLISH STUDIES FOR OVERSEAS STUDENTS – postgraduate courses (for others, see above) especially intended for overseas students (1 yr for diploma, unless otherwise indicated): *Applied Linguistics, Phonetics and the Teaching of English*, Essex – see page 155.
English as a Second or Foreign Language, Wales (Bangor University College, for graduates with teaching experience).
English for Overseas Graduates, Wales (Swansea University College, College diploma for graduates in English who wish to pursue postgraduate work in English).
English Studies, Edinburgh (for foreign students), Leeds (for those who are, or wish to become, lecturers and tutors in English) and Nottingham.

Research facilities	At all universities offering first degree courses. Birmingham: Shakespeare Institute (sixteenth and seventeenth century literature) and Centre for Contemporary Cultural Studies.

First degrees	CNAA degrees are offered at the following (3 yrs). Birmingham P. Cambridgeshire C Art T. East Sussex CHE, with *Art, History, Music* or *Religious Studies*. Edge Hill CHE (validated by U of Lancaster). Goldsmiths' C. King Alfred's C, with *History* or *Drama*. Kingston P, *Modern Arts– English, French* and *History*. Newcastle upon Tyne P, *English* and *History*. P of North London. Portsmouth P, *English* with *French Literature* (4 yrs S), and *Latin Literature*. Roehampton IHE. West London IHE, *English and Linguistics*. English is usually available as a subject in general Arts degrees (see page 90).
Diploma course	City of London P, certificate in English as a Foreign language (3 yrs). Ealing TC, diploma in English Studies for foreign students (1 yr).
Research facilities	Middlesex P. Newcastle upon Tyne P.

Environmental Studies

See also Education; Public and Industrial Health; and Town and Country Planning

First degrees	Degrees with specialisation awarded by the following universities: *Agricultural and Environmental Science*, Newcastle upon Tyne. *Archaeology with Environment*, London (Institute of Archaeology). *Architecture and Environmental Design*, Nottingham. *Architecture, Planning, Building and Environmental Studies*, London (University College). *Art and Environment* (with Geography), Lancaster. *Biology of Man and His Environment*, Aston in Birmingham (alone or with another subject). *Earth and Environmental Science* (provisional), Stirling. *Ecology*, see under 'Biology'. *Energy and Environment*, London (Westfield College). *Environmental Biology*, Liverpool, London (Chelsea and Queen Mary Colleges), Nottingham, Wales (Aberystwyth and Swansea University Colleges) and York (Human and Environmental Biology).

Environmental Chemical Engineering, Exeter.

Environmental Chemistry, Brunel (Medicinal, Agricultural and Environmental Chemistry, 4 yrs S), Edinburgh and London (Wye College).

Environmental Engineering, Bath, The City (Environmental Engineering (Buildings), 4 yrs S), London (University College, Civil, Structural and Environmental Engineering), Loughborough U of Technology (4 yrs S), Newcastle upon Tyne (Natural Environmental Engineering, also Civil and Environmental Engineering) and Strathclyde.

Environmental Health, Aston in Birmingham (4 yrs S) and Strathclyde.

Environmental Physics, Kent at Canterbury (Environmental Physical Science) and New U of Ulster.

Environmental Planning, Aston in Birmingham.

Environmental Plant Geography, Reading.

Environmental Science, Bradford (also with Chemistry and Pollution Control, each 4 yrs S), London (Bedford and Westfield Colleges), Sheffield (Natural Environmental Science), Sussex (School of Molecular Sciences), New U of Ulster and Wales (Aberystwyth University College and – with Pure and Applied Chemistry – Institute of Science and Technology).

Environmental Sciences, East Anglia, Lancaster (alone or as part of Geophysics), Salford, Southampton and Warwick (alone or with one of certain other subjects).

Environmental Studies, Dundee, London (University College) and Wales (with another subject at Cardiff University College, Civil Engineering and Environmental Studies at Swansea University College).

Health Physics and Environmental Physics, Salford.

Human Environmental Studies, London (King's College).

Rural Environment Studies, London (Wye College).

Science of Resources, Birmingham.

Urban Studies, Kent at Canterbury.

Water Resources (Engineering) (with another subject), Aston in Birmingham.

Environmental Studies may also be included in final yr of BSc courses at Birmingham (Chemistry) and The City (Marine Environment Studies, for degree in Systems and Management).

Postgraduate courses   Courses (1 yr and for master's degree, unless otherwise indicated) at the following universities and at Cranfield IT and Royal College of Art:

Advanced Functional Design Techniques for Buildings (Environmental option), Bristol (12 months full-time or 3 yrs – modular course – part-time).

Building Science and Environmental Design, Newcastle upon Tyne (2 yrs, for MPhil in Architecture).

Combustion Science and Pollution Control, Sheffield.

Energy Conservation and the Environment, Cranfield IT (1 or 2 yrs).

Environmental and Energy Aspects of Automative Engine Design and Operation, Southampton (12 months).

Environmental Aspects of Building Design, Manchester.

Environmental Conservation, Heriot-Watt (diploma, also – 9 months full-time plus 12 months' non-residential study – MSc).

Environmental Control Engineering and Resource Utilisation and *Environmental Control in Industry,* Strathclyde (diploma 1 yr, MSc 1 or 2 yrs).

Environmental Design, Royal College of Art (2 yrs).

Environmental Design and Engineering, London (University College, option in MSc in Architecture).

Environmental Engineering, Southampton (option for diploma – 9 months – or MSc – 12 months – in Sound and Vibration Studies).

Environmental Planning, Nottingham (2 yrs) and Reading (diploma 21 months, MPhil 24 months).

Environmental Planning and Design, Aston in Birmingham.

Environmental Planning for Developing Countries, Nottingham (2 yrs).

Environmental Pollution Control, Leeds (12 months).

Environmental Psychology, Surrey (12 months).

Environmental Resources, Salford.

Environmental Technology, London (Imperial College, for MSc and/or DIC).

Human Environment, London (Institute of Archaeology).

Integrated Land Resources Survey, Reading (2 yrs).

Land Policy and the Environment, Cambridge (option in Development Studies course).

Pollution and Environmental Control, Manchester (University and Institute of Science and Technology, MSc or diploma).

Radiation and Environmental Protection, Surrey (MSc minimum 12 months, diploma 9 months).

Resource Management, Edinburgh (diploma 9 months, MSc 12 months).

Urban and Regional Studies, Sussex.

Urban Design, Heriot-Watt (also diploma) and Manchester.

Urban Studies, Salford.

Urban Studies (Developing Countries), London (University College, College diploma). See also under 'Transport'.

Research facilities   At the following universities: Birmingham (Centre for Urban and Regional Studies), Bradford, East Anglia (including Centre of East Anglian Studies), Exeter, Glasgow (Building Services Research Unit), Heriot-Watt, Kent at Canterbury (including Centre for Research in the Social Sciences), Lancaster, London (Chelsea and University Colleges and – including Countryside Planning Unit – Wye College), Loughborough U of Technology (Centre for Transport Engineering Practice), Manchester (Pollution Research Centre, Centre for Urban and Regional Research), Newcastle upon Tyne, Reading, Southampton, Surrey (Conservation Science Group), Sussex (Centre for Contemporary European Studies, Institute of Development Studies, Science Policy Research Unit), New U of Ulster and Warwick; and at Cranfield IT (including Centre for Transport Studies).

First degrees   CNAA degrees are offered at the following: Derby C Art and T, *Earth and Life Sciences* (3 yrs). Huddersfield P, *Human Ecology*. Leeds P, *Environmental Health* (4 yrs S). Leicester P, *Science and the Environment* (3 yrs). Plymouth P, *Environmental Sciences* (3 yrs). Roehampton IHE, *Environmental Sciences* (3 yrs) (U of London degree). P of the South Bank, *Environmental Engineering* (4 yrs S). Sunderland P, *Environmental Studies* (3 yrs). Thames P, *Environmental Health*. West London IHE, *Environmental Sciences*.

Courses in *Environmental Studies* are available as part of Science degrees at the following: Lanchester P, *Physical Science/Materials Technology*. Oxford P, *Science*.

Many teacher training establishments offer options in Environmental Studies in their degree and certificate courses – see *Handbook of Institutions providing . . . Teacher Training . . .* (page 265).

College diplomas   Highbury TC, *Environmental Health Inspector's* Diploma (3 yrs S). Sheffield P, CNAA diploma *Water Engineering and Pollution Control* ($2\frac{1}{2}$ terms). P of the South Bank, diploma in *Environmental Engineering* (2 yrs S), postgraduate diploma in *Environmental Engineering and Design* (1 yr).

Postgraduate course   Edinburgh C Art (MSc Heriot-Watt University), *Environmental Conservation* (1 yr).

*Research
facilities*

P of Central London. Plymouth P. P of the South Bank.

Ergonomics and Cybernetics

First degrees

Degrees with specialisation awarded by the following universities: *Cybernetics Science*, Kent at Canterbury (Computers and Cybernetics) and Reading (also Cybernetics and Control Engineering); *Ergonomics*, Aston in Birmingham (with another subject), Loughborough U of Technology (Ergonomics (Applied Human Sciences)) and Wales (Institute of Science and Technology, Occupational Psychology – Personnel Psychology and Ergonomics, 3 yrs or 4 yrs S). At the following universities Ergonomics and/or Cybernetics are included in the first degree courses indicated: Birmingham (Engineering Production), Brunel (various) and Nottingham (Production Engineering).

*Postgraduate
courses*

Courses (1 yr and for MSc, unless otherwise indicated) at the following universities:
Applied Psychology for Engineers, Aston in Birmingham (12 months).
Cybernetics and Instrument Technology, Reading (12 months).
Ergonomics, Loughborough U of Technology (MSc or associateship).
Ergonomics (Human Factors in Work, Design and Production), London (intercollegiate course, 1
    yr full-time or 2 yrs part-time, jointly by Birkbeck and University Colleges, Guy's and
    Royal Free Hospital Medical Schools and London School of Hygiene and Tropical
    Medicine).
Industrial Psychology (including Engineering Psychology and Ergonomics), Hull.
Work Design and Ergonomics, Birmingham.
    At London (Queen Mary College) Ergonomics and Cybernetics are included in MSc course in Systems Engineering and at Wales (Institute of Science and Technology) Ergonomics is included in diploma (9 months) and MSc (2 yrs) courses in Psychology.

*Research
facilities*

At the following universities: Aston in Birmingham, Bath, Birmingham, Brunel (Cybernetics), London (Ergonomics at Birkbeck College, Cybernetics at Chelsea College), Loughborough U of Technology (Centre for Transport Engineering Practice, Institute for Consumer Ergonomics), Reading (Cybernetics), Southampton and Wales (Institute of Science and Technology).

Estate and Farm Management

First degrees

Degrees with specialisation awarded by the following universities:
Estate Management, Heriot-Watt (4 yrs, or 5 yrs S).
Land Economy, Aberdeen and Cambridge (2 yrs for candidates who have obtained Honours in
    another Tripos, which will usually be Part I Economics).
Land Management, Reading.
    At Reading and Wales (Bangor University College) *Farm Management* is included in degree courses in Agriculture/Agricultural Economics.

*Postgraduate
courses*

Courses (1 yr and for master's degree, unless otherwise indicated) at the following universities:
Agricultural Management, Reading.
Agriculture (Farm Management), Leeds (diploma).

Farm Business Administration, London (diploma, Wye College).
Farm Business Economics, Belfast.
Forestry and its Relation to Land Management, Oxford.
Land Economy, Cambridge.
Land Policy and the Environment, Cambridge (option in Development Studies course).
Recreational Land Management Studies, Reading.
Rural and Regional Resources Planning, Aberdeen (21 months).
Rural Planning Studies and *Urban Land Appraisal,* Reading (each 12 months).

Research facilities

At the universities of Aberdeen (Land Economy), Belfast, London (Wye College) and Reading.

First degrees

CNAA degrees are offered at the following polytechnics and colleges (3 yrs unless otherwise indicated).
Estate Management, Leicester P. Oxford P. P of the South Bank (4 yrs S). Thames P.
Housing Administration, Bristol P.
Land Administration, North East London P. Portsmouth P, *Urban Land Administration.*
Land Economics, Paisley CT (4 yrs). Sheffield P, *Urban Land Economics,* also *Housing Studies* (both 4 yrs S).
Urban Estate Management, P of Central London. Liverpool P. P of Wales.
Valuation and Estate Management, Bristol P.

TEC HD courses

Leicester P, *Estate Management.* North East London P, *Estate Management* (3 yrs S). Trent P, *Estate Management and Valuation* (2 yrs).

College diplomas

(3 yrs unless otherwise indicated) Birmingham P. Bristol P, *Valuation and Estate Management,* also *Housing Management.* Kingston P. Leicester P, Technician course (2 yrs). Royal AgC, *Rural Estate Management.* Sheffield P, *Land Administration* (2 yrs). P of the South Bank, postgraduate diploma *Property Development Studies* (2 yrs). Trent P, with *Valuation* (2 yrs). Ulster C, Northern Ireland P. Willesden CT (4 yrs).

Post-diploma courses

Courses in *Farm Management* (1 yr): North of Scotland CAg. Royal AgC. Seale-Hayne AgC.

Research facilities

P of the South Bank.

Professional courses

A number of colleges and polytechnics offer courses leading to the examinations of the Incorporated Society of Valuers and Auctioneers. For full details, one should contact the Society.

European Studies

See also separate languages/studies – French, German, etc; also Art and Design, and Law

First degrees

Degrees with specialisation in *European Studies* awarded by the following universities (some courses may include a period of study abroad): Bath (majoring in French or German with Italian or Russian as minor language, or jointly in French and either German or Spanish), Birmingham (European Integration in BSocSc School of International Studies), Bradford (3 main options –

Eastern Europe with German or Western Europe with either French or German, also European Industrial Studies – French with either Communications or Textiles, all 4 yrs S), Brunel (Economics or Government and European Studies, both involving economics, government studies and languages, also Engineering, Social and European Studies, all 4 yrs S), East Anglia (European Literature and History with France, Germany, Italy, Russia or Scandinavia as main countries, also joint programme in European and Social Studies), Edinburgh (European Institutions and the European Movement or European Economic Law for MA or LLB, also joint Honours courses in French or German with (Contemporary) European Institutions or European History), Hull (including study of 2 languages and with specialisation in later yrs in either literature, history or social science), Kent at Canterbury (specialising in one of: economics, politics and government, sociology, history, French, German, Italian, also BA in Renaissance Studies), Lancaster, London (combining language-based course with French, German, Russian or Spanish, or with Classical Studies, at Queen Mary College, also Central European or South-East European Regional Studies at School of Slavonic and East European Studies), Loughborough U of Technology (Modern European Studies, also – in Department of European Studies – Government taken with either applied economics or a language), Manchester (Institute of Science and Technology, majoring in French or German or Russian, alone or with Mathematics), Southampton (Modern European and American History), Sussex (with wide choice of major subject(s)), New U of Ulster (East European Studies with emphasis on non-literary subjects after 1st yr, or West European Studies involving French or German languages, culture and society plus a range of options in other fields) and Warwick (Spanish and European Studies including history, literature and theatre, also English or French or Italian and European Literature).

Most degree courses in subjects such as economics, geography, history and political science, and also some courses in individual European languages/studies, include courses relating to Europe (Essex: School of Comparative Studies, especially for degrees in Art History and Theory, History and Literature).

The independent University College at Buckingham (see page 32) awards a licence in the School of European Studies.

Postgraduate courses . Courses (1 yr and for master's degree, unless otherwise indicated) at the following universities:

Area Studies (Europe), London (University College and – the Impact of Religious Change on Society in Early Modern Europe – Royal Holloway College).

Area Studies of Eastern Europe and Russia (economics, history, politics etc), London (School of Slavonic and East European Studies, 9 months or 12 months).

Comparative Literary Studies, Manchester and St Andrews (diploma 1 yr, MLitt 2 yrs).

Comparative Literature, East Anglia and Sussex.

Contemporary European Studies, Sussex.

European Community Studies, London (Queen Mary College) and Manchester (including various options in law, politics, economics, geography, social policy and administration).

European Economic Studies, Exeter.

European History, East Anglia, Oxford (BPhil, 2 yrs) and Wales (Cardiff University College).

European Land Use Studies, Reading (2 yrs).

European Legal Studies, Exeter (12 months).

European Literature, East Anglia.

European Political Studies, Leicester.

European Politics, Hull (BPhil).

European Studies, London (London School of Economics, 1 or 2 yrs) and Reading (MA 1 yr, MPhil 2 yrs, in Graduate School of Contemporary European Studies – wide range of options).

International Relations, Oxford (BPhil, 2 yrs).

Language Studies (for modern language graduates interested in careers as professional linguists in international organisations), Bath (diploma).
Politics and Government of Western Europe, London (London School of Economics, for MSc in Politics).
Western European Politics, Essex (12 months).

At Edinburgh, teaching in the structures and law of the European communities is provided for all postgraduate students in relevant fields; and at many other universities postgraduate courses in subjects such as economics, geography, history and political science include courses relating to Europe.

Research facilities   At most of the universities named in the paragraphs above, and at Aberdeen and Sheffield. Edinburgh: Centre of European Governmental Studies (of which library is a depository library for the European communities). Exeter: Centre for European Legal Studies. London: London School of Economics; Queen Mary College (European Documentation Centre); Wye College (Centre for European Agricultural Studies); Institute of Historical Research; School of Slavonic and East European Studies. Reading: Graduate School of Contemporary European Studies. Sussex: Centre for Contemporary European Studies; Institute of Manpower Studies. Essex, Nuffield College (Oxford) and Strathclyde are members of the European Consortium for Political Research.

First degrees   CNAA degrees are offered at the following polytechnics and colleges (3 yrs). Brighton P, *British Studies* (3 yrs or 4 yrs S). Cambridgeshire C Arts and T, Joint Honours *Arts* with option in *European Thought and Literature*. Ealing CHE, *Modern European Studies*. La Sainte Union CHE, *Modern Languages and European Studies* (4 yrs). Leeds P, *European Languages and Institutions* (4 yrs). Middlesex P, *European Business Administration* (4 yrs S). North East London P, *Social Studies (Modern France)* (4 yrs S). P of North London, *Contemporary European Studies*. Trent P, *Modern European Studies*. Wolverhampton P, *European Studies* (4 yrs).

Postgraduate course   Leeds P, *European Management Programme* (2 yrs).

Other courses   Brighton P, certificate in *British Studies* (1 yr).

Research facilities   Brighton P. Huddersfield P. Portsmouth P.

The sections *Arts (General)* and *Language Studies* should also be consulted.

Food Science and Technology
See also Dietetics and Nutrition

First degrees   Degrees with specialisation awarded by the following universities:
Brewing, Heriot-Watt (3 yrs, or, with Biochemistry or Microbiology, 4 yrs).
Food Science, Belfast, Leeds (alone, or with Biochemistry or Microbiology or Physiology), London (Queen Elizabeth College, with Chemistry or Physics or Physiology, also Food and Management Science), Nottingham (including Microbiology), Reading (also Food Science and Food Economics, and Chemistry and Food Science), Strathclyde and

Surrey (Nutrition (Food Science), 4 yrs S, also included in BSc courses in Hotel and Catering Administration, Home Economics, Microbiology and Nutrition).
Food Technology, Loughborough U of Technology (Food Processing Technology, 3 yrs, or – for BSc and DIS – 4 yrs S) and Reading (4 yrs S, at National College of Food Technology).

Postgraduate courses Courses (1 yr and for MSc, unless otherwise indicated) at the following universities:
Brewing, Birmingham (Brewing Science) and Heriot-Watt (diploma).
Food and Management Science, London (Queen Elizabeth College).
Food Engineering, Leeds (12 months).
Food Resources Related to Community Development, London (Queen Elizabeth College, diploma).
Food Science, Leeds (MSc 12 months, diploma 1 or 2 yrs) and Reading (12 months, options in General Food Science, Dairy Science, Public Health, Analysis of Food and Drugs).
Food Science and Microbiology, Strathclyde (1 or 2 yrs).
Food Technology, Reading (12 months, at National College of Food Technology, options in Food Microbiology, Food Quality Control, Food Process Engineering).
Meat Science, Bristol (expected to begin 1978 or 1979) and Nottingham (12 months).

Research facilities At the following universities: Birmingham, Heriot-Watt, Leeds, London (Queen Elizabeth College, also Wye College – Hop Research laboratories and experimental gardens), Loughborough U of Technology, Nottingham, Reading, Strathclyde and Surrey; also at Scottish Universities Research and Reactor Centre, East Kilbride.

First degrees CNAA degree in *Food Science* at P of the South Bank (4 yrs S).

HND courses (2 yrs unless otherwise stated):
Applied Biology (Food Science), South Glamorgan IHE (3 yrs S).
Baking Technology, P of the South Bank. South Glamorgan IHE (3 yrs S).
Food Technology, Bristol P. Glasgow C Food Technology. Grimsby CT (3 yrs S). Loughry C Agriculture and Food Technology (3 yrs). Manchester P. Seale-Hayne AgC (3 yrs S). West of Scotland AgC (3 yrs).

Diplomas and certificates *Bakery and Confectionery*, South Glamorgan IHE (1 yr).
Bakery Supervisors/Technicians diploma, Manchester P (1 yr).
Confectionery Design and Decoration, P of the South Bank (1 yr).
Fish Processing, Grimsby CT (1 yr).
Meat Technology, advanced certificate, Manchester P (1 yr), also advanced diplomas in *Meat Hygiene*, *Meat Technology* and *Food Technology* (all 1 yr).

Postgraduate course Plymouth P, MSc *Fish Biology* (1 yr).

French

See also European Studies

First degrees Degrees with specialisation in *French* awarded by the following universities (some courses may include a period of study abroad): Aberdeen, Aston in Birmingham (with another subject), Bath (for Honours in European Studies), Belfast, Birmingham, Bradford (with German or Russian or Spanish), Bristol, Cambridge, Dundee, Durham, East Anglia (Honours in School of European

Studies with specialisation in French, or Honours in Comparative Literature), Edinburgh, Essex (School of Comparative Studies, for degree in Language and Linguistics), Exeter (also Medieval Studies – English or French), Glasgow, Heriot-Watt (with Spanish or German or Russian, for BA in Languages (interpreting and translating)), Hull (French Language and Literature, or French Studies), Keele (with another principal subject), Kent at Canterbury (also Renaissance Studies), Lancaster (French Studies), Leeds, Leicester, Liverpool, London (Colleges as listed under 'English Language and Literature', also French Studies at London School of Economics, and French and Rumanian at School of Slavonic and East European Studies), Loughborough U of Technology (for BA in Modern European Studies, also in courses in Business Administration or Government with a Modern Language), Manchester (University, also – Language Studies (French) with Mathematics – Institute of Science and Technology), Newcastle upon Tyne, Nottingham, Oxford, Reading, St Andrews, Salford (with another main language), Sheffield, Southampton, Stirling, Strathclyde, Surrey (Linguistic and International Studies (French)), Sussex (French Studies or French Literature as major subjects in School of European Studies, French Studies as major subject in School of African and Asian Studies), New U of Ulster, Wales (Aberystwyth – also Romance Studies – and Bangor, Cardiff, Swansea and St David's University Colleges) and Warwick (French Studies, also French taken with European Literature, History or Theatre Studies).

At many of the universities offering degrees with specialisation in this subject alone, French may also be studied with another principal subject for a Joint (or Combined) Honours degree. Combinations of French with an engineering/technological subject available at Aston in Birmingham (French and Control and Instrumentation), Bath (Engineering with French), Bradford (French with Communications or Textiles for BA in European Industrial Studies, 4 yrs S), Leeds (Civil Engineering and French) and Surrey (French with Materials Technology or Metallurgy). In addition, less specialised study of French may be included in first degree courses at many of the universities named above and also (as part of single-subject or combined-subject courses in Language) York.

The independent University College at Buckingham (see page 32) awards a licence in the School of European Studies.

Postgraduate courses   Courses (1 yr and for MA, unless otherwise indicated) at the following universities:
Comparative Literary Studies, St Andrews (diploma 1 yr, MLitt 2 yrs).
Comparative Literature, Sussex and Warwick.
French, Birmingham (wide range of courses in different topics), Exeter, London (Bedford, Birkbeck, King's, Queen Mary, Royal Holloway and Westfield Colleges), Manchester, Newcastle upon Tyne (MA 1 yr, MPhil 2 yrs) and Reading (MA 1 yr, MPhil 2 yrs, options in Graduate School of Contemporary European Studies).
French and History, Liverpool (BPhil, 1 or 2 yrs).
French and Romance Studies, Wales (Aberystwyth University College).
French Classical Drama and Theatre History, Bristol.
French Language and Literature, Liverpool (BPhil, 1 or 2 yrs) and Sheffield (Language or Literature).
French Renaissance c.1500–c.1600, Birmingham.
French Renaissance Literature, Liverpool (BPhil, 1 or 2 yrs).
French Studies, Kent at Canterbury, Lancaster (also 2 yrs part-time), Reading (12 months full-time or 24 months part-time), Sussex and Warwick.
French Theatre Studies, Lancaster.
General and Comparative Literature of 2 or 3 languages, Oxford (BPhil, 2 yrs).
Medieval French Language Studies, Edinburgh (diploma).
Medieval French Studies, Hull (BPhil/MA).
Medieval Studies, Aberdeen (including Medieval French or Anglo-Norman or Provençal, for MLitt), Leeds and St Andrews (diploma 1 yr, MLitt 2 yrs).

Middle English and Medieval French, Lancaster.
Modern French Literature: Poetry, Novel and Drama, Hull (BPhil/MA).
Modern French Studies, Belfast.
Renaissance Studies, Warwick (MA 1 yr, MPhil 2 yrs).

*Research
facilities*

At most of the universities named above.

First degrees

CNAA degrees are offered at the following polytechnics: Portsmouth P, *French Studies* (4 yrs). Roehampton IHE (3 yrs) (U of London degree).
   French is often offered as a subject in general Arts degrees at polytechnics (see page 90). The sections *European Studies* and *Language Studies* should also be consulted.

Fuel Technology

See also Engineering, Chemical

First degrees

Degrees with specialisation awarded by the following universities:
Fuel and Combustion Science, Fuel and Energy Engineering, also *Chemistry and Fuel Science* (Combined Studies), Leeds.
Fuel Technology, Heriot-Watt (Chemistry with special reference to Fuel Technology) and Sheffield (Chemical Engineering and Fuel Technology).
Gas Engineering, Heriot-Watt (Civil Engineering for Gas Engineers) and Salford (Natural Gas Engineering, 4 yrs S).
Petroleum Engineering, London (Imperial College).
   Some study of Fuel Technology also included in first degree courses in Chemical Engineering at the universities of Aston in Birmingham, Birmingham, Bradford, London, Newcastle upon Tyne, Nottingham and Surrey.

*Postgraduate
courses*

Courses (1 yr and for master's degree, unless otherwise indicated) at the following universities and Cranfield IT:
Combustion, Cranfield IT (1 or 2 yrs, option for MSc in Engineering Thermodynamics).
Combustion and Energy, Leeds (minimum 12 months).
Combustion Science and Pollution Control, Sheffield.
Fuel and Combustion Science, Leeds (diploma, 1, 2 or 3 yrs) and Newcastle upon Tyne (option in Chemical Engineering Science course).
Fuel and Energy Engineering, Leeds (diploma, 1, 2 or 3 yrs).
Fuel Technology and Power Engineering, Belfast (12 months).
Fuels, Surrey (included in diploma course in Chemical Engineering).
Internal Combustion, London (King's College, for MSc or College diploma).
Internal Combustion Engineering, Bath.
Petroleum Engineering, Heriot-Watt and London (Imperial College, MSc and/or DIC).

*Research
facilities*

At most of the universities named in the paragraphs above and at Manchester (Institute of Science and Technology) and Strathclyde.

First degree

CNAA degree at Middlesex P, *Engineering* with *Fuel Technology* option (4 yrs S).

HND courses

In *Mechanical Engineering* with *Fuel Technology* option (3 yrs S): Middlesex P. Warley CT.

*Postgraduate
course*

Portsmouth P, MSc *Fuel Technology* (1 yr).

Genetics

First degrees
Degrees with specialisation in *Genetics* awarded by the universities of Aberdeen, Birmingham (Honours in School of Biological Sciences with specialisation in groups of relevant subjects), Cambridge, Edinburgh, Glasgow, Hull (Plant Biology or Botany and Zoology with Genetics), Leeds (alone or with another subject), Leicester (Honours in Biology with specialisation in a group of relevant subjects), Liverpool, London (with Botany or Microbiology at Queen Mary College, with Botany or Microbiology or Zoology at University College), Manchester (Genetics and Cell Biology), Newcastle upon Tyne (with another subject), Nottingham, Sheffield, Strathclyde (with Biology or Microbiology), Wales (Swansea University College, alone or with another subject) and York. At many universities (including Wales – Cardiff University College) less specialised study of Genetics may be included in first degree courses in Science (Oxford, including Human Sciences), or Agriculture, or Veterinary Science.

Postgraduate courses
Courses (1 yr and for MSc, unless otherwise indicated) at the following universities:
Applied Genetics and *Conservation and Utilisation of Plant Genetic Resources*, Birmingham.
Epigenetics, Edinburgh (diploma).
Gene Technology in Micro-organisms, Essex (12 months).
Genetics, Cambridge (certificate of postgraduate study) and Edinburgh (diploma).
Genetics and Plant Breeding, Wales (Aberystwyth University College).
Human Genetics, Edinburgh.

Research facilities
At the following universities: Aberdeen, Birmingham, Cambridge, Dundee, Durham, East Anglia (also at John Innes Institute which is recognised by the university for purposes of postgraduate study), Edinburgh, Essex, Glasgow, Kent at Canterbury, Lancaster, Leicester, Liverpool, London (Queen Mary and University Colleges), Manchester, Newcastle upon Tyne, Nottingham, Oxford, Reading, Sheffield, Southampton, Stirling, Strathclyde, Sussex, New U of Ulster, Wales (Aberystwyth, Bangor, Cardiff and Swansea University Colleges) and York.

Geography

First degrees
Degrees with specialisation awarded by the following universities:
Environmental Plant Geography, Reading.
Geography (at a number of those universities which have separate faculties – of arts, science, etc – these degree courses may be available in more than one faculty – e.g. in arts or social sciences and in science – and there may be differences between faculties both in the requirements for admission and in the syllabus or choice of options): Aberdeen, Belfast, Birmingham, Bradford (with Economics, History or Politics), Bristol, Cambridge, Dundee, Durham, East Anglia, Edinburgh, Exeter, Glasgow, Hull, Keele (with another principal subject), Lancaster, Leeds, Leicester, Liverpool, London (Bedford, Birkbeck (part-time), King's, Queen Mary and University Colleges, London School of Economics and School of Oriental and African Studies, also Goldsmiths' College), Loughborough

U of Technology, Manchester, Newcastle upon Tyne, Nottingham, Oxford, Reading, St Andrews, Salford, Sheffield, Southampton, Strathclyde, Sussex (major subject in Schools of African and Asian or Cultural and Community or European Studies, and of Social or Biological Sciences), New U of Ulster and Wales (Aberystwyth, Swansea and St David's University Colleges).

History of Resource Management, New U of Ulster.

Human Geography, Belfast and New U of Ulster (Economics, Human Geography and Planning).

Topographic Science (Cartography and Photogrammetry), Glasgow and Wales (Swansea University College, with another subject).

At many of these universities Geography may also be studied with another principal subject for a Joint (or Combined) Honours degree; and at many of them, also at Stirling, Surrey and Wales (Cardiff University College and – Maritime Geography – Institute of Science and Technology), less specialised study of Geography may be included in courses leading to first degrees.

The University of London awards an academic diploma (2 yrs) in Geography (courses at Goldsmiths' College).

Postgraduate courses
Courses (normally 1 yr and for master's degree, unless otherwise indicated) at the following universities:

Advanced Regional Geography of Western Europe, Reading (MA 1 yr, MPhil 2 yrs, in Graduate School of Contemporary European Studies).

Applied Geography, Newcastle upon Tyne.

Biogeography, London (Bedford College).

Cartography, Glasgow (diploma) and Wales (Swansea University College, diploma).

Contemporary European Studies, Sussex.

Development Studies (Britain and Overseas), Durham.

Geographical Education, Southampton (12 months).

Geography, Edinburgh (diploma), Glasgow (diploma) and London (Bedford and King's Colleges and London School of Economics and – Geography of countries of Monsoon Asia and of Africa and the Middle East – School of Oriental and African Studies).

Geography in Education, London (Institute of Education).

Geography of Middle East and Mediterranean, Durham.

Integrated Land Resources Survey, Reading (2 yrs).

Natural Resources Research, Sheffield.

Planning Studies, London (London School of Economics).

Polar Studies, Cambridge (diploma).

Rural and Regional Resources Planning, Aberdeen (21 months).

Urban and Regional Studies, see 'Town and Country Planning'.

Research facilities
At most of the universities which offer first degree courses. Hull: Centre for South-East Asian Studies.

First degrees
CNAA degrees in *Geography* are offered at the following (4 yrs unless otherwise stated): Cambridgeshire C Arts T. East Sussex CHE. Edge Hill CHE (degree validated by U of Lancaster). Huddersfield P. Kingston P. Lanchester P (4 yrs S), also *Modern Studies* with option in *International Studies* and *Geography.* Middlesex P, also *Economics and Geography.* Newcastle upon Tyne P. P of North London, also *Geography and History.* North Staffordshire P. Plymouth P. Portsmouth P. Roehampton IHE. St Mary's and St Paul's C's, Cheltenham, with *Geology.*

Geography is also offered as an option in many combined studies degrees, see *Arts (General)* and *Science and Technology.*

TECHD   Luton CT, *Geographical Techniques* (3 yrs S). Sheffield P, *Land Use Studies* (2 yrs).
courses.

College   Oxford P, *Cartography* (2 yrs).
diplomas

Research   City of London P. Huddersfield P. Kingston P. Newcastle upon Tyne P. Plymouth P.
facilities   Portsmouth P.

Geology
See also Mining and Mineral Sciences

First degrees   Degrees with specialisation awarded by the following universities:
Applied Geology, Newcastle upon Tyne (Engineering Geology) and Strathclyde.
Applied Geophysics and Engineering Geology, Exeter.
Geological Sciences, Birmingham and Leeds.
Geology, Aberdeen, Aston in Birmingham, Belfast, Bristol, Cambridge, Dundee, Durham, East
    Anglia, Edinburgh, Exeter, Glasgow, Hull, Keele (with another principal subject, but
    Geology alone possible in final yr), Leicester, Liverpool, London (Bedford, Birkbeck
    (part-time), Chelsea, Imperial, King's, Queen Mary and University Colleges, also – with
    another subject – Goldsmiths' College), Manchester, Newcastle upon Tyne, Notting-
    ham (also Exploration Sciences), Oxford, Reading, St Andrews, Sheffield, Southampton
    and Wales (Aberystwyth, Cardiff and Swansea University Colleges).
Geophysics, Durham (with Geology), Edinburgh, Exeter (Physics with Geophysics), Lancaster,
    Leicester (Geology with Geophysics), Liverpool, Newcastle upon Tyne (with Planetary
    Physics), Reading (Geological Geophysics) and Southampton (Geophysical Sciences).
Mining Geology, Leeds, Leicester and London (Imperial College).
At many of these universities Geology (Leeds: Earth Sciences, except in combination
Geography – Geology) may also be studied with another principal subject for a Joint (or
Combined) Honours degree; and at many of them, also at Surrey and New U of Ulster, less
specialised study of Geology may be included in first degree courses. Some study of Geophysics
may also be included in first degree courses in Science (usually Geology) at the universities of
Birmingham, Bristol, Cambridge, Durham, Glasgow, Leicester, Liverpool and London
(Imperial College).

Postgraduate   Courses (1 yr and for MSc, unless otherwise indicated) at the following universities:
courses   *Applied Geophysics*, Birmingham, Leeds (diploma, 1, 2 or 3 yrs) and Wales (Cardiff University
    College).
Coal Petrology and Organic Geochemistry, Newcastle upon Tyne.
Engineering Geology, Durham, London (Imperial College, MSc and/or DIC) and Newcastle
    upon Tyne.
Engineering Geology and Geotechnics, Leeds (minimum 12 months).
Geochemistry, Leeds (minimum 12 months) and Oxford.
Geophysics, Durham, Leeds (minimum 12 months) and London (Imperial College, MSc and/or
    DIC).
Geophysics and Planetary Physics, Newcastle upon Tyne.
Hydrogeology, Birmingham and London (University College, MSc or College diploma).
Marine Earth Science, London (University College).
Marine Geotechnics, Wales (Bangor University College, also diploma).

Micropalaeontology, London (University College, MSc or College diploma) and Wales (Aberystwyth University College, MSc or diploma).
Micropalaeontology (Palynology), Sheffield.
Mineral Chemistry, Birmingham.
Mineral Exploration, Leicester and London (Imperial College, MSc and/or DIC).
Mining Geology, Leicester.
Mining Geostatistics, Leeds (12 months).
Petroleum Exploration and Production Studies, Aberdeen.
Petroleum Geology, London (Imperial College, MSc and/or DIC).
Physics of the Earth's Environment, Exeter.
Rock Mechanics and Excavation Engineering, Newcastle upon Tyne.
Sedimentology and its Applications, Reading (12 months).
Structural Geology and Rock Mechanics, London (Imperial College, MSc and/or DIC).

Research facilities *Geology:* at most of the universities which offer first degree courses (at Keele, postgraduate certificate in Education may be taken concurrently with research for PhD). *Geophysics:* at Birmingham, Bristol, Cambridge, Durham, Edinburgh, Exeter, Glasgow, Liverpool, London (Chelsea, Imperial and King's Colleges), Newcastle upon Tyne, Oxford, Reading, Southampton and Strathclyde.

First degrees CNAA degrees (3 yrs) are offered at the following polytechnics and colleges: City of London P, part of modular degree. Kingston P. Luton CHE, part of modular Science degree. Plymouth P, *Environmental Sciences.* Portsmouth P, also *Engineering Geology.* St Mary's and St Paul's C's, Cheltenham, with *Geography.*
   Geology is usually available as an optional subject in Combined Studies or Science degrees (see *Science (General)*).

TEC HD course South London C, *Geological Technology,* options in *Oil* or *General Techniques* (2 yrs).

College diploma South London College, college diploma in *Advanced Geology Techniques* including specialist option in *Oil Exploration Techniques* (1 yr).

Research facilities City of London P. Huddersfield P. P of North London. Plymouth P. Portsmouth P. P of Wales.

Germanic Languages and Studies

See also European Studies; and Language Studies

First degrees Degrees with specialisation in *German* awarded by the following universities (some courses may include a period of study abroad): Aberdeen, Aston in Birmingham (with another subject, also Communication Science and Linguistics (German)), Bath (for Honours in European Studies), Belfast, Birmingham, Bradford (with French or Russian or Spanish), Bristol, Brunel (Applied Chemistry and German, 4 yrs S), Cambridge, Dundee (with another principal subject), Durham, East Anglia (German Studies in School of European Studies, also Honours in Comparative Literature), Edinburgh, Essex (School of Comparative Studies, for degree in Language and Linguistics), Exeter, Glasgow, Heriot-Watt (with French or Spanish or Russian for BA in Languages (interpreting and translating)), Hull, Keele (with another principal subject), Kent at Canterbury, Lancaster (German Studies), Leeds, Leicester, Liverpool, London (at colleges listed under 'English Language and Literature', above, also School of Slavonic and East European Studies), Loughborough U of Technology (for BA in Modern European Studies, also in courses in Business Administration or Government with a Modern Language), Manchester (University and – Language Studies (German) with Mathematics – Institute of Science and Technology), Newcastle upon Tyne, Nottingham, Oxford, Reading, St Andrews, Salford (with another main language), Sheffield, Southampton, Stirling, Strathclyde, Surrey (Linguistic and International Studies (German)), Sussex (major subject in School of European Studies), New U of Ulster, Wales (Aberystwyth, Bangor, Cardiff, Swansea and St David's University Colleges, also, at Bangor University College, German Language and Modern Germany) and Warwick (German Studies).

Many of the universities offering degrees with specialisation in German alone also provide courses in which German may be studied with another principal subject for a Joint (or Combined) Honours degree. Combinations of German with an engineering/technological subject (see also above) available at Aston in Birmingham (German and Control and Instrumentation), Bath (Engineering and German) and Surrey (German with Materials Technology or Metallurgy). Less specialised study of German may be included in first degree courses at many of the universities named above and (as part of single-subject or combined-subject course in Language) at York.

First degrees with specialisation in other Germanic languages/studies:

Danish, Cambridge, London (University College, with German) and Newcastle upon Tyne.

Dutch, Cambridge, Liverpool (German with Dutch) and London (Bedford College).

Icelandic, London (University College, with Norwegian).

Norwegian, Cambridge, Glasgow (with another subject), London (University College, with German or Icelandic) and Newcastle upon Tyne.

Scandinavian Studies, East Anglia (School of European Studies), Hull and London (University College).

Swedish, Aberdeen (Swedish Studies, or Swedish with one of certain other subjects), Cambridge, Hull (alone, or with another principal subject), London (University College, with German), Newcastle upon Tyne and Wales (Aberystwyth University College, with another subject).

Less specialised courses in these and other Germanic languages/studies available at Aberdeen (Norwegian, Swedish), Belfast (Swedish, for degree in German), East Anglia (Danish, Norwegian and Swedish, for Honours in Comparative Literature), Edinburgh (Icelandic), Hull (Dutch for degree in German, Old Norse for degree in English or German), Glasgow (Norwegian), Leeds (Old or Modern Icelandic, for degree in English), Liverpool (Dutch), London (Dutch History and Institutions for degree in History, also Modern Faroese and Modern Icelandic, at University College, Swedish at King's College), Newcastle upon Tyne (Danish, Norwegian, Swedish), Reading (Dutch and Old Norse, options for degree in German), Salford (Dutch and Swedish, for degree in Modern Languages), Sheffield (Danish and Dutch, for degree in German), Stirling (Swedish) and Wales (for degrees in German – Dutch and Norwegian at Bangor, Norwegian at Swansea, and Swedish at Aberystwyth and Cardiff University Colleges, also Old Norse at Swansea for degree in English and Medieval Studies).

Postgraduate courses Courses (1 yr and for MA, unless otherwise indicated) at the following universities:

Comparative Literary Studies, St Andrews (diploma 1 yr, MLitt 2 yrs).

Comparative Literature, Sussex and Warwick.

Danish Literature of the Nineteenth Century, Newcastle upon Tyne.

General and Comparative Literature of 2 or 3 languages, Oxford (BPhil, 2 yrs).

German, Liverpool (BPhil, 1 or 2 yrs), London (Bedford (optional syllabuses), Birkbeck (1 yr full-time or 2 yrs part-time), King's, Queen Mary, Royal Holloway, University and Westfield Colleges), Reading (MA 1 yr or MPhil 2 yrs in Graduate School of

Contemporary European Studies, and MA 12 months or MPhil 24 months in Graduate Centre for Medieval Studies) and Southampton.
German Language and Literature, Sheffield (Language or Literature) and Wales (Aberystwyth and Cardiff University Colleges).
German Studies, Sussex and Warwick (MA 1 yr, MPhil 2 yrs).
History and Structure of the German Language, Wales (Bangor University College).
History, Thought and Literature of Norway in the Nineteenth Century, Newcastle upon Tyne.
Icelandic Studies, Leeds (MA or diploma).
Linguistics and German Language, Surrey (diploma).
Literature and Society in Twentieth Century Germany, Newcastle upon Tyne.
Medieval Studies, Aberdeen (MLitt), Leeds and St Andrews (diploma 1 yr, MLitt 2 yrs).
Modern German Studies, New U of Ulster.
Swedish Literature in the Nineteenth and Twentieth Centuries, Newcastle upon Tyne.
Twentieth Century German Drama, Bristol.

Research facilities *German:* at many of the universities named above (London: colleges named in first paragraph, and Institute of Germanic Studies – a research institute open to all suitably qualified graduates). *Dutch:* at Cambridge. *Scandinavian Studies:* at Cambridge and London (University College).

First degrees CNAA degrees in *German* are offered at the following polytechnics: Kingston P, with *Chemistry* or *Business Administration* (4 yrs). Portsmouth P, *German Studies* (4 yrs).
 German is often available as a subject in general Arts degrees at polytechnics (see page 90). The sections *European Studies* and *Language Studies* should also be consulted.

Greek and Latin
See also Archaeology, and History

First degrees Degrees with specialisation in *Classics* (Greek and Latin) and/or *Classical Studies* awarded by the following universities: Aberdeen, Belfast, Birmingham, Bristol (also Ancient Mediterranean Studies), Cambridge, Durham, Edinburgh, Exeter, Glasgow, Hull, Keele, Kent at Canterbury, Lancaster, Leeds, Leicester, Liverpool, London (Bedford, Birkbeck (part-time), King's, Queen Mary, Royal Holloway, University and Westfield Colleges), Manchester, Newcastle upon Tyne, Nottingham, Oxford, Reading, St Andrews, Sheffield, Southampton, Sussex (Classical and Medieval Studies in School of European Studies) and Wales (Aberystwyth, Bangor, Cardiff, Swansea and St David's University Colleges). At New U of Ulster students may specialise in *Latin* taken with another subject; and a number of the other universities named above also offer degrees with specialisation in either *Latin* or *Greek,* taken alone or in combination with another principal subject (in some instances Classics/Classical Studies may itself be offered as one of two principal subjects). Less specialised study of Classics (Greek and/or Latin) may be included in first degree courses in arts at many of the universities named above and (Latin only) at Salford (for degree in modern languages) and Warwick (English and Latin Literature).
 Degrees with specialisation in *Ancient Civilisation* (Greek, Roman) awarded by the following universities: Exeter (Latin and Ancient History), Kent at Canterbury (Classical Civilisation with another subject), Leeds (Greek or Roman Civilisation with one of certain other subjects), Wales (Ancient History and Civilisation alone or with another subject at Swansea University College, Greek and Roman Civilisation with another subject at St David's University College, also Classical Studies – mainly literature and civilisation – at Cardiff and – with another subject – Bangor and St David's University Colleges) and Warwick (Classical Civilisation).

First degrees with specialisation in *Modern Greek* awarded by Birmingham (BA in Combined Subjects and in Ancient and Modern Greek), Cambridge, London (King's College) and Oxford (Medieval and Modern Greek); and less specialised study of Modern Greek may be included in first degree curricula at Aberdeen (1-yr course for MA Ordinary, also Byzantine and Modern Greek as optional subject for Honours in Classics or in English-Greek) and Birmingham (Byzantine and Modern Greek in Schools of Classics and of Greek).

Postgraduate courses

Courses (normally 1 yr and for MA, unless otherwise indicated) at the following universities:
Aegean and Anatolian Prehistory, Bristol.
Ancient Greek Mythology and Modern Greek Folklore, Birmingham.
Ancient History, see 'History'.
Byzantine Studies, Birmingham.
Classics, Glasgow (MPhil, 2 yrs), Hull (BPhil), Keele, Lancaster (also 2 yrs part-time), Leicester, London (Bedford, Birkbeck, Queen Mary, Royal Holloway, University and Westfield Colleges), Nottingham, Reading (for teachers, 12 months full-time or 24 months part-time), St Andrews (diploma, also, with Ancient History, MLitt, 2 yrs), New U of Ulster and Wales (colleges as above).
Comparative Ancient and Modern Greek Poetry, Birmingham.
Contemporary Classical Studies, Southampton.
General and Comparative Literature of 2 or 3 languages, Oxford (BPhil, 2 yrs).
Greek, Lancaster and Leeds.
Greek and Latin, Liverpool (BPhil, 1 or 2 yrs).
Greek and Latin Languages and Literature, Oxford (BPhil, 2 yrs).
Greek Lyric and Elegiac Poetry and Epigram or *Greek Philosophy*, Sheffield.
Greek Regional Studies, Birmingham.
Greek Tragedy, Sheffield.
The History of the Greek Language, Birmingham.
Homeric and Mycenaean Studies, Sheffield.
Late Roman Studies, Bristol.
Latin, Lancaster, Leeds and Sheffield.
Latin Language or *Latin Literature*, Manchester.
Medieval Studies, Manchester (MA or diploma) and St Andrews (diploma 1 yr, MLitt 2 yrs).
Roman Law, see under 'Law'.
Textual Criticism of Classical Greek Authors, Sheffield.
Theory of Textual Criticism, Birmingham.

Research facilities

At most of the universities which offer first degree courses. Birmingham: Centre for Byzantine Studies. London: Institute of Classical Studies provides facilities for advanced study and research and for training of postgraduate students in Classics and cognate subjects, and Warburg Institute for postgraduate study and research (including seminars) in the character and history of the classical tradition; King's College, also Byzantine Studies. Oxford: including Bodleian Library, Ashmolean Museum and Library.

History

First degrees

Degrees with specialisation in *History* awarded by the following universities (at some of which students may further specialise in one or more of Ancient, Medieval and Modern History): Aberdeen, Belfast, Birmingham (also Medieval and Renaissance Studies), Bradford (with one of certain other subjects), Bristol (also Ancient Mediterranean Studies, and Social History taken with Philosophy or Sociology), Brunel (Government, Politics and Modern History), Cambridge,

Dundee, Durham, East Anglia (English History in School of English and American Studies, or European Political, Social and Intellectual History in School of European Studies), Edinburgh, Essex (School of Comparative Studies), Exeter (also Medieval Studies (Medieval History and Latin) and English Medieval Studies), Glasgow, Heriot-Watt (Government and Modern History), Hull, Keele (with another principal subject), Kent at Canterbury (also Renaissance Studies), Lancaster (also Medieval Studies and Social History), Leeds, Leicester, Liverpool, London (colleges as for 'English Language and Literature', also London School of Economics, School of Oriental and African Studies and School of Slavonic and East European Studies), Loughborough U of Technology (also Modern Social History), Manchester (various schemes including one in Medieval Studies), Newcastle upon Tyne, Nottingham, Oxford, Reading (also Medieval Studies with Classical Studies or Latin), St Andrews, Salford (Contemporary History in Social Studies course, also Politics and History of Industrial Societies), Sheffield, Southampton, Stirling, Strathclyde, Sussex (major subject in all Arts and Social Studies Schools, also Intellectual History in Schools of European and of English and American Studies), New U of Ulster (also History of Resource Management), Wales (Aberystwyth, Bangor, Cardiff, Swansea and St David's University Colleges, also Welsh History with another subject at Aberystwyth, Bangor and Cardiff, and Medieval Studies with another subject at Swansea), Warwick and York. At many of the universities offering degrees with specialisation in this subject alone, History may also be studied with another principal subject for a Joint (or Combined) Honours degree; and at most of them less specialised study of History may be included in courses leading to first degrees.

The independent University College at Buckingham (see page 32) awards a licence in the School of History, Politics and English Literature.

Postgraduate courses   Courses (1 yr and for master's degree, unless otherwise indicated) at the following universities:
African Studies, Sussex.
American History, Sheffield.
American History and Literature, East Anglia.
American Politics and History, Liverpool (BPhil, 1 or 2 yrs).
American Studies, Sussex.
Ancient History, Liverpool (with Classical Archaeology, BPhil, 1 or 2 yrs), Newcastle upon Tyne, Oxford (BPhil, 2 yrs) and St Andrews (with Classics, 2 yrs).
British History, Leeds (12 months full-time or 24 months part-time).
Combined Historical Studies: The Renaissance, London (Warburg Institute, 2 yrs).
Commonwealth and American History, Oxford (BPhil, 2 yrs).
Commonwealth History, London (Birkbeck College, 1 yr full-time or 2 yrs part-time).
Comparative History, Essex (12 months).
Comparative Labour History and *Comparative Social History*, Warwick.
Contemporary European History, etc, Reading (MA 1 yr, MPhil 2 yrs, in Graduate School of Contemporary European Studies).
East European, Russian and Soviet History, London (School of Slavonic and East European Studies).
Eighteenth Century Studies, Newcastle upon Tyne.
English and European History, London (Queen Mary and – Twelfth and Thirteenth Centuries – University Colleges).
English Government and Society before the Civil War, Birmingham.
English History, Wales (Cardiff University College).
English History and Literature, East Anglia and – 1880–1920 – Sheffield.
English Local History, Leicester.
English Society and Culture in later Middle Ages, Birmingham.
English with some European History, London (King's College).
European History, East Anglia, Oxford (BPhil, 2 yrs) and Wales (Cardiff University College).

French and History, Liverpool (BPhil, 1 or 2 yrs).
French Renaissance c. 1500–c. 1600, Birmingham.
Historical Studies, Cambridge (diploma).
History, Belfast (1½–2 yrs) and Sussex.
History of Dress, London (Courtauld Institute of Art, Institute certificate, 2 yrs).
History of the USA, Wales (Cardiff University College).
Intellectual History, Sussex.
International History, London (London School of Economics).
Law, Government and Society in England before the Restoration, Birmingham.
Medieval English and European History, London (Westfield College).
Medieval History, Birmingham (Medieval Literature and History, 1 or 2 yrs) and St Andrews (diploma 1 yr, MLitt 2 yrs).
Medieval Studies, Aberdeen, Leeds, Liverpool (BPhil, 1 or 2 yrs), Manchester (MA or diploma), Reading (MA 12 months, MPhil 24 months), St Andrews (diploma 1 yr, MLitt 2 yrs) and York (12 months).
Modern British Social History, Birmingham.
Modern History, Liverpool (BPhil, 1 or 2 yrs) and London (Queen Mary College).
Modern Social History, Lancaster.
Oriental and African History, London (School of Oriental and African Studies).
Prehistory, see under 'Archaeology'.
Renaissance Studies, Warwick.
Scottish History, St Andrews (2 yrs).
Social and Demographic History, Liverpool (BPhil, 1 or 2 yrs).
Social and Political Thought, Sussex.
Social History, Birmingham (Economic and Social), Essex (12 months), Manchester (Economic and Social) and Wales (Swansea University College).
Social History of Wales, Wales (Aberystwyth University College).
Southern African Studies, York (12 months).
Studies in Dark Age Britain, Wales (Aberystwyth University College).
United States History and Institutions, Keele.
Victorian Studies, Keele (2 yrs) and Leicester.
Welsh History, Wales (Cardiff University College).

Research facilities At most of the universities which offer first degree courses, also (Industrial History) Bath (Centre for the Study of the History of Technology). East Anglia: Centre of East Anglian Studies. Hull: Centre for South-East Asian Studies. London: several Colleges, Schools and Institutes, including Institute of Historical Research (facilities for advanced study and research, including training of postgraduate students in many fields) and Warburg Institute (fields pertaining to the Character and History of the Classical Tradition). Reading: Graduate Centre for Medieval Studies, Graduate School of Contemporary European Studies. Warwick: Centre for the Study of Social History. York: Centre for Medieval Studies, Centre for Southern African Studies, Borthwick Institute of Historical Research.

First degrees First degrees in *History* (CNAA unless otherwise stated) are offered at the following (3 yrs): Cambridgeshire C Arts T, *Modern History*. East Sussex CHE, *History* with *Art, English, Geography* or *Religious Studies* (U of Sussex degree). Edge Hill CHE, *History* (U of Lancaster degree). King Alfred's C, *History* with *Drama* or *English*. Newcastle upon Tyne P, *Humanities (English and History)*. P of North London, *Geography and History*. Portsmouth P, *Historical Studies*.
History is also offered as an option in *Combined Arts* degrees. See *Arts (General)*, also *European Studies*.

Postgraduate Architectural Association S Architecture, *Housing, Social Institutions and Theory of History*
course (1 or 2 yrs).

Research Newcastle upon Tyne P. Portsmouth P.
facilities

History and Philosophy of Science
(including History of Technology)

First degrees Degrees with specialisation in *History and/or Philosophy of Science* awarded by the universities
of Belfast (with Mathematics or Philosophy or Psychology), Cambridge (option for Part II of
Natural Sciences Tripos), Lancaster (History of Science taken with Philosophy and either
Chemistry, Mathematics, Physics or Psychology), Leeds (History of Science, History of
Scientific Thought or Philosophy taken with one of certain other subjects), London (Chelsea
College, Mathematics and Philosophy of Mathematics) and Sussex (Science, Technology and
Society with Physics, also Logic with Mathematics or Physics). Less specialised study of
History and/or Philosophy of Science may also be included in first degree courses in arts and/or
science at these universities and at Aberdeen, Bristol, Bradford (for BA, 4 yrs S, in Human
Purposes and Communication), The City, Durham, East Anglia, Edinburgh, Glasgow,
Heriot-Watt, Hull, Kent at Canterbury, Leicester (History and Social Relations of Science, also
Logic and Scientific Method), London (London School of Economics, Scientific Method),
Loughborough U of Technology, Manchester (History, also Social and Economic Aspects, of
Science in Liberal Studies in Science course), Oxford, Sheffield. Southampton and Wales
(Aberystwyth, Cardiff and Swansea University Colleges).

Postgraduate Courses (normally 1 yr and for master's degree, unless otherwise indicated) at the following
courses universities:
History and Philosophy of Science, Cambridge (2 yrs), Leeds (diploma, 1 yr full-time or 2 yrs
part-time) and London (Chelsea – 1-yr course followed in 2nd yr by thesis or dissertation
– and University Colleges).
History and Social Studies of Science, Sussex.
History of Science, London (Imperial College, MSc and/or DIC).
History of Science and Technology, Manchester (Institute of Science and Technology, MSc or
diploma).
History of Technology, London (Imperial College, MSc and/or DIC).
History, Philosophy and Social Studies of Science, Kent at Canterbury (12 months).
Logic and Science, Birmingham.
Logic and Scientific Method, London (London School of Economics) and Sussex.
Philosophy of Science and Mathematics, London (Chelsea College, 1 yr full-time or 2 yrs
part-time).
Structure and Organisation of Science and Technology, Manchester (MSc or diploma).

Research At the following universities: Bath (Centre for the Study of the History of Technology),
facilities Cambridge (Whipple Museum of History of Science), Edinburgh (Science Studies Unit),
Glasgow, Kent at Canterbury, Lancaster, Leicester, London (London School of Economics and
Chelsea, Imperial and University Colleges), Loughborough U of Technology, Manchester
(History of Science and Technology in Institute of Science and Technology, Liberal Studies in
Science in Faculty of Science) and Sussex (Science Policy Research Unit).

First degrees   A study of *History* and/or *Philosophy of Science* is included in CNAA degree courses in Arts or Science at the following polytechnics: Middlesex P, *Humanities*. Teesside P, *Humanities*. Thames P, *Combined Studies*. Wolverhampton P, *Humanities*.

Home Economics

See also Education; and Hotel and Institutional Management

First degrees   Degrees in *Home Economics* awarded by the universities of Surrey (4 yrs S) and Wales (Cardiff University College).

Research facilities   At University of Surrey.

First degrees   First degrees in *Home Economics* are offered at the following (3 yrs). Bath CHE (U of Bath degree). City of Manchester CHE (U of Manchester degree). F L Calder CE (U of Liverpool degree). Queen Margaret C (CNAA). Robert Gordon's IT (CNAA). Roehampton IHE (U of London degree).

Diploma courses   Courses (3 yrs) leading to a diploma in *Home Economics*, designed for home economists working in industry and commerce. Birmingham C Food and Domestic Arts. Croydon C Design and Technology. P of North London. The Queen's C. Queen Margaret C (1 yr). Sheffield P.

Hospital and Health Service Administration

First degrees   At the University of Manchester *Medicine in Modern Society* may be included in course for BA(Econ) with specialisation in Social Administration.

Postgraduate courses   Courses (1 yr and for diploma, unless otherwise indicated) at the following universities:
Health Administration, Hull (MSc, 12 months).
Health and Welfare Services Management, Aston in Birmingham (option for MSc/diploma in Public Sector Management).
Health Services Administration, Leeds.
Health Services Management, Manchester (also 2-yr course designed primarily for graduates who have been accepted for (non-university) 3-yr training course for the Hospital Service).
Health Service Studies, Leeds (MA, 12 months).
　　Also, at Brunel, Health option in MA course in Public and Social Administration; and, at Exeter, an area of specialisation for MSc in Information Processing which involves study of the public sector of the economy including the National Health Service.

Research facilities   At the following universities: Brunel, Hull (Institute for Health Studies), Kent at Canterbury (Health Services Research Unit of Centre for Research in the Social Sciences) and Manchester.

Professional courses   London: International Hospital Centre, course for senior hospital and health service administrators from overseas (3 months); P of the South Bank, diploma course in *Hospital Administration,* for overseas students (2 yrs).

The Institute of Health Service Administrators awards a diploma by examination which is the generally accepted qualification in this profession in the National Health Service. For information apply to the Secretary.

Hotel and Institutional Management
(including Catering)
See also Food Science and Technology

First degrees Degrees with specialisation awarded by the following universities:
Hotel and Catering Administration, Surrey (4 yrs S).
Hotel and Catering Management, Strathclyde.
Institutional Management, Wales (Cardiff University College).

Postgraduate courses Courses in *Tourism* at the universities of Strathclyde (diploma 9 months, MSc 12 months) and Surrey (diploma 1 academic yr, MSc minimum 12 months).

Research facilities At University of Surrey.

First degrees CNAA degrees (4 yrs S) at Huddersfield P, *Hotel and Catering Administration.* P of North London, *Institutional Management.* Sheffield P, *Catering Systems.* Ulster C, Northern Ireland P, *Institutional Management.*

HND courses *Hotel and Catering Administration* (3 yrs S), Blackpool CT Art. Bournemouth CT. Brighton P. Dorset IHE. Ealing CHE. Glasgow C Food and Technology (3 yrs). Highbury TC. Huddersfield P. Llandrillo TC. Manchester P. Middlesex P. Napier CC and T. Norwich City C. Portsmouth P. Robert Gordon's IT (3 yrs). South Devon TC. South Glamorgan IHE. Ulster C, Northern Ireland P. Westminster C.
Hotel Catering and Institutional Management (3 yrs S). Birmingham C Food and Domestic Arts. Duncan of Jordanstone C Art (3 yrs). Leeds P. North Gloucestershire CT. Oxford P. Sheffield P.
Institutional Management (3 yrs S). Duncan of Jordanstone C Art. Leeds P (also 2 yrs). Manchester P. P of North London. Queen's C. Queen Margaret C. Robert Gordon's IT. Ulster C, Northern Ireland P.

Professional courses Courses leading to the final membership examination of the Hotel, Catering and Institutional Management Association (1 yr or 2 yrs S). Birmingham C Food and Domestic Arts. Blackpool CT Art. Bournemouth CT. Brighton TC. Colchester IHE. Dorset IHE. Ealing CHE. Glasgow C Food Technology. Henley CFE. Highbury TC. Llandrillo TC. Manchester P. Middlesex P. Napier CC and T. North Gloucestershire CT. Norwich City C. Oxford P. Robert Gordon's IT. Slough CHE. South Devon TC. South Glamorgan IHE. Thomas Danby C. Westminster C.
The following colleges offer courses leading to the HCIMA certificate in Institutional Management (1 yr). Bath TC. Leeds P. Manchester P. Queen's C. Queen Margaret C. Radbrook C.

College diplomas Bournemouth CT, college diploma in *Tourism Studies* (1 yr). Manchester P, postgraduate diploma in *Hotel and Catering Administration* or *Tourism* (1 yr). Queen's C, diploma *Residential Management* (1 yr). Ulster C, Northern Ireland P, diploma *Catering Education.*

Irish, Scottish and Welsh Studies
(including Celtic)

First degrees Degrees with specialisation awarded by the following universities:
Celtic/Celtic Studies, Aberdeen, Belfast, Cambridge (Anglo-Saxon, Norse and Celtic Tripos), Edinburgh, Glasgow (alone or for Combined Honours) and Wales (Aberystwyth University College).
Irish Studies, New U of Ulster and Wales (Aberystwyth University College, Irish with another subject).
Scottish Studies, Edinburgh (Scottish Historical Studies), Glasgow (Medieval or Modern Scottish History) and Stirling (with English Studies or History).
Welsh, Wales (Aberystwyth, Bangor, Cardiff, Swansea and St David's University Colleges).
  Less specialised study may also be included in first degree syllabuses at most of these universities (Wales: including Breton and Cornish) and at Manchester (Irish, Welsh).

Postgraduate Courses (1 yr and for master's degree, unless otherwise indicated) at the following universities:
courses *Anglo-Irish Literature*, Leeds and New U of Ulster.
Anglo-Irish Studies, Belfast.
Celtic Studies, Aberdeen (Medieval Studies including Celtic or Middle Scots), Edinburgh (2 yrs), Leeds (MA or diploma) and Oxford (diploma, also for BPhil in General and Comparative Literature of 2 or 3 languages, each 2 yrs, and for diploma in Comparative Philology, 2 yrs in most cases).
Scottish History, St Andrews (2 yrs).
Scottish Literature, Aberdeen.
Scottish Studies, Stirling.
Social History of Wales, Wales (Aberystwyth University College).
Welsh, Wales (Bangor University College).
Welsh History, Wales (Cardiff University College).

Research At most of the universities named in the paragraphs above (St Andrews: Scottish History).
facilities. Edinburgh: School of Scottish Studies and Linguistic Survey of Scotland.

Diploma P of Wales, *Oral Welsh* (1 yr).
course

Italian
See also European Studies

First degrees Degrees with specialisation in *Italian* awarded by the following universities (some courses may include a period of study abroad): Aberdeen, Belfast, Birmingham, Cambridge, Edinburgh, Exeter (with another subject), Glasgow, Hull, Kent at Canterbury (also Renaissance Studies), Lancaster (with another principal subject), Leeds, Leicester, Liverpool, London (Bedford and University and – part-time – Birkbeck Colleges), Manchester, Oxford, Reading, Salford (with another main language), Sheffield (with another principal subject), Strathclyde (with another principal subject), Sussex (major subject in School of European Studies), Wales (Aberystwyth –

also Romance Studies, Cardiff, Swansea and – with another language – Bangor University Colleges) and Warwick (with European Literature or Renaissance Studies or Theatre Studies). At some of the universities offering degrees with specialisation in this subject alone, Italian may also be studied with another principal subject for a Joint (or Combined) Honours degree; and at a number of them, also at Bath, Durham, London (Royal Holloway College), Nottingham and Southampton, less specialised study of Italian may be included in courses leading to first degrees in Arts.

Postgraduate courses   Courses (1 yr and for MA, unless otherwise indicated) at the following universities:
Comparative Literature, Warwick.
Contemporary European Studies, Reading (MA 1 yr, MPhil 2 yrs, in Graduate School of Contemporary European Studies).
General and Comparative Literature of 2 or 3 languages, Oxford (BPhil, 2 yrs).
Italian, Wales (Cardiff University College).
Italian Renaissance, Liverpool (BPhil, 1 or 2 yrs).
Italian Renaissance Studies, Hull (BPhil).
Machiavelli, Birmingham.
Medieval Studies (including Italian), Aberdeen (MLitt) and Leeds.
Modern Italian Studies, Hull.
Petrarch and Petrarchism in Renaissance Italy and France, Birmingham.
Renaissance Studies, Warwick.

Research facilities   At many of the universities named above. Reading: Centre for Advanced Study of Italian Society, also Graduate School of Contemporary European Studies.

First degrees   The study of *Italian* is included in some CNAA Modern Language degrees including those offered at: Cambridgeshire C Arts and T. P of Central London. Leeds P, *European Languages and Institutions*.

Landscape Architecture

See also Town and Country Planning

First degrees   Heriot-Watt University awards a BA in *Landscape Architecture* (normally 5 yrs S) and University of Sheffield a BSc in Natural Environmental Science with *Landscape Studies*.

Postgraduate courses   Courses (2 yrs and for diploma, unless otherwise indicated) at the following universities:
Landscape Architecture, Edinburgh.
Landscape Design, Manchester, Newcastle upon Tyne (MSc or BPhil) and Sheffield (MA or diploma, 1 or 2 yrs).
Landscape Ecology, Design and Maintenance, London (Wye College, MSc, 1 yr).
Landscape Studies, Sheffield (certificate, 1 yr).
Royal College of Art offers MA course (2 yrs) in *Urban Landscape Design*.

Research facilities   At the following universities: Heriot-Watt, Manchester (Centre for Urban and Regional Research) and Sheffield.

First degree   Edinburgh C Art, *Landscape Architecture* (Heriot-Watt University). Leeds P (3 yrs).

Professional   The 4-yr full-time diploma courses of the following institutions give partial or complete
courses   exemption from Parts 1–3 of the four-part examinations of the Institute of Landscape
Architects. the parts exempted are noted in brackets: Gloucestershire C Art and Design (Parts 1,
2 and 3). Leeds P (Parts 1, 2 and 3). Manchester P (Parts 1, 2 and 3). Thames P (Parts 1 and 2).
Part-time courses are also available and a full list of courses may be obtained from the Institute.

Research   Thames P.
facility

Language Studies

First degrees   Degrees with specialisation in the study of Language (as distinct from the study of a particular
language, for which see under the relevant headings) awarded by the following
universities:
Applied Language Studies, Manchester (Institute of Science and Technology).
Human Communication, Aston in Birmingham (3 yrs, or 4 yrs S).
Language, York (alone or with another subject).
Language and Linguistics, Essex (School of Comparative Studies, including Modern English
and either one or two of certain foreign languages).
Linguistics, Aston in Birmingham (with another subject), Birmingham (with one of certain
other subjects), Edinburgh, Essex (alone or with Language Pathology, Literature,
Philosophy or Sociology), Exeter (with a language subject), Glasgow (Linguistics and
Phonetics jointly with another main subject), Hull (alone or with one of certain other
subjects), Lancaster (alone or with one or two other subjects), London (School of
Oriental and African Studies and – alone or with one of certain other subjects –
University College), Manchester (with French), Newcastle upon Tyne, Nottingham
(with one of certain other subjects), Reading (alone, or with Language Pathology or one
of certain other subjects), Sheffield (with certain other subjects), Sussex (major in
School of Social Sciences), New U of Ulster (with another subject) and Wales (Bangor
University College, alone or with one of certain other subjects, also Linguistics and the
Structure of English).
Bradford, Heriot-Watt and Salford offer modern language courses (see also under the separate
headings) in which the emphasis is on the practical use of the language (Bradford, particularly
Translation and Interpreting; Heriot-Watt, BA in Languages (Interpreting and Translating)
requiring a yr to be spent at translators' or interpreters' college abroad), combined in each case
with social, economic and political studies of the relevant countries. Final yr of BA Honours
course in European Studies at Bath (see also 'European Studies') may include specialist course
in interpreting, translating and précis-writing (for those wishing to become professional
linguists – languages are studied together with the contemporary society of the relevant
countries, in the context of Europe as a whole).
Less specialised study of Language/Linguistics may be included in first degree courses at the
following universities: Aberdeen, Birmingham, Bradford, Cambridge, East Anglia, Exeter,
Glasgow, Hull, Lancaster, Leeds, Leicester, Liverpool, London (University College –
Phonetics of European languages, Psycho-linguistics and Experimental Phonetics and
Linguistics, including special course in Phonetics of English for foreign students – and School
of Oriental and African Studies – General and Comparative Linguistics and Phonetics,
Phonetics and Phonology of Asian and African languages, and General Linguistics and

Phonetics), Manchester, Newcastle upon Tyne (including English Linguistic Studies), Nottingham, St Andrews, Salford, Sheffield (Applied Linguistics), Southampton, Surrey (Linguistic and International Studies – French, German and Russian), New U of Ulster and Wales (Bangor, Cardiff and Swansea University Colleges). At Essex there is a certificate course (10 weeks) in Applied Linguistics and the Teaching of English (see under 'English as a Foreign Language').

PHILOLOGY – English, French, German and Classical – may be studied at many universities. Special branches which may be included in first degree courses:

Comparative, Aberdeen (for Honours in Classics), Cambridge (Historical and Comparative), Edinburgh, Manchester (Comparative Semitic, Comparative Slavonic) and Reading.

Romance, Aberdeen, Birmingham, Edinburgh, Leeds, London (several institutions), Reading and Wales (in Romance Studies course at Aberystwyth University College).

Slavonic, London (several institutions including School of Slavonic and East European Studies), Manchester (Comparative Slavonic) and Reading.

Postgraduate courses Courses (1 yr and for master's degree, unless otherwise indicated) at the following universities:

Applied Linguistics, Edinburgh (MLitt 2 yrs, MSc 12 months), Essex (for MA in Linguistics, also diploma in Applied Linguistics, Phonetics and the Teaching of English, and 10-week certificate course in Applied Linguistics and the Teaching of English – see under 'English as a Foreign Language'), Exeter (General and Applied Linguistics), Kent at Canterbury (MA or diploma), Manchester (BLing), Reading (MA 1 yr full-time or 2 yrs part-time, MPhil 2 yrs full-time or 4 yrs part-time, also diploma in General and Applied Linguistics) and New U of Ulster (General and Applied Linguistics).

Comparative Indo-European Linguistics (with special reference to Greek and Anatolian group), Sheffield.

Comparative Philology (diplomas), London (University College and – Comparative Slavonic Philology – School of Slavonic and East European Studies, each 2 yrs) and Oxford (2 yrs in most cases).

Dialectology, Leeds.

English Language and General Linguistics, Newcastle upon Tyne (MA 1 yr, MPhil 2 yrs).

English Linguistics, Wales (Institute of Science and Technology, Institute diploma).

General Linguistics, Edinburgh (MLitt, 2 yrs), Exeter (General and Applied Linguistics), London (School of Oriental and African Studies, 2 yrs), Manchester (BLing, also – various options – MA), Reading (General and Applied Linguistics, diploma) and New U of Ulster (General and Applied Linguistics).

Hittite and Cognate Anatolian Languages: Philology and Linguistics, Sheffield.

Interpreting and Translating, Bradford (diploma).

Language, York.

Language in Education, see 'Education'.

Language Studies, Bath (diploma for modern language graduates interested in careers as professional linguists in international organisations).

Linguistics, Cambridge, Essex (12 months or 1 academic yr – see also 'Phonetics', below), Leeds, London (School of Oriental and African Studies and University College, MA – usually 2 yrs – or diploma), Reading (MA 1 yr full-time or 2 yrs part-time, MPhil 2 yrs full-time or 4 yrs part-time), St Andrews (MLitt or diploma, 2 yrs) and Wales (Bangor University College, diploma/MA).

Linguistics and English Language Teaching, Leeds.

Linguistics and German Language, Surrey (diploma).

Linguistics and Phonetics (diplomas), Glasgow and London (School of Oriental and African Studies, 2 yrs).

Linguistics for English Language Teaching, Lancaster.

Linguistics for Language Teaching, Wales (Bangor University College).
Logic and Language, Birmingham.
Logic and Linguistics, St Andrews (2 yrs).
Phonetics, Edinburgh (for graduates and those who have reached a similar standard), Essex (Linguistics and Phonetics – 12 months for MA in Linguistics, also 10-week certificate course for qualified teachers, speech therapists, and others concerned with speech and language), Leeds (MA and diploma) and London (School of Oriental and African Studies and University College).
Russian Language and Literature (Philology), London (School of Slavonic and East European Studies).
Russian Studies (Philology), Birmingham.
Theoretical Linguistics, Essex (for MA in Linguistics, 12 months).
Vocational Techniques for Career Linguists, Kent at Canterbury (diploma).

Research facilities   At most of the universities named in the paragraphs above (London: also – Applied Linguistics – Birkbeck College; Surrey: Applied, Contrastive and Descriptive Linguistics with special reference to French, German, Russian). Essex: Language Centre. St Andrews: Centre for Latin-American Linguistics. York: including Language Teaching Centre, with language laboratory and audio-visual aids.

First degrees   CNAA degrees in *Modern Languages* are offered at the following (4 yrs). Bristol P. Cambridgeshire C Arts T. P of Central London, 2 languages chosen from *Arabic, Chinese, French, German, Italian, Russian* and *Spanish*. Ealing CHE, *Applied Language Studies*. Kingston P, *Languages, Economics and Politics*. Lanchester P. Leeds P, *European Languages and Institutions*. Liverpool P. Manchester P, *Modern Languages and Literature* (2 languages chosen from *French, German* and *Spanish*). Newcastle upon Tyne P, *Modern Languages and Economic Studies*. Portsmough P, courses in *French, German, Russian* and *Spanish Studies*. Sheffield P, *Modern Languages* with *Political Studies*. P of the South Bank, courses in *French, German* and *Spanish* with *Regional Studies* and *International Relations*. Wolverhampton P, 2 languages chosen from *French, German, Russian* and *Spanish*.

HND courses   In Business Studies with emphasis on modern language studies are offered by more than 20 polytechnics and colleges; see *A Compendium of Advanced Courses in Colleges of Further and Higher Education* (page 265).

College diplomas   Aberdeen CC, *Interpreters/Translators* course (2 yrs). Birmingham P, *Foreign Languages for Business* (3 yrs). Bradford C, *Translators/Interpreters* and for *Foreign Correspondents* (2 yrs). P of Central London, college diplomas in *Arabic/English Translation* (2 yrs), *Technical and Specialised Translation* (1 yr), *Conference Interpretation Techniques* (7 months), *Russian* (1 yr). Chelmer IHE, *European Languages* (2 yrs). Hammersmith and West London C, *Business Studies with Modern Languages* (3 yrs). Leeds P, *Modern Languages with Business Studies* (2 yrs). Luton CHE, certificate *French* or *German for Business* (1 yr). Napier CC and T, postgraduate diploma *European Marketing and Languages* (1 yr). Oxford P, *Language Studies* (3 yrs). Scottish C Textiles, postgraduate diploma *European Marketing and Languages* (1 yr). Wolverhampton P, *Languages for Business* (2 yrs).

Research facilities   P of Central London. Leeds P. Middlesex P. P of North London. Portsmouth P. Wolverhampton P.

Linguistic and secretarial studies   Secretarial courses combined with modern languages, and lasting from 2 terms to 2 yrs, are available at polytechnics, CC's and CT's throughout the country; see *Secretarial Studies* (page 243).

Laryngology and Otology

First degrees   Degree courses in Medicine (for list of awarding universities, see page 198) include *Laryngology and Otology*.

Postgraduate courses   Basic science course (3 months, twice yearly) at University of London Institute of Laryngology and Otology, also clinical instruction throughout the yr; information about short/part-time courses is given in 'Summary of Postgraduate Diplomas and Courses in Medicine' – see page 266. MSc courses (full-time) in *Audiology* at universities of Manchester (Clinical Audiology, 1 yr, for registered medical practitioners, qualified and experienced teachers of the deaf, etc – see also 'Education'), Salford (modular course, to be completed in 1, 2 or exceptionally 3 yrs) and Southampton (12 months, also certificate, 6 months, in Medical Audiology).

Research facilities   At the universities of Cambridge, Dundee, Glasgow, Liverpool (MChOtol), London (Institute of Laryngology and Otology), Manchester, Newcastle upon Tyne, Oxford and Wales (Welsh National School of Medicine).

Postgraduate courses   A postgraduate diploma in *Laryngology and Otology* is awarded by the Examining Board in England of the Royal College of Physicians of London and the Royal College of Surgeons of England. Particulars from the Secretary of the Examining Board in England.
  Diplomas of Fellowship are awarded by the Royal College of Surgeons of England, the Royal College of Surgeons of Edinburgh, and the Royal College of Physicians and Surgeons of Glasgow, by examination, with *Otolaryngology* as a special subject.

Latin American Studies

First degrees   Degrees with specialisation in *Latin American Studies* awarded by the universities of Essex (School of Comparative Studies, either Latin American Studies or Latin American specialisation in certain subjects), Glasgow (for Honours in Hispanic Studies, or with another principal subject), Liverpool, London (King's and University Colleges, Modern Iberian and Latin American Regional Studies), Newcastle upon Tyne (also Spanish and Latin American Studies), Southampton (Iberian and Latin American Studies) and Warwick (Comparative American Studies covering both North and South America, alone or with English). Latin American Studies may also be included in first degree courses, usually in Spanish or Hispanic Studies, at the universities of Aberdeen (Latin American Literature), Birmingham (also in Special Honours course in American Studies), Bristol, Cambridge (Historical Tripos, Modern Languages Tripos), Edinburgh, Hull (also in History and in Sociology and Social Anthropology), Lancaster (History), Leeds, London (Latin American Regional History at University College, Latin American Literature at King's, Queen Mary and University Colleges, also Latin America as approved geographical region for study for BSc or BSc(Econ)), Manchester, Nottingham, Oxford (Spanish-American Literature), St Andrews, Sheffield, Strathclyde and Wales (Aberystwyth University College).

Postgraduate courses   Courses (1 yr and for MA, unless otherwise indicated) at the following universities:
  Latin American Area Studies, London (1 or 2 yrs, details from Institute of Latin American Studies).
  Latin American Government and Politics and *Latin American Literature* (MA scheme in Literature), Essex (each 12 months).

Latin American Studies, Cambridge (diploma), Glasgow (MPhil, 1 or 2 yrs), Liverpool (BPhil, 1 or 2 yrs), Newcastle upon Tyne (MA 1 yr, MPhil 2 yrs), Oxford (BPhil, 2 yrs) and St Andrews (options for MLitt in Spanish, 2 yrs).

Pre-Columbian and Colonial Art in Central and South America, Essex (for MA in History of Art, 12 months).

Quechua Studies, St Andrews (diploma).

Sociology of Latin America, Essex (12 months).

Spanish and Latin American Studies (Hispanic Drama), Newcastle upon Tyne.

Research facilities

At the universities of Bristol, Essex (Latin American Centre), Glasgow (Institute of Latin American Studies), Liverpool (Centre for Latin American Studies), London (London School of Economics, King's and University Colleges, and Institute of Latin American Studies, which also promotes and co-ordinates Latin American Studies at postgraduate level within the university), Manchester, Newcastle upon Tyne, Oxford (including Taylor Institution, Latin American Centre, St Antony's College), St Andrews (Centre for Latin American Linguistics) and Warwick.

First degree

CNAA degree: Portsmouth P, *Latin American Studies* (4 yrs). Course includes Spanish History, Economics, Geography, Sociology and Literature.

Law

See also Criminology

First degrees

First degrees in *Law* (courses normally 3 yrs and for LLB, unless otherwise indicated) awarded by the following universities: Aberdeen* (4th yr for Honours, also MA Joint Honours in Jurisprudence and Philosophy or Politics or International Relations), Belfast (normally 4 yrs), Birmingham, Bristol, Brunel (also major option for degree in Social Sciences, both 4 yrs S), Cambridge (BA Law Tripos, usually followed in 4th yr by LLB examination which is open to those who have obtained Honours in Law Tripos or to graduates who are barristers or solicitors), Dundee* (4th yr for Honours, also LLB Honours or MA Honours in Jurisprudence with one of certain other subjects), Durham (BA Honours, alone or with Economics or Politics or Sociology), East Anglia, Edinburgh* (4th yr for Honours, alone or with one of certain other subjects), Exeter (also BA Combined Honours in Law and Sociology and BSc in Chemistry and Law, each of which may be followed by 4th yr for BA(Law) – see also 'Accountancy'), Glasgow* (4th yr for Honours), Heriot-Watt (BA in Business Law), Hull (also BA in Law with Philosophy or Politics or Sociology), Keele (BA Honours, only with another principal subject), Kent at Canterbury (BA Honours in Faculty of Social Sciences with specialisation in Law in Part II), Leeds, Leicester, Liverpool, London (King's, Queen Mary and University Colleges, London School of Economics and School of Oriental and African Studies), Manchester, Newcastle upon Tyne, Nottingham (also BA), Oxford (BA Honour School of Jurisprudence), Reading, Sheffield (also, for candidates transferring to Faculty of Law after 1st-yr examination in another Faculty, BA(Law)), Southampton (also BSc (Social Sciences) with Law as main subject), Strathclyde* (LLB or – with another subject – BA, each with 4th yr for Honours), Sussex (BA Honours with Law as major subject in Schools of English and American or European Studies, and of Social Sciences), Wales (Aberystwyth and Cardiff University Colleges and Institute of Science and Technology) and Warwick. At Surrey Law may be offered as an option in Linguistic

*It should be noted that the degree in Law of a Scottish university is based on Scots Law.

and International Studies courses, and at some other universities also Law may be studied as an optional subject for a first degree in arts, economics, etc.

Courses in *International Law* (*Public* and/or *Private*) and *European/European Community Law* may be included in the LLB curriculum at many of the universities which award this degree.

The independent University College at Buckingham (see page 32) awards a licence in the Schools of Law and of Law, Economics and Politics; and Law is also studied in the School of European Studies.

Postgraduate courses Courses for the degree of *LLM* are provided by the universities of Bristol, Exeter, Glasgow, Leicester, London (London School of Economics, King's, Queen Mary and University Colleges, and School of Oriental and African Studies), Manchester, Newcastle upon Tyne, Sheffield and Southampton. LLM regulations vary considerably from one university to another, but the LLM awarded by Belfast, Cambridge (open only to Cambridge graduates), Dundee, Edinburgh, Hull, Keele, Liverpool, Manchester, Wales and Warwick is taken mainly by individual study or research (at Bristol and Sheffield the degree may also be taken by that method).

Oxford provides a course (normally 2 yrs, but 1 yr for exceptionally well-qualified candidates) leading to *BCL* (Bachelor of Civil Law); the BCL awarded by Durham is a research degree.

Other postgraduate courses in Law/Legal Studies (normally 1 yr and for diploma, unless otherwise indicated) at the following universities:

Advanced Legal Studies, Newcastle upon Tyne.

African Law, London (in LLM courses at School of Oriental and African Studies).

Comparative Law, Brunel (MA) and Hull.

Economics and the Law, Wales (Cardiff University College).

European Legal Studies, Exeter (LLM).

Hindu Law and *Indian Criminal Law*, London (in LLM courses at School of Oriental and African Studies).

International Business Legal Studies, Exeter (LLM).

International Law, Cambridge, Hull, Liverpool (for graduates and other approved candidates), London (University College), Manchester and Wales (Aberystwyth University College, International Law and Relations) – may also be studied for LLM at London (London School of Economics and – LLM or MSc – University College).

Law, The City (diploma of first degree standard, primarily for graduates wishing to become barristers but – see also below – without qualifying law degree) and London (postgraduate).

Laws, Belfast (1 or 2 yrs).

Legal Studies, Cambridge.

Marine Law and Policy, Wales (Institute of Science and Technology, MSc).

Muhammedan Law, London (in LLM courses at School of Oriental and African Studies).

Roman Law, Edinburgh and Glasgow.

Shipping Law, London (University College).

Sociology and Law/the Law, Brunel (MA, 1 yr full-time or $2\frac{1}{2}$ yrs part-time) and Wales (Cardiff University College).

Soviet and Yugoslav Law, London (School of Slavonic and East European Studies, for MA in Area Studies).

Welfare Law, Leicester (LLM).

Research facilities At most of the universities that award first degrees in Law (London, including Institute of Advanced Legal Studies).

The higher doctorate, *LLD* (Doctor of Laws), is awarded by most of the universities that award the LLB, but regulations vary considerably from one university to another. Oxford also awards a *DCL* (Doctor of Civil Law), open only to Oxford BCLs of at least 15 terms' standing.

Apart from university courses for degrees in Law (which do not in themselves give a student the right to practise), training for the legal profession varies according to whether the student wishes to become a Barrister-at-Law or a Solicitor.

Barristers
In ENGLAND AND WALES a person seeking to be called to the Bar must first obtain admission to one of the four Inns of Court: Lincoln's Inn, the Inner Temple, the Middle Temple or Gray's Inn, and the normal educational requirement for Admission is a United Kingdom degree, except for certain categories of mature students. Thereafter he must pass or obtain exemption from Parts I and II of the Bar Examinations (graduates with a law degree from a United Kingdom university or CNAA degree are usually exempt from Part I, as will be Buckingham licentiates in law). The former Part I examinations have been phased out and since October 1977 replaced by a qualifying examination conducted by the City University and the Polytechnic of Central London leading to the Diploma in Law Examination.

In addition to passing the prescribed examinations the Bar student is normally required to 'keep' eight terms before Call by dining in the Hall of his Inn of Court on any three days in each term. There are four dining terms in each year. There are concessions for students exempted from Part I of the examination whereby dining six times in one term may count as keeping two terms.

Lectures and tutorial classes are provided in the Inns of Court School of Law in all the subjects of the Bar Part II Examinations. Attendance on the Part II course is compulsory for those intending to practise at the Bar. Students must register for these courses, which start in September.

No student may normally be called to the Bar until he is 21 years of age.

All persons wishing to join an Inn must apply direct to the Under-Treasurer of any of the Inns and further information on the examinations and training required may be obtained from the Council of Legal Education, 4 Gray's Inn Place, London WC1R 5DX.

Solicitors
Changes in the system of training are to be introduced in 1978 for graduates (and their equivalent) and in 1980 for non-graduates. Under the existing Regulations a candidate is required to have obtained the requisite standard of general education, to have passed both parts of the Law Society's Qualifying Examination and to have served for a period under articles of clerkship.

Exemption may be granted from Part I of the Qualifying Examination to the extent that the heads of that examination have been covered in a degree or other comparable examination.

The term of articles varies. For a non-graduate it is 4 years and for a graduate either 2 or 2½ years, depending on whether Part I of the Qualifying Examination has been passed before entry into articles. With certain exceptions a non-graduate must attend a recognised course of legal education before attempting Part I, and must have passed at least 3 heads of Part I before becoming articled. Concessions in relation to the period of service under articles and examination exemptions are granted to former barristers and to those who have completed 10 years bone fide service as solicitor's clerks. The new system of training for graduates will consist of two stages:
(a) the academic stage which will be completed either by graduating with an acceptable law degree or attending a one-year course in preparation for the Common Professional Examination and
(b) the vocational stage which will be completed by attendance on a one-year course in preparation for the new final examination and two years articles.

The standard of general education which the non-graduate must obtain before he is eligible to commence to qualify will be increased in 1980 and thereafter. In effect, non-graduates who embark on a one-year Part I course in the autumn of 1979 will be the last non-graduates to commence to qualify under the current regulations. Transitional provisions have been made for certain categories of prospective solicitors who will have commenced to qualify but will not have completed their training before the introduction of the new system. Full details may be obtained from the Law Society.

In SCOTLAND the legal profession is divided into Advocates and Solicitors. Full information about requirements for admission can be obtained from the Clerk of the Faculty of Advocates and the Secretary of the Law Society of Scotland respectively.

In NORTHERN IRELAND the legal profession is organised in much the same way as in England. Information about the call to the Bar may be obtained from the Honourable Society of the Inn of Court, and about admission as solicitor from the Incorporated Law Society of Northern Ireland.

First degrees CNAA degrees in *Law* are offered at the following polytechnics and colleges (3 yrs). Birmingham P. Bristol P. P of Central London. Chelmer IHE. City of London P, *Business Law*. Ealing CHE. Kingston P. Lanchester P, also *Business Law*. Leeds P. Leicester P. Liverpool P. Manchester P. Middlesex P. Newcastle upon Tyne P. North East London P. P of North London. North Staffordshire P. P of the South Bank. Trent P, also *Legal Studies* (4 yrs S). Wolverhampton P.

Professional courses The following polytechnics offer full-time Law Society courses Part I and Part II (various periods of study, usually 1 yr for Part I and 5–7 months for Part II). There must be a year's interval between passing Part I and attempting Part II. Graduates with a Law degree can be admitted directly to Part II courses.
Bristol P. Chelmer IHE. City of London P (Part II only). Leeds P. Liverpool P (Part II only). Manchester P (Part I only). Newcastle upon Tyne P. Trent P. P of Wales.

Postgraduate course City of London P, MA *Business Law* (1 yr). Leeds P, *European Community Law and Integration* (1 yr).

Research facilities P of Central London. Kingston P. Leeds P. Trent P. Wolverhampton P.

Librarianship and Information Science

First degrees/ diplomas Degrees with specialisation awarded by the following universities:
Information Science, Belfast (BLS – Library and Information Studies), The City (Psychology and Information Processing, 3 yrs, or 4 yrs S) and Loughborough U of Technology (3 yrs, or – BSc and DPS – 4 yrs S).
Librarianship, Strathclyde (principal subject for BA Pass or, with another main subject, for BA Joint Honours) and Wales (with an arts or science academic subject for BLib, course offered jointly at Aberystwyth University College and College of Librarianship Wales).
Library Studies, Belfast (BLS – Library and Information Studies) and Loughborough U of Technology (BA or BSc Honours, 3 yrs, also with Education for BA Honours, 4 yrs S).
The City University also offers a BSc course in Systems and Management which includes study of *Information and Communication.*
Full-time diploma courses at universities for which candidates need not necessarily be graduates:
Library and Information Studies, Belfast (2 yrs, graduates 1 yr).
The Study of Records and Administration of Archives, Liverpool (1 or 2 yrs).

Postgraduate courses Courses (1 yr and for master's degree, unless otherwise indicated) at the following universities:
Archive/Library/Information Studies and Education, Loughborough U of Technology.
Archive Studies, London (University College – School of Library, Archive and Information Studies, MA or diploma).
Information Science, The City (MSc or diploma) and London (University College).
Information Studies, Loughborough U of Technology (12 months full-time or 9 months full-time plus 1 yr part-time) and Sheffield (also Information Studies (Social Sciences)).
Information Systems, London (London School of Economics).
Librarianship, Sheffield, Strathclyde (diploma) and Wales (jointly at Aberystwyth University College and College of Librarianship Wales, diploma).
Library and Information Studies, London (University College – School of Library, Archive and Information Studies, MA or diploma) and Loughborough U of Technology (diploma).
Library Studies (MLS), Belfast and Loughborough U of Technology (12 months full-time, i.e. 3 months full-time – or 1 yr part-time – following diploma course in Library and Information Studies).
Palaeography and Archives Administration, Wales (Aberystwyth and Bangor University Colleges, diploma).
Teacher Librarians (see also 'Education'), London (Institute of Education, diploma, 1 yr full-time or 2 yrs part-time).
At Durham there are some facilities for the study of Archive Administration in the department of Palaeography and Diplomatic.

Research facilities At the following universities: Belfast, The City, London (University College), Loughborough U of Technology, Manchester (Archives), Sheffield, Strathclyde and Wales (Aberystwyth University College and College of Librarianship Wales). Wales awards a degree of MLib (by thesis).

First degrees CNAA degrees (3 yrs unless otherwise stated). Birmingham P (3 yrs S). Brighton P, with *Modern Languages*. Leeds P, also *Information Science*. Liverpool P. Manchester P, *Library Studies*. Newcastle upon Tyne P. P of North London. Robert Gordon's IT.

Postgraduate courses (1 yr) Aberystwyth (C of Librarianship Wales). Birmingham P. Ealing CHE. Leeds P, also MA *Librarianship*. Liverpool P. Manchester P. Newcastle upon Tyne P. P of North London. Robert Gordon's IT. Sheffield P, MSc *Management Information Systems*.

Professional examinations Information about courses leading to the professional examinations of the Library Association can be obtained from the Association. Courses at certain institutions have also been approved by the Institute of Information Scientists as providing possible exemption from the period of practical experience necessary for Corporate Membership. For details, one should contact the Institute.

Mass Media and Communication Studies
See also *Printing and Publishing*

First degrees May be included in first degree courses at the following universities:
Aspects of Communication, Bradford (one of the themes for BA in Human Purposes and Communication, 4 yrs S).
Films, and Radio and Television Drama, Bristol (in Drama courses).

Film Studies, Kent at Canterbury (minor component of certain Combined Honours courses). University of Surrey awards a BMus(Tonmeister) in *Music with Applied Physics* (4 yrs S).

Postgraduate courses

Courses (1 yr unless otherwise indicated) at the following universities and Royal College of Art: *Educational Broadcasting,* York (diploma for experienced teachers, 1 term full-time plus 2 terms part-time).
Film and Television, Royal College of Art (MA 3 yrs, also 1-yr course – limited entry, certificate of attendance awarded).
Journalism, Wales (Cardiff University College, Centre for Postgraduate Studies in Journalism, diploma).
Radio, Television and Film, Bristol (certificate).
Sociology of Education and Mass Communication, Leicester (MA(Ed)).

Research facilities

At the following universities: Birmingham (Centre of Contemporary Cultural Studies), Leicester (Centre for Mass Communication Research), London (University College, Film Studies in Slade School of Fine Art) and New U of Ulster (Communications Media and their application to learning studies).

First degrees

CNAA degrees (3 yrs unless otherwise indicated) are offered at the following. P of Central London, *Media Studies.* Harrow CT Art, *Applied Photography, Film and TV.* London C Printing, *Visual Communication,* also *Media and Production Design.* North East London P, *Communication Design.* P of North London, *Electronic and Communications Engineering.* Plymouth P, *Communication Engineering* (4 yrs S). St Martin's S Art, *Fine Art,* option in *Film.* Sheffield P, *Communication Studies.* Sunderland P, *Communication Studies.* P of Wales, *Communications.*

BEd and certificate of education courses

The following institutions of education offer options in Communication Studies as part of their Certificate of Education (3 yrs) and/or BEd courses. Crewe and Alsager CHE, *Communication Studies* (BEd). Edge Hill CHE, *Communication in Contemporary Society* (BEd). Hull CHE, *Drama and Communication Media* (BEd, Cert Ed). C Ripon and York St John, *Film and Television* (BEd, Cert Ed). C St Hild and St Bede, *Film and Television* (BEd). Trinity and All Saints C, *Communication Arts and Media* (BEd). Ulster C, Northern Ireland P, *Communication Studies* (BEd).

HND courses

Glasgow CT, *Communication Studies* (2 yrs). Napier CC and T, *Communication Studies* (2 yrs). Oldham CT, *Electrical and Electronic Engineering* with *Radio, TV and Communications* options (3 yrs S).

Diploma courses

Birmingham P, CNAA diploma *Communication Studies* (3 yrs). Hull CHE, diploma *TV Design* (3 yrs). Loughry C Agriculture and Food Technology, diploma *Agricultural Communication* (1 yr). Southampton C Art, diploma *Creative Communication Studies* (3 yrs). Watford CT, postgraduate diploma *Advertising* (1 yr), diploma *Advertising Writing* (1 yr).

Broadcasting (sound and television)

The Thomson Television College provides two 16-week courses each year concentrating on Broadcast Engineering for practising members of broadcasting organisations in developing countries. Enquiries should be made through a British High Commissioner's Office, Embassy or legation, or a British Council office overseas. A limited number of scholarships are available.
    The British Broadcasting Corporation provides the following training for members of overseas broadcasting organisations, whose applications must be sponsored by their employers.
(i)   Courses in radio production techniques through the medium of practical exercises. There are one general course and one specialised course for experienced broadcasters a year. Each

lasts 12 weeks and may be followed by up to 2 weeks attachments to BBC output departments.

(ii) Courses in television production, including studio and film direction, lighting and sound, planning and design and colour techniques. There are two 12-week courses a year followed by up to 2 weeks attachments.

(iii) One 3-month newswriting course a year for editorial staff in radio and television news.

(iv) Places on various BBC domestic courses in broadcasting engineering, followed by attachments.

(v) One 8-week course most years in broadcasting management for middle and senior executives.

(vi) Training courses in the programme and engineering fields may be arranged on the premises of overseas broadcasting stations.

Applications by broadcasting organisations proposing themselves to meet the cost of training should be made direct to the BBC (Head of Personnel and Administration, International Relations). (Address on p 284).

Organisations seeking British Government Technical Cooperation funds, should apply through their own governments to the local British Embassy or High Commission, or to their local British Council office.

Film and television   Harrow CT Art, diploma *Photography* with specialisation in *Film and TV* (3 yrs). London International Film School, diploma courses (2 yrs) (film only, candidates from overseas must normally be graduates). National Film School, courses in *Film Production, Direction, Camera, Editing, Writing* and *Sound* (all 3 yrs). Ravensbourne C Art, *Television Production* (2 yrs). West Surrey C Art and Design, diploma in *Television and Film Production* (3 yrs).

Journalism   Darlington CT, international diploma *Journalism* (1 yr). Harlow TC, professional course *Journalism Studies* (1 yr). London C Fashion, college diploma *Fashion Writer's* course (1 yr). Preston P, professional course for certificate of National Council for the Training of Journalists (1 yr).

A number of colleges provide pre-entry college diploma courses in Journalism in preparation for the National Council for the Training of Journalists course (1 yr). Full details can be obtained from the Council.

The Thomson Foundation provides three 3-month courses each year in journalistic techniques for practising journalists and newspaper executives from developing countries. The courses are based in Cardiff and a limited number of scholarships are available. Applications must be made through the British Council, a British Embassy or High Commission, or the Commonwealth Press Union. The Thomson Foundation awards scholarships in suitable cases covering tuition and all costs, except fares, to applicants sponsored by their newspapers.

Materials Science and Technology

See also Engineering, Chemical; Metallurgy; and Polymer Science and Technology

First degrees   Degrees with specialisation awarded by the following universities:
Ceramics, Leeds and Sheffield.
Engineering Materials Technology, Aston in Birmingham.
Glasses (Science and Technology of), Sheffield.
Materials, Birmingham (with Metallurgy), Reading (Chemical Physics (Materials and Molecules)) and Wales (Swansea University College, with Economics).

Materials Engineering, The City (Mechanical/Materials Engineering, 3 yrs or 4 yrs S) and Loughborough U of Technology (3 yrs or – BSc and DIS – 4 yrs S).

Materials Science, Aston in Birmingham (Metals and Materials Science with another subject), Bath (3 yrs, or 4 yrs S), Cambridge, Lancaster (Science of Materials), Leeds, Liverpool (Materials Science (Chemistry) or (Physics)), London (Imperial and Queen Mary Colleges), Manchester (University and Institute of Science and Technology), Nottingham (Chemistry or Metallurgy and Materials Science), Oxford (Metallurgy and Science of Materials), Sussex, Wales (Bangor University College, Science of Materials, also Materials Science with Physics) and Warwick (Materials Science and Physics, also Materials and Engineering Sciences).

Materials Science and Technology, Bradford (4 yrs S), Brunel (4 yrs S), Sheffield and Wales (Swansea University College).

Materials Technology, Brunel (with Management, 4 yrs S), Manchester (University and Institute of Science and Technology, Metals and Materials Technology), Nottingham (Production and Materials Technology) and Surrey (alone, or with French or German and Regional Studies, or with Business Economics – 4 yrs including industrial training yr which is spent abroad if language option taken).

Paper Science, Manchester (Institute of Science and Technology).

Physics of Materials, Manchester.

Science of Engineering Materials, Newcastle upon Tyne.

Less specialised study of Materials Science may also be included in first degree courses (usually in Engineering and/or Metallurgy) at some of the universities named above and at Belfast, Dundee, Glasgow, Heriot-Watt, Salford (also Electrical Materials Science in Electronics course), Southampton and Wales (Cardiff University College).

Postgraduate courses   Courses (1 yr and for master's degree, unless otherwise indicated) at the following universities and Cranfield IT:

Advanced Mechanics of Materials, Strathclyde (option for MSc in Mechanical Engineering).

Ceramics, Leeds (diploma, 1, 2 or 3 yrs) and Sheffield (MScTech or – open to suitably qualified candidates – diploma).

Electronic Materials and Devices, Wales (Bangor University College, also diploma).

Electronic Science of Materials, Salford.

Exploitation of Materials, Leeds (12 months).

Glass Technology, Sheffield (diploma 1 yr, MScTech 1 or 2 yrs).

Materials (with options in Materials (General), Metallic Materials, Polymeric Materials, Welding Technology), Cranfield IT (1 or 2 yrs).

Materials and Construction Management, Birmingham.

Materials Protection, Loughborough U of Technology in association with Manchester (Institute of Science and Technology).

Materials Technology, Cambridge, London (Imperial College, MSc and/or DIC) and Sheffield (diploma).

Mechanical Properties of Solids, Newcastle upon Tyne.

Mechanics and Materials, The City (1 yr full-time or 2 yrs part-time).

Metallic and Ceramic Materials, Manchester (Institute of Science and Technology, MSc or diploma).

Non-Destructive Testing of Materials, Brunel (1 yr full-time or $2\frac{1}{2}$ yrs part-time).

Optical and Electrical Properties of Materials, London (Royal Holloway College).

Physics of Materials, Bristol.

Polymer and Fibre Science, Manchester (Institute of Science and Technology, MSc or diploma).

Powder Technology, Bradford (diploma) and London (King's College).

Science and Applications of Electric Plasmas, Oxford (for MSc in Engineering Science).

Science of Materials, London (Imperial College, MSc and/or DIC, particularly as applied to the Chemical, Electrical, Mechanical and Metallurgical industries).
Technology of Engineering Materials, Aston in Birmingham.
Theory of Materials, Sheffield (1 or 2 yrs).

Research facilities
At the following universities: Bath, Birmingham (Centre for Materials Science), Bradford, Bristol, Brunel, Cambridge, Dundee, Glasgow, Lancaster, Liverpool, London (Imperial and Queen Mary Colleges), Loughborough U of Technology, Manchester (including Paper Science at Institute of Science and Technology), Newcastle upon Tyne, Nottingham, Oxford, Reading, Salford, Sheffield (including Ceramics, Glass Technology), Southampton, Strathclyde, Surrey, Sussex, Wales (Bangor, Cardiff and Swansea University Colleges) and Warwick; and at Cranfield IT.

First degrees
CNAA degrees in *Materials Science* are offered at the following (4 yrs S). Lanchester P, *Materials Technology*. North Staffordshire P, *Ceramic Technology*. Royal Military C Science, *Applied Science* (*Materials Science*) (3 yrs). Sunderland P. Thames P.

HND courses
Nene C, *Leather Technology* (2 yrs). Sunderland P, *Metallurgy* (*Materials Science*) (2 yrs).

Postgraduate courses
North Staffordshire P, MSc *Electro-Ceramics* (1 yr). Oxford P, MSc *Technology and Economics of Chemical Processes* (1 yr). Portsmouth P, MSc *Biodeterioration of Materials* (1 yr). Thames P, *MSc Molecular Science of Materials* (1 yr).

Other courses
Birmingham P, diploma *Ceramics* (3 yrs). Brighton P, certificate *Industrial Ceramics* (3 yrs). P of North London, Associateship of the National C of Rubber Technology (1 yr).

Research facilities
Brighton P. Lanchester P. Newcastle upon Tyne P. North East London P. North Staffordshire P. Plymouth P. Wolverhampton P.

Mathematics

See also Statistics

First degrees
Degrees with specialisation awarded by the following universities:
Actuarial Mathematics and Statistics, Heriot-Watt.
Actuarial Science, The City and London (London School of Economics).
Applied Mathematics, Hull, Leeds, London (Queen Mary College), Reading, St Andrews, Sheffield, Wales (Aberystwyth, Bangor and Swansea University Colleges) and Warwick.
Engineering Mathematics, Bristol, Nottingham (Mathematics – with – Engineering), Southampton, Sussex and Warwick (Mathematical Engineering, diverges from Engineering Science course during 2nd yr).
Mathematical Chemistry, Essex.
Mathematical Economics, Birmingham, Essex and Nottingham.
Mathematical Physics, Birmingham, Edinburgh, Liverpool and Sussex.
Mathematical Sciences, Bradford, Glasgow, Newcastle upon Tyne (in conjunction with computing laboratory), Reading and Strathclyde.
Mathematical Statistics, see 'Statistics'.
Mathematical Studies, Bath (3 yrs, or 4 yrs S), Heriot-Watt, Hull and Loughborough U of Technology (3 yrs, or – for BSc and DIS – 4 yrs S).

Mathematics (at some of those universities which have separate faculties – of arts, science, etc – these degree courses may be available in both the arts faculty and the science faculty, and there may be differences between faculties both in the requirements for admission and in the syllabus or choice of options), Aberdeen, Aston in Birmingham (3 yrs, or 4 yrs S), Belfast, Birmingham, Bradford (4 yrs S), Bristol, Brunel (4 yrs S), Cambridge, The City (3 yrs, or 4 yrs S), Dundee, Durham, East Anglia, Edinburgh, Essex, Exeter, Glasgow, Heriot-Watt, Hull, Keele (with another principal subject, but Mathematics alone possible in final yr, also for BSc in Integrated Physical Science), Kent at Canterbury, Lancaster, Leeds, Leicester, Liverpool, London (Bedford, Birkbeck (part-time), Chelsea, Imperial, King's, Queen Elizabeth, Queen Mary, Royal Holloway, University and Westfield Colleges, and London School of Economics, also Goldsmiths' College), Manchester (University and Institute of Science and Technology), Newcastle upon Tyne, Nottingham, Oxford, Reading, St Andrews, Salford (Mathematics with Modern Applications, 4 yrs S, or Mathematics with one of certain other subjects), Sheffield, Southampton, Stirling, Strathclyde, Surrey (with Computing Science or with Statistics), Sussex, New U of Ulster, Wales (Aberystwyth, Bangor, Cardiff and Swansea University Colleges, also – Mathematics and its Applications, 3 yrs, or 4 yrs S – Institute of Science and Technology), Warwick and York.

Modern Mathematics, Surrey (3 yrs, or 4 yrs S).

Pure Mathematics, Birmingham, Hull, Leeds, Liverpool, London (Queen Mary College), Reading, Sheffield and Wales (Aberystwyth, Bangor, Cardiff and Swansea University Colleges).

Technological Mathematics, Surrey (4 yrs S).

At many universities a Mathematical subject may also be studied with another principal subject for a Joint (or Combined) Honours degree, and less specialised study of Mathematics may be included in first degree courses in arts and/or science.

Postgraduate courses Courses (normally 1 yr and for master's degree, unless otherwise indicated) at the following universities and Cranfield IT:

Applicable Mathematics, Cranfield IT (1 or 2 yrs).

Applied Mathematics, Exeter, London (Imperial College for MSc and/or DIC, Royal Holloway College, also – in wide variety of topics and largely on intercollegiate basis – Bedford and Westfield Colleges), Manchester (with Fluid Mechanics, minimum 1 yr), Southampton (Applied Mathematics and Theoretical Physics, 12 months), Wales (Bangor University College) and York (various topics, 12 months).

Applied Mathematics and Mathematical Physics, London (Chelsea College) and Wales (Cardiff University College).

Applied Numerical Analysis and Optimisation, Edinburgh.

Biometry, Reading (diploma or MSc, 12 months).

Elementary Particle Theory, Kent at Canterbury.

Engineering Mathematics, Newcastle upon Tyne.

Fluid Mechanics, Bristol and Manchester (with Applied Mathematics, minimum 1 yr).

Functional Analysis and Differential Equations, Dundee.

Industrial Applied Mathematics, Hull and Sheffield jointly.

Industrial Mathematics and Statistics, Aston in Birmingham (12 months).

Information Processing, Exeter.

Mathematical Economics, Liverpool (BPhil, 1 or 2 yrs).

Mathematical Education, see 'Education'.

Mathematical Logic, East Anglia (MA 1 yr, BPhil 2 yrs).

Mathematical Logic and Foundations of Mathematics, Bristol and London (London School of Economics, 1 yr full-time or 2 yrs part-time).

Mathematical Psychology, Stirling.

Mathematical Statistics, see 'Statistics'.

Mathematical Techniques and their Applications, Newcastle upon Tyne.

Mathematics, Aberdeen, Cambridge (Mathematical Tripos, Part III), The City (1 yr full-time or 2 yrs part-time), Leeds (minimum 12 months), London (1 yr full-time or 2 yrs part-time at Birkbeck and Chelsea Colleges and London School of Economics, also courses in selected topics at Bedford, King's and Queen Mary Colleges, and diploma course at Chelsea College), Manchester (also – Mathematics (Applied and Pure) – diploma), Nottingham, Oxford (wide range of main subjects), Sussex (options include Algebra, Analysis and Differential Equations, Fluid Mechanics) and Warwick.

Mathematics and Mathematical Education, York (2 yrs).

Mathematics of Modern Control Systems, Loughborough U of Technology (MSc or associateship).

Mathematics with Applications, Brunel (1 yr full-time or 2½ yrs part-time).

Methods of Applied Mathematics, Liverpool.

Numerical Analysis, see 'Computer Science and Technology'.

Numerical and Statistical Mathematics, Lancaster.

Numerical Solutions of Differential Equations, Reading (12 months full-time or 24 months part-time).

Operational Mathematics, Liverpool.

Practical Analysis for Applied Mathematics, Wales (Aberystwyth University College).

Probability and Statistics, Sheffield.

Pure Mathematics, Birmingham, Durham (jointly with Newcastle upon Tyne), Hull (12 months), Kent at Canterbury, London (Chelsea College, Imperial College for MSc and/or DIC, Royal Holloway College, also – in wide variety of topics and largely on intercollegiate basis – Bedford, Queen Elizabeth and Westfield Colleges), Newcastle upon Tyne, Wales (Aberystwyth – for MSc or College diploma – and Bangor University Colleges) and York (various topics, 12 months).

Relativity and Quantum Theory, Newcastle upon Tyne.

Solid State Theory, Wales (Cardiff University College).

Statistics and Numerical Method, London (Chelsea College).

Theoretical and Applied Mechanics, Manchester (Institute of Science and Technology, MSc or diploma).

Theoretical Mechanics, East Anglia.

Theory and Technology of the Mechanics of Solids, Cranfield IT (1 or 2 yrs).

Topology, Liverpool.

Research facilities
At almost all universities (at Keele, postgraduate certificate in education may be taken concurrently with research for PhD). Essex: Fluid Mechanics Research Institute. Loughborough U of Technology: Centre for Advancement of Mathematical Education in Technology. Warwick: Mathematics Research Centre.

First degrees
CNAA degrees in *Mathematics* are offered at the following (4 yrs S unless otherwise indicated): Hatfield P. Lanchester P. Leicester P. Middlesex P, *Mathematics for Business.* Newcastle upon Tyne P. P of North London, *Mathematics and Computing.* North Staffordshire P, *Mathematical Analysis for Business.* Paisley CT. Portsmouth P. Robert Gordon's IT, *Mathematical Sciences* (3 yrs). Royal Military C Science, *Applied Science* (*Mathematics and Mathematical Methods*) (3 yrs). P of the South Bank, *Mathematics and Computing.* Teesside P, modular degree *Mathematical and Computer Sciences* (4 yrs). Thames P, also *Mathematics, Statistics and Computing* (3 yrs). Wigan CT. P of Wales, with *Computer Science.*

Mathematics is also offered as an optional subject within the CNAA Combined Studies and Science degrees (see *Science* (*General*)).

HND courses | Mathematics, Statistics and Computing (normally 2 yrs), see Computer Science and Technology.

Quantitative Methods for Management, Aberdeen CC (2 yrs), Bell CT (2 yrs).
Applicable Mathematics, Dundee CT (3 yrs S).
Mathematics, Napier CC and T (2½ yrs S).

Postgraduate courses and college diplomas | Leicester P (1 yr). Teeside P, MSc Applicable Mathematics (4 terms S). Sheffield P, associateship course (1 yr after HND).

Professional courses | Information about the Graduateship of the Institute of Mathematics and its Applications can be obtained from the Institute.

Research facilities | Available at most of the polytechnics mentioned above.

Medical/Health Physics
See also Engineering, Medical; and Radiology

First degrees | Degrees with specialisation awarded by the following universities:
Health Physics and Environmental Physics, Salford.
Physics with Medical Applications, London (Queen Elizabeth College).
Physics with Medical Physics, Sussex.

Postgraduate courses | Courses (1 yr and for MSc, unless otherwise indicated) at the following universities (candidates must be suitably, but not necessarily medically, qualified):
Biophysics and Medical Physics, Manchester (for MSc or diploma in Physics).
Clinical Measurement, London (St Bartholomew's Hospital Medical College).
Health Physics, Salford (modular course).
Medical Biophysics, London (intercollegiate course at Guy's, Middlesex and St Mary's Hospital Medical Schools).
Medical Electronics, London (St Bartholomew's Hospital Medical College).
Medical Physics, Aberdeen and Surrey (minimum 12 months full-time or 24 months collaboratively).
Nuclear Reactor Science and Engineering, London (Imperial and Queen Mary Colleges jointly, MSc and/or College diplomas).
Radiation and Environmental Protection, Surrey.
Radiation Biology, London (1 yr full-time or 2 yrs part-time, jointly at Guy's, Middlesex, Royal Free and St Bartholomew's Hospital Medical Schools).
Radiation Physics, London (1 yr full-time or 2 yrs part-time, Middlesex and St Bartholomew's Hospital Medical Schools).
Radiological Health and Safety, Salford.

Research facilities | At the universities of Aberdeen, Dundee (Medical Biophysics), Edinburgh, Exeter, Glasgow, Leeds, London, Newcastle upon Tyne and Surrey.

Medical Laboratory Technology

First degrees   Included in University of Bradford BTech (4 yrs S) in *Medical Sciences.*

First degree   Portsmouth P, Joint Honours in *Medical Laboratory Sciences* and *Physiology.*

HND courses   *Medical Laboratory Subjects* (3 yrs S): Birmingham P. Bristol P. South Glamorgan IHE.

Professional courses   Day release, part-time courses are also available, usually for those employed in medical laboratories. Details of these can be obtained from the Institute of Medical Laboratory Sciences.

A State Register of Medical Laboratory Technicians is maintained by the Council for Professions Supplementary to Medicine.

Medicine and Surgery
See also under special subjects such as Anaesthetics, Cardiology, etc.

Note. Medical Schools are at present meeting heavy demands from British students and consequently there can be only a limited number of vacancies for students from overseas.

Qualifying degrees and diplomas   First degrees in *Medicine and Surgery* – MB, ChB unless otherwise indicated – are awarded by the universities of Aberdeen, Belfast (MB, BCh, BAO), Birmingham, Bristol, Cambridge (MB, BChir), Dundee, Edinburgh, Glasgow, Leeds, Leicester, Liverpool, London (MB, BS – for Medical Schools, see page 269), Manchester, Newcastle upon Tyne (MB, BS), Nottingham (BM, BS), Oxford (BM, BCh), Sheffield, Southampton (BM) and Wales (MB, BCh – Welsh National School of Medicine). The regulations are generally uniform: satisfactory attendance is required during at least 5 yrs (generally 6) at recognised courses of study and hospital practice. After qualification, graduates must spend a further year in specified appointments in recognised hospitals before they can apply for full medical registration.

At Cambridge and Oxford students normally qualify for the BA at the end of their first 3 yrs, before beginning their clinical studies (which they may take either at the university concerned or at another approved clinical school); Nottingham awards a BMedSci at the end of the 3-yr Medical Sciences course, which is followed by 2 yrs' clinical study before qualification; and at some universities medical students may qualify for BSc in one of various science subjects – e.g. Anatomy, Biochemistry, Physiology (Aberdeen: BMedBiol) – by intercalating 1 yr's (Glasgow: 2 yrs') additional study between the pre-clinical and clinical parts of their course.

Other registrable qualifications (which are taken by many medical students at universities as an alternative or additional qualification to a degree) are the diplomas awarded by the Royal College of Physicians of London and the Royal College of Surgeons of England (LRCPLond, MRCSEng), by the Society of Apothecaries of London (LMSSALond) and by the Conjoint Board of the Royal College of Physicians of Edinburgh, the Royal College of Surgeons of Edinburgh and the Royal College of Physicians and Surgeons of Glasgow (LRCP(Edin), LRCS(Edin), LRCPS(Glas)).

First degrees in medical science(s)   Degrees in *Medical Science/Sciences* (usually BSc(MedSci), BMedSci, etc), which do not qualify holder for medical registration, awarded by the universities of Aberdeen (BMedBiol – see above), Bradford (BTech, 4 yrs S), Dundee (1 yr, may be intercalated at various times during normal medical course, but not before 2nd professional MB, ChB examination), Edinburgh (may be taken by medical students, at end of first 3 yrs, who have followed prescribed courses),

Newcastle upon Tyne (for selected candidates who have passed stage I examinations), Nottingham (see above), St Andrews (3 yrs for Ordinary degree, Honours – by special arrangement the graduates then study in Manchester clinical s MB, ChB of University of Manchester) and Sheffield (may be taken by medical student passing 2nd MB examination at satisfactory standard, who have followed prescribed cou

Higher qualifications

Higher qualifications in Medicine. Except at Birmingham, Bristol and Southampton the degr of MD (Nottingham, Oxford and Southampton: DM), which may be conferred by all those universities offering first degrees in Medicine and Surgery, is open only to the universities' own graduates in Medicine and Surgery (or in some cases, to suitably qualified graduates of other universities who hold teaching, research or hospital appointments in or near the university concerned). At Birmingham, Bristol and Southampton, graduates in Medicine and Surgery from other approved universities may qualify for the MD/DM by undertaking 2 yrs' approved research within the university (at Birmingham such graduates must also have held, for at least 5 yrs before presenting themselves for the MD, an approved degree that is also recognised for registration by the General Medical Council). At most of the universities which offer first degree courses, suitably qualified graduates of other universities may undertake research in Medicine leading to PhD (Dundee, also MMSc; Sheffield, also MMedSci); also, in Medical Sciences, at Bradford (facilities normally restricted to doctors living or working in the area).

The Royal Colleges of Physicians of London and of Edinburgh and the Royal College of Physicians and Surgeons of Glasgow together award a Diploma of Membership (MRCP(UK)) by common examinations. (The Fellowship of these bodies (FRCP) is conferred by election, not by examination.)

Particulars may be obtained from the Secretary of the Royal College of Physicians of London, the Secretary of the Royal College of Physicians of Edinburgh, and the Secretary of the Royal College of Physicians and Surgeons of Glasgow.

Higher qualifications in Surgery. Except at Bristol and Southampton the degree of ChM (Cambridge: MChir; London, Newcastle upon Tyne and Southampton: MS; Belfast, Oxford and Wales: MCh), which may be conferred by most of the universities offering first degrees in Medicine and Surgery, is open only to the universities' own graduates in Medicine and Surgery (or in some cases to suitably qualified graduates of other universities who hold teaching, research or hospital appointments in or near the university concerned). At Bristol and Southampton the conditions for graduates of other universities are similar to those for the MD/DM (see above). At Birmingham, Glasgow and Nottingham, which do not offer a separate degree of Master of Surgery, the degree of MD may be conferred for work relevant to either Medicine or Surgery; but only at Birmingham – see also above – is this degree open (subject to certain requirements) to graduates of other universities.

The Royal College of Surgeons of England, the Royal College of Surgeons of Edinburgh and the Royal College of Physicians and Surgeons of Glasgow each grant a Fellowship (FRCSEng, FRCSEd, FRCSGlas) by examination. The examination consists of two parts. The first part deals with the basic medical sciences: Applied Anatomy, Applied Physiology and Pathology (for courses, see under separate headings). The second part is in Clinical Surgery. Regulations can be obtained from the Secretary of the Examining Board in England of the Royal College of Physicians of London and the Royal College of Surgeons of England (FRCSEng), the Clerk of the Royal College of Surgeons of Edinburgh (FRCSEd), and the Secretary of the Royal College of Physicians and Surgeons of Glasgow (FRCSGlas).

Postgraduate courses (full-time) in:

General Medicine, universities of Edinburgh (18 weeks) and London (Royal Postgraduate Medical School, 10 weeks).

General Surgery, Edinburgh Postgraduate Board for Medicine (15 weeks) and University of London (St Thomas's Hospital Medical School, 8 weeks), also Royal College of Surgeons of Edinburgh (Surgical Pathology and Operative Surgery, 9 weeks).

University of London (Middlesex, Royal Free, St Thomas's and Royal
Medical Schools and Institute of Cancer Research, 1 yr for MSc).
urses, and/or part-time courses of varying lengths, are also provided by some
offering first degrees in Medicine and Surgery and at Postgraduate Medical
versity of Exeter; fuller information is given in 'Summary of Postgraduate
Courses in Medicine' – see page 266.
sh Postgraduate Medical Federation, a School of the University of London, is
onsible for the development of postgraduate medical education in the University. The
Federation comprises 13 specialist Institutes associated with postgraduate teaching hospitals–
(see under separate subjects, e.g. Cardiology).
The Scottish Council for Postgraduate Medical Education has been set up to plan and correlate
the facilities for postgraduate education in Scotland. Details of courses available in Scotland
from the Secretary of the Council.

A National Advice Centre is administered by the Council for Postgraduate Medical Education
in England and Wales and may be consulted on specific training problems.

Medicine, Forensic

See also Pharmacy

First degrees   Degree courses in Medicine (for list of awarding universities, see page 198) and also, at some
universities, in Law, include some study of *Forensic Medicine* or *Medical Jurisprudence*.

Postgraduate   Provision for course (10 weeks) at University of Glasgow (may be held if sufficient number of
courses   applications received).

Research   At the universities of Belfast, Dundee, Edinburgh, Glasgow, Liverpool and London (Guy's and
facilities   St George's Hospital Medical Schools).

Diploma   A diploma in *Medical Jurisprudence* is awarded by the Society of Apothecaries. The
course   examination is in two parts of which Part II can be taken in clinical medicine or pathology.

Metallurgy

See also Materials Science and Technology

First degrees   Degrees with specialisation awarded by the following universities:
Engineering Metallurgy, Salford (4 yrs S).
Metallurgical Engineering, Loughborough U of Technology (with Management, 4 yrs S) and
      Wales (Cardiff University College).
Metallurgy, Aston in Birmingham (4 yrs S), Birmingham (with Materials), Brunel (alone or with
      Management, each 4 yrs S), Cambridge (Natural Sciences Tripos), Leeds, Liverpool,
      London (Imperial College for BSc(Eng) and associateship of Royal School of Mines),
      Manchester (University – also with Chemistry – and Institute of Science and
      Technology – also with Mechanical Engineering), Newcastle upon Tyne, Nottingham
      (with Materials Science), Oxford (Metallurgy and Science of Materials), Sheffield,
      Strathclyde, Surrey (alone, or with French or German and Regional Studies, or with
      Business Economics, 4 yrs including industrial training yr which is spent abroad if
      foreign language option taken) and Wales (Cardiff and Swansea University Colleges,
      BSc and College diplomas).

Metals, Aston in Birmingham (with Materials Science and another subject) and Manchester (University and Institute of Science and Technology, Metals and Materials Technology).

Postgraduate courses Courses (normally 1 yr and for master's degree, unless otherwise indicated) at the following universities and Cranfield IT:
Corrosion Science, Manchester (Institute of Science and Technology, MSc or diploma).
Extraction Metallurgy, London (Imperial College, MSc and/or DIC).
Industrial Metallurgy and Management Techniques, Aston in Birmingham.
Mechanical Properties of Solids, Newcastle upon Tyne.
Metallic Materials, Cranfield IT (1 or 2 yrs, option for MSc in Materials) and Manchester (Institute of Science and Technology, MSc or diploma in Metallic and Ceramic Materials).
Metallurgical Processes and Management, Birmingham.
Metallurgical Quality Control, Brunel (1 yr full-time or 2½ yrs part-time).
Metallurgy, Cambridge (certificate of postgraduate study, 1 yr, in exceptional circumstances 2 yrs), Dundee (for diploma in Mechanical Engineering), Leeds (diploma, 1, 2 or 3 yrs) and Sheffield (diploma 1 yr, MMet 1 or 2 yrs).
Surface Technology and Management, Aston in Birmingham.
Terotechnology, Manchester (University and Institute of Science and Technology, MSc or diploma).
Welding Technology, Aston in Birmingham (Welding Technology and Management) and Cranfield IT (1 or 2 yrs, option for MSc in Materials).

Research facilities At most of the universities named above (Manchester – Institute of Science and Technology: Corrosion and Protection Centre) and at Warwick; also Scottish Universities Research and Reactor Centre, East Kilbride.

First degrees CNAA degrees are offered at the following polytechnics (4 yrs S): City of London P, *Metallurgy and Materials.* Sheffield P, *Metallurgy and Microstructural Engineering.*

HND courses *Metallurgy* (3 yrs S). Manchester P. North East Wales IHE. Sheffield P. P of the South Bank, *Applied Chemistry (Metal Finishing)* (2 yrs). Sunderland P, *Metallurgy (Materials Science)* (4 yrs S). Teesside P.
Foundry Technology (3 yrs S). Bolton IT. Chesterfield CT. West Bromwich CC and T, *Cast Metals Technology (Foundry or Diecasting).*

Postgraduate courses City of London P, MSc *Corrosion Science and Engineering* (1 yr). Sheffield P, MSc *Metallurgical Process Management* (1 yr).

College diplomas Courses 1 yr after HND: Bolton IT (also *Foundry Studies* diploma, 2 yrs S). City of London P, advanced diploma in *Metallurgy* (1 yr). Manchester P. North East Wales IHE, post-HND diploma (1 yr).

Other courses Bolton IT, associateship in *Foundry Technology* (6 months). Sheffield P, Associateship in Metallurgy (1 yr). P of the South Bank, Graduateship of the Institute of Metal Finishing (1 yr). Information on membership of the Institute of Metal Finishing and the Institution of Metallurgists can be obtained from the bodies concerned.

Research facilities City of London P. Lanchester P. Manchester P. North Staffordshire P. Sheffield P. Teesside P.

Meteorology (including Climatology)

First degrees University of Reading awards a BSc in *Meteorology* (3½ yrs S, also with Physics, 3 yrs). Less specialised study of Meteorology may be included in first degree courses at Cambridge (Geographical Tripos), Edinburgh (MA, BSc), New U of Ulster (for degree in Geography) and Wales (Institute of Science and Technology, with Oceanography for BSc(Tech) in Maritime Studies).

Climatology may be included in first degree courses (in Geography) at Birmingham (with Biogeography), Reading (for degrees in Geography and in Environmental Plant Geography) and Wales (Aberystwyth University College).

Postgraduate Courses (1 yr and for MSc, unless otherwise indicated) at the following universities:
courses *Atmospheric Physics and Dynamics*, London (Imperial College, MSc and/or DIC).
Meteorology, Reading (12 months).
Meteorology and Climatology, Birmingham.

Research At the following universities: Birmingham, Cambridge, Heriot-Watt (Satellite Radiometry),
facilities London (Imperial College and – Applied Climatology – University College), Reading, Southampton and New U of Ulster (Applied Meteorology, Micro-Climatology).

Microbiology

See also Bacteriology

First degrees Degrees with specialisation in *Microbiology* awarded by the following universities: Aberdeen, Bath (in Applied Biology course, 4 yrs S), Belfast, Birmingham (Honours in School of Biological Sciences with specialisation in groups of relevant subjects), Bradford (special subject in Applied Biology course), Bristol, Dundee, Edinburgh, Glasgow, Heriot-Watt, Kent at Canterbury, Leeds (alone or with one of certain other subjects), Leicester (Honours in Biology with specialisation in a group of relevant subjects), Liverpool, London (Chelsea, Imperial, Queen Elizabeth, Queen Mary and University Colleges, also – with Botany – Bedford College, and – with Biochemistry or Botany – Royal Holloway College), Loughborough U of Technology (with Chemistry, 4 yrs S for BSc and DIS), Reading, Sheffield (alone or with other principal subjects), Stirling, Strathclyde (Applied, also Microbiology with Genetics), Surrey (also Plant Microbiology, each 3 yrs or 4 yrs S), Wales (Aberystwyth, Cardiff and Swansea University Colleges) and Warwick (Microbiology and Virology). Less specialised study of Microbiology may also be included in first degree courses at many of these universities and at East Anglia, Essex, Hull, Lancaster, Nottingham, Sussex, New U of Ulster and York.

Postgraduate Courses (1 yr and for MSc, unless otherwise indicated) at the following universities:
courses *Applied Microbiology*, Heriot-Watt and Strathclyde (diploma).
Food Microbiology, Reading (option for MSc in Food Technology, 12 months).
Food Science and Microbiology, Strathclyde (1 or 2 yrs).
Gene Technology in Micro-organisms, Essex (12 months).
Industrial Microbiology, Heriot-Watt (diploma).
Microbiological Chemistry, Newcastle upon Tyne.

Research At the following universities: Aberdeen, Birmingham, Bradford, Bristol, Cambridge, Dundee,
facilities East Anglia, Edinburgh, Essex, Glasgow, Heriot-Watt (Biochemical Microbiology), Kent at Canterbury, Lancaster, Leeds, Liverpool, London (Bedford, Birkbeck, Chelsea, Imperial,

King's, Queen Elizabeth, Queen Mary and University Colleges, certain Medical Schools including King's, St Bartholomew's, St Mary's and St Thomas's, and London School of Hygiene and Tropical Medicine, also National Institute for Medical Research and Rothamsted Experimental Station), Loughborough U of Technology, Manchester, Newcastle upon Tyne, Nottingham, Oxford, Reading, Sheffield, Southampton, Stirling, Strathclyde, Surrey, Sussex, New U of Ulster, Wales (Aberystwyth, Cardiff and Swansea University Colleges), Warwick and York.

First degrees The study of *Microbiology* is included in most CNAA degrees in Applied Biology (see *Biology*).

Mining and Mineral Sciences
See also Fuel Technology, and Geology

First degrees Degrees with specialisation awarded by the following universities:
Mineralogy and Petrology, Cambridge (Natural Sciences Tripos).
Mineral Processing, Leeds (alone or with Chemistry) and Wales (Cardiff University College).
Minerals Engineering (Coal or Metal), Birmingham.
Mineral Technology, London (Imperial College – course also leads to associateship of Royal School of Mines).
Mining, Leeds, London (Imperial College – course also leads to associateship of Royal School of Mines).
Mining Engineering, Newcastle upon Tyne, Nottingham (also Exploration Sciences), Strathclyde and Wales (Cardiff University College).
Mining Geology, Leeds, Leicester, London (Imperial College) and Wales (Cardiff University College).
Less specialised study of Mineralogy may be included in first degree courses in science (usually Geology) at many universities.

Postgraduate courses Courses (1 yr and for MSc, unless otherwise indicated) at the following universities:
Coal Preparation, Newcastle upon Tyne (certificate).
Engineering Rock Mechanics, London (Imperial College, MSc and/or DIC).
Mineral Exploration, Leicester and London (Imperial College, MSc and/or DIC).
Mineral Process Design, London (Imperial College, MSc and/or DIC).
Mineral Processing, Leeds (diploma, 1, 2 or 3 yrs).
Mineral Production Management, London (Imperial College, MSc and/or DIC).
Minerals Engineering, Birmingham (2 yrs).
Mining Geology, Leicester.
Mining Geostatistics, Leeds (12 months).
Ore Dressing, Newcastle upon Tyne (certificate).
Rock Mechanics and Excavation Engineering, Newcastle upon Tyne.

Research facilities At the following universities:
Mineralogy, Aberdeen, Birmingham (Minerals Engineering), Cambridge, Hull, Leeds (including Mineral Processing), Leicester, London (Imperial and King's Colleges), Manchester, Newcastle upon Tyne, Reading and Southampton.
Mining, Leeds, London (Imperial College, Rock Mechanics), Nottingham, Strathclyde and Wales (Cardiff University College).

First degrees CNAA degrees (3 yrs) are available at: Camborne School of Mines, *Mining*, also *Mineral Processing Technology*. North Staffordshire P, *Mining Engineering* (4½ yrs). Portsmouth P, *Engineering Geology* includes a *Mining* bias.

HND courses In *Mining* (3 yrs S): Doncaster Metropolitan IHE, *Mining Engineering*. Kirkcaldy TC, *Mining Engineering*. North Staffordshire P, *Mining Engineering*. Trent P. P of Wales.

Postgraduate courses Camborne School of Mines, *Mineral Technology* (*Applied Geochemistry, Mineral Processing, Economic Geology, Mining Economics*) (1 yr).

College diplomas Camborne School of Mines, diploma in *Mineral Industries* (2 yrs). Doncaster Metropolitan IHE, *Quarrying* (2 yrs S) also *Minerals Processing* and *Minerals Reclamation* (both 3 yrs). Sheffield P, *Minerals Processing and Materials Reclamation* (3 yrs S), also Associateship in *Minerals Surveying* (4 yrs S).

Research facilities Camborne School of Mines.

Museum Studies

Postgraduate courses Courses (1 yr unless otherwise indicated) at the following universities:
Art Gallery and Museum Studies, Manchester (diploma).
Museum Studies, Leicester (MA or MSc, 2 yrs including at least 6 months' full-time museum employment, also certificate).

Research facilities At the universities of Leicester and Manchester (Manchester Museum, Whitworth Art Gallery).

Music

First degrees Degrees in *Music* – BMus (Cambridge and Manchester, MusB) – awarded by the following universities (see below for BMus as higher degree): Aberdeen, Belfast, Birmingham, Cambridge (1 yr after Honours in Music Tripos), Durham (external candidates only), Edinburgh, Exeter (by transfer in 3rd yr from BA course in Music, for students whose performance has been satisfactory), Glasgow, Hull, London (King's and Royal Holloway Colleges, also Royal Academy of Music, Royal College of Music, Trinity College of Music and Goldsmiths' College), Manchester, Nottingham, Sheffield, Surrey (Academic and Practical Applications of Music, also – 4 yrs S – Music with Applied Physics (Tonmeister)) and Wales (Aberystwyth, Bangor and Cardiff University Colleges). The following award other first degrees – BA, unless otherwise indicated – with specialisation in Music (at some universities only in combination with another subject): Aberdeen (MA), Birmingham, Bristol, Cambridge, The City (BSc, 3 yrs, or 4 yrs S), Durham, East Anglia, Exeter, Glasgow (MA), Hull, Keele, Lancaster, Leeds, Leicester (Musicianship – Music with another subject plus a third – minor – subject), Liverpool, London (Royal Holloway College, also Goldsmiths' College), Newcastle upon Tyne, Nottingham, Oxford, Reading, St Andrews (MA), Sheffield, Southampton, Sussex (major subject in Schools of Cultural and Community or English and American Studies), Wales (colleges as above) and York. Less specialised study of Music can also be included in first degree courses in arts at many universities (but not at Brunel, Dundee, Essex, Heriot-Watt, Kent at Canterbury, Loughborough U of Technology or Strathclyde).

Most first degree courses in Music include *Musicology*. For *Music Teaching/Education*, see under 'Education'.

At Wales Cardiff University College also offers a College diploma (2 yrs) in Music.

Postgraduate courses
Courses for the degree of *MMus* (or, as indicated, BMus) which are open to suitably qualified graduates of other universities (normally 1 yr) are provided by the universities of Bristol (2 yrs), East Anglia, Edinburgh, Exeter, Liverpool (BMus, in Composition, Musicology or, Performance), London (King's and Royal Holloway Colleges, Musicology, Composition, Musical Analysis or Folk Music), Manchester (Musicological Studies or Performance), Newcastle upon Tyne, Reading (BMus), Southampton (BMus in Musical Composition), Surrey (Advanced Composition or Performance) and Wales (Aberystwyth, Bangor and Cardiff University Colleges). At Aberdeen, Durham and Hull the MMus is taken mainly by individual study/research; and the BMus at Leeds and Oxford and the MusM at Cambridge are open only to those universities' own graduates.

Courses in Music leading (unless otherwise indicated) to *MA* (normally 1 yr) at the universities of Belfast (Social Anthropology (Ethnomusicology), MA or diploma), Birmingham, Durham, Keele (American Music), Leeds, Newcastle upon Tyne, Nottingham (Renaissance and Baroque Music), Oxford (BPhil, 2 yrs), Sussex, Wales (Bangor University College, also, at Cardiff University College, Analysis of Modern Music or Electronic and Contemporary Music or Mediaeval Music or Sources of Classical Style or Baroque Music) and York (12 months); also, at London (King's College), certificate course (1 yr) in Advanced Musical Studies.

In addition to the courses specifically mentioned above, most higher degree courses (and certificate course at King's College, London) include facilities for the study of *Musicology*.

Research facilities
At all those universities – except New U of Ulster – which offer first degree courses (London, including Indian and African Music at the School of Oriental and African Studies; Nottingham, including MPhil in Composition; Surrey, Music and Technology; Wales, Aberystwyth, Bangor and Cardiff University Colleges; York, MPhil and DPhil in Musical Composition); also in *Musicology* at Aberdeen, Birmingham, Liverpool, London (King's College), Surrey, Wales (Aberystwyth – in conjunction with National Library of Wales – and Cardiff University Colleges) and York.

The higher doctorate, *DMus* (Cambridge and Manchester, MusD), is awarded by most of the universities which award the BMus or MusB; but only at Edinburgh, Glasgow and Manchester is the doctorate open to graduates of other universities.

First degrees
CNAA degrees in *Music* (3 yrs). Colchester IHE. Dartington C Arts. Huddersfield P. Roehampton IHE. Bath CHE (Newton Park C) 3 yr BA *Music* degree validated by Bath U.

A number of colleges provide courses leading to the BMus of the U of London and/or Durham (3 yrs). These are Goldsmiths' C (followed by a teacher training course of 1 yr), Royal Academy of Music, Royal College of Music and Trinity C of Music.

Performers' courses
Aberdeen C Commerce, professional course LTCL (Licentiate Diploma Trinity C) (2 yrs). Birmingham P, diplomas in all musical subjects, leading to ABSM (Associate) and GBSM (Graduate).

Cambridgeshire C Arts and T, diploma in Music (3 yrs).

Chichester CFE, diploma in Music (2 yrs).

City of Leeds C Music, diploma of Proficiency in Light Music (3 yrs).

Colchester IHE, courses leading to diplomas of the Royal Academy and the Royal C of Music, also college certificate in Music (2 yrs).

Coventry TC, Advanced course in Music (2 yrs). Courses in all subjects leading to college diploma and diplomas of the Royal Academy, Royal C of Music and Guildhall S of Music and Drama.

Early Music Centre, London, performers course for advanced students of renaissance lute (1 yr).

Guildhall S of Music and Drama, courses in all subjects leading to LGSM (Licentiate) and AGSM (Associate). Private tuition in single subjects.

Huddersfield P, college graduate diploma in Music (3 yrs).

London C of Music, courses for GLCM (3 yrs) and LLCM (2 yrs).

Mabel Fletcher TC, courses leading to Associateship of the Royal C of Music (ARCM) and Licentiateship of the Guildhall S of Music and Drama (LGSM) (2 yrs).

Napier CC and T, college diploma in Music (2 yrs).

Newcastle C Arts and T, professional diploma courses in Music and Light Music (both 3 yrs).

Royal Academy of Music, courses in all subjects leading to LRAM(Licentiate) and GRSM (Graduate of the Royal Schools of Music). Special courses in the training of conductors, opera and the playing of early classical music.

Royal C of Music, courses in all subjects leading to ARCM (Associate) and GRSM. Specialist classes in a wide range of subjects, including conducting and opera.

Royal Northern C of Music, courses leading to GRNCM and ARNCM.

Royal Scottish Academy of Music and Drama, courses in all subjects leading to DRSAM and other recognised professional diplomas (3 and 4 yrs). Advanced postgraduate course (1 yr).

Trinity College of Music, course leading to GTCL and Licentiate diploma (LTCL) (3 yrs) also 1 yr advanced course.

Welsh C of Music and Drama, diploma course (3 yrs), advanced certificate course (1 yr).

Instrument Making and Technology

Royal National C for the Blind, residential course in piano tuning, repairing and allied subjects, including piano and organ playing (3 yrs).

London C of Furniture, Department of Musical Instrument Technology, (3 yrs), course includes early keyboard instrument making; fretted instrument, violin and early woodwind making; piano construction, tuning and maintenance; electronics course in piano tuning and maintenance (2 yrs). Course in stringed keyboard instrument design and repair (3 yrs).

Newark TC, full-time courses in music, piano-tuning, piano, violin and wood-wind making and repair.

Teacher training courses

CNAA degree, Kingston P (3 yrs).

All the colleges which provide courses for performers also provide courses for intending teachers of music in schools. The courses last 3 years except those at the Welsh College of Music and Drama and Colchester IHE, which last 2 years and are followed by a 1 year course at a specified college of education. This procedure can also be followed at Huddersfield P.

Supplementary specialist courses in Music for qualified teachers (1 yr). Birmingham P. Bulmershe CHE. Dartington C Arts, 1 yr course for teachers in primary education, followed by 2 yrs at Rolle C, Exmouth, also DipHE course *Music in the Community* (2 yrs). Huddersfield P, diploma for intending specialist music teachers (1 yr). Northern S Music. Trinity C Music, London. Ulster C, Northern Ireland P, teacher's diploma (1 yr). Westminster C, Oxford.

Courses at colleges of education for students with musical qualifications (1 yr) as follows. Bath CHE. Bretton Hall C. City of Manchester CHE. Edge Hill CHE. Rolle C. South Glamorgan IHE.

Many institutions of education offer a music option in their BEd and certificate courses. The *Handbook of Institutions providing Teacher Training* (see page 265) should be consulted.

Nautical Studies

First degrees   Degrees with specialisation awarded by the following universities:
Maritime Studies, Wales (Institute of Science and Technology, with options in International
Transport, Maritime Commerce or Maritime Technology, 3 yrs or 4 yrs S, and – 3 yrs –
Maritime Geography).
Nautical Studies, Southampton (5 yrs S, in conjunction with Southampton School of
Navigation).

Postgraduate   Courses at University of Wales (Institute of Science and Technology) in:
courses   *Marine Law and Policy* (MSc, 1 yr).
Ocean Resource Management and *Shipping Economics and Policy* (options for MSc in
Management and Technology).
Port and Shipping Administration (Institute diploma, 1 yr, for graduates and others with suitable
qualifications and experience and Department of Trade and Industry certificates of
competency for First Mates and Masters).
For *Maritime Civil Engineering* see 'Engineering, Civil'.

Research   At University of Wales (Institute of Science and Technology).
facilities

First degrees   CNAA degrees are offered at the following polytechnics: Liverpool P (3 yrs, also 4 yrs S).
Plymouth P (4 yrs S). Sunderland P (3 yrs).
Southampton University BSc degree in *Nautical Studies* is offered at Southampton School of
Navigation (3 yrs).

HND courses   In *Nautical Science* (3 yrs S): Plymouth P. Southampton School of Navigation.

Postgraduate   Liverpool P, MSc *Shipping and Maritime Studies* (1 yr). Plymouth P, diploma in *Management*
course   *Studies* (*Shipping*) (1 yr).

Research   Liverpool P. Plymouth P.
facilities

Neurology
See also Biology, and Physiology

First degrees   Degree courses in Medicine (for list of awarding universities see page 198) include *Neurology*.

Postgraduate   Courses (12 months and for MSc, unless otherwise indicated) at the following universities:
courses   *Neurochemistry*, London (Institute of Neurology jointly with Institutes of Psychiatry and
Ophthalmology).
Neurocommunications, Birmingham (instruction in neurology in addition to neurochemistry,
psychology and analytical methods).
Neurological Science, London (University College, 12 months or 24 months).
Also, at University of London Institute of Neurology, clinical neurology and the anatomy,
physiology and pathology of the nervous system, some instruction in neurosurgery, neuro-
radiology and electroencephalography, clinical teaching throughout the yr, and 10-week course
in *Neurophysiology*.

Research
facilities

At the universities of Aberdeen, Belfast, Birmingham, Cambridge, Dundee, Edinburgh, Glasgow, Keele (Department of Communication – postgraduate certificate in Education may be taken concurrently with research for PhD), Leeds, London (Institute of Neurology and King's College Hospital Medical School), Manchester, Newcastle upon Tyne, Oxford, Southampton and Wales (Welsh National School of Medicine).

Nursing

Note – This section provides information on degree, diploma and post-registration courses in Nursing, and does not describe the provision that is made for basic nurse training leading to State Registration. Three-year courses leading to State Registration in either General, Paediatric, Mental or Mental-Subnormality Nursing, and integrated courses ($4\frac{1}{2}$ yrs) which lead to registration on more than one part of the Register, are undertaken throughout the country in training hospitals approved by the statutory bodies for nurses. These statutory bodies, from which specific details may be obtained, are the General Nursing Council for England and Wales, the General Nursing Council for Scotland and the Northern Ireland Council for Nurses and Midwives.

First degrees
with State
Registration

Courses (normally 4–5 yrs) in which academic study at the university may be combined with Nursing training/practical Nursing in hospitals are provided by the following universities, but overseas students are warned that universities may be unable to consider applications from them for these courses (e.g. because very few places are available or because an interview is an essential part of the selection procedures): Brunel (Mental Nursing), The City, Edinburgh, Glasgow, Hull, Liverpool, London (Bedford and Chelsea Colleges and London School of Economics), Manchester, Surrey, New U of Ulster and Wales (Welsh National School of Medicine).

Post-
registration
courses at
universities

Courses for *Health Visitor's* certificate (see also below) at universities of Bradford, Hull, Leeds, Southampton, Surrey and Wales (Welsh National School of Medicine), also – combined with BNurs course – Manchester. *Nurse Teachers* certificate courses at New U of Ulster (Institute of Continuing Education, certificate of competence for intending Nurse Tutors, 1 yr) and Wales (Cardiff University College, Education (Further Education) for Nurse Tutors). *Nursing* courses at Manchester (diploma in Advanced Nursing Studies, or MSc, 1 yr for suitably experienced registered nurses – MSc candidates taking 'Education' elective may apply for registration as Nurse Tutors); London awards a Nursing diploma – examination only. *Nursing Education* courses, Edinburgh (MSc or diploma). MSc/diploma course in Public Sector Management (Health and Welfare Services Management option) at Aston in Birmingham is suitable for senior nursing officers seeking a managerial qualification.

Research
facilities

At the universities of Edinburgh, Hull, London (Chelsea College: Nursing Education Research Unit), Manchester, Surrey and Wales (Welsh National School of Medicine).

First degrees
with State
Registration

CNAA degrees in *Nursing/Nursing Studies* at: Dundee CT (4 yrs S). Leeds P. Newcastle upon Tyne P. P of the South Bank.

Post-registration courses

Specialised Nursing courses

Community Nursing: Courses for National Certificate in District Nursing (4 months) and Health Visitor's Certificate (1 yr). Details from local Health Authority/Council for Education and Training of Health Visitors.

Midwifery: Training (1 yr) at hospitals approved by Central Midwives Boards or Northern Ireland Council for Nurses and Midwives.

Ophthalmic Nursing: (9 months) for Advanced Nursing Diploma.

Orthopaedic Nursing: (1 yr) for certificate of Joint Examination Board of the British Orthopaedic Association and Central Council for the Disabled.

Thoracic Nursing: for certificate of the British Thoracic and Tuberculosis Association.

Occupational Health Nursing: Courses in 12 centres throughout the United Kingdom in preparation for the Royal College of Nursing Occupational Health Nursing Certificate.

Post-Basic Clinical Nursing Studies: Training in many clinical specialties for nationally recognised certificate of Joint Board of Clinical Nursing Studies (Scotland: Committee for Clinical Nursing Studies) and Northern Ireland Council for Nurses and Midwives at centres approved by these bodies.

Management and Education courses

University of London Sister Tutor's diploma, Royal College of Nursing (2 yrs). P of the South Bank (2 yrs).

Clinical Teacher's courses (RCN) (6 months unless otherwise stated). Belfast CT. Birmingham P. Bristol P. Dundee CT (diploma, 1 yr). Foresthill C (1 yr). Glasgow CT (diploma, 1 yr). Gwent CHE. Huddersfield P. Ipswich Civic C. Mabel Fletcher TC. Newcastle upon Tyne P. Queen Margaret C (diploma, 1 yr). Royal College of Nursing. Sheffield P. P of the South Bank.

Nurse Teacher's course (62 weeks), Jordanhill CE.

Nurse Tutor's course (1 yr) leading to certificate in education. Bolton CE. Huddersfield P. Garnett C. Wolverhampton TTC.

Royal College of Nursing, certificate courses in Advanced Nursing Administration (1 yr); Clinical Teaching (6 months) (preparation for this certificate is undertaken by 12 other centres throughout the United Kingdom); Community Health Nurse Teaching (1 yr); international course for teachers of nursing (1 yr); Occupational Health Nurse Teacher's course (1 yr).

Obstetrics and Gynaecology

First degrees

Degree courses in Medicine (for list of awarding universities see page 198) include *Obstetrics and Gynaecology*. At Belfast a degree of BAO is awarded with the degrees of MB, BCh.

Postgraduate courses

Information about the short and/or part-time courses provided by some universities (London: Institute of Obstetrics and Gynaecology) is given in 'Summary of Postgraduate Diplomas and courses in Medicine' – see page 266.

Research facilities

At the universities of Aberdeen, Belfast (including degree of MAO), Birmingham, Bristol, Cambridge, Dundee, Edinburgh, Glasgow, Liverpool, London (various Medical Schools and Institute of Obstetrics and Gynaecology), Manchester, Newcastle upon Tyne, Nottingham, Oxford, Sheffield, Southampton and Wales (Welsh National School of Medicine).

Postgraduate qualifications

The Royal College of Obstetricians and Gynaecologists awards a diploma in *Obstetrics* (DObst, RCOG) upon examination. The Membership of the College of Obstetricians and Gynaecologists (MRCOG) is by examination in two parts, Part 1 including basic sciences – for courses see Anatomy. Particulars of the regulations for both the diploma and Membership may be obtained from the Royal College of Obstetricians and Gynaecologists.

Occupational Therapy

Postgraduate courses University of Southampton awards an MSc (15 months) and a diploma (12 months) in *Remedial Therapy.*

Professional courses A State Register of Occupational Therapists is maintained by the Council for Professions Supplementary to Medicine. The British Association of Occupational Therapists award a diploma in *Occupational Therapy,* recognised for State Registration. Courses of training (3 yrs) are available at:
Derby School of Occupational Therapy. Dorset House School of Occupational Therapy, Oxford. Edinburgh: Astley Ainsley Hospital, Occupational Therapy Training Centre. Exeter: St Loye's School of Occupational Therapy. Glasgow School of Occupational Therapy. Grampian School of Occupational Therapy, Aberdeen. Liverpool College of Occupational Therapy (Liverpool) Ltd. London School of Occupational Therapy. Newcastle upon Tyne P. Northampton School of Occupational Therapy, St Andrew's Hospital. Salford School of Occupational Therapy, Salford CT. Ulster C, Northern Ireland P School of Occupational Therapy. Welsh School of Occupational Therapy, Cardiff. Wolverhampton School of Occupational Therapy. York School of Occupational Therapy, C Ripon and York St John. Applications for places should in all cases except Ulster C be made through the Occupational Therapy Clearing House (British Association of Occupational Therapists).
Further information is available from the British Association of Occupational Therapists.

Oceanography

First degrees Degrees with specialisation in *Oceanography* awarded by the universities of Liverpool and Wales (with another subject at Bangor – Physical Oceanography – and Swansea University Colleges). Less specialised study of Oceanography may be included in first degree courses at Reading (in Meteorology course, also Hydrodynamics in courses in School of Mathematical Sciences), Southampton (Chemistry with Oceanography, also Environmental Sciences), Stirling and Wales (Aberystwyth University College as special subject in Honours courses, Bangor University College for General degree, and – with Meteorology – Institute of Science and Technology for BSc(Tech) in Maritime Studies).

Postgraduate courses Courses (1 yr and for MSc, unless otherwise indicated) at the following universities:
Applied Marine Science, Wales (Swansea University College).
Marine Geotechnics, Wales (Bangor University College).
Marine Pollution Chemistry, Liverpool (diploma, 6 months).
Oceanography, Southampton.
Physical Oceanography, Wales (Bangor University College, MSc or diploma).
Underwater Science and Technology, Salford (modular course, 1 yr full-time or 2 yrs part-time).

Research facilities At the following universities: Bath (including Marine Geophysics), Birmingham (including Marine Geophysics, Underwater Acoustics), Essex, Heriot-Watt (Underwater Technology), Liverpool, Southampton and Wales (Bangor – Marine Science Laboratory, Menai Bridge – and Swansea University Colleges).

Operational Research

See also Business and Management Studies; and Engineering, Production

First degrees Degrees with specialisation in *Operational Research* awarded by the following universities: Aston in Birmingham (in Managerial and Administrative Studies course), Bath (with Mathematics or Statistics), Exeter (with Mathematical Statistics, also with Chemistry or Physics), Keele (Applied Statistics and Operational Research with another principal subject), Kent at Canterbury (Computing, Operational Research and Statistics), Lancaster (Management Sciences (Operational Research), also with Computer Studies or with Mathematics), Leeds (with one of certain other subjects), London (Chelsea College, with Mathematics), Manchester (Institute of Science and Technology, with Statistics), Salford (Business Operation and Control, 4 yrs S), Strathclyde (alone, or with another business studies subject, also in Technology and Business Studies course), Sussex (Applied Sciences with Management Science), New U of Ulster (with Mathematics) and Warwick (with Mathematics, Statistics and Economics). Less specialised study of Operational Research may be included in first degree courses at Belfast, Bradford (with Marketing, Financial and Production Management), Brunel, Essex, Exeter, Lancaster, London (London School of Economics for BSc and BSc(Econ), Imperial College in Mining and in Mechanical Engineering), Loughborough U of Technology, Nottingham, Reading (Mathematics or Computer Science and Statistics), Stirling (in Technological Economics course), Surrey (Chemical Engineering) and Wales (Aberystwyth University College for BSc in Statistics and for BScEcon, Cardiff University College with Mathematics).

Postgraduate courses Courses (1 yr and for master's degree, unless otherwise indicated) at the following universities and Cranfield IT:
Information Processing, Exeter.
Information Systems, London (London School of Economics).
Operational Mathematics, Liverpool.
Operational Research, Aston in Birmingham (Operational Research and Management, MSc or diploma), Birmingham, Bradford (for diploma in Management and Administration, or MBA, 1 or 2 yrs), Cambridge (Control Engineering and Operational Research), Cranfield IT (Management Science and Operational Research, 1 or 2 yrs, option for MSc in Industrial Engineering and Administration), Essex (Statistics and Operational Research, MSc 12 months, diploma 9 months), Hull, Lancaster (MA 12 months, diploma 9 months), Leeds (with Computing, minimum 12 months), London (London School of Economics, 1 or 2 yrs, also – for MSc/DIC in Management Science or Statistics – Imperial College), Loughborough U of Technology (Statistics and Operational Research, MSc or associateship, 1 yr full-time or 2 or 3 yrs part-time), Oxford, Southampton, Stirling (as part of MSc course in Technological Economics designed for graduates with experience in science-based industry and scientific departments of the public service), Strathclyde (MSc or diploma, also with Marketing, diploma, 1 yr full-time or 3 yrs part-time), Surrey (for MSc in Economics or Quantitative Business Methods, minimum 12 months), Sussex and Warwick (Management Science and Operational Research).
Systems Analysis, Aston in Birmingham (12 months) and London (London School of Economics, School diploma).

Research facilities At the following universities: Birmingham, Brunel, Exeter, Heriot-Watt, Hull, Lancaster (including Simulation Centre), London, Loughborough U of Technology, Manchester, Reading, Strathclyde, Surrey, Sussex, Wales (Aberystwyth and Cardiff University Colleges, and Institute of Science and Technology) and Warwick; and at Cranfield IT.

First degrees   CNAA degrees in *Operational Research with Computing* are offered at the following (4 yrs S):
Leeds P. Paisley CT (also 3 yrs).
Degrees in Business Studies with an option in *Operational Research* are offered at the
following: Hatfield P. Kingston P. Portsmouth P. Trent P.

Postgraduate   Paisley CT (2 yrs). Southampton CT (1 yr). Thames P (1 yr).
diplomas

Ophthalmic and Dispensing Optics
See also Orthoptics

First degrees   Degrees in *Ophthalmic Optics* awarded by the following universities: Aston in Birmingham,
Bradford, The City (also BSc in Visual Science), Manchester (Institute of Science and
Technology) and Wales (Institute of Science and Technology).

Postgraduate   Courses (1 yr and for MSc, unless otherwise indicated) at the following universities:
courses   *Applied Optics*, London (Imperial College, MSc and/or DIC).
Applied and Modern Optics, Reading (12 months).
Methods of Ophthalmic Investigation, Aston in Birmingham.

Research   At all the universities named in the paragraphs above.
facilities

Degree and   Bradford C Art and Technology, diploma in *Dispensing Optics* (2 yrs). Glasgow College of
diploma   Technology, CNAA degree (BSc) in *Ophthalmic Optics* 4 yrs); also diploma in *Dispensing*
courses   *Optics* (2 yrs). Facilities can be arranged for postgraduate research and higher degrees. London:
City and East London College for FE, diploma in *Dispensing Optics* (2 yrs).
   To qualify for registration with the General Optical Council a candidate must obtain the
appropriate diploma of the British Optical Association, the Worshipful Company of Spectacle
Makers, the Scottish Association of Opticians or the Association of Dispensing Opticians. This
involves at least 1 yr of practical work after taking the relevant degree or college course. Details
may be obtained from the General Optical Council.

Ophthalmology

First degrees   Degree courses in Medicine (for list of awarding universities see page 198) include
Ophthalmology.

Postgraduate   At University of London (Institute of Ophthalmology, 4 months – clinical teaching throughout
courses   the yr); also short courses, about which information is given in 'Summary of Postgraduate
Diplomas and Courses in Medicine' (see page 266).

Research   At the universities of Birmingham, Cambridge, Dundee, Glasgow, Liverpool, London
facilities   (Institute of Ophthalmology), Manchester (including Institute of Science and Technology),
Newcastle upon Tyne and Oxford.

Postgraduate qualifications A postgraduate diploma (DO) is awarded by the Examining Board in England of the Royal College of Physicians of London and Royal College of Surgeons of England. Particulars from the Secretary of the Examining Board in England.

Diplomas of Fellowship are awarded by the Royal College of Surgeons of England, the Royal College of Surgeons of Edinburgh and the Royal College of Physicians and Surgeons of Glasgow by examination with Ophthalmology as a special subject.

Oriental Languages and Studies

Arabic

First degrees Degrees with specialisation in *Arabic* awarded by the universities of Aberdeen (with Hebrew for MA in Semitic Languages), Cambridge, Durham (Classical Arabic and Islamic Studies, or Modern Arabic Studies alone or with Persian or Turkish), Edinburgh (with one of certain other languages for MA in Modern Languages, or with Hebrew for MA in Semitic Languages), Exeter (with French, Hebrew Studies, Islamic Studies or Spanish), Glasgow (with Hebrew for MA in Semitic Languages, also with a modern language or one of certain other subjects), Lancaster (Arabic and Islamic Studies, also Arabic, Islamic and Other Religious Studies), Leeds (Semitic Languages and Literatures including Arabic, also Arabic with one of certain other subjects), London (School of Oriental and African Studies, alone or with one of certain other subjects, also BA in Semitic Studies), Manchester (for BA in Oriental Studies, also Classical Arabic with Spanish), Oxford and St Andrews (Classical and Modern). Less specialised study of Arabic may be included in first degree courses at most of the universities named above and at Belfast and Wales (Bangor University College). Leeds also offers certificate course (usually 2 yrs) in Arabic.

Postgraduate courses Courses (1 yr and for master's degree, unless otherwise indicated) at the following universities:
Arabic, Durham (diploma).
Arabic Studies, St Andrews (diploma, also MLitt 2 yrs).
Medieval Arabic Philosophy, Oxford (2 yrs, for BPhil in Oriental Studies).
Medieval Studies, Leeds.
Modern Arabic, St Andrews (diploma).
Semitic Languages and Literature, Leeds.
Semitic Studies, Leeds (diploma).

Research facilities At the universities of Cambridge, Durham, Edinburgh, Exeter, Glasgow, Lancaster (Institute of Arabic and Islamic Studies), Leeds, London (School of Oriental and African Studies and University College), Manchester, Oxford and St Andrews.

First degree P of Central London, CNAA Modern Languages degree with *Arabic* option (4 yrs).

Chinese

First degrees Degrees with specialisation in *Chinese* awarded by the universities of Cambridge (Oriental Studies Tripos), Durham (Chinese Studies), Edinburgh, Leeds (Chinese Studies, alone or with certain other subjects), London (School of Oriental and African Studies) and Oxford. Less specialised study of Chinese may be included in degree courses in Language at York.

Postgraduate courses University of Glasgow offers MPhil course (2 yrs) in *Modern Chinese Studies*.

Research facilities   At the universities of Cambridge, Edinburgh, Leeds, London (School of Oriental and African Studies) and Oxford.

First degree   P of Central London, CNAA Modern Languages degree with *Chinese* option (4 yrs).

Postgraduate course   Ealing CHE, postgraduate diploma in *Modern Chinese* (*Mandarin*) (1 yr).

Hebrew

First degrees   Degrees with specialisation in *Hebrew* awarded by the universities of Aberdeen (with Arabic for MA in Semitic Languages, or with Old Testament Studies for BD), Belfast (Semitic Studies, or with Greek or Latin), Cambridge, Durham (Classical Hebrew and Old Testament Studies), Edinburgh (with Arabic as secondary subject), Exeter (Arabic and Hebrew Studies), Glasgow (with Arabic for MA in Semitic Languages, also with one of certain other subjects), Leeds (Semitic Languages and Literatures, including Hebrew Language and Literature of all periods), Liverpool, London (School of Oriental and African Studies – also Modern Hebrew, and University College – also Jewish History alone or with Hebrew Literature), Manchester (Ancient Semitic or Modern Hebrew for BA in Oriental Studies), Oxford, St Andrews (with another language or with Biblical or Theological Studies) and Wales (Cardiff University College). At several of the universities offering degrees with specialisation in this subject alone, Hebrew may also be studied with another principal subject for a Joint (or Combined) Honours degree. Less specialised study of Hebrew may be included in first degree courses in arts, theology or religious studies at many of the universities named above and at Birmingham (School of Ancient Near Eastern Studies), Bristol, Hull, London (King's College), Newcastle upon Tyne, Nottingham and Wales (Bangor and St David's University Colleges). Leeds also offers diploma course (usually 2 yrs) in Hebrew.

Postgraduate courses   Courses (1 yr and for master's degree, unless otherwise indicated) at the following universities:
Hebrew, London (School of Oriental and African Studies, 2 yrs).
Hebrew and Old Testament Studies, Edinburgh (12 months).
Modern Jewish Studies, Oxford (2 yrs, for BPhil in Oriental Studies).
Semitic Languages and Literatures, Leeds and Wales (Cardiff University College, 1 or 2 yrs).
Semitic Studies, Leeds (diploma).

Research facilities   At the universities of Aberdeen, Cambridge, Edinburgh, Exeter, Leeds, London (King's and University Colleges and School of Oriental and African Studies), Manchester, Oxford, St Andrews and Wales (Bangor and Cardiff University Colleges).

First degrees   Jews' College, *Hebrew* as part of CNAA degree *Jewish Studies* (3 yrs). Facilities for study for MPhil and PhD, London, in *Hebrew and Jewish Studies*.

Japanese

First degrees   Degrees with specialisation in *Japanese* awarded by the universities of Cambridge, London (School of Oriental and African Studies), Oxford and Sheffield (with one of certain other subjects). At Edinburgh, Modern Japanese Written Language may be included in first degree courses in arts, and at Stirling Japanese Religions is available as option in General degree course.

Postgraduate courses   Courses for higher degrees at universities of London (School of Oriental and African Studies) and Sheffield (MA, 2 yrs, in *Japanese Studies* – language and one other subject, also certificate in Japanese Language on successful completion of first yr of course).

Research facilities   At the universities of Cambridge, London (School of Oriental and African Studies), Oxford and Sheffield (Centre of Japanese Studies).

Other Oriental Languages and Studies

First degrees   Degrees with specialisation awarded by the following universities – for University of London, see separate paragraph below:

Akkadian, Liverpool and Manchester (for BA in Oriental Studies (Cuneiform Studies)).

Ancient Mediterranean Studies, Bristol.

Ancient Near Eastern Studies, Birmingham and Wales (Cardiff University College).

Aramaic/Syriac, Cambridge and Leeds (Semitic Languages and Literatures).

Assyriology, Cambridge.

Cuneiform Studies, Manchester (for BA in Oriental Studies).

Egyptian, Oxford.

Egyptology, Durham and Liverpool.

Ethiopic, Manchester (for BA in Oriental Studies).

Indian Studies, Cambridge.

Iranian, Cambridge.

Islamic Studies, Oxford.

Modern Middle Eastern Studies (Modern Arabic or Persian or Turkish with either Politics or Geography), Durham.

Persian, Cambridge, Durham (Modern Turkish and Persian Studies, see also 'Modern Middle Eastern Studies'), Edinburgh (with Arabic as secondary subject), Manchester (for BA in Oriental Studies) and Oxford.

Sanskrit, Edinburgh (with a related or a European language, or Latin or Greek) and Oxford.

Southeast Asian Studies (specialising in certain aspects – law, politics and government, or sociology), Kent at Canterbury.

Turkish, Cambridge, Durham (Modern Turkish and Persian Studies, see also 'Modern Middle Eastern Studies'), Edinburgh (with Arabic as secondary subject), Manchester (for BA in Oriental Studies) and Oxford.

    Less specialised study may be included in first degree courses as follows (see also University of London below):

Akkadian, Birmingham, Manchester, Oxford and Wales (Cardiff University College).

Ancient Near Eastern Studies, Belfast.

Aramaic/Syriac, Aberdeen (including Ugaritic, for Honours students only), Birmingham, Oxford and Wales (Bangor and Cardiff University Colleges).

Armenian, Birmingham and Oxford.

Egyptian, Manchester and Oxford (Ancient Egyptian, including Coptic).

Ethiopic, Manchester.

Georgian, Birmingham.

Hindi, York (as part of degree courses in Language).

Hittite, Birmingham.

Indian Religions, Stirling (for degree in Religious Studies).

Near Eastern Religion, Manchester.

Pali, Cambridge, Manchester and Oxford.

Persian/Iranian, Manchester and Oxford.

Prakrit, Cambridge and Oxford.

Sanskrit, Cambridge, Hull and Oxford.

Sinhalese, York (as part of degree courses in Language).

South East Asian Economics or *Geography* or *History* or *Politics* or *Sociology and Social Anthropology,* Hull.

Sumerian, Birmingham.

Turkish, Manchester and Oxford.

At Sussex BA with major in one of various subjects (e.g. Economics, Geography) may be taken in School of African and Asian Studies (Asian languages are *not* taught).

University of London. School of Oriental and African Studies: courses in many Oriental languages including the following, the study of most of which may lead to BA († = BA Honours) and higher degrees: Akkadian†, Aramaic, Armenian, Bengali†, Burmese†, Cambodian, Sino-Tibetan languages, Georgian, Gujarati†, Hindi†, Indonesian† and other Austronesian languages, Iranian languages, Khmer, Korean, Kurdish, Malay†, Marathi†, Mon, Mongolian, Nepali, Oriya, Pali†, Panjabi, Pashto, Persian†, Prakrit, Sanskrit†, Sinhalese†, Syriac, Thai†, Tamil†, Telugu, Tibetan, Turkish†, Urdu†, Vietnamese; also BA Honours in South-East Asian Studies (with a choice of one language from the following options: Burmese; Malay and Indonesian; Thai); courses in the history, economic and political institutions, geography, law and culture of many Oriental regions, in Oriental art, archaeology, philosophy and social anthropology, and in general linguistics and comparative grammar (some of these courses may lead to degrees and/or School diplomas).

London School of Economics: undergraduate teaching in the Social Anthropology, Politics and Economics of some areas (details from the Registrar).

University College: BA Joint Honours in Hebrew and Akkadian or Egyptian.

Postgraduate courses   For University of London, see above. Other courses (1 yr and for master's degree, unless otherwise indicated) at the following universities:

Ancient History of Mesopotamia or *Cuneiform Studies,* Oxford (2 yrs, for BPhil in Oriental Studies).

Eastern Christian Studies, Oxford (BPhil, 2 yrs).

Hittite Studies or *Indian Studies* or *Modern Middle Eastern Studies,* Oxford (2 yrs, for BPhil in Oriental Studies).

Mongol Language and Mongolian Studies, Leeds (diploma, mainly for graduates in Chinese, Japanese or Russian Studies).

Mongolian Studies, Leeds (for those with appropriate qualifications in Mongol Language and Mongolian Studies).

Semitic Languages and Literatures, Leeds.

Semitic Languages and Studies (including Akkadian, Aramaic), Wales (Cardiff University College, 1 or 2 yrs).

Semitic Studies, Leeds (diploma).

Southeast Asian Studies, Kent at Canterbury (designed to provide graduates in any of the social sciences or in history with a liberal foundation for understanding the contemporary South-East Asian scene).

Research facilities   At the universities of Birmingham, Cambridge, Durham (Centre for Middle Eastern Studies), Edinburgh, Hull (Centre for South-East Asian Studies – areas within Malaysia, Indonesia, the Philippines), Lancaster (Institute of Arabic and Islamic Studies), London (see below), Manchester, Oxford (Oriental Institute) and Sussex.

University of London: the five Area Studies Centres (Africa, Far East, Near and Middle East, South Asia, South East Asia) based on the School of Oriental and African Studies are primarily concerned with postgraduate teaching and interdisciplinary research and with the organisation of MA Area Studies programmes throughout the university (their work includes humanities, social sciences, historical studies and contemporary developments). Also, at London School of Economics, graduate research facilities in the Social Anthropology, Politics and Economics of some areas (details from the Registrar).

Orthopaedics

First degrees   Degree courses in Medicine (for list of awarding universities see page 198) include *Orthopaedics.*

Postgraduate courses   At the universities of Liverpool (MChOrth, 12 months) and London (Institute of Orthopaedics, clinical teaching throughout the yr; information about short/part-time courses is given in 'Summary of Postgraduate Diplomas and Courses in Medicine' – see page 266).

Research facilities   At the universities of Birmingham, Cambridge, Dundee, Edinburgh, Glasgow, Liverpool, London (Institute of Orthopaedics), Manchester, Newcastle upon Tyne, Nottingham, Oxford, Sheffield, Southampton and Wales (Welsh National School of Medicine).

Orthoptics
No university courses

Professional courses   The British Orthoptic Council and Society awards a diploma (DBO) and an additional qualification (DBO(T)) to teachers of orthoptics. Courses (3 yrs) for the DBO are available at: Birmingham and Midland Eye Hospital. Cardiff Royal Infirmary. Cheltenham General Hospital. Chester Royal Infirmary. Coventry and Warwickshire Hospital. Glasgow Eye Infirmary. London: Moorfields Eye Hospital (both branches). Manchester: Royal Eye Hospital. Reading: Royal Berkshire Hospital. Sheffield: United Sheffield Hospitals.

Full particulars may be obtained from the British Orthoptic Council.

Paediatrics

First degrees   Degree courses in Medicine (for list of awarding universities see page 198) include *Paediatrics.*

Postgraduate courses   At the following universities:
Paediatrics, London (Institute of Child Health, 8/9-week series of 1-week courses in special subjects) and Sheffield (3 months).
Tropical Child Health, Liverpool (diploma, 6 months for candidates with approved postgraduate experience and training). Information about short/part-time courses is given in 'Summary of Postgraduate Diplomas and Courses in Medicine' – see page 266.

Research facilities   At the universities of Aberdeen, Belfast, Birmingham (Institute of Child Health), Bristol, Cambridge, Dundee, Edinburgh, Glasgow, Liverpool, London (Guy's – Paediatric Research Unit – and King's and University College Hospital Medical Schools, and Institute of Child Health), Manchester, Newcastle upon Tyne, Nottingham, Oxford, Salford (Postgraduate Medical Institute), Sheffield, Southampton and Wales (Welsh National School of Medicine).

Postgraduate qualifications   Postgraduate diplomas in *Child Health* (DCH) are awarded by the Examining Board in England of the Royal College of Physicians of London and Royal College of Surgeons of England, and also by the Royal College of Physicians and Surgeons of Glasgow. Particulars may be obtained from the Secretary of the Examining Board in England and from the Royal College in Glasgow.

The clinical and oral sections of Part II of the MRCP (UK) – see *Medicine and Surgery* – can be taken in paediatrics.

Palaeography

See also Librarianship and Information Science

First degrees   Degree courses (usually in History) may include some study of *Palaeography* at the universities of Belfast, Edinburgh, Exeter (History and Medieval Studies courses), Glasgow (non-graduating courses), Liverpool (also in diploma course in Study of Records and Administration of Archives), Manchester (History and Medieval Studies courses) and St Andrews.

Postgraduate courses   Courses for research students at the universities of Birmingham, Durham, Manchester and Oxford. At London, School of Oriental and African Studies awards special School diplomas (1 yr for graduates or equivalent) in *Indian* or *Hebrew Palaeography and Epigraphy*; also training in *Slavonic Palaeography* at School of Slavonic and East European Studies. University of Wales awards a diploma (1 yr) in *Palaeography and Archives Administration* (courses at Aberystwyth and Bangor University Colleges), and Cardiff University College awards College diplomas (1 yr, mainly for graduates) in *Semitic Palaeography* and in *Medieval and Modern Writing*.

Palaeography is also included in the courses indicated at Aberdeen (MLitt in Medieval Studies), Cambridge (Faculty of History), East Anglia (MA in English History), Leeds (MA in Bibliography and Textual Criticism and in Medieval Studies), London (courses, for graduates or equivalent, in Palaeography and Diplomatic and the Study of Archives at King's College, in Arabic and Hebrew and Indian Palaeography at School of Oriental and African Studies, in Palaeography and Historical Method at Institute of Historical Research, in Papyrology and Greek and Latin Palaeography at Institute of Classical Studies, and in Rumanian Palaeography at School of Slavonic and East European Studies), Manchester (MA or diploma in Medieval Studies), Reading (MA and MPhil in Graduate Centre for Medieval Studies) and Southampton (MA in Medieval Studies).

Research facilities   At the universities of Cambridge, Durham, London (Schools, etc, as above) and Manchester.

Parasitology

First degrees   University of Glasgow awards a degree with specialisation in *Parasitology*. Parasitology is also included in courses in departments of Biology or Zoology at most universities (London, special course for BSc Zoology at Imperial and King's Colleges; Wales, in Zoology/Applied Zoology courses at Bangor University College).

Postgraduate courses   Courses (1 yr and for MSc, unless otherwise indicated) at the following universities:
Animal Parasitology, Wales (Bangor University College, also diploma).
Medical Parasitology, London (School of Hygiene and Tropical Medicine).
Nematology, London (Imperial College, MSc and/or DIC).
Parasitology and Applied Biology, Liverpool.

Some courses included in curricula for diplomas in Public Health (see page 236), also included in diploma courses in Tropical Medicine and Hygiene at Liverpool and London (see page 261).

Research facilities   At the universities of Birmingham, Cambridge (Molteno Institute of Biology and Parasitology), Exeter, Glasgow (Wellcome Institute for Experimental Parasitology), Liverpool (School of Tropical Medicine and Hygiene), London (Imperial, King's and Queen Mary Colleges, and School of Hygiene and Tropical Medicine), Manchester, Wales (Bangor and – Department of Agriculture (Animal Husbandry) – Aberystwyth University Colleges) and York.

Pathology

First degrees Degrees with specialisation awarded by the following universities:
Cellular Pathology, Bristol.
Pathobiology, Reading.
Pathology (open only to students already enrolled in medical (or veterinary) degree courses), Belfast, Edinburgh, Glasgow and Nottingham. Pathology is also included in courses for first degrees in Medicine (for list of awarding universities see page 198).

Postgraduate Courses (1 yr) at the following universities:
courses *Aquatic Pathobiology*, Stirling (MSc – offered in alternate yrs, next 1978–79).
Clinical Pathology, London (Royal Postgraduate Medical School, diploma).
Immunology, Birmingham (MSc).
Revision courses (full-time) in the basic medical sciences, including Pathology (suitable for one or more of: Primary FRCS, Primary FFA, Primary FDS, MRCOG Part I), are organised by the Edinburgh Postgraduate Board for Medicine (16 weeks) and the University of London Institute of Basic Medical Sciences (including 12 weeks for Primary FRCS, 8 weeks for Primary FDS). Information about part-time courses is given in 'Summary of Postgraduate Diplomas and Courses in Medicine' – see page 266.

Research At the universities of Aberdeen, Belfast, Birmingham, Bristol, Cambridge, Dundee, Edinburgh,
facilities Glasgow, Leeds, Liverpool, London (various Medical Schools and Institute of Basic Medical Sciences), Manchester, Newcastle upon Tyne, Nottingham, Oxford, Sheffield, Southampton and Wales (Welsh National School of Medicine).

Postgraduate The Royal College of Pathologists conducts examinations for its diploma (DRCPath) and for
qualifications Membership (MRCPath). The Examining Board in England of the Royal College of Physicians of London and the Royal College of Surgeons of England awards a diploma in *Pathology* (DPath) of which details may be obtained from the Secretary, Conjoint Board.

Peace and Conflict Studies

For International Relations, see also Political Science

First degrees University of Bradford awards a BA in Peace Studies (4 yrs S). Peace and/or Conflict Studies may also be included in first degree courses at the following universities: Birmingham (course option on Critical World Problems in certain BSocSc courses), The City (options in Conflict Analysis and in Strategic Aspects of International Relations for final yr of BSc in Systems and Management), Hull (option for BA in Politics), Keele (for degree in International Relations), Lancaster (Peace and Conflict Studies, Strategic Studies), Manchester (options for BA and BA(Econ)), Oxford (Military History and Theory of War as special subject in Honour School of Modern History) and Surrey (Conflict Analysis option in final yr of degree courses in Linguistic and International Studies).

Postgraduate Courses (normally 1 yr and for master's degree, unless otherwise indicated) at the following
courses universities:
Peace Studies, Bradford (MA or diploma).
Strategic Studies, Aberdeen and Wales (Aberystwyth University College).
War Studies, London (King's College, MA or diploma).

Research At the universities of Birmingham, Bradford, Keele, Lancaster, London (King's College),
facilities Manchester, Oxford and Surrey.

Pharmacology

See also Pharmacy

First degrees Degrees in *Pharmacology* awarded by the following universities: Aberdeen, Aston in Birmingham (Physiology and Pharmacology with another subject), Bath (4 yrs S), Bradford (4 yrs S), Bristol, Dundee, Edinburgh, Glasgow, Leeds (alone or with Biochemistry or Physiology), Liverpool (alone or with Chemistry), London (Chelsea, King's and University Colleges), Manchester (alone, or with Physiology or Psychology), Nottingham (with Chemistry, Psychology or Zoology), Strathclyde (Biochemistry and Pharmacology) and Wales (Cardiff University College). Pharmacology is also included in first degree courses in Medicine (for list of awarding universities see page 198); at Sheffield in BMed Sci course (see page 198); and at Southampton in degree course in Physiology and Biochemistry. *Applied Pharmacology* is included in BPharm courses at London (School of Pharmacy) and Wales (Institute of Science and Technology).

Postgraduate courses Courses (1 yr and for master's degree, unless otherwise indicated) at the following universities:
Biochemical Pharmacology, Southampton.
Biology (Pharmacology) and *Chemical Pharmacology*, Edinburgh (diplomas).
Clinical Pharmacology, Manchester (1–2 yrs full-time or 2 yrs part-time).
Experimental Pharmacology, Bradford (minimum 12 months).
Pharmacology, Cambridge, London (Chelsea College), Manchester (MSc or diploma, 1 or 2 yrs) and Strathclyde.
  Reading offers MSc course (12 months) in Food Science with option in *Analysis of Food and Drugs*, and Wales (Institute of Science and Technology) MSc course (12 months) in Pharmaceutical Sciences with option in *Applied Pharmacology.*

Research facilities At the universities of Aberdeen, Belfast, Birmingham (pre-clinical and clinical), Bradford, Bristol, Cambridge, Dundee, Edinburgh, Glasgow, Leeds, Liverpool, London (Chelsea, King's and University Colleges, School of Pharmacy, various Medical Schools and Institute of Basic Medical Sciences), Manchester, Newcastle upon Tyne, Nottingham, Oxford, Sheffield, Southampton, Strathclyde and Wales (Institute of Science and Technology and Welsh National School of Medicine).

First degrees CNAA degrees in *Pharmacology*: Portsmouth P. Sunderland P (both 3 yrs).
The study of *Pharmacology* is included in Applied Biology degrees at: Lanchester P. Hatfield P, *Physiology/Pharmacology.* North East London P.

Research facilities Portsmouth P. Sunderland P.

Pharmacy
See also Pharmacology

First degrees   Degrees in *Pharmacy* (BPharm, unless otherwise indicated) awarded by the following universities: Aston in Birmingham (BSc), Bath, Belfast (BSc), Bradford (3 yrs, or 4 yrs S), Heriot-Watt (BSc), London (Chelsea College and School of Pharmacy), Manchester (BSc), Nottingham, Strathclyde (BSc) and Wales (Institute of Science and Technology). Loughborough U of Technology awards degree in *Medicinal and Pharmaceutical Chemistry* (3 yrs or – for BSc and DIS – 4 yrs S).

Postgraduate courses   Courses (1 yr and for MSc, unless otherwise indicated) at the following universities:
Clinical Pharmacy, Bradford (MPharm, 12 months full-time or 24 months part-time) and Strathclyde.
Cosmetic Science, Wales (Institute of Science and Technology, option for MSc in Pharmaceutical Sciences).
Forensic Science, Strathclyde (12 months or 21 months) and Wales (Institute of Science and Technology, option for MSc in Pharmaceutical Sciences).
Hospital Pharmacy, Belfast and Heriot-Watt (1 yr full-time or 2 yrs part-time).
Medicinal Chemistry, Loughborough U of Technology (MSc or associateship, 1 yr full-time or 3 yrs part-time).
Pharmaceutical Analysis, Strathclyde (12 months or 21 months) and Wales (Institute of Science and Technology, option for MSc in Pharmaceutical Sciences).
Pharmaceutical Sciences, Aston in Birmingham (2 yrs) and Wales (Institute of Science and Technology).
Pharmaceutics (*Pharmaceutical Technology*), London (Chelsea College, 1 yr full-time or 2 yrs part-time, MSc/College diploma).
Pharmacy (Hospital Pharmacy and Pharmaceutical Analysis), Manchester (MSc or diploma).

Research facilities   At all the universities which offer first degree courses.

First degrees   CNAA degrees in *Pharmacy* (3 yrs, unless otherwise indicated) at: Brighton P. Leicester P. Liverpool P. Portsmouth P. Robert Gordon's IT (4 yrs). Sunderland P.

Research facilities   Brighton P. Leicester P. Liverpool P. Portsmouth P. Sunderland P.

College diploma   Leicester P, *Formulation* (3 yrs S).

Professional registration   Graduates must complete 12 months' preregistration experience under the direct supervision of a pharmacist before they are eligible to apply to the Pharmaceutical Society for registration to practise as pharmacists.

Philosophy
See also History and Philosophy of Science

First degrees   Degrees with specialisation in *Philosophy* awarded by the following universities: Aberdeen, Belfast, Birmingham, Bristol, Cambridge, The City (3 yrs, or 4 yrs S), Dundee, Durham, East Anglia, Edinburgh, Essex (with one of certain other subjects), Exeter, Glasgow, Hull, Keele (with another principal subject), Kent at Canterbury, Lancaster, Leeds, Leicester, Liverpool, London (Bedford, Birkbeck (part-time), King's and University Colleges, also Mathematics and Philosophy of Mathematics at Chelsea College and as special subject for BSc(Econ) at London School of Economics), Manchester, Newcastle upon Tyne, Nottingham, Oxford, Reading, St Andrews, Sheffield, Southampton, Stirling, Surrey (with Psychology and Sociology), Sussex (major subject in Schools of African and Asian, English and American, European, or Cultural and Community Studies, and of Social Sciences, also Logic in School of Mathematical and Physical Sciences), New U of Ulster, Wales (Aberystwyth, Bangor, Cardiff, Swansea and St David's University Colleges), Warwick and York. Bradford awards a BA in *Human Purposes and Communication* (4 yrs S). At many of the universities offering degrees with specialisation in this subject alone, Philosophy may also be studied with another principal subject for a Joint (or Combined) Honours degree; and at many of them, also at Strathclyde, less specialised study of Philosophy may be included in first degree courses in arts.

Postgraduate courses
Courses (1 yr and for master's degree, unless otherwise indicated) at the following universities:
Contemporary European Philosophy, etc, Reading (MA 1 yr, MPhil 2 yrs, in Graduate School of Contemporary European Studies).
Greek Philosophy, Sheffield.
Human Purposes, Bradford (diploma 11 months, further 9 months full-time or 18 months part-time for MA).
Intellectual History, Sussex.
Logic and Ethics or *Logic and Language*, Birmingham.
Logic and Linguistics, St Andrews (2 yrs).
Logic and Science, Birmingham.
Logic and Scientific Method, London (London School of Economics) and Sussex.
Mathematical Logic, East Anglia (MA 1 yr, BPhil 2 yrs).
Medieval Studies, Aberdeen and Leeds.
Moral and Social Philosophy, Exeter.
Philosophy, Cambridge (2 yrs), East Anglia (MA 1 yr, BPhil 2 yrs), Edinburgh (2 yrs), Glasgow (2 yrs), Keele, Kent at Canterbury, Lancaster, Leeds (2 yrs), Liverpool (BPhil, 1 or 2 yrs), London (Bedford College), Nottingham (1 yr full-time or 2 yrs part-time), Oxford (BPhil, 2 yrs), St Andrews (also Philosophy and Psychology, diploma 1 yr, MLitt 2 yrs), Sheffield, Surrey, Sussex, Wales (Cardiff University College), Warwick (MA 1 yr, MPhil 2 yrs) and York (12 months).
Philosophy of Education, see under 'Education'.
Philosophy (Socialist Studies), Kent at Canterbury.
Social and Political Thought, Sussex.

Research facilities
At most of the universities offering first degree courses.

First degrees
CNAA degree in *Philosophy* at: P of North London (3 yrs).
Philosophy is offered as an optional subject in Humanities degrees at: Bolton IT. Hatfield P. Huddersfield P. Middlesex P. P of North London. Thames P. P of Wales.

Photography

Postgraduate courses MA course (2 yrs) at Royal College of Art.

First degrees CNAA degrees offered at the following (3 yrs): P of Central London, *Photographic Arts and Photographic Science*. Falmouth S Art, *Fine Art (Photography)*.

Other courses Normally 3 yrs (diplomas unless otherwise indicated). Birmingham P. Bournemouth and Poole C Art. P of Central London, *Professional Photography*. Ealing TC. Glasgow C Building and Printing. Guildford C Arts. Harrow TC. London C Printing, higher diploma *Creative Photography*. Maidstone C Art. Manchester P. Medway C Design, *Photography*. Napier CC and T, HND (3 yrs), college diploma (1 yr), IIP diploma *Photography* (2 yrs). Salisbury C Art. Trent P (jointly with Derby C Art). Ulster C, Northern Ireland P. West Surrey C Arts. Wimbledon S Art, certificate course (1 yr).

Physical Education and Sports Science

See also Recreation Studies

First degrees Degrees with specialisation awarded by the following universities:
Education with Physical Education, Wales (Bangor University College).
Physical Education, Birmingham (alone or with another subject).
Physical Education and Sports Science, Loughborough U of Technology (alone or with another subject, also Physical Education, Sports Science and Recreation Management).
Physical Education may also be offered as a subject for the degree of BEd; and as a 1-yr course for a first degree in arts or science at St Andrews. Salford awards a BSc Joint Honours in *Human Movement Studies and Physiology*.

Postgraduate courses Courses in *Physical Education* (1 yr and for master's degree, unless otherwise indicated) at the universities of Birmingham (12 months), Leeds (12 months, also diploma) and Manchester. At some universities Physical Education may be offered as a subject for the postgraduate diploma or certificate in Education (Wales (Bangor University College): postgraduate certificate in Education with special emphasis on *Outdoor Activities*).

Research facilities At the following universities: Belfast, Birmingham, Leeds, Loughborough U of Technology, St Andrews (Exercise Physiology), Salford and Wales (Bangor University College).

First degree Liverpool P, *Sports Science* (3 yrs).

Teacher training *Physical Education* is offered as a specialist subject at a number of colleges of education as part of a BEd or certificate course. These colleges are listed below (M = men only, W = women only) (specialist courses in brackets); the addresses are on pages 278–281.
Aberdeen CE (M). Avery Hill C. Bath CHE. Bedford CHE. Bingley C. Birmingham P, Anstey Dept of Physical Education (W). Birmingham P, Bordesley Dept of Teacher Education and Training. Bishop Grosseteste C. Brighton P. Buckinghamshire CHE. Bulmershe CHE. Calendar Park CE (M). Chelmer IHE. Chester C. Christ Church C. City of Liverpool CHE. City of Manchester CHE. College of All Saints (W). Coventry CE. Crewe and Alsager CHE. De La

Salle C. Derby Lonsdale CHE. East Sussex CHE (W). Eaton Hall CE (W). Edge Hill CHE. Gloucestershire IHE, St Mary's C (W), St Paul's C (M). Goldsmiths' C. Gwent CHE. Hertfordshire CHE. Hull CHE. I M Marsh C of Physical Education (W) (also *Outdoor Education*, 1 yr). Jordanhill CE (M). King Alfred's CHE (M). Kingston P. Leeds P. Leicester P. Liverpool IHE. Madeley CE. Manchester P, Didsbury Faculty. Matlock CE. Nene C. New C, Durham. Newman C. Nonington C of Physical Education. Normal C (*Outdoor Education* (M)). North East London P, Barking Precinct. North East Wales IHE. P of North London. North Riding CE. North Worcestershire C. Northumberland CHE. Oxford P (also *Movement Studies*). Padgate CHE. Portsmouth P. Ripon and York St John CHE. Roehampton IHE. C of St Hild and St Bede. C of St Mark and St John (M). St Mary's C, Newcastle upon Tyne (*Outdoor Education*). St Mary's C, Twickenham. Sheffield P. South Glamorgan IHE (M, *Movement and Physical Recreation Studies*). Sunderland P. Trinity and All Saints' C. Ulster C, Northern Ireland P. P of Wales (W, *Human Movement Studies*). West London IHE. West Midlands CHE. West Sussex IHE. Wolverhampton P. Worcester CHE.

Physics

See also Astronomy and Space Science, Geology, and Medical/Health Physics

First degrees   Degrees with specialisation awarded by the following universities:

Applied Physics, Bradford (4 yrs S), Brunel (4 yrs S), The City (3 yrs, or 4 yrs S), Durham, Essex, Heriot-Watt (with Solid State Electronics), Hull, Lancaster (with Electronics), London (Chelsea and University Colleges), Nottingham (with Physics), Salford (4 yrs S), Strathclyde, Sussex (major subject in School of Engineering and Applied Sciences), New U of Ulster and Wales (Swansea University College and – 3 yrs, or 4 yrs S – Institute of Science and Technology).

Chemical Physics, Bristol, Edinburgh, Essex, Glasgow, Kent at Canterbury, Manchester (University and Institute of Science and Technology), Reading (Chemical Physics (Materials and Molecules)), Sheffield, Sussex (major subject in School of Molecular Sciences) and Wales (Bangor University College).

Electronic Physics, London (Royal Holloway College) and Wales (Aberystwyth University College).

Engineering Physics, Loughborough U of Technology (4 yrs S).

Environmental Physics, see 'Environmental Studies'.

Mathematical Physics, Birmingham, East Anglia, Edinburgh, Liverpool, Manchester (Institute of Science and Technology), Nottingham and Sussex.

Molecular Physics and Chemistry, London (Queen Elizabeth College).

Physical Electronics, Bradford (4 yrs S) and Warwick.

Physics, Aberdeen (Natural Philosophy), Aston in Birmingham (3 yrs, or 4 yrs S), Bath (3 yrs, or 4 yrs S), Belfast, Birmingham, Bristol, Brunel (with Computer Science, Education or Electronics, 4 yrs S), Cambridge (Natural Sciences Tripos), The City (with Electronics, 3 yrs, or 4 yrs S), Dundee, Durham, East Anglia, Edinburgh, Essex, Exeter, Glasgow (Natural Philosophy), Heriot-Watt, Hull, Keele (with another principal subject but Physics alone possible in final yr, also BSc in Integrated Physical Sciences), Kent at Canterbury, Lancaster, Leeds, Leicester, Liverpool, London (colleges as listed under 'Chemistry'), Loughborough U of Technology (3 yrs, or 4 yrs S), Manchester (University and Institute of Science and Technology), Newcastle upon Tyne, Nottingham, Oxford, Reading, St Andrews, Salford, Sheffield, Southampton, Stirling, Strathclyde, Surrey (3 yrs, or 4 yrs S, also Physical Science), Sussex, New U of Ulster, Wales (Aberystwyth, Bangor, Cardiff and Swansea University Colleges), Warwick and York.

Physics for Advanced Technology, Salford.
Physics of Materials, Manchester.
Physics of Natural Resources, Salford.
Radiation Physics, Liverpool (for Combined Studies degree).
Solid State Physics, Wales (Institute of Science and Technology, 3 yrs, or 4 yrs S).
Theoretical Physics, Cambridge, Essex, Kent at Canterbury, Lancaster, Leicester (Physics with Theoretical Physics), London (Queen Mary College), St Andrews (with one of certain other subjects) and Stirling (with Mathematics).

At many universities Physics (Hull, also Physics Studies; Surrey, also Physical Science) may also be studied with another principal subject for a Joint (or Combined) Honours degree, and less specialised study of Physics may be included in first degree courses in science.

Courses in *Optics* are given in most universities' Physics departments.

Postgraduate courses   Courses (1 yr and for master's degree, unless otherwise indicated) at the following universities:
Applied and Modern Optics, Reading (12 months).
Applied Cryophysics, Lancaster.
Applied Optics, London (Imperial College, MSc and/or DIC).
Applied Physics, Hull (diploma).
Applied Radiation Physics, Birmingham.
Atmospheric Physics and Dynamics, London (Imperial College, MSc and/or DIC).
Atomic and Molecular Processes, Belfast.
Atomic Collisions in Solids (modular course), Salford.
Chemical Physics, East Anglia.
Combustion and Energy, Leeds (12 months).
Cryogenics and its Applications, Southampton (12 months or in 3 parts over 36 months).
Experimental Space Physics, Leicester.
Fluid Dynamics, Edinburgh (MSc or diploma).
Ionization Physics, Wales (Swansea University College, also diploma).
Mathematical Physics, London (Imperial College, DIC) and Wales (Swansea University College, College diploma).
Non-Destructive Testing of Materials, Brunel (1 yr full-time or $2\frac{1}{2}$ yrs part-time).
Nuclear and Elementary Particle Physics, London (Bedford and Westfield Colleges, joint course).
Nuclear Instrumentation, Edinburgh (diploma 1 yr, MSc 12 months).
Nuclear Physics, London (Bedford College, College diploma) and Manchester (option for MSc/diploma in Physics).
Optical and Electrical Properties of Materials, London (Royal Holloway College).
Optoelectronics, Belfast and Essex.
Physical Methods of Analysis, Aston in Birmingham.
Physics, Aberdeen (certain branches), Cambridge (certificate of postgraduate study), Exeter, Lancaster, Leeds (minimum 12 months), London (Imperial College, DIC) and Manchester (many branches, for diploma or MSc).
Physics and Education, see 'Education'.
Physics and Technology of Nuclear Reactors, Birmingham.
Physics of Amorphous Materials, Glasgow, Edinburgh and Dundee in collaboration (12 months, including 6 months' course-work).
Physics of Materials, Bristol.
Physics of the Upper Atmosphere, Wales (Aberystwyth University College).
Physics of the Earth's Environment, Exeter.
Principles of Instrument Design, Aberdeen.
Quantum Electronics, Essex (12 months).
Science and Applications of Electric Plasmas, Oxford (for MSc in Engineering Science).

Science Education, see under 'Education'.

Semiconductor Devices, Lancaster.

Semiconductor Physics and Technology, Brunel (1 yr full-time or $2\frac{1}{2}$ yrs part-time).

Solid State Physics, London (Chelsea with Bedford and Westfield Colleges, 1 yr full-time or 2 yrs part-time), Sheffield and Wales (Swansea University College, also diploma).

Techniques in Molecular Physics, Manchester (MSc or diploma).

Theoretical Mechanics, East Anglia.

Theoretical Physics, Essex (12 months), Hull (diploma for Honours graduates in Physics or Mathematics or equivalent) and Southampton (Applied Mathematics and Theoretical Physics, 12 months).

Vacuum Physics and Technology, Brunel (1 yr full-time or $2\frac{1}{2}$ yrs part-time).

Research facilities

At most universities (including, for Liverpool and Manchester, (joint) Universities Research Reactor), and at Cranfield IT and Scottish Universities Research and Reactor Centre, East Kilbride. At Keele, postgraduate certificate in Education may be taken concurrently with research for PhD.

First degrees

CNAA degrees in *Physics* or *Applied Physics* (4 yrs S unless otherwise indicated). Brighton P (3 yrs and 4 yrs S). Lanchester P, *Physical Science/Materials Technology.* Liverpool P. Newcastle upon Tyne P, *Physical Electronics.* P of North London, *Physics and Technology of Electronics.* Paisley CT (4 yrs). Portsmouth P. Robert Gordon's IT (3–4 yrs). P of the South Bank. Sunderland P.

CNAA degrees in *Physical Science* (3 yrs). Lanchester P (4 yrs S). Robert Gordon's IT (3–4 yrs). Physics is also included as part of courses in Combined Studies or Science in a number of polytechnics and colleges.

HND courses

In *Applied Physics* (3 yrs S, unless otherwise stated). Glasgow CT. Kingston P (2 yrs). Lanchester P (2 yrs). Middlesex P (2 yrs). Napier CC and T, *Applied Physics with Electronics.* North Staffordshire P (2 yrs). Portsmouth P (2 yrs). Preston P. Sheffield P.

Professional courses

A number of institutions run courses leading to the Graduateship examination of the Institute of Physics. For full details, one should contact the Institute.

Postgraduate courses

Brighton P, MSc *Applied Solid State Physics* (1 yr). Portsmouth P, MSc *Microwave and Solid State Physics* (1 yr). P of the South Bank, *MSc Applied Nuclear Physics* (1 yr).

Research facilities

At all polytechnics mentioned above.

Physiology

For Plant Physiology, see Biology; for Animal Physiology, see also Agriculture and Forestry

First degrees

Degrees with specialisation in *Physiology* awarded by the universities of Aberdeen, Aston in Birmingham (Physiology and Pharmacology taken with another subject), Belfast, Birmingham (Honours in School of Biological Sciences with specialisation in groups of relevant subjects), Bristol, Cambridge (Natural Sciences Tripos), Dundee, Edinburgh, Glasgow, Leeds, Leicester (Honours in Biology with specialisation in a group of relevant subjects), London (Bedford, Chelsea, King's, Queen Elizabeth, Queen Mary and University Colleges, and Medical Schools, also at Chelsea Immunology with Physiology), Manchester, Newcastle upon Tyne, Nottingham (with Chemistry or Psychology, or as integral part of BMedSci course), Oxford, Reading (integrated course with Biochemistry), St Andrews, Salford (with Biological Chemistry or Chemistry or Human Movement Studies), Sheffield, Southampton (integrated course with Biochemistry) and Wales (Cardiff University College). At some of the universities offering degrees with specialisation in this subject alone, Physiology may also be studied with another principal subject for a Joint (or Combined) Honours degree; and it is also included in first degree courses in Medicine (for list of awarding universities see page 198). *Animal* or *Comparative Physiology* is included in first degree courses in Biology or Zoology at most universities.

Postgraduate courses   Courses (for MSc) at University of London in *Neurobiology* (Bedford and Chelsea Colleges, 1 yr) and in *Physiology* (University College, 1 or 2 yrs, suitable for graduates in other sciences). Revision courses (full-time) in the basic medical sciences, including Physiology (suitable for one or more of: Primary FRCS, Primary FFA, Primary FDS, MRCOG Part I), are organised by Edinburgh Postgraduate Board for Medicine (16 weeks) and University of London Institute of Basic Medical Sciences (including 12 weeks for Primary FRCS, 8 weeks for Primary FDS). Similar courses, but on a part-time/day-release basis, are offered by several universities; further information is given in 'Summary of Postgraduate Diplomas and Courses in Medicine' – see page 266.

Research facilities   At most of the universities which offer first degree courses (London, also Birkbeck College), and at Keele (Neurophysiology and Sensory Communication, Department of Communication – postgraduate certificate in Education may be taken concurrently with research for PhD) and Liverpool.

First degrees   CNAA degrees in Applied Biology at the following polytechnics provide opportunities for the study of *Physiology*: Hatfield P. Lanchester P. North East London P. Thames P.

Physiotherapy

Postgraduate courses   University of Southampton awards an MSc (15 months) and a diploma (12 months) in *Remedial Therapy.*

Professional courses   The Chartered Society of Physiotherapy awards by examination a certificate of Membership (MCSP) and a diploma for Teachers of Physiotherapy. Those who obtain the Society's qualification, after taking its examination, are eligible for registration with the Council for Professions Supplementary to Medicine, which maintains a State Register of physiotherapists.

Courses in *Physiotherapy* (3 yrs) are available in Schools of Physiotherapy recognised by the Chartered Society of Physiotherapy in Aberdeen, Bath, Birmingham, Bradford, Bristol, Cambridge, Cardiff, Coventry, Edinburgh, Glasgow, Leeds, Liverpool, London, Manchester, Middlesbrough, Newcastle upon Tyne, Nottingham, Oswestry, Salford, Sheffield and Wolverhampton and at †Northern Ireland P. All recognised Physiotherapy training schools are attached to hospitals. Blind students are accepted at the †North London School of Physiotherapy for the Visually Handicapped.

†Applications should be made direct. Applications for places should in all other cases be made through the Physiotherapy Training Clearing House of the Chartered Society.

Political Science

First degrees   Degrees with specialisation awarded by the following universities:
Government, Brunel (Government, Politics and Modern History, 4 yrs S), Essex (including, in School of Comparative Studies, comparative syllabus or area specialisation), Heriot-Watt (Government and Modern History), Kent at Canterbury (Politics and Government), London (London School of Economics), Loughborough U of Technology (with Applied Economics or a language), Manchester and Wales (with Law, Philosophy or Sociology at Cardiff and with Political Theory at Swansea University Colleges).

International Relations, Aberdeen (with one of certain other subjects), Birmingham, Keele, Leeds (International History and Politics), Reading (with another subject), Sussex (major subject in Schools of African and Asian or English and American or European Studies or of Social Sciences) and Wales (International Politics at Aberystwyth University College).

International Studies, Birmingham, Southampton (with Politics) and Warwick.

Political Science/Politics, Aberdeen, Aston in Birmingham (Political Studies with another subject), Belfast (with Modern History, Philosophy or Economics, also as major subject for BSSc), Birmingham (BSocSc), Bradford (with one of certain other subjects for Honours in Social Sciences), Bristol, Brunel (Government, Politics and Modern History), Cambridge (Social and Political Sciences Tripos, or with Economics), Dundee, Durham, Edinburgh (with one of certain other subjects), East Anglia, Essex (with Mathematics), Exeter, Glasgow, Hull (also with reference to South-East Asia), Keele (with another principal subject, also Joint Honours in Philosophy, Economics and Politics), Kent at Canterbury (with Government), Lancaster, Leeds (Political Studies), Leicester, Liverpool (Political Theory and Institutions), London (Queen Mary and – with History and Economic History – Royal Holloway Colleges), Manchester (with Modern History, also Political Theory for BA(Econ)), Newcastle upon Tyne (with Economics, History or Social Administration), Nottingham, Oxford (with Philosophy and/or Economics), Reading, Salford (with one of certain other subjects, also Politics and History of Industrial Society), Sheffield (Political Theory and Institutions), Southampton (as main subject for BSc (Social Sciences), or with Philosophy, or with Modern History plus Economics), Stirling (Political Studies), Strathclyde, Sussex (major subject in Schools of African and Asian, English and American or European Studies, or of Social Sciences), Wales (for BScEcon at Aberystwyth University College and Institute of Science and Technology, also – Political Theory and Government – Swansea University College), Warwick and York.

At many of the universities offering degrees with specialisation in this subject alone, *Politics/Political Science* may also be studied with another principal subject for a Joint (or Combined) Honours degree; and at many of them less specialised study of Political Science/Politics may be included in first degree courses in arts, economics or social studies.

Less specialised study of *International Relations* may be included in first degree courses in arts or social studies at some universities, including Aberdeen, Birmingham (BCom, BSocSc), The City (for BSc in Systems and Management), Lancaster, Leicester, London (London School of Economics), Oxford, Southampton (Politics and International Studies) and Surrey (Linguistic and International Studies: French, German and Russian).

The independent University College at Buckingham (see page 32) awards a licence in the Schools of Law, Economics and Politics, and of History, Politics and English Literature; and European Institutions are studied in the School of European Studies.

Postgraduate courses   Courses (1 yr and for master's degree, unless otherwise indicated) at the following universities: *American Politics and History,* Liverpool (BPhil, 1 or 2 yrs).

Area Studies (International Relations), London (University College).
British Foreign Policy, Wales (Aberystwyth University College).
Comparative Politics, Sussex.
Contemporary European Politics, etc, Reading (MA 1 yr, MPhil 2 yrs, in Graduate School of
   Contemporary European Studies).
Contemporary European Studies, Sussex.
European Political Studies, Leicester.
European Politics, Hull (BPhil).
Formal Political Analysis, Essex (12 months).
Government, Kent at Canterbury (with Politics) and Manchester (MA (Econ) or diploma).
International Relations, London (London School of Economics, University College and School
   of Slavonic and East European Studies), Oxford (BPhil, 2 yrs), Sussex and Wales
   (Aberystwyth University College, International Law and Relations, diploma).
International Studies, Southampton.
Latin American Government and Politics, Essex (12 months).
Local Government, Kent at Canterbury.
Modern British Politics, Sheffield.
Political Behaviour, Essex (12 months).
Political Philosophy, Hull (BPhil).
Political Science/Politics, Birmingham (12 months), Glasgow (2 yrs), Kent at Canterbury (with
   Government), Lancaster (MA 12 months, diploma 9 months), Leeds (MA 1 yr, MPhil 2
   yrs), Liverpool (BPhil, 1 or 2 yrs), London (including History of Political Thought,
   Politics and Government of United Kingdom or Russia or Western Europe or Africa,
   Comparative Government, and Political Sociology, at London School of Economics,
   also Political Characteristics of Contemporary Asian and African Societies at School of
   Oriental and African Studies, and Politics with reference to Eastern Europe and Russia
   at School of Slavonic and East European Studies), Oxford (BPhil, 2 yrs), Strathclyde and
   Warwick.
Political Theory and Government, Wales (Swansea University College, 2 yrs).
Political Theory and Institutions, Sheffield.
Politics (Theory), Durham.
Politics with Sociology, London (Birkbeck College, 1 yr full-time or 2 yrs part-time).
Social and Political Thought, Sussex.
Social Theory and Public Policy, Aberdeen.
Sociology and Politics of Development, Cambridge (option in Development Studies course).
Sociology with Politics, London (Birkbeck College, 1 yr full-time or 2 yrs part-time).
Southern African Studies, York (12 months).
Soviet Government, London (School of Slavonic and East European Studies).
Soviet Government and Politics, Essex (12 months).
United States Government and Politics, Essex (12 months).
Western European Politics, Essex (12 months).

Research facilities Political Science/Politics: at most of the universities named above (Hull, Centre for South-East Asian Studies; Kent at Canterbury, Centre for Research in the Social Sciences; London, Birkbeck College, London School of Economics, School of Oriental and African Studies and School of Slavonic and East European Studies; Reading, Graduate School of Contemporary European Studies; Sussex, Centre for Contemporary European Studies, Institute of Development Studies; York, Centre for Southern African Studies). Essex, Nuffield College (Oxford) and Strathclyde are members of the European Consortium for Political Research. *International Relations:* at Birmingham, Keele, London, Reading and Sussex.

First degrees   CNAA degrees are offered at the following polytechnics (3 yrs): Birmingham P, *Government.* City of London P, *Politics and Government.* Kingston P, *Languages, Economics and Politics* (4 yrs). Newcastle upon Tyne P, *Government.* Thames P, *Political Economy.* Portsmouth P, *Politics.* Sheffield P, *Modern Languages with Political Studies* (4 yrs).

Politics is offered as an optional subject in Modern Studies and Humanities degrees at the following. Ealing CHE. Huddersfield P. Lanchester P. Leicester P. Manchester P. North Staffordshire P. Sheffield P. Teesside P. Thames P. Trent P. Ulster C, Northern Ireland P.

Other courses   Two residential colleges of adult education in Oxford, Plater College and Ruskin College, have courses leading to the Special Diploma in Social Studies of the University of Oxford (2 yrs). For other courses at adult education colleges see page 281–283.

Research facilities   Kingston P. Sheffield P.

Polymer Science and Technology

First degrees   Degrees with specialisation awarded by the following universities:

Macromolecular Science, Liverpool.

Polymer Chemistry, Belfast (Polymer and Colour Science for BSc in Industrial Chemistry) and Manchester (Institute of Science and Technology).

Polymer Chemistry and Technology, Wales (Institute of Science and Technology, 3 yrs, or 4 yrs S).

Polymer Engineering, Manchester (Institute of Science and Technology).

Polymer Science, Sussex.

Polymer Science and Engineering, London (Queen Mary College).

Polymer Science and Technology, Aston in Birmingham (with another subject), Sheffield and Wales (Institute of Science and Technology, Applied Science with special reference to).

Polymer Science and Technology (*Chemistry*) or (*Physics*), Manchester (Institute of Science and Technology).

Polymer Science/Technology, Loughborough U of Technology (with Chemistry, 3 yrs, or 4 yrs S).

Polymer Technology, Brunel (alone or with Management, each 4 yrs S).

Postgraduate courses   Courses (1 yr and for MSc, unless otherwise indicated) at the following universities and Cranfield IT:

Applied Polymer Engineering, Loughborough U of Technology.

Chemistry and Technology of Polymers, Aston in Birmingham (12 months).

Polymeric Materials, Cranfield IT (1 or 2 yrs, option for MSc in Materials).

Polymer Science, Bradford and Manchester (University and – Polymer and Fibre Science – Institute of Science and Technology, MSc or diploma).

Polymer Science and Engineering, London (Imperial College, for MSc and/or DIC in Applied Mechanics).

Polymer Science and Technology, Lancaster.

Polymer Technology, Loughborough U of Technology and Sheffield (diploma 1 yr, MScTech 2 yrs).

Research facilities   At most of the universities named in the paragraphs above (Loughborough U of Technology: Institute of Polymer Technology), and at Birmingham, Bristol and Essex (Institute of Polymer Science), and Cranfield IT.

First degrees CNAA degrees in *Polymer Science*. Kingston P, *Applied Chemistry*, option in *Polymer Chemistry* (4 yrs S). Manchester P, *Polymer Science and Technology* (4 yrs S). P of North London (National College of Rubber Technology) (3 yrs, or 4 yrs S). P of the South Bank, *Chemical Technology and Polymer Technology (Plaster or Surface Coatings)* (4 yrs S).

HND course P of the South Bank, *Applied Chemistry* with option in *Polymer Chemistry* (2 yrs).

Professional courses For information on courses leading to the Graduateship of the Plastics and Rubber Institute, one should contact the Institute.

College and postgraduate course Leicester P, diploma in *Polymer Science* (2 yrs) and MSc in *Polymer and Adhesion Science* (1 yr). P of North London (National C Rubber Technology), MSc *Adhesion Science and Technology*, and *Polymer Science and Technology* (both 1 yr).

Research facilities Kingston P. Manchester P. P of North London. P of the South Bank.

Portuguese

First degrees Degrees with specialisation in *Portuguese* awarded by the universities of Cambridge, Leeds (with another main subject), Liverpool, London (King's College), Oxford and Wales (Cardiff University College, in Hispanic Studies course or with another subject). Less specialised study of Portuguese may be included in courses leading to first degrees (usually for students taking Spanish) at the universities of Aberdeen (only for Honours students in Spanish), Belfast, Birmingham, Bristol, Durham, Essex (particularly for Latin American specialisations), Glasgow, Hull, Leeds, Manchester, Newcastle upon Tyne (in Spanish or Latin American Studies courses), Nottingham, St Andrews (in Hispanic Languages and Literatures course), Salford, Sheffield and Southampton (in unit course scheme with options in other modern European languages, Classics, and Philosophy).

Postgraduate courses Courses (2 yrs) at the universities of Oxford (for BPhil in *General and Comparative Literature* of 2 or 3 languages) and St Andrews (MLitt in *Portuguese Studies*).

Research facilities At the universities of Cambridge, London (King's College), Manchester and Oxford.

Printing and Publishing

First degrees University of Reading awards a BA in *Typography and Graphic Communication*.

Postgraduate courses MA courses in *Graphic Design* and in *Printmaking* (each 3 yrs) and in *Graphic Information* (2 yrs) at Royal College of Art.

Research facilities At University of Reading and Royal College of Art (Readability of Print Research Unit).

First degrees CNAA degree in *Packaging Technology* and *Printing Technology* (4 yrs S) at Watford CT.

HND courses (3 yrs S): Glasgow C Building and Printing, *Printing (Administration and Production)* (3 yrs). London C Printing, also *Business Studies (Printing)*, for those entering printing and related industries. Napier CC and T, *Printing Administration and Production* (3 yrs). Stockport CT, *Package Design* and *Advertising Design* (both also 3 yrs). Trent P, *Printing Technology*.

TEC HD course Watford CT, *Printing (Administration and/or Technology)* (2 yrs).

College diplomas Cambridgeshire C Arts T, *Graphic Design (Typography, Illustration)* (3 yrs). London C Printing, diploma *Typographic Design* (3 yrs), Certificate *Advanced Typographic Design* (1 yr). Manchester P, diploma *Printing* (3 yrs), also *Graphic Reproduction* (2 yrs). Napier CC and T, *Book and Periodical Publishing* (3 yrs). Oxford P, *Book Publishing* (3 yrs). Watford CT, *Printing* options in *Administration* or *Technology* (2 or 3 yrs).

Postgraduate courses London C Printing, diploma in *Printing Studies* (20 weeks), CNAA MPhil and PhD degrees can also be offered. Croydon C Design and T, *Printmaking* and *Typography* (both 1 yr).

Psychological Medicine (Psychiatry)
See also Psychology

First degrees Degree courses in Medicine (for list of awarding universities see page 198) include *Psychological Medicine*.

Postgraduate courses Full-time courses (for medically qualified candidates) at the following universities: *Psychiatry*, London (Institute of Psychiatry, MPhil, also – see below – for MRCPsych and DPM); *Psychotherapy*, Aberdeen (diploma, 1 yr full-time or 20 months part-time) and Sheffield (diploma, 2 yrs full-time or 4 yrs part-time). Part-time and/or short courses, including courses for diploma in Psychological Medicine (DPM) and/or MRCPsych (see below), are offered by several universities; fuller information is given in 'Summary of Postgraduate Diplomas and Courses in Medicine' – see page 266.

Research facilities At the universities of Aberdeen, Belfast, Birmingham, Bristol, Cambridge, Dundee, Glasgow, Liverpool (including MPsyMed), London (Institute of Psychiatry), Manchester, Newcastle upon Tyne, Nottingham, Sheffield and Southampton.

Postgraduate qualifications The Royal College of Psychiatrists awards a diploma of Membership (MRCPsych) by examination. The Examination Board of the Royal College of Physicians of London and Royal College of Surgeons of England awards a diploma in *Psychological Medicine* (DPM).

Psychology

See also Ergonomics and Cybernetics; and Psychological Medicine

First degrees
Degrees with specialisation awarded by the following universities:

Applied Social Psychology, Wales (Institute of Science and Technology, 3 yrs, or 4 yrs S).

Developmental Psychology, Sussex (major subject in Schools of Cultural and Community Studies and of Social Sciences).

Experimental Psychology, Oxford and Sussex (major subject in School of Biological Sciences).

Human Psychology, Aston in Birmingham.

Industrial Psychology, Bradford (with Industrial Sociology, for Honours in Business Studies).

Occupational Psychology, Wales (Institute of Science and Technology, 3 yrs, or 4 yrs S).

Psychology (at a number of those universities which have separate faculties – of arts, science, etc – these degree courses may be available in more than one faculty – e.g. in arts or social sciences and in science – and there may be differences between faculties both in the requirements for admission and in the syllabus or choice of options), Aberdeen, Aston in Birmingham (4 yrs S, for BSc in Behavioural Science), Belfast, Birmingham, Bradford, Bristol, Brunel (4 yrs S), Cambridge (Natural Sciences Tripos), The City (3 yrs, or 4 yrs S), Dundee, Durham, Edinburgh, Exeter, Glasgow, Hull, Keele (with another principal subject), Lancaster, Leeds, Leicester, Liverpool, London (Bedford and University and – part-time – Birkbeck Colleges, also Goldsmiths' College), Loughborough U of Technology, Manchester, Newcastle upon Tyne, Nottingham, Oxford (with either Philosophy or Physiology), Reading, St Andrews, Salford, Sheffield, Southampton, Stirling, Strathclyde, Surrey (with Philosophy and Sociology), New U of Ulster, Wales (Bangor, Cardiff and Swansea University Colleges), Warwick and York.

Social Psychology, Bradford, London (London School of Economics), Loughborough U of Technology (with a minor subject) and Sussex (major subject in Schools of Social Sciences and of African and Asian Studies).

At many of the universities offering degrees with specialisation in this subject alone, Psychology may also be studied with another principal subject for a Joint (or Combined) Honours degree; and at many of them (London: also Chelsea College) less specialised study of Psychology (Birmingham, Bradford and Exeter, also Social Psychology) may be included in first degree courses in arts, science, social studies, or education. Less specialised study of Industrial Psychology may be included in first degree courses at Edinburgh (BSc), Glasgow (for students taking Psychology for MA) and Nottingham (BA Honours in Industrial Economics).

Postgraduate courses
Courses (1 yr and for master's degree, unless otherwise indicated) at the following universities:

Abnormal Psychology, Belfast (2 yrs), London (Institute of Psychiatry) and Oxford (2 yrs).

Applied Child Psychology, Stirling (diploma, 2 yrs).

Applied Psychology, Aston in Birmingham (also Applied Psychology for Engineers, each 12 months), Liverpool (diploma, 1 or 2 yrs, for graduates in Psychology or other suitably qualified and approved candidates) and Wales (Cardiff University College and – diploma 9 months, MSc 2 yrs – Institute of Science and Technology).

Child Psychology, Birmingham (diploma in Psychology of Childhood, for graduates and other suitably qualified persons) and Nottingham.

Clinical Psychology (2 yrs), Aberdeen, Birmingham, Edinburgh (24 months), Glasgow (for Honours graduates), Leeds (24 months), Liverpool (BPhil), London (Institute of Psychiatry), Newcastle upon Tyne and Surrey.

Cognitive Studies and Computing Studies, Sussex.

Computer Applications in Psychology, Belfast.

Developmental and Educational Psychology, Belfast (1–2 yrs).

Developmental Psychology, Sussex.

Educational Psychology, Aberdeen, Birmingham, Edinburgh (12 months), Exeter (for candidates

with degree in Psychology and some teaching experience), Glasgow (diploma or –
Educational Psychology and Child Guidance – MAppSci, 1 or 2 yrs), London (12
months full-time or 21 months part-time at Institute of Education – Psychology of
Education – and 1 or 2 yrs at University College), Manchester (Educational Psychology
(Child Guidance), for suitably qualified and experienced graduate teachers), Newcastle
upon Tyne (normally 2 yrs), Sheffield, Southampton (1 yr, also 4-yr integrated scheme,
both restricted intake), Strathclyde, Sussex (2 yrs) and Wales (Swansea University
College).

Environmental Psychology, Surrey (12 months).

Experimental Psychology, Sussex.

Industrial Psychology, Hull.

Manpower Studies, London (Birkbeck College, 1 yr full-time or 2 yrs part-time).

Mathematical Psychology, Stirling.

Neurocommunications, Birmingham.

Occupational Psychology, Belfast, Liverpool (BPhil, 2 yrs) and Sheffield.

Organisational Psychology, Lancaster (MA 12 months, diploma 9 months).

Psychology, Manchester (MSc or diploma), St Andrews (Philosophy and Psychology, diploma 1
yr, MLitt 2 yrs) and Wales (Institute of Science and Technology, diploma).

Psychology of Delinquency, Liverpool (BPhil, 2 yrs).

Psychology of Education, see 'Education'.

Psychology of Mental Handicap, Keele.

Psychology of Reading, Dundee (diploma).

Research Methods in Developmental and Social Psychology, Strathclyde.

Social and Psychological Aspects of Science and Technology in Industry, London (Imperial
College, MSc and/or DIC).

Social Psychology, London (London School of Economics).

Psychology may also be included in higher degree and diploma courses in Education, also at
Dundee in diploma course in Social Administration and at St Andrews in diploma course in
Pastoral and Social Studies.

Research
facilities   At most of the universities which offer first degree courses; and including Industrial Psychology
at Aston in Birmingham, Birmingham, Bradford, Brunel, Cambridge and London (Birkbeck and
University Colleges and London School of Economics). Cambridge: Psychological laboratory
with research facilities in general Experimental Psychology.

First degrees   CNAA degrees in *Psychology* are offered at the following polytechnics and college (3 yrs):
Bolton IT. Hatfield P. Huddersfield P, *Behavioural Sciences* (4 yrs S). Manchester P. Newcastle
upon Tyne P. North East London P. Plymouth P. Portsmouth P. Preston P. Ulster C, Northern
Ireland P.

Psychology is offered as an optional subject in Humanities degrees at a number of colleges and
polytechnics.

Postgraduate   North East London P, MSc *Educational Psychology* (1 yr).
courses   The British Psychological Society awards a diploma in *Clinical Psychology* and a Diploma in
Developmental and Educational Psychology

Research   City of London P. Hatfield P. North East London P.
facilities

Public Administration and Finance

First degrees Degrees with specialisation in *Public Administration and/or Finance* awarded by the following universities: Aston in Birmingham (in Managerial and Administrative Studies course), Bath (Economics and Government, 4 yrs S), Bradford (Public and Social Policy, 4 yrs S), Brunel (Government and Public Administration option in Government, Politics and Modern History course, 4 yrs S), Dundee (in Administrative Studies course), Durham (Social and Public Administration), Kent at Canterbury (Public Administration and Management or Social Policy, also Social Policy and Administration) and Leeds (Social and Public Administration). Public Administration and Finance may also be included in first degree courses in arts, commerce or social studies, etc, at the following universities: Bath, Birmingham (Public Finance option in BCom (Accounting) course), Exeter (Economics, Politics, Social Administration and Social Policy), Heriot-Watt, Leeds, Leicester (Public Finance only), Liverpool, London (with Economics at Bedford College), Manchester, Newcastle upon Tyne, Nottingham, Reading (options in Politics and Sociology courses), Sheffield and Strathclyde (Public and Social Administration with another subject).

Postgraduate courses Courses (1 yr and for master's degree, unless otherwise indicated) at the following universities:

Development Administration, Birmingham (diploma, only for overseas candidates who are graduates or established public servants) and Manchester (diploma).

Financial Studies, Heriot-Watt (diploma) and Strathclyde (diploma or MSc).

Local Government, Birmingham (12 months, also 4-month course, at Institute of Local Government Studies, mainly for students from developing countries), Bradford (Local Government Management option for diploma in Management and Administration or MBA) and Kent at Canterbury.

Management (diploma) and *Management Studies* (12 months), Heriot-Watt.

Port and Shipping Administration, Wales (Institute of Science and Technology, Institute diploma, open to graduates and to others with appropriate qualifications and experience).

Public Administration, Liverpool (1 or 2 yrs), London (Theory and Practice of, London School of Economics, for MSc in Politics) and Manchester (in Department of Administrative Studies for Overseas Visiting Fellows, for senior serving officials in overseas central or local government, certificates for overseas government officers and in Methodology of Public Administration Training, also – each 3 months – Special Aspects of Public Administration and course for Overseas University Administrators).

Public and Social Administration, Brunel.

Public Finance, Cambridge (in Economic Policy and Planning option in Development Studies course) and York (Economics with special reference to, 12 months).

Public Sector Management, Aston in Birmingham (MSc or diploma, 1 yr full-time or 2 yrs part-time, options in Health and Welfare Services or Urban Management).

Social Research and Social Policy, Oxford (2 yrs).

Social Theory and Public Policy, Aberdeen.

Research facilities At the following universities: Aston in Birmingham, Birmingham, Brunel, Exeter, Kent at Canterbury (Centre for Research in the Social Sciences), Leicester (Public Sector Economics Research Centre), London (London School of Economics), Manchester, Oxford, Strathclyde, Sussex (Institute of Development Studies) and New U of Ulster (Institute of Continuing Education).

First degrees CNAA degrees in *Public Administration* (4 yrs S): Leicester P. Manchester P. Sheffield P. Teesside P. Trent P.

HND course HND *Business Studies* with a specialist option in *Public Administration* are offered at Crawley CT, Croydon C Design T, Derby Lonsdale IHE, Dorset IHE, Hammersmith and West London C, Huddersfield P, Luton CHE, Newcastle upon Tyne P, Preston P, Sheffield P, Teesside P, Thames P, P of Wales.
Public Administration, Wolverhampton P.

Other courses South Devon TC, special course for overseas students (mainly for those already in government service in developing countries): *Diploma in Development Administration* (1 yr).

The Royal Institute of Public Administration provides five 3-month courses for students from overseas. *Management Services for Officers from Developing Countries. Training Techniques for Senior Officers. Organisation, Methods and Job Evaluation. Personnel Work in Public Administration Overseas. Government Administration for National Development.*

Public and Industrial Health

See also Engineering, Public Health and Municipal

First degrees Degrees with specialisation awarded by the following universities:
Environmental Health, Aston in Birmingham (4 yrs S) and Strathclyde.
Environmental Sciences or *Health Physics and Environmental Physics,* Salford.
Safety and Health, Aston in Birmingham (3 yrs, or 4 yrs S).
Public Health is included in courses leading to first degrees in Medicine (for list of awarding universities see page 198); and at most of the universities offering such degrees the courses also include *Industrial* and/or *Social* or *Community Medicine,* etc. At Bradford, BTech (4 yrs S) in Industrial Technology and Management includes *Safety Factors in Plant Design.*

Postgraduate courses Full-time courses (1 yr unless otherwise indicated) leading to diploma in *Public Health* (DPH), and normally open only to candidates holding a registrable medical qualification, at the universities of Bristol, Glasgow, Leeds and (if sufficient candidates available) Sheffield; part-time DPH courses also offered at several universities.

Other postgraduate courses (1 yr and for MSc, unless otherwise indicated) for candidates with an approved medical qualification:
Community Medicine, Edinburgh (diploma).
Industrial Health, Dundee (diploma or certificate, 3 months), London (School of Hygiene and Tropical Medicine, 3 months for Conjoint Board diploma – see below) and Manchester (for Conjoint Board diploma – see below – 1 yr full-time or equivalent part-time).
Occupational Medicine or *Social Medicine* (2 yrs) or *Tropical Public Health,* London (School of Hygiene and Tropical Medicine).
Tuberculosis and Chest Diseases, Wales (Welsh National School of Medicine, diploma, 6 months).

Postgraduate courses (for MSc unless otherwise indicated) not necessarily restricted to medically qualified candidates:
Community Health, Glasgow (MPhil, 2 yrs full-time or 3 yrs part-time, primarily for those without medical qualifications) and Liverpool (MCommH, 1 yr).
Community Medicine, Nottingham (MMedSci, 2 yrs).
Industrial Safety, London (Imperial College, MSc and/or DIC).
Occupational Hygiene, London (School of Hygiene and Tropical Medicine) and Newcastle upon Tyne.
Occupational Safety and Hygiene, Aston in Birmingham.

Public Health, Dundee (MPH, minimum 12 months) and Reading (option for MSc, 12 months, in Food Science).
Safety and Hygiene, Aston in Birmingham (diploma, 6 months).

Research facilities   At most of the universities named above, also at others which award first degrees in Medicine (see page 198), and at Kent at Canterbury (Health Services Research Unit of Centre for Research in the Social Sciences) and Surrey.

First degree   CNAA degree: P of the South Bank, *Occupational Hygiene* (3 yrs).

Medical postgraduate qualifications   Postgraduate diplomas in *Industrial Health* are awarded by the Examining Board in England of the Royal College of Physicians of London and the Royal College of Surgeons of England, by the Royal College of Physicians and Surgeons of Glasgow, and by the Society of Apothecaries of London.

A postgraduate diploma in *Public Health* is granted by the Examining Board in England of the Royal College of Physicians of London and the Royal College of Surgeons of England.

Particulars of these diplomas are available from the Secretary of the Examining Board in England.

The Faculty of Community Medicine of the Royal College of Physicians of the UK awards a diploma of Membership by examination.

Non-medical postgraduate courses   London: British Examining Board in Occupational Hygiene awards a diploma of Professional Competence and a certificate of Operational Competence in *Comprehensive Occupational Hygiene.* Details from the Secretary of the Board.

Royal Institute of Public Health and Hygiene provides courses including a diploma in *Environmental Control* (4 months).

College diplomas   (3 yrs S): Liverpool P, *Public Health Inspection.* Highbury TC, *Environmental Health Inspector's* diploma. Salford CT, *Public Health Inspection.*

Radiobiology
See also Medical/Health Physics

First degrees   Some study of *Radiobiology* included in first degree courses at the universities of Belfast (courses may be provided by special arrangement with departments of Physiology and Chemistry) and Bristol (Microbiology).

Postgraduate courses   Courses (for MSc) at the universities of Birmingham (55 weeks, primarily as preparation for PhD candidature) and London (1 yr intercollegiate course in Radiation Biology jointly at Guy's, Middlesex, Royal Free and St Bartholomew's Hospital Medical Schools, and in Radiation Physics jointly at Middlesex and St Bartholomew's Hospital Medical Schools).

Research facilities   At the universities of Birmingham, Cambridge, London (Queen Mary College and St Bartholomew's Hospital Medical College), Manchester, Reading (National Institute for Research in Dairying, attached to the University, and at ARC Letcombe Laboratory, Wantage, an associated institution), Salford (Nuclear Science Building), Wales (Cardiff University College) and York.

Radiography

See also Radiology
No university courses

Professional courses

The College of Radiographers awards certificates of qualification in both radiography (R) and radiotherapy (T) by examination. Holders of a certificate are entitled to apply for membership of the Society. Training for each takes a minimum of two years. Students who have obtained one of the certificates and wish to sit for the second are required to spend one year studying in approved centres after obtaining the first. Training is available in a large number of hospitals. Details may be obtained from the Secretary of the College of Radiographers.

Those who obtain the College's qualification after taking its examinations are eligible for registration with the Council for Professions Supplementary to Medicine, which maintains a State Register of radiographers. The College also organises (1) a Higher Examination for persons who have been eligible for State Registration in the United Kingdom for not less than four years; (2) Examinations leading to the Teacher's Diploma; and (3) (a) Diploma in Nuclear Medicine. (b) Diploma in Medical Ultrasound. Details of these examinations are obtainable from the Secretary of the College.

Radiology
(Radiodiagnosis or Radiotherapy)

Note. In the United Kingdom the two specialities of Radiodiagnosis and Radiotherapy are quite separate. There are postgraduate courses in each, and postgraduate students cannot cover the study of both specialities in one course.

First degrees

Degree courses in Medicine (for list of awarding universities see page 198) include the study of *Radiodiagnosis* and *Radiotherapy.*

Postgraduate courses

Courses (2 yrs – in some cases 3rd yr may be available for FRCR) leading to university diplomas at Aberdeen (in *Medical Radiodiagnosis* for registered medical practitioners of at least 1 yr's standing) and Edinburgh (*Medical Radiodiagnosis* or *Medical Radiotherapy*), and to the diplomas of the Conjoint Board (see below) at the universities of Birmingham, Bristol, Glasgow, London (Schools of the university in co-operation with Royal College of Radiologists) and Manchester (2 yrs for DMRD, 3 yrs for FRCR).

Research facilities

Radiodiagnosis and *Radiotherapy*: at the universities of Belfast, Birmingham, Bristol, Cambridge, Dundee, Edinburgh, Glasgow, Leeds, Liverpool (MRad, open only to holders of Liverpool DMR(D) or DMR(T)), London, Manchester, Newcastle upon Tyne, Nottingham, Sheffield and Wales (Welsh National School of Medicine).

Professional courses

The Examining Board in England of the Royal College of Physicians of London and the Royal College of Surgeons of England awards a postgraduate diploma in *Radiodiagnosis* (2 yrs) and a postgraduate diploma in *Radiotherapy* (2 yrs); particulars may be obtained from the Secretary of the Examining Board in England.

The diploma of Fellowship (FRCR) is awarded by the Royal College of Radiologists.

Recreation Studies

See also Physical Education and Sports Science

First degrees Loughborough U of Technology awards a BSc Honours in *Physical Education, Sports Science and Recreation Management.*

Postgraduate courses Courses (1 yr and for master's degree, unless otherwise indicated) at the following universities: *Countryside Recreation Resources,* Salford (special option for MSc in Environmental Resources); *Recreational Land Management,* Reading (12 months); *Recreation Management,* Loughborough U of Technology; *Tourism,* Strathclyde (diploma 9 months, MSc 12 months) and Surrey (diploma 1 academic yr, MSc minimum 12 months), also post-experience course (3 months) in Tourism Projects at Bradford (Project Planning Centre for Developing Countries). Recreation Studies also included in Physical Education and Urban and Regional Studies courses at Birmingham.

Research facilities At the following universities: Birmingham, Loughborough U of Technology, Manchester (Centre for Youth Studies) and Reading (in relation to Land Management).

First degree Bingley C, *Recreational Studies* (4 yrs S).

Diploma courses P of Central London, *Administration of the Arts and Leisure* (1 yr). Dunfermline C Physical Education, *Recreation and Leisure Practice* (1 yr). Luton CHE, diploma *Management Studies* (option in *Recreational Management,* 1 yr). P of North London, *Management Studies* (option in *Recreational Management,* 1 yr). Teesside P, *Management Studies* (option in *Leisure Management,* 1 yr).

Religious Studies

First degrees Degrees in *Divinity* (BD) awarded by the universities of Aberdeen, Belfast, Glasgow, London (Heythrop and King's Colleges), Wales and – BD Ordinary – Edinburgh and St Andrews (also MTheol). At other universities the BD is open only to graduates (see below).

First degrees in arts with specialisation in theological/religious subjects are awarded as follows:

Biblical Studies, Manchester, Newcastle upon Tyne, Sheffield and Wales (Bangor and Cardiff University Colleges).

Religious Studies, Aberdeen, Bristol (Religion with Literature), Cambridge (Theology and Religious Studies), Edinburgh, Glasgow (with another subject), Lancaster, Leeds (in various two-subject schemes), London (King's College, also – Islamic Religion – School of Oriental and African Studies), Manchester, Newcastle upon Tyne, Stirling, Sussex (major subject in Schools of African and Asian or Cultural and Community or English and American or European Studies) and Wales (Cardiff and – with one of various other subjects – Aberystwyth University Colleges, also – Religion and Ethics in Western Thought – St David's University College).

Theology, Birmingham, Bristol, Cambridge (Theology and Religious Studies), Durham, Exeter, Hull, Kent at Canterbury, Leeds (in various two-subject schemes), Manchester, Nottingham, Oxford, Southampton and Wales (St David's University College) (for St Andrews see above).

Several of the universities offering degrees with specialisation in theological/religious subjects alone also provide courses in which Theology, or Biblical or Religious Studies, may be studied with another principal subject for a Joint (or Combined) Honours degree. In addition less specialised study of theological/religious subjects may be included in certain first degree courses at Bradford (Human Purposes and Communication), Durham (Theology), Edinburgh (Biblical Studies), Exeter, Glasgow, Keele (Theology), Lancaster, Leicester (Study of Religion), London (Theology), Manchester (Biblical Studies, Comparative Religion, Near Eastern Religion, Theology), Newcastle upon Tyne (Religious Studies), Nottingham, St Andrews (Biblical and Theological Studies) and Wales (Religious Studies at Aberystwyth and Biblical Studies at Bangor, Cardiff and St David's University Colleges).

Other qualifications open to non-graduates (certificates unless otherwise indicated): *Biblical Knowledge*, Manchester (1 yr).

Christian Education and *Mission Studies*, Edinburgh (each 1 yr).

Pastoral Studies, Edinburgh (2 yrs), Glasgow (1 or 2 yrs) and Wales (Cardiff University College, College diploma, 1 yr full-time or 3 yrs part-time).

Theology (normally 3 yrs and for licence/licentiate, unless otherwise indicated), Aberdeen, Edinburgh, Glasgow, Manchester (certificate), St Andrews and Wales (diploma, at Bangor, Cardiff and St David's University Colleges).

Postgraduate courses

Courses for degrees in *Divinity* (BD, 3 yrs unless otherwise indicated) that are open only to graduates or, in some cases, to holders of equivalent qualifications, are offered by the following universities (for BD as a first degree, see above): Aberdeen, Edinburgh (BD Honours), Leeds (2 yrs), Manchester (minimum 2 yrs), Oxford (2 yrs) and St Andrews (BD Honours). The BD may also be taken, by individual study/research, at Birmingham, Cambridge (open only to Cambridge graduates), Durham (candidates who are not Durham graduates must hold Durham diploma in Theology, see below) and Hull.

Other postgraduate courses (1 yr and for MA, unless otherwise indicated) offered by the following universities:

Biblical Studies, Durham (diploma), Sheffield and Wales (Bangor and Cardiff University Colleges).

Christian Dogmatics, Edinburgh (MTh, 12 months).

Christian Education, Edinburgh (diploma, 1 yr, 15 months or 2 yrs).

Christian Ethics and Practical Theology or *Divinity*, Edinburgh (MTh, 12 months).

Eastern Christian Studies, Oxford (BPhil, 2 yrs).

Ecclesiastical History, Edinburgh (MTh, 12 months).

Ecumenical Studies, St Andrews (diploma).

Hebrew and Old Testament Studies, Edinburgh (MTh, 12 months).

The Impact of Religious Change on Society in Early Modern Europe, London (Royal Holloway College, for MA in Area Studies (Europe)).

Liturgy and Architecture, Birmingham (diploma).

Medieval Studies, Leeds.

Mission Studies, Edinburgh (diploma).

New Testament Language, Literature and Theology, Edinburgh (MTh, 12 months).

Pastoral Studies (diplomas), Aberdeen (Pastoral Studies and Applied Theology, 2 yrs), Birmingham, Edinburgh (1 or 2 yrs), Glasgow (1 or 2 yrs), St Andrews (Pastoral and Social Studies, 2 yrs) and Wales (Cardiff University College, College diploma, 1 yr full-time or 3 yrs part-time).

Political Theology or *Problems of Biblical Interpretation in Modern Study*, Bristol.

Religion and Humanism, Birmingham.

Religion and Society in the Nineteenth Century, Bristol.

Religion in Primal Societies, Aberdeen (MLitt).

Religious Education, see 'Education'.

Religious Studies, Lancaster (12 months full-time or 24 or 36 months part-time), Leeds and Sussex.

Religious Studies and Education, Lancaster.

Social and Pastoral Theology, Manchester (diploma).

Sociology of Religion, Lancaster.

The Study of Religion in Relation to Society, Bristol.

Theology, Belfast, Birmingham (also diploma, normally 2 yrs), Cambridge (MPhil 2 yrs, also diploma and certificate 1 yr), Durham (for graduates in Theology, also diploma 2 yrs), Exeter (diploma), Glasgow (MTh), Hull (certificate and diploma), Leeds (also diploma, 2 yrs), London (MTh), Manchester (MA(Theol), length of course varies according to qualifications), Nottingham (MTh, also, for graduates in other subjects, diploma), Oxford (diploma) and Wales (MTh at Bangor and Cardiff University Colleges, College diploma or licence – 2 yrs – at St David's University College).

Research facilities
At many of the universities named above.

The higher doctorate in *Divinity* (DD) is conferred by all those universities that award a BD, and by Exeter, but only Manchester permits graduates of other universities to become candidates. In Scottish universities, except Edinburgh, the DD is conferred only as an honorary degree.

Professional courses
Training courses for the Ministry or Priesthood vary in length from 4 to 7 years, according to the regulations of the Church concerned and the candidate's age and qualifications. Some Churches require a candidate to hold or obtain a university degree before starting on his professional training at a theological college. Details may be obtained from the Churches, as follows. Baptist Church: Baptist Union of Great Britain and Ireland. Catholic Church: the Bishop of the Diocese concerned. Church of England: Advisory Council for the Church's Ministry. Church of Scotland: The Secretary, Department of Education. Methodist Church: The Candidates' Secretary, Division of Ministries. United Reformed Church: The Secretary of the Ministerial Training Committee.

Other courses
Jews' College, London, CNAA BA *Jewish Studies* (3 yrs), Rabbinical Diploma *Theology* (4 yrs), Diploma *Jewish Studies* (1 yr).

Spurgeon's College, London, CNAA degree *Theology* (3 yrs).

London Bible College, CNAA degree in *Theology* (3 yrs). Facilities for study for higher Theological degrees. Diplomas in Biblical Studies, Theology and Religious Knowledge (1–3 yrs).

Science and Technology

Science, General

First degrees
As well as providing courses leading to first degrees with Honours (or Special degrees) in a *single* science subject, or Joint (or Combined) Honours degrees in two science subjects (see page 89), many universities also offer less specialised degree courses which involve the study of *several* science subjects. It is not possible to include in this handbook details of the varying structures and titles of these less specialised degrees but summarised information is set out in one of the Tables in the annual *Compendium of University Entrance Requirements* (see page 265). These degrees are usually called either 'General' or 'Ordinary' degrees, and at some universities General degrees may be awarded with Honours – see also page 28.

First degrees CNAA degrees (3 yrs unless otherwise indicated). Brighton P, *Applied Science* (also 4 yrs). Cambridgeshire C Arts T, *Science* (Joint Honours). P of Central London, modular degree *Science and Mathematics*. City of London P, modular degree. Dundee CT. Kingston P, *Applied Science*. Lanchester P, *Combined Science*. Leicester P, *Combined Studies* (*Science*). Luton CHE. North East London P, modular degree. P of North London, *Combined Science* (also 4 yrs S). Oxford P, modular degree. Paisley CT. Preston P, *Combined Sciences*. Royal Military C Science, *Applied Science*. Sheffield P, *Applied Science* (4 yrs S). Sunderland P, *Combined Studies in Science*. Ulster C, Northern Ireland P, *Combined Sciences*. West London IHE, modular degree. Wolverhampton P, *Combined Studies, Science and Engineering*.

In BA and BSc modular degrees (CNAA), students choose a pattern of modules that relate either to a single subject and thus to a specialised degree or to a combination of modules that constitute a broader education. Initially the students take three or four basic courses and subsequently select advanced modules (usually related to the basic course) chosen from the subject areas.

Dip HE courses (2 yrs). Science subjects are offered as part of free-ranging DipHE programmes at a number of colleges and polytechnics. See also under Arts (General), page 90. The DipHE programmes listed below are among those having a special science/technology bias. Brighton P (Computer Science). King Alfred's C (Social/Environmental Problems). La Sainte Union CE (Environmental Systems and Planning Studies). Leicester P (Electronics). Oxford P.

Science/Technology and Society

First degrees Degree courses involving interdisciplinary or 'problem-oriented' studies with emphasis on Science/Technology in its social context are offered by the following universities: Birmingham (Science and Modern Society option in certain BSocSc courses), Bradford (BTech in Science and Society, 4 yrs S), Brunel (BSc Joint Honours in Engineering, Social and European Studies, 4 yrs S), Edinburgh (BSc in Science Studies – Physics or Zoology in its social context), Kent at Canterbury (a science – Biochemistry or Chemistry or Physics – with Liberal Studies), Leicester (History and Social Relations of Science for BSc in Combined Studies), Manchester (BSc Honours in Liberal Studies in Science – Life Sciences or Physical Sciences programme), Salford (Sociology of Science and Technology for BSc in Social Studies or Sociology – not available every yr), Surrey (BSc Combined Studies in Science – Science and Society with Physical Science and either Business Economics or Science Education) and York (BA Honours in Chemistry, Technology and Economics, or in Chemistry, Resources and the Environment).

Postgraduate courses At the following universities:
Social Aspects of Science and Technology, Aston in Birmingham (MSc, 12 months).
Sociology of Science and Technology, Salford (MSc, 12 months).
Structure and Organisation of Science and Technology, Manchester (MSc or diploma, 10–12 months).
Technology and Development, London (Imperial College, MSc and/or DIC, 1 yr).

Research facilities At the universities of Bradford, Keele, Leicester, Manchester, Oxford and Salford.

First degrees CNAA degrees (3 yrs unless otherwise indicated). Middlesex P, *Society and Technology*. Newcastle upon Tyne P, *Social and Physical Sciences*. Napier CC and T, *Science with Industrial Studies,* or *Technology with Industrial Studies* (both 4 yrs S). Plymouth P, combined studies in *Science* and/or *Social Science* (4 yrs S). Portsmouth P.

Secretarial Studies

First degrees At University of Strathclyde *Office Organisation* may be offered with another Business Studies subject for BA.

Postgraduate Diploma course (1 yr) in *Secretarial Studies* at University of Strathclyde.
courses

Research At University of Strathclyde.
facilities

HND courses At the following colleges, also with an option in languages (both 2 yrs). Aberdeen CC. Bell CT. Dundee CC. Glasgow CT. Inverness TC. Kirkcaldy TC. Napier CC and T. Perth TC. Scottish C Textiles.

Postgraduate At the following polytechnics and colleges (1 yr unless otherwise indicated). Aberdeen CC (also
courses *Secretarial/Linguistics*). Barking CT. Bell CT. Bristol P, bilingual course, also *Secretarial, Business and Management Studies*. Cassio C. Colchester IHE. Dundee CC. Guildford County CT. Harrow CT, also bilingual course, also intensive course (9 months). Loughborough TC (2 terms). Napier CC and T, also bilingual course. Preston P, bilingual course. Salford CT. P of South Bank, *Secretarial/Linguistics*. South Glamorgan IHE, also with *Linguistics*. Southampton CT.

Other courses The colleges and polytechnics listed below offer a variety of certificate and diploma courses, including courses for bilingual secretaries, advanced courses and personal assistants courses (usually 1 or 2 yrs). A number of colleges offer courses leading to the examinations of the Royal Society of Arts. For further details of these, one should contact the Society. Barking CT. Barnsley CT. Bristol P. Buckinghamshire CHE. Cambridgeshire C Arts T. Canterbury CT. Chelmer IHE. Chichester CFE. City of London P, also part of modular degree. Crawley CT. Doncaster Metropolitan IHE. Ealing CHE. Farnborough CT. Hull CHE. Guildford County CT. Ipswich Civic C. Llandrillo TC. Loughborough TC. Medway and Maidstone CT. Newcastle upon Tyne P. Norfolk C Arts T, also intensive course (6 months). Norwich City C. North East Surrey CT. North East Wales IHE. North Hertfordshire C. P of North London. Preston P. Richmond upon Thames C. Salford CT. Salisbury CT. Slough CHE. South Glamorgan IHE. Stockport CT. Thurrock TC. P of Wales. West Glamorgan IHE. West London IHE.

Secretaryship, Chartered and Incorporated

No university courses

Professional Full time courses providing tuition from all four parts (unless otherwise indicated) of the
courses examination scheme of the Institute of Chartered Secretaries and Administrators (ICSA) are held at the following colleges. Bristol P (Parts 2, 3 and 4). Buckinghamshire CHE. Chelmer IHE. Derby Lonsdale CHE. Farnborough CT. Glasgow CT (parts 2, 3 and 4) Guildford County CT (Parts 2, 3 and 4). Hull CHE. Leeds P. Newcastle upon Tyne P. P of North London. Redditch C. Sheffield P. South West London C. Stevenage C (Parts 1 and 2). Ulster C, Northern Ireland P (Parts 2 and 3). West Bromwich CCT. Details of all colleges offering courses leading to the ICSA examinations are available from the Institute.

Slavonic and other East European Languages and Studies

See also European Studies, and Language Studies

First degrees   Degrees with specialisation in *Russian* awarded by the following universities (some courses may include a period of study abroad): Aberdeen, Aston in Birmingham (with another subject), Belfast, Birmingham (BA Combined or Special Honours – Language, Literature, History – and BCom, BSocSc – Language, Social Sciences), Bradford (with French or German or Spanish), Bristol, Cambridge, Durham, East Anglia (Russian Literature, also for degree in Comparative Literature), Edinburgh (also Russian Studies), Essex (School of Comparative Studies for degree in Language and Linguistics, also Russian Studies or Russian specialisation in certain subjects, including compulsory Russian language course), Exeter, Glasgow, Heriot-Watt (with French, German or Spanish, for BA in Languages (interpreting and translating)), Hull (Russian Studies), Keele (Russian Studies with another principal subject), Lancaster (Russian and Soviet Studies), Leeds (Russian Studies), Liverpool, London (Russian at Queen Mary College, Russian Language and Literature or Russian Studies or Russian with Polish or with History at School of Slavonic and East European Studies, also German and Russian or French and Russian at the School and King's College jointly, and Russian and French at London School of Economics), Manchester (University or – as major in European Studies course, also Language Studies (Russian) with Mathematics – Institute of Science and Technology), Nottingham (also Slavonic Studies), Oxford, Reading (Russian Studies), St Andrews (Russian Language and Literature, or Modern Russian Studies), Salford (as one of two main languages), Sheffield (Russian and Slavonic Studies), Strathclyde (with another principal subject), Surrey (for degree in Linguistic and International Studies), Sussex (Russian Studies), New U of Ulster (Combined Honours, also certificate of competence in Russian, 1 yr) and Wales (Bangor, Swansea and – with another main subject – Aberystwyth University Colleges).

Many of the universities offering degrees with specialisation in *Russian* or *Russian Studies* alone also provide courses in which this subject may be studied with another principal subject for a Joint (or Combined) Honours degree. Less specialised courses in Russian/Russian Studies (Nottingham: also Soviet Studies) are also available at most of the universities which offer degrees with specialisation (including, at Exeter, classes in Scientific Russian), and at Bath and Southampton; and Russian/Soviet Government, Politics, etc, may be included in first degree courses at London (London School of Economics, for BSc(Econ)), Reading (in Politics course) and Wales (Swansea University College, for BScEcon).

First degrees with specialisation in other East European languages/studies: *Bulgarian* or *Finnish* language and literature, or *Finnish Studies*, London (School of Slavonic and East European Studies); *Czech* and/or *Slovak* or *Hungarian* or *Polish* language and literature, Cambridge, Glasgow (Czech or Polish with a modern language or one of certain other subjects), Lancaster (Czechoslovak Studies, also joint courses including Czechoslovak Studies, and Yugoslav Studies) and London (School of Slavonic and East European Studies); *East European Studies*, New U of Ulster; *Rumanian*, London (School of Slavonic and East European Studies, also – jointly with Westfield College – Rumanian and French, and – jointly with University College – Italian with Rumanian); *Serbo-Croat*, London (School of Slavonic and East European Studies, language and literature) and Nottingham (with Russian for degree in Slavonic Studies). Less specialised courses may be included in first degree syllabuses as follows: Bulgarian – Leeds; Central and South Eastern European (non-language) Studies – Lancaster; Czech – Glasgow, Lancaster and Leeds; Polish – Glasgow and Salford; Serbian/Serbo-Croat – Birmingham, Lancaster, Nottingham, New U of Ulster and Wales (Swansea University College).

Postgraduate   Courses (1 yr and for MA or MSc, unless otherwise indicated) at the following universities:
courses   *Area Studies*, London (School of Slavonic and East European Studies).

Comparative Literature and *Contemporary European Studies,* Sussex.
Czech and Slovak Language and Literature and *East European, Russian and Soviet History,* London (School of Slavonic and East European Studies).
General and Comparative Literature of 2 or 3 languages, Oxford (BPhil, 2 yrs).
Politics and Government of Russia, London (London School of Economics, for MSc in Politics).
Russian, Exeter, Liverpool (BPhil, 1 or 2 yrs), St Andrews (MLitt, 2 yrs, Language and Literature options, both including Modern Russian Language) and Surrey (diploma, for graduate scientists and technologists).
Russian and East European Studies (options include History of Russia, Poland, Rumania, Hungary, Czechoslovakia, Yugoslavia, Bulgaria, Greece), Oxford (BPhil, 2 yrs).
Russian and Slavonic Studies, Sheffield.
Russian Language, Strathclyde (diploma).
Russian Language and Literature, London (School of Slavonic and East European Studies).
Russian Language for Social Scientists, Glasgow (diploma).
Russian Studies, Birmingham (Literature, or Philology, or Literature and Society), Sussex and Wales (Swansea University College).
Slavonic Studies, Glasgow (diploma) and Oxford (diploma – Russian, Polish, Czech, Serbo-Croat, Bulgarian).
Sociology of USSR, Essex (12 months).
Soviet and East European Studies, Birmingham (MSocSc, 12 months or 24 months).
Soviet Government, London (School of Slavonic and East European Studies).
Soviet Government and Politics, Essex (12 months).
Soviet Literature, New U of Ulster.
Soviet Studies, Glasgow (diploma 1 or 2 yrs, MPhil 2 yrs) and London (School of Slavonic and East European Studies).
Yugoslav Studies (including language instruction in Serbo-Croat or Macedonian), Bradford.

Research facilities　*Russian/Russian Studies,* at the following universities: Aberdeen, Belfast, Birmingham (Centre for Russian and East European Studies), Cambridge, Edinburgh, Essex, Exeter, Glasgow, Keele, Lancaster (Comenius Centre), Liverpool, London (London School of Economics – including Soviet Law – and School of Slavonic and East European Studies), Manchester, Oxford, Reading, Sheffield, Surrey, Sussex (Centre for Contemporary European Studies), New U of Ulster and Wales (Swansea University College – Centre for Russian and East European Studies). *Other East European languages and studies:* Bradford (Yugoslav Studies), Cambridge, Lancaster (Central and South-Eastern European Studies), London (School of Slavonic and East European Studies, also – Modern Polish History – Queen Mary College, and – Archaeology of Central and Eastern Europe – Institute of Archaeology) and Oxford.

First degrees　CNAA degree: Portsmouth P, *Russian and Soviet Studies* (4 yrs).
Russian is offered as an optional subject in Modern Languages degrees at the following: P of Central London. Ealing TC, *Applied Language Studies, Humanities* and *Modern European Studies.* Leeds P. Liverpool P. Wolverhampton P.

College diploma　P of Central London, polytechnic diploma in *Russian* (2 yrs).

Social Work

See also Sociology, and Youth Services

Note – The university courses listed below are those which are of particular relevance for students planning a social work career, but the university qualifications to which they lead do not all entitle the holder to recognition by the relevant *professional bodies.*

First degrees/ diplomas Degree courses which include some provision for practical training in social work or the social services are offered by the following universities: Bath (in final yr of Sociology course), Belfast (Social Science), Birmingham (Social Administration for BSocSc or – with Physical Education – for BA), Bradford (Applied Social Studies and Public and Social Policy, both 4 yrs S), Bristol (Social Administration and either Politics or Sociology), Dundee, Durham (Social Administration with Sociology, also Social and Public Administration), Edinburgh (Social Administration and Politics), Exeter (Social Administration and Social Policy), Glasgow (1-yr or 2-yr Social Administration courses in MA curriculum), Hull (Social Studies, also Sociology and Social Administration), Keele (Social Studies in 'tied' combination with Sociology for degree with diploma in Applied Social Studies), Kent at Canterbury (Social Policy and Administration), Lancaster (Social Administration, 3 yrs, also Social Work, 4 yrs with larger practical content), London (Bedford College and London School of Economics, Social Science and Administration, also Goldsmiths' College), Manchester (Social Administration), Nottingham (Social Administration), St Andrews (Practical Theology with Social Studies, for MTheol), Southampton (options in Sociology and Social Administration course), Stirling (Sociology and Social Administration), Strathclyde (Social Administration), Surrey (Economics, Sociology and Statistics course, 3 yrs, or 4 yrs S), Sussex (Social Administration as major subject in School of Cultural and Community Studies), New U of Ulster (Social Administration) and Wales (Bangor – Social Theory and Institutions – and Cardiff – Social Administration – University Colleges).

Diploma/certificate courses for which applicants need not be graduates (normally 2 yrs) at the universities of Bristol (certificate in Social Work), Leeds (for CCETSW certificate – see below) and Wales (Swansea University College, for College diploma in Social Administration). See also 'Postgraduate courses', below.

Postgraduate courses Courses (1 yr and for diplomas, unless otherwise indicated) at the following universities (many of these courses may also be open to non-graduates with suitable qualifications and/or experience):

Advanced Social Work (*Mental Health*), Surrey (MSc, minimum 12 months).

Applied Social Studies, Aberdeen (2 yrs, certificate), Bath (starting mid-February), Bristol (certificate, for those with Social Administration qualification), Brunel (MA, 2 yrs), Hull, Keele (certificate, 1 or 2 yrs), Leeds (MA or certificate, 12 months), Leicester (certificate, 1 or 2 yrs), Liverpool, London (Bedford College for College diploma, 14 months for graduates in Sociology, 2 yrs for other graduates), Newcastle upon Tyne, Oxford (MSc, 2 yrs), Sheffield (24 months), Southampton, Surrey (diploma, minimum 12 months, or MSc, maximum 36 months), New U of Ulster (MSc, 1 or 2 yrs depending on qualifications), Wales (Swansea University College, also College diploma course for overseas candidates with some social work experience) and Warwick (MA, 12 months).

Mental Health Social Work, Leeds (MSc, minimum 12 months).

Pastoral and Social Studies, St Andrews (2 yrs).

Psychiatric Social Work, Liverpool (for diploma in Applied Social Studies), London (London School of Economics, diploma in Social Work Studies – special field Mental Health), Manchester (also MSc, 2 yrs full-time or 1 yr full-time plus 2 yrs part-time), Newcastle upon Tyne (diploma in Applied Social Studies, minimum age 21 yrs) and Southampton (additional option for diploma in Applied Social Studies).

Residential Social Work with Children and Young People, Bristol (certificate, for senior staff of establishments providing residential care for children with special needs).

Social Administration, Birmingham (MSocSc, 12 months), Bristol, Brunel (Public and Social Administration, MA, 1 yr full-time or 2½ yrs part-time), Dundee, Edinburgh (12 months), Hull, Keele (advanced diploma for practising social workers), Liverpool, London (London School of Economics, for School diploma, also option for MSc), Manchester (MA(Econ) or diploma, also diplomas in Social Administration and Social Work – 2 yrs – and in Social Service Administration – 1 yr full-time or 2 yrs part-time), Southampton, New U of Ulster, Wales (Bangor University College, intended as conversion course for graduates who aim subsequently to undertake professional social work training) and York (12 months, also MA 1 yr, MPhil 2 yrs).

Social and Community Work Studies, Bradford (MA, 1 yr full-time or 2 yrs part-time).

Social Planning, Wales (Swansea University College, MScEcon).

Social Policy, Wales (Swansea University College, for overseas candidates already in senior positions in their own country's social services).

Social Research and Social Policy, Oxford (MSc, 2 yrs).

Social Science, Belfast.

Social Service Planning, Essex (MA, 12 months).

Social Studies, Wales (Bangor University College, for College diploma) (see also under 'Sociology').

Social Work, Belfast, Birmingham (12 months or 24 months), Dundee, East Anglia (MA, 2 yrs), Edinburgh (12 months), Exeter (providing professional social work qualification for graduates in Social Administration or an allied subject, also BPhil – 2 yrs – for graduates in subjects other than social studies, or in social studies only and with no practical experience), Glasgow (1 or 2 yrs, providing professional training), Kent at Canterbury (21 months), Lancaster (2 yrs), Leicester (MA, 2 yrs), London (Bedford College – MSc, 2 yrs – and London School of Economics – Social Work Studies, also option for MSc), Manchester (MA(Econ) or diploma, 2 yrs, in Social Administration and Social Work), Nottingham (MA, 12 months, or 2 yrs for graduates who have not previously studied social science subjects), Stirling (2 yrs, professional training course), Sussex (MSW, 2 yrs), Wales (Bangor University College – MA, 15 months, leading to certificate of qualification for graduates with social work experience – and Cardiff University College – diploma 1 or 2 yrs, MScEcon 1 yr) and York (diploma or MSW, 2 yrs, leading to professional qualification in a number of fields, including probation, and medical and psychiatric social work).

Research facilities   At many of the universities named above and at Cranfield IT.

First degrees   CNAA degrees offered at the following polytechnics and colleges provide an option in *Social Work* (4 yrs). Birmingham P, *Sociology,* community work option. Edge Hill CHE, *Applied Social Science* (3 yrs). Hatfield P, *Applied Social Studies.* Lanchester P, *Applied Social Studies.* Middlesex P, *Applied Social Science.* North East London P, *Sociology* with *Professional Studies* (4 yrs S). P of North London, *Applied Social Studies.* Paisley CT, *Social Studies.* Plymouth P, *Social Policy and Administration.* Preston P, *Applied Social Studies.* Sheffield P, *Applied Social Studies.* Trent P, *Applied Social Studies.* Ulster C, Northern Ireland P, *Social Administration* or *Social Work.*

Postgraduate courses   (Normally 1 yr). Goldsmiths' C. Leeds P. Manchester P. Middlesex P (2 yrs). Preston P. Queen's C. P of the South Bank (2 yrs). Trent P.

Professional Two year courses recognised by the Central Council for Education and Training in Social Work
courses leading to the Certificate of Qualification in Social Work are provided at the following colleges. A minimum of 5 'O' levels (or equivalent qualifications) are required for those under 25. For those over 25, formal educational requirements are relaxed though in all cases students are expected to perform beyond 'A' level standard and high academic as well as personal demands are made of them. Birmingham P. Bristol P. Buckinghamshire CHE. Bulmershe CHE. Chelmer IHE. Croydon C Design T. Dundee CE. Hull CHE. Jordanhill CE. Lanchester P. Leeds P. Leicester P. Liverpool P. Manchester P. Medway and Maidstone CT. Middlesex P. Moray House CE. Newcastle upon Tyne P. North East London P. North East Wales IHE. P of North London. Oxford P. Plymouth P. Portsmouth P. Preston P. Queen Margaret C. Robert Gordon's IT. Sheffield P. South Glamorgan IHE. Stevenage CFE. Suffolk CFHE. Teesside P. Trent P. Ulster C, Northern Ireland P. West London IHE.

There are also courses for students of 30 and over who wish to switch to social work from an unrelated career, offered at P of Central London, Huddersfield P, Jordanhill CE, Kingston P, Sunderland P, Wolverhampton P.

For full details of these and other courses, one should contact the Central Council for Education and Training in Social Work.

Sociology
See also Anthropology, and Social Work

First degrees Degrees with specialisation awarded by the following universities:
and diplomas *Applied Social Studies,* Bradford (4 yrs S).
Human Sciences, Oxford.
Planning Studies (Social Planning/Policy in Developing Countries), Wales (Swansea University College).
Politics and History of Industrial Society, Salford.
Social Administration, Bristol (with Politics or Sociology), Dundee, Durham (with Politics or Sociology, also Social and Public Administration), Exeter (Social Administration and Social Policy), Hull (with Sociology), Kent at Canterbury (Social Policy and Administration), Leeds (Social and Public Administration), Loughborough U of Technology, Manchester, Newcastle upon Tyne (with Sociology or Economics or Politics), Nottingham, Southampton (with Sociology), Stirling (with Sociology), Strathclyde (with another principal subject), New U of Ulster and Wales (Cardiff and Swansea University Colleges).
Social Policy, Bradford (Public and Social Policy) and London (Bedford College).
Social Science and Administration, London (London School of Economics, also Goldsmiths' College).
Social Statistics (with Sociology), Exeter.
Sociology/Social Studies, Aberdeen, Aston in Birmingham (BSc in Behavioural Science with specialisation in Sociology, 4 yrs S, also Sociology with another subject, 3 yrs), Bath (Sociology or Social Sciences), Belfast, Birmingham, Bradford (with one of certain other subjects), Bristol, Brunel (4 yrs S), Cambridge (Sociology/Social Anthropology in Social and Political Sciences Tripos), The City (Sociology alone or with one of certain other subjects, also Social Sciences – 3 yrs, or 4 yrs S), Durham (Sociology alone or with Social Administration), East Anglia, Edinburgh, Essex (School of Social Studies, also School of Comparative Studies with comparative syllabus or area specialisation), Exeter, Glasgow, Hull (Social Studies, also Sociology with one of certain other

subjects), Keele (with another principal subject), Kent at Canterbury, Lancaster, Leeds, Leicester, Liverpool, London (Bedford College and London School of Economics, also Goldsmiths' College), Loughborough U of Technology, Manchester, Newcastle upon Tyne (Sociology and Social Administration, or Social Studies), Nottingham, Oxford (Honour School of Human Sciences), Reading (Sociology or Combined Social Sciences), Salford, Sheffield, Southampton, Stirling, Strathclyde, Surrey (with Economics and Statistics, 3 yrs, or 4 yrs S, or with Philosophy and Psychology, 3 yrs), Sussex (as major subject in Schools or African and Asian, English and American, Cultural and Community or European Studies, or of Social Sciences), New U of Ulster (Social Anthropology and Sociology), Wales (Aberystwyth, Cardiff and Swansea University Colleges, and – Social Theory and Institutions, also Sociology or Social Theory with another subject – Bangor University College), Warwick and York.

Urban Studies, see 'Town and Country Planning'.

Many of the universities offering degrees with specialisation in Sociology, Social Studies, etc, alone also provide courses in which the subject may be studied with another principal subject for a Joint (or Combined) Honours degree; and at many of them (London, also Chelsea College) less specialised study of Sociology/Social Studies may be included in first degree courses. The study of *Race Relations* may be included in the first degree courses indicated in brackets at the universities of Edinburgh (Social Anthropology), London (Anthropology, at London School of Economics and University College) and Nottingham (Sociology).

Diploma/certificate courses open to non-graduates (normally 2 yrs and for diploma, unless otherwise indicated):

Social Administration, Wales (Swansea University College, for College diploma).

Social Studies, Hull and Wales (Social Study, at Swansea University College).

Postgraduate courses

Courses (normally 1 yr and for diploma, unless otherwise indicated) at the following universities (some of these courses may also be open to non-graduates with suitable qualifications and/or experience – for courses which may lead to either higher degrees or diplomas see below):

Applied Social Studies, Aberdeen (2 yrs, certificate), Bristol (certificate), Liverpool, London (London School of Economics, School diploma), Sheffield (12 or 24 months), Southampton, Surrey (diploma minimum 12 months or MSc maximum 36 months) and Wales (Swansea University College).

Community Development, see 'Development Studies'.

Population Growth Studies, Wales (Cardiff University College, College diploma).

Social Administration, see under 'Social Work'.

Social Policy, Wales (Swansea University College, College diploma for overseas candidates in senior positions in social service and preferably with graduate training in social science).

Social Studies, Belfast, London (Chelsea College, for College diploma in Modern Social and Cultural Studies), Sheffield (1 or 2 yrs) and Wales (Bangor University College, for College diploma, and – Social Study – Swansea University College).

Sociology, Belfast, Bristol, East Anglia, Kent at Canterbury, London (Bedford College), Manchester and Reading (conversion course for graduates in another discipline, 1 yr full-time or 2 yrs part-time).

At London, diploma courses in Anthropology include *Race Relations*.

Courses (normally 1 yr and for master's degree, unless otherwise indicated) at the following universities and Cranfield IT:

Applied Social Studies, Leeds.

Contemporary Cultural Studies, Birmingham (12 months).

Contemporary European Sociology, etc, Reading (MA 1 yr, MPhil 2 yrs, in Graduate School of Contemporary European Studies).

Demography, London (London School of Economics, 1 or 2 yrs).

Medical Demography, London (School of Hygiene and Tropical Medicine).
Political Sociology, London (London School of Economics).
Politics with Sociology, London (Birkbeck College, 1 yr full-time or 2 yrs part-time).
Race Relations, Bristol.
Race Relations and Community Studies, Bradford (12 months full-time or 24 months part-time for diploma, minimum 18 months full-time or 30 months part-time for MSc).
Rural Social Development, Reading (11 months, also diploma 9 months).
Social Administration, see under 'Social Work'.
Social and Psychological Aspects of Science and Technology in Industry, London (Imperial College, MSc and/or DIC).
Social History, see under 'History'.
Social Planning, Wales (Swansea University College).
Social Policy and Institutions, Cranfield IT (1 or 2 yrs).
Social Service Planning, Essex (12 months).
Social Statistics, Birmingham.
Sociological Studies (several options), Sussex.
Sociology, Belfast, Birmingham (12 months), East Anglia, Essex (12 months), Kent at Canterbury, Leeds (12 months), Leicester, London (London School of Economics), Manchester, Oxford (BPhil, 2 yrs), Reading (12 months full-time or 24 months part-time), Sheffield, Warwick and York (12 months).
Sociology and Law, Brunel (1 yr full-time or 2½ yrs part-time).
Sociology and Politics of Development, Cambridge (option in Development Studies course).
Sociology as applied to Medicine, London (Bedford College).
Sociology of Education, see under 'Education'.
Sociology of Industrial Societies, Bradford (12 months).
Sociology of Latin America, Essex (12 months).
Sociology of Literature, Essex (12 months).
Sociology of Religion, Lancaster.
Sociology of Science and Technology, Salford.
Sociology of the USSR, Essex (12 months).
Sociology with Politics, London (Birkbeck College, 1 yr full-time or 2 yrs part-time).
Statistics and Sociology, London (London School of Economics).

Research facilities   *Sociology/Social Studies:* at most of the universities providing first degree courses, and (Social Policy and Institutions) at Cranfield IT. Hull: Centre for South-East Asian Studies. Kent at Canterbury: Centre for Research in the Social Sciences. London: Bedford, Birkbeck, Chelsea and – Industrial Sociology – Imperial Colleges and London School of Economics. Sussex: Institute of Development Studies. *Race Relations:* at Bradford, Bristol, Edinburgh, London (London School of Economics, School of Oriental and African Studies, University College and Institute of Commonwealth Studies), Oxford, Sussex and Warwick.

First degrees   CNAA degrees are offered as follows (3 yrs unless otherwise indicated).
Behavioural Studies (*Psychology and Sociology*), Huddersfield P.
Social Administration, Leeds P. Plymouth P (*Social Policy and Administration*). Portsmouth P. Teesside P. Ulster C, Northern Ireland P.
Social Science, Bristol P. P of Central London (modular degree). Edge Hill CHE (*Applied Social Science*). Glasgow CT. Hatfield P. Kingston P. Lanchester P (*Applied Social Sciences*) (3 or 4 yrs). Manchester P. Middlesex P (4 yrs). Sheffield P. P of the South Bank. Sunderland P, with *Economics.* Trent P. Ulster C, Northern Ireland P.
Social Studies, Hatfield P (*Applied Social Studies, Policy*). Liverpool P. North East London P (*Social Studies, Modern France*, 4 yrs). P of North London (*Applied Social Studies*).

Oxford P. Paisley CT (4 yrs). Preston P (*Applied Social Studies*). Sheffield P (*Applied Social Studies*, 4 yrs S). P of the South Bank. Trent P (*Applied Social Studies*).
Sociology, Birmingham P. Buckinghamshire CHE. City of London P (modular degree). Kingston P. Newcastle upon Tyne P. North East London P, with *Professional Studies*. P of North London. North Staffordshire P. Portsmouth P. Thames P.
Degree Courses of the University of London in *Social Administration* and *Sociology* are offered at Roehampton IHE.

Research facilities   Newcastle upon Tyne P. North East London P. Oxford P. P of the South Bank. Thames P. P of Wales.

Other courses   The following are among the courses offered at residential colleges of adult education (see pages 281–283): Loughborough: Co-operative College, University of Nottingham diploma in *Political, Economic and Social Studies* (1 yr). Oxford: Plater College (Catholic Workers' College) and Ruskin College, University of Oxford Special Diploma in *Social Studies* (2 yrs).

Soil Science
(including Soil Conservation)
See also Agriculture

First degrees   Degrees with specialisation in *Soil Science* awarded by the universities of Aberdeen, Newcastle upon Tyne, Reading and Wales (Bangor University College, with Biochemistry). Less specialised study of Soil Science may also be included in courses leading to first degrees in Agriculture/Agricultural Sciences at Aberdeen (also in Forestry degree course and in BSc Ordinary curriculum), Belfast, Edinburgh (Forestry), London (Wye College), Nottingham, Oxford, Reading (also Horticultural Botany and Horticulture) and Wales (Aberystwyth University College).

Postgraduate courses   Courses (1 yr and for MSc, unless otherwise indicated) at the following universities and Cranfield IT:
Pedology, Cambridge (in MPhil course in Applied Biology) and (with Soil Survey) Reading (12 months).
Soil and Water Engineering, Cranfield IT (MSc 1 or 2 yrs, diploma 9 months, option in Agricultural Engineering course at National College of Agricultural Engineering, Silsoe).
Soil Biology, Nottingham (1 or 2 yrs).
Soil Chemistry, Reading (12 months).
Soil Science, Aberdeen, Newcastle upon Tyne, Oxford (diploma, 4 terms), Reading (MAgrSc, 2 yrs) and Wales (Aberystwyth University College, diploma).

Research facilities   At the universities of Aberdeen (also Macaulay Institute for Soil Research), Cambridge, London (University and Wye Colleges, also – Soil Mechanics – Imperial College, and – soils as they apply to archaeological studies – Institute of Archaeology), Manchester, Newcastle upon Tyne, Reading and Wales (Bangor University College); and at Cranfield IT (National College of Agricultural Engineering, Silsoe).

Spanish

See also European Studies, and Latin American Studies

First degrees Degrees with specialisation in *Spanish* awarded by the following universities (some courses may include a period of study abroad): Aberdeen, Bath, Belfast, Birmingham, Bradford (with French or German or Russian), Bristol, Cambridge, Durham, Edinburgh, Essex (School of Comparative Studies, for degree in Language and Linguistics), Exeter, Glasgow, Heriot-Watt (with French or German or Russian for BA in Languages (interpreting and translating)), Hull, Leeds, Liverpool (Hispanic Studies), London (Birkbeck (part-time), King's, Queen Mary, University and Westfield Colleges), Manchester (Hispanic Studies or Spanish Studies), Newcastle upon Tyne (with Latin American Studies), Nottingham, Oxford, St Andrews (Hispanic Languages and Literature, also Spanish with another main language), Salford (with another main language), Sheffield (Hispanic Studies), Southampton, Stirling (with another subject), Strathclyde, New U of Ulster (with 1 or 2 other subjects), Wales (Aberystwyth – also Romance Studies, Cardiff – also Hispanic Studies, and – with another subject – Swansea University Colleges) and Warwick (with European Studies or English). At many of these universities, and in addition to the combined courses already mentioned, Spanish may be studied with another subject for a Joint (or Combined) Honours degree; and at many of them less specialised study of Spanish may be included in first degree courses in arts.

Postgraduate courses Courses (1 yr and for MA, unless otherwise indicated) at the following universities:
General and Comparative Literature of 2 or 3 languages, Oxford (BPhil, 2 yrs).
Hispanic Studies, Wales (Cardiff University College).
Modern Spanish Poetry, Essex (for MA scheme in Literature, 12 months – not available 1978–79).
Spanish, Aberdeen (for MLitt in Medieval Studies), Exeter, Leeds (also for MA in Medieval Studies), London (King's, Queen Mary and Westfield Colleges), St Andrews (MLitt 2 yrs, also for diploma – 1 yr – or MLitt – 2 yrs – in Medieval Studies) and Sheffield. Also included in postgraduate courses in Latin American Studies (see separate heading).

Research facilities At most of those universities which offer first degree courses.

First degrees CNAA degree in *Spanish* at Portsmouth P (4 yrs).
Spanish is available as an optional subject in many general Arts degrees (see page 89). The sections *European Studies* and *Language Studies* should also be consulted.

Speech Therapy

See also Education

First degrees Degrees with specialisation awarded by the following universities:
Linguistics and Language Pathology, Essex and Reading.
Speech, Newcastle upon Tyne.
Speech Pathology and Therapy, Manchester.
Speech Science, Sheffield.
  Also, at Glasgow, option for BEd course provided in conjunction with Jordanhill CE.

Postgraduate MSc course (1 yr full-time or 2 yrs part-time) in *Human Communication* at University of London
courses (Guy's Hospital Medical School). University of Essex offers certificate (10 weeks) in Linguistics
and Phonetics for qualified speech therapists, etc, also diploma (1 yr) in Applied Linguistics,
Phonetics and the Teaching of English – see under 'Language Studies'.

Research At the universities of Essex, Manchester and Reading.
facilities

First degrees City of Manchester CHE, *Speech Pathology and Therapy* (3 yrs). Ulster C, Northern Ireland P,
Speech Therapy (4 yrs).

Professional Apart from the above the recognised professional qualification for speech therapists trained in
qualifications Great Britain is the Diploma of Licentiate of the College of Speech Therapists. Courses (3 yrs)
are available at the following. Birmingham P. Central School of Speech and Drama. Leeds P.
Leicester P. National Hospitals C of Speech Sciences. Queen Margaret C. School for the Study
of Disorders of Human Communication. South Glamorgan IHE.
Licentiates of the College may proceed to Membership (MCST) by examination and
fellowship (FCST) by dissertation. Further information is available from the College of Speech
Therapists.

Statistics
See also Mathematics

First degrees Degrees with specialisation awarded by the following universities:
Mathematical Statistics, Birmingham, Exeter (with Operational Research, or with Biology or
Psychology), Hull and Liverpool.
Statistics, Aberdeen, Bath (3 yrs or 4 yrs S), Belfast (with Mathematics or Computer Science),
Birmingham (with Mathematics and Economics, for BSocSc), Bradford (4 yrs S), Bristol
(Economics or Mathematics with Statistics), Brunel (with Computer Science or
Mathematics, each 4 yrs S), The City (3 yrs or 4 yrs S), Dundee (with one of certain other
subjects), Edinburgh, Essex, Exeter (with Economics or Geography, also Social
Statistics with Sociology), Glasgow, Heriot-Watt (also Actuarial Mathematics and
Statistics), Hull (special subject for BSc(Econ)), Keele (Applied Statistics and
Operational Research with another principal subject), Kent at Canterbury (Social
Statistics or Quantitative Social Science, also Computing, Operational Research and
Statistics), Lancaster (with Numerical Analysis), Leeds, Liverpool (Computational and
Statistical Science), London (Queen Mary and University Colleges and London School
of Economics, also – with Computer Science, Mathematics, Physics or Chemistry –
Royal Holloway College), Manchester (with Operational Research at Institute of
Science and Technology, also Econometrics and Social Statistics for BA(Econ)),
Newcastle upon Tyne, Reading (with Computer Science, Economics or Mathematics),
St Andrews, Salford (with Mathematics and Numerical Analysis, 4 yrs S, also
Computational Mathematics and Statistics), Sheffield (Probability and Statistics),
Southampton (main subject for BSc (Social Sciences)), Surrey (Mathematics with
Statistics, or Economics/Sociology/Statistics, each 3 yrs, or 4 yrs S), Sussex (with
Mathematics), New U of Ulster, Wales (Institute of Science and Technology, 3 yrs or 4
yrs S, also Aberystwyth and Swansea University Colleges), Warwick (integrated course
in Mathematics, Operational Research, Statistics and Economics, also Statistics with

Applied Mathematics, Computing or Mathematics) and York (Social and Economic Statistics with Economics or Politics or Sociology).

At a number of the universities offering degrees with specialisation in this subject alone, Statistics may also be studied with another principal subject for a Joint (or Combined) Honours degree. Less specialised study of Statistics may also be included in first degree courses in arts, science, economics or social studies at many of these universities (Exeter and Leicester, also Mathematical Statistics), and at Cambridge, London (Imperial College, also – part-time only and in science combination – Birkbeck College), Loughborough U of Technology, Nottingham, Oxford and Stirling; also in certain diploma/certificate courses in Public or Social Administration, or Social Studies.

Postgraduate courses Courses (1 yr and for master's degree, unless otherwise indicated) at the following universities:
Applied Statistics, Bath (MSc or diploma, 12 months full-time or 2 yrs part-time), Oxford (MSc or diploma) and Southampton (diploma 9 months, MSc 12 months).
Biometry, Reading (MSc or diploma, 12 months).
Computational and Statistical Methodology in the Analysis of Large-Scale Data, Hull (12 months).
Econometrics/Economic Statistics, see under 'Economics'.
Industrial Mathematics and Statistics, Aston in Birmingham (12 months).
Mathematical Statistics, Birmingham, Cambridge (diploma), Exeter, Manchester (12 months) and Wales (Swansea University College, with Computational Analysis, for College diploma).
Medical Statistics, London (School of Hygiene and Tropical Medicine).
Numerical and Statistical Mathematics, Lancaster.
Quantitative Social Science, Kent at Canterbury.
Social Statistics, Birmingham (12 months), Exeter (Economic and Social Statistics, diploma), Manchester (MA(Econ) or – Economic and Social Statistics – diploma) and Southampton.
Statistics, Aberdeen, Brunel (1 yr full-time or $2\frac{1}{2}$ yrs part-time), Edinburgh (diploma 1 yr, MSc 12 months), Essex (Statistics and Operational Research, 12 months), Kent at Canterbury (MSc 1 yr, diploma 9 months), Leeds (minimum 12 months), London (for MSc and/or DIC at Imperial College, alone or with Sociology at London School of Economics, for MSc or diploma – 1 yr full-time or 2 yrs part-time – at University College), Loughborough U of Technology (Statistics and Operational Research, MSc and associateship, 1 yr full-time or 2 or 3 yrs part-time), Manchester (University and Institute of Science and Technology, MSc 12 months, diploma 1 academic yr), Newcastle upon Tyne, Oxford (BPhil 2 yrs, also a main subject for MSc in Mathematics), Sheffield, Sussex (option for MSc in Mathematics), Wales (Aberystwyth University College, MSc or diploma) and Warwick (diploma).

Statistics also included in postgraduate courses at Belfast, Lancaster (study and application of statistical techniques, for MA in Marketing and in Operational Research) and – Vital Statistics and Epidemiology – Liverpool (diplomas in Tropical Medicine and Hygiene and Venereology); also in certain diploma courses in Public or Social Administration, or Social Studies.

Research facilities At many of the universities named above (London, at Birkbeck, Imperial, Queen Mary, Royal Holloway and University Colleges, and London School of Economics; Oxford, Institute of Economics and Statistics; Manchester and Sheffield, joint School of Probability and Statistics; Wales, Aberystwyth, Cardiff and Swansea University Colleges); also, in Medical Statistics and Epidemiology, at Birmingham and London (St Thomas's Hospital Medical School and School of Hygiene and Tropical Medicine).

First degrees CNAA degrees in *Statistics and Computing* (4 yrs S unless otherwise stated). Liverpool P. P of North London. Thames P, *Mathematics, Statistics and Computing.* Sheffield P, *Applied Statistics.*
Courses in *Statistics* are available as part of degrees in Business Studies.
Statistics is offered as part of a modular degree at City of London P.

HND courses For HNDs in *Mathematics, Statistics and Computing* see *Computer Science,* page 111. Dorset IHE, *Statistics.*

Professional courses A number of colleges and polytechnics conduct courses leading to the examinations of the Institute of Statisticians. For full details, one should contact the Institute.

Research facilities City of London P. Hatfield P. Lanchester P. Leicester P. P of North London.

Surveying
(including Quantity Surveying)
See also Mining and Mineral Sciences; and Surveying, Land

First degrees Degrees in *Quantity Surveying* awarded by the following universities: Heriot-Watt (Building Economics and Quantity Surveying, 4 yrs, or 5 yrs S), Reading (also Building Surveying) and Salford (Quantity Surveying and Construction Economics, also Building Surveying, each 4 yrs S). Quantity Surveying is also included in courses leading to degrees in Architecture and Building (Aston in Birmingham, Building Economics and Measurement course), and in Land Management degree course at Reading.

Postgraduate courses MSc courses (12 months) in *Building Maintenance Management,* in *Construction Management* and in *Urban Land Appraisal* at University of Reading.

Research facilities At the universities of Reading and Salford.

First degrees CNAA degrees in *Surveying* (4 yrs S unless otherwise indicated) are offered at the following:
Building Surveying, Leicester P. Liverpool P. Thames P (3 yrs).
General Practice Surveying, Newcastle upon Tyne P.
Quantity Surveying, Bristol P. P of Central London (3 yrs). Dundee CT. Glasgow C Building and Printing. Glasgow CT. Kingston P. Leeds P. Liverpool P. Newcastle upon Tyne P. Portsmouth P (3 yrs). Robert Gordon's IT. P of the South Bank (part of degree in *Building*). Thames P (3 yrs). Trent P. P of Wales.
Urban Estate Surveying, Trent P.

HND courses Specialisation in *Quantity Surveying* and *Surveying* is allowed in HND courses in *Building* at Leicester P, P of the South Bank, Trent P and Willesden CT.

College diplomas Birmingham P, *Quantity Surveying* (4 yrs S). Cauldon CFE, *Quantity Surveying* (3 yrs). Glasgow C Building and Printing, *Building Surveying* (4 yrs S). Sheffield P, Associateship in *Minerals Surveying* (4 yrs S). Trent P, postgraduate diploma *Design Cost Control* (1 yr). Ulster C, Northern Ireland P, diploma *Quantity Surveying* (4 yrs S). Willesden CT, *Quantity Surveying* (4 yrs S).

Courses at the colleges listed above give full or partial exemption from the examinations of the Royal Institution of Chartered Surveyors and the Institute of Quantity Surveyors. Full information can be obtained from these Bodies.

Research   P of the South Bank. Thames P.
facilities

Surveying, Land
(including Geodesy and Photogrammetry)

First degrees Degrees with specialisation awarded by the following universities: *Surveying,* Newcastle upon Tyne; *Topographic Science* (Cartography and Photogrammetry), Glasgow and Wales (Swansea University College). *Land Surveying* is included in first degree courses (usually in Geography or in Civil or Municipal Engineering) at many universities and *Photogrammetry* is included in first degree courses (in Civil Engineering, Geology, Geography or Mining/Minerals) at the universities of Aberdeen, Birmingham, Bristol, Cambridge, Glasgow, Leeds, London, Newcastle upon Tyne, Reading, Sheffield and Surrey.

Postgraduate Courses (1 yr and for master's degree, unless otherwise indicated) at the following universities:
courses   *Geodesy,* Oxford.
                  Integrated Land Resources Survey, Reading (24 months).
                  Photogrammetry, Glasgow (diploma) and London (University College, MSc or College diploma).
                  Surveying, Glasgow (diploma) and London (University College, MSc or College diploma).
                  Topographic Science, Glasgow (1 or 2 yrs full-time, 2 or 3 yrs part-time).

Research   At the universities of Cambridge, Glasgow, London (Imperial and University Colleges),
facilities   Newcastle upon Tyne, Nottingham, Oxford and Reading.

First degrees CNAA degrees at North East London P, *Land Surveying Sciences* (3 yrs).

TEC HD   North East London P (3 yrs S).
course

College   Plymouth P, postgraduate diploma in *Hydrographic Surveying* (1 yr).
diplomas

Professional   Most of the degrees of universities mentioned above the line and the CNAA degree give
courses   exemption from the professional examination of the Royal Institution of Chartered Surveyors
                  (Land Surveying Section). Further information can be obtained from the Institution.

Research   North East London P.
facilities

Textiles

First degrees Degrees with specialisation awarded by the following universities:
Fibre Science, Strathclyde (also in Technology and Business Studies course).
Textile and Colour Chemistry, Manchester (Institute of Science and Technology).
Textile Chemistry, Leeds.
Textile Design, Bradford (4 yrs S) and Leeds.
Textile Design and Design Management or *Textile Economics and Management,* Manchester
(Institute of Science and Technology).
Textile Engineering or *Textile Industries,* Leeds.
Textile Management, Bradford (4 yrs S) and Leeds.
Textile Physics or *Textile Process Engineering,* Leeds.
Textile Science, Bradford (4 yrs S).
Textile Technology, Bradford (4 yrs S), Manchester (Institute of Science and Technology) and
Strathclyde (with Accountancy or Marketing or Economics for BSc in Technology and
Business Studies).
Bradford also offers a BA (4 yrs S) in European Industrial Studies with Textiles.

Postgraduate Courses (normally 1 yr and for diploma, unless otherwise indicated) at the following universities
courses and Royal College of Art:
Clothing Technology, Leeds (12 months).
Fibre Science and Technology, Leeds (MSc, 1 or 2 yrs depending upon qualifications) and
Manchester (Institute of Science and Technology, Polymer and Fibre Science, MSc or
diploma).
Textile Design, Manchester (Institute of Science and Technology) and Royal College of Art
(Knit, Print, Tapestry or Weave, MDes, 2 yrs).
Textile Engineering, Manchester (Institute of Science and Technology, for MSc or diploma in
Textile Technology).
Textile Evaluation, Strathclyde (MSc or diploma).
Textile Industries, Leeds (1 or 2 yrs).
Textile Physics and *Textile Processing,* Manchester (Institute of Science and Technology, for
MSc or diploma in Textile Technology).
Textile Technology, Bradford (MSc or diploma) and Manchester (Institute of Science and
Technology, MSc or diploma).

Research At all the universities named above, and at Royal College of Art (Textile Research Unit).
facilities

First degrees CNAA degrees (4 yrs S). Goldsmiths' C, *Textiles/Embroidery* (3 yrs). Huddersfield P, *Textile
Design.* Kidderminster CFE, *Design of Carpets and Related Textiles.* Leicester P, *Textile
Technology.* Liverpool P, *Fashion and Textiles* (3 yrs). Manchester P, *Textiles/Fashion* (3 yrs).
Trent P, *Knitwear Design,* also *Textile Design* (3 yrs). Winchester S Art, *Textile Design* (3 yrs).
Wolverhampton P, *Design of Carpets and Related Textiles.*

HND courses Bolton IT (2 or 3 yrs). C for the Distributive Trades, *Business Studies* with option in *Textile
Buying.* Salford CT, *Business Studies* with option in *Textile Marketing* (2 yrs).

TEC HD Blackburn CT and Design (2 yrs). Huddersfield P (2 yrs).
courses

Postgraduate Manchester P, MA *Textiles/Fashion* (4 terms).
course

Professional courses Full courses leading to the Associateship of the Textile Institute (ATI (Technology)) are offered at Belfast CT (4 yrs S), Bolton IT (3-4 yrs), Huddersfield P (4 yrs S), Leicester P (3-4 yrs) and Scottish C Textiles (4 yrs). Courses leading partway to the final ATI requirement and ATI (Design) are available at a number of other colleges, details of which can be obtained from the Institute. Some colleges offer courses leading to the Associateships of the Clothing Institute and the Society of Dyers and Colourists. Details can be obtained from these Bodies.

Other courses Dundee CT, diploma *Textiles* (3 yrs), also certificate in *Jute Manufacture* (2 yrs). Huddersfield P, diploma *Printed and Woven Textiles* (2 yrs). Kidderminster CFE, diploma *Carpet Technology* (3 yrs), also Advanced Diploma *Carpet Studies* (9 months). Leicester P, certificate *Textiles*, also diploma *Textile and Knitwear Technology* (1–2 yrs). London C Fashion, diploma *Clothing Management* (4 yrs S). Mabel Fletcher TC, Technician's Certificate *Clothing Manufacture* (3 yrs), advanced diploma *Clothing Machine Engineering* (2 yrs). Manchester P, advanced diploma *Clothing Technology* (1 yr). Scottish C Textiles, Associateship *Textile Design* (4 yrs S). Trent P, diploma *Textile Technology* (3 yrs), also postgraduate diploma *Textiles* (1 yr).

Research facilities Huddersfield P. Leicester P.

Town and Country Planning

See also Estate and Farm Management; Environmental Studies; Landscape Arthitecture; and Transport

First degrees Degrees with specialisation awarded by the following universities:
Applied Urban and Regional Planning, Aberdeen (for degree in Land Economy).
Architecture, Planning, Building and Environmental Studies, London (University College).
Town and Country Planning, Manchester and Newcastle upon Tyne.
Town and Regional Planning, Dundee.
Town Planning, Heriot-Watt.
Town Planning Studies, Wales (Institute of Science and Technology, BSc/diploma, 5 yrs including 1 yr in professional practice).
Urban Planning, Aston in Birmingham (with another subject).
Urban Studies, Kent at Canterbury and Sussex (School of Cultural and Community Studies).

Postgraduate courses Courses (normally 1 yr and for master's degree, unless otherwise indicated) at the following universities:
Advanced Functional Design Techniques for Buildings (Functional Planning and Environmental options), Bristol (12 months full-time or 3 yrs – modular course – part time).
Civic Design, Liverpool (MCD, 2 yrs).
Development Planning, London (University College, diploma).
Environmental Design, Newcastle upon Tyne (2 yrs).
Environmental Design and Engineering, London (University College, option in MSc in Architecture).
Environmental Planning, Heriot-Watt (2 yrs), Nottingham (2 yrs) and Reading (diploma 21 months, MPhil 24 months).
Environmental Planning and Design, Aston in Birmingham.
Environmental Planning for Developing Countries, Nottingham (2 yrs).

Land Economy, Cambridge (diploma).
Land Policy and the Environment, Cambridge (option in Development Studies course).
Operational Urban Design and Management, Newcastle upon Tyne (1 yr full-time plus 2 terms part-time).
Planning Studies (Developing Countries), Edinburgh (diploma).
Planning of Urban Regions, Newcastle upon Tyne (2 yrs).
Recreational Land Management Studies, Reading (12 months).
Regional and Urban Planning Studies, London (London School of Economics) and Reading (12 months).
Rural and Regional Resources Planning, Aberdeen (21 months).
Rural Planning Studies, Reading (12 months).
Town and Country Planning, Belfast (MSc 24 months, diploma 18 months) and Newcastle upon Tyne (2 yrs, MSc or – for holders of approved qualifications – BPhil).
Town and Regional Planning, Glasgow (diploma or MPhil, 2 yrs) and Sheffield (MA or diploma, 1 or 2 yrs).
Town Planning, London (University College, 2 yrs), Manchester (BTP 2 yrs, MTP 2–3 yrs, also BPl – 1 yr – open only to holders of Manchester BA) and Wales (Institute of Science and Technology, 2 yrs, including special study of planning in Asian countries).
Urban and Regional Planning, Strathclyde (with emphasis on City-Region, 2 yrs).
Urban and Regional Studies, Birmingham (diploma 12 months, MSocSc 24 months) and Sussex.
Urban Design, Heriot-Watt (diploma, also – 9 months full-time plus 12 months non-residential study – MSc) and Manchester.
Urban Design and Regional Planning, Edinburgh (diploma, also MPhil 2 yrs).
Urban Geography and Planning, Durham.
Urban Land Appraisal, Reading (12 months).
Urban Management, Aston in Birmingham (option for MSc/diploma in Public Sector Management).
Urban Planning Design, Newcastle upon Tyne (2 yrs).
Urban Science, Birmingham.
Urban Studies, Salford.
Urban Studies (Developing Countries), London (University College, College diploma).

Research facilities	At most of the universities named above. Birmingham: Centre for Urban and Regional Studies. Kent at Canterbury: Centre for Research in the Social Sciences. Manchester: Centre for Urban and Regional Research.

First degrees	CNAA degrees are offered at the following (4 yrs unless otherwise indicated):

Town and Country Planning, Edinburgh C Art (in conjunction with Heriot-Watt U), Glasgow School of Art. Liverpool P (4 yrs S). Trent P.
Town and Regional Planning, Duncan Jordanstone C of Art (in conjunction with U of Dundee).
Town Planning, Birmingham P. Bristol P. Chelmer IHE (*Planning*). Leeds P. Oxford P (*Planning Studies*, 3 yrs). P of the South Bank.
Urban and Regional Planning, Lanchester P (5 yrs S).
Urban Land Administration, Portsmouth P (3 yrs).
Urban Land Economics, Sheffield P (4 yrs S, also *Housing Studies*).

Professional courses	In addition to the courses listed above, there are a number of diploma courses which either lead to or give exemption from the final examinations of the Royal Town Planning Institute. These are listed below (normally 2 yrs). Birmingham P. Gloucestershire IHE (4 yrs). Kingston P. Leeds P. Oxford P. Trent P.
For further details of these and part-time courses, one should contact the Institute.

Postgraduate courses	*Regional Planning*, Lanchester P MA (1 yr) (also diploma *Local Planning*, 1 yr). *Town Planning*, Leeds P diploma (2 yrs). Kingston P (2 yrs). P of North London (2 yrs). *Town and Country Planning*, Edinburgh C Art (MSc, Heriot-Watt U, 2 yrs). Trent P (2 yrs). *Town and Regional Planning*, Duncan Jordanstone C Art (MSc or PhD Dundee U, 1–3 yrs S). *Rural and Regional Planning*, Duncan Jordanstone C Art (MSc 2 yrs) (also diploma *Urban Design*, 1 yr). *Planning and Urban Design*, Architectural Association S Architecture diploma (2 yrs). *Urban Design*, Oxford P MA (2 yrs) (also *Urban Planning Studies*, 1 yr diploma, 2 yrs MSc).
College diplomas	*Housing Management*, Bristol P (3 yrs). *Planning*, Chelmer IHE (4 yrs).
Research facilities	Birmingham P. Edinburgh C Art. Lanchester P. Leeds P. Liverpool P. Oxford P. Sheffield P.

Transport

See also Engineering, Aeronautical; and Engineering, Civil

First degrees	Degrees with specialisation awarded by the following universities: *International Transport*, Wales (Institute of Science and Technology, 3 yrs for BSc or 4 yrs S for BSc(Tech) in Maritime Studies). *Transport Management and Planning*, Loughborough U of Technology (3 yrs, or 4 yrs S). *Transport Planning and Operation*, Aston in Birmingham (with another subject). Some study of Transport included in first degree courses at the universities of Leicester (BA in Economics), London (London School of Economics, BSc(Econ)), Nottingham (Civil Engineering) and Salford (Transport Administration in Social Studies courses).
Postgraduate courses	Courses (1 yr and for master's degree, unless otherwise indicated) at the following universities and Cranfield IT: *Civil Engineering (Highways and Transport)*, The City (12 months full-time or 3 yrs part-time). *General Highway and Traffic Engineering*, Birmingham. *Highway and Traffic Engineering*, Newcastle upon Tyne (diploma and certificate). *Highway Engineering*, Salford (1 yr full-time or 2 yrs part-time). *Highway Engineering for Developing Countries*, Birmingham. *Rail Transport Engineering*, Cranfield IT (1 or 2 yrs). *Traffic and Highway Engineering*, Strathclyde (diploma 1 yr, MSc 1 or 2 yrs). *Transport*, London (Imperial College, MSc and/or DIC, also course in Traffic Flow and Transport Planning at University College). *Transportation*, Bradford (MSc 1 or 2 yrs, diploma 1 yr). *Transportation and Traffic Engineering*, Sheffield (MEng, diploma, also short courses). *Transportation and Traffic Planning*, Birmingham. *Transportation Planning and Engineering*, Southampton (diploma 9 months or MSc 12 months or in 3 parts over 33 months for diploma or 36 months for MSc). *Transport Design*, Liverpool (MTD 1 or 2 yrs, diploma 1 yr). *Transport Economics*, Leeds. *Transport Engineering*, Newcastle upon Tyne (12 months). *Transport Engineering and Planning*, Salford (1 yr full-time or 2 yrs part-time). *Transport Planning*, Loughborough U of Technology. *Transport Planning and Engineering*, Leeds (minimum 12 months).

Transport Studies (including engineering, socio-economic assessment, planning, mathematical modelling, methodology), Cranfield IT.
Transport Systems, Cranfield IT (1 or 2 yrs).

Research facilities At most of the universities named above and at Manchester, Oxford, Reading, Surrey and Warwick, and Cranfield IT. Leeds, Newcastle upon Tyne and Salford: Centres for Transport Studies. Loughborough U of Technology: Centre for Transport Engineering Practice. Oxford: Transport Studies Unit. Warwick: Urban Transport Research Group.

First degree Lanchester P, *Industrial Design/Transportation* (4 yrs S).

HND courses Dorset IHE, *Business Studies (Transport)* (2 yrs). Newcastle upon Tyne P, *Business Studies (Transport and Physical Distribution)*. North Worcestershire C, *Transport* (3 yrs S).

Diploma courses Chelsea C Aeronautical and Automobile Engineering, diploma *Transport Administration and Engineering* (3 yrs). Middlesex P, *Engineering Design Methods* (3 months). North Worcestershire C, *Road Transport Engineering* (3 yrs S), *Motor Trade Management, Road Transport Engineering Management* (both 6 months). Willesden CT, *Transport Engineering* (3 yrs S), *Transport Management* (2 yrs).

Postgraduate courses P of Central London, MSc *Transportation Planning and Management* (1 yr or 15 months).

Research facilities P of Central London.

Tropical Medicine and Hygiene

Postgraduate courses Courses (1 yr and for diploma, unless otherwise indicated) at the following universities:
Clinical Tropical Medicine, London (School of Hygiene and Tropical Medicine, MSc).
Tropical Child Health, Liverpool (6 months for candidates with approved postgraduate experience and training).
Tropical Public Health, London (School of Hygiene and Tropical Medicine).
Tropical Medicine and Hygiene, Liverpool (3 months) and London (5 months for Conjoint Board diploma – see below – in School of Hygiene and Tropical Medicine).

Research facilities At the universities of Liverpool and London.

Postgraduate diploma The Examining Board in England of the Royal College of Physicians of London and the Royal College of Surgeons of England awards a postgraduate diploma in *Tropical Medicine and Hygiene.* Particulars from the Secretary of the Examining Board in England.

United States Studies

First degrees Degrees with specialisation in (North) *American Studies* awarded by the following universities: Belfast (alone or with English), Birmingham, Dundee, East Anglia (American Studies, or English and American Literature or History, also American and/or English Literature with

European Literature for degree in Comparative Literature), Essex (US Government or Literature or Sociology, each alone or with History, also History alone, Government and Sociology), Hull (alone or with another main subject), Keele (with another principal subject), Kent at Canterbury (with specialisation in Literature or History or Politics), Manchester (alone or with Russian Studies, also English and American Literature), Nottingham (alone or with English), Sussex (options in History, Literature or Social Studies), Wales (Single or Joint Honours at Aberystwyth University College, Joint Honours at Swansea University College) and Warwick (Comparative American Studies covering both North and South America, alone or with English, also English and American Literature).

Less specialised American Studies courses included in first degree syllabuses at Cambridge (History Tripos, Part II), Durham, Exeter (American and Commonwealth Arts with English), Leicester (for Combined Studies degree), Manchester (for Combined Studies degree), Nottingham (for Part I examinations in most arts and social science subjects) and Reading (options in degree courses in History and in Politics).

At most universities some study of North America is included in first degree courses in Geography (but not at New U of Ulster) and History (Oxford, aspects as further subjects and special subjects in Honour School of Modern History; Warwick, some History students spend some time studying American History at an American university). Courses in *Economic History and Government* of the USA are included in BSc(Econ) syllabus at London (London School of Economics), and in *American Literature* in English degree syllabuses at Exeter, Kent at Canterbury, London, Sheffield, Stirling, New U of Ulster, Wales (Swansea University College) and Warwick.

Postgraduate courses

Courses (usually 1 yr, and for MA, unless otherwise indicated) at the following universities:

American History, Sheffield.

American History and Literature, East Anglia.

American Literature, Keele, Leeds and Wales (Aberystwyth University College, American Literature since 1945).

American Music, Keele.

American Poetry, Essex (MA scheme in Literature, 12 months).

American Politics and History, Liverpool (BPhil, 1 or 2 yrs).

American Studies, Manchester (any 4 of 6 options), Nottingham (1 yr full-time or 2 yrs part-time) and Sussex.

Area Studies (United States), London (12 months, seminars at Institute of United States Studies).

Commonwealth and American History, Oxford (BPhil, 2 yrs).

Economic History of the USA, London (London School of Economics, option in MSc in Economic History).

English and American Literature, Kent at Canterbury and Leicester (Modern English and American Literature).

English and American Literature of the Twentieth Century, Newcastle upon Tyne.

History of the USA, Wales (Cardiff University College).

North American Architecture (from colonial times to the present day), Manchester.

North American Studies (USA and/or Canada), Edinburgh (MPhil or MLitt, 2 yrs).

United States Government and Politics, Essex (12 months).

United States History and Institutions, Keele.

Research facilities

At the universities of Birmingham, East Anglia, Edinburgh, Essex, Glasgow (Centre for Research in North American History), Hull, Keele, Kent at Canterbury, Manchester, Nottingham, Sussex and Warwick. At London, the Institute of United States Studies promotes and co-ordinates United States Studies within the university.

Urology and Venereology

First degrees   Included in first degree courses in Medicine (for list of awarding universities see page 198).

Postgraduate courses   Courses in *Sexually Transmitted Diseases* (12 weeks) at University of London (British Postgraduate Medical Federation; also, at Institute of Urology, clinical teaching throughout the yr) and in *Venereology* (3 months, for diploma) at University of Liverpool.

Research facilities   *Urology*: at the universities of Belfast, Cambridge, Edinburgh, Glasgow, Leeds, London (Institute of Urology and University College Hospital Medical School), Manchester, Newcastle upon Tyne, Oxford, Southampton and Wales (Welsh National School of Medicine). *Venereology*: at the universities of Glasgow and London (Middlesex Hospital Medical School).

Postgraduate diploma   The Society of Apothecaries of London awards a postgraduate diploma in *Venereology*.

Veterinary Medicine and Surgery

First degrees   Degrees in *Veterinary Science/Medicine and Surgery* awarded by the universities of Bristol (BVSc), Cambridge (VetMB), Edinburgh (BVM&S), Glasgow (BVMS), Liverpool (BVSc) and London (BVetMed, Royal Veterinary College); at Belfast, *Veterinary Studies* included in BAgr course.
Animal Husbandry usually included in first degree courses in Agriculture.

Postgraduate courses   Courses (1 yr and for master's degree, unless otherwise indicated) at the following universities:
Animal Health, London (Royal Veterinary College).
Applied Parasitology, Liverpool.
Aquatic Veterinary Studies, Stirling (MSc or diploma, offered in alternate yrs, next 1978–79).
Avian Medicine, Liverpool.
Diagnostic Veterinary Pathology or *Neurophysiology* (in Veterinary Medicine) or *Tropical Animal Health and Production*, Edinburgh (12 months, also diplomas).
Tropical Veterinary Medicine (diploma) or *Tropical Veterinary Science* (12 months), Edinburgh.
Veterinary Pathology, London (Royal Veterinary College, offered in alternate yrs, next 1979–80).
Veterinary Public Health (12 months) or *Veterinary State Medicine* (diploma), Edinburgh.

Research facilities   At the universities of Bristol (Langford Research Station, Somerset), Cambridge, Edinburgh, Glasgow (including MVM, DVM, DVS), Liverpool (including MVSc) and London (Royal Veterinary College, including DVetMed); also Belfast (Veterinary research farm), Surrey (Veterinary Microbiology) and Wales (Aberystwyth University College, Animal Health).

Professional courses   Full information about obtaining Membership of the Royal College of Veterinary Surgeons may be obtained from the Registrar of the Royal College of Veterinary Surgeons.

Youth Services

Diplomas/ certificates

Courses (1 yr unless otherwise indicated) at the following universities:

Youth and Community Work, (Community and Youth Work, 2 yrs, primarily for those intending to work in Britain), Sheffield (for experienced teachers) and Wales (Swansea University College, diploma in Adolescent Development for experienced teachers including those interested in combining teaching with Youth Work, and special option in Youth Work for postgraduate certificate in Education).

Youth Leadership and Organisation, Wales (Swansea University College, for College diploma).

Professional courses

Full-time courses in *Careers Guidance* for graduates or those with relevant qualifications:

Local Government Training Board Diploma (1 yr) at Birmingham P, also postgraduate diploma in *Community Work.* Bristol P. Huddersfield P. Kent C for the Careers Service. Manchester P. Napier CC and T. Newcastle upon Tyne P. Paisley CT. P of the South Bank. Trent P. Ulster C, Northern Ireland P. P of Wales.

For further information, one should contact the Board.

Youth and Community Work, Crewe and Alsager CHE (2 yrs). Manchester P (1 yr). North East London P (2 yrs, certificate *Community Work* (2 yrs S). Roehampton IHE, certificate *Community Work* (2 yrs S). Sunderland P (2 yrs). Ulster C, Northern Ireland P.

Careers Education and Guidance, Hatfield P (1 yr).

Vocational Guidance/Counselling, North East London P (1 yr). Paisley CT (1 yr). P of Wales (1 yr).

Youth Employment Service Training Board Diploma, Birmingham P (1 yr).

Many establishments of education include training in youth work in their BEd and certificate of education courses (see the *Handbook of Institutions providing ... Teacher Training ...*). Information about all courses is available from the Local Government Training Centre (see page 286).

SOURCES OF ADDITIONAL INFORMATION

Commonwealth Universities Yearbook (Association of Commonwealth Universities, annual). 1977–78 edition, £25. Includes a survey of British universities in general and a chapter on each university.

A Compendium of Advanced Courses in Colleges of Further and Higher Education (Regional Advisory Councils for Further Education, annual). 1977 edition, £1·50.

Compendium of Information (Scottish Universities Council on Entrance, annual). 50p (UK), £1·50 (overseas).

Compendium of University Entrance Requirements for First Degree Courses in the United Kingdom (Association of Commonwealth Universities for Committee of Vice-Chancellors and Principals of the Universities of the United Kingdom, annual). 1978 edition, about £4. Gives details in terms of GCE and other UK certificates.

Directory of Day Courses (in Scotland) (Scottish Education Department, annual). Free.

Directory of First Degree Courses (CNAA) (Council for National Academic Awards, annual). Free.

Directory of Further Education (Careers Research and Advisory Centre, Cambridge). £20 (paperback), £22·50 (hardback).

Directory of Postgraduate Courses (CNAA) (Council for National Academic Awards, annual). Free.

Graduate Studies (Careers Research and Advisory Centre, Cambridge). £35.

Guide to the DipHE (Careers Consultants Ltd, Richmond). 1977 edition. Free.

Handbook of Institutions providing both Teacher Training and other full-time Advanced Courses (England and Wales) (Lund Humphries for National Association of Teachers in Further and Higher Education, annual). 1978 edition, £3·95. Also annually, *Summary of Teacher Training Courses*, 75p, and *Summary of Diversified Courses in Institutions providing Teacher Training*, 40p. Combined price for both summaries is £1·00, and information booklet, *MW1*, describing relevant application procedures. All available from the Central Register and Clearing House Ltd.

Polytechnic Courses in England and Wales (Lund Humphries for the Committee of Directors of Polytechnics). 1978–79 edition, £3·60.

Handbook of the Scottish Central Institutions (Committee of Principals and Directors of Central Institutions). Free.

How to Apply for Admission to a University (Universities Central Council on Admissions, annual). Issued free with UCCA application form.

How to Live in Britain (Longman Group Ltd for the British Council, biennial). 25p.

Information Sheets for School Leavers (Department of Education and Science). Free.

Memorandum on Entry Requirements for Admission to Courses of Teacher Training in Scotland (HM Stationery Office for the Scottish Education Department, 1975). 73p.

Schedule of Postgraduate Courses in United Kingdom Universities (Association of Commonwealth Universities for Committee of Vice-Chancellors and Principals of the Universities of the United Kingdom, annual). 1977–78 edition, £2·10.

Research in British Universities, Polytechnics and Colleges: Vol 1 – *Physical and Biological Sciences*. Vol 2 – *Applied Sciences and Technologies*. Vol 3 – *Medical Sciences*. Vol 4 – *Social Sciences*. Being compiled by the British Library for publication in 1978 (to replace *Scientific Research in British Universities and Colleges*, last published in 1975).

Universities in Britain (Central Office of Information for British Information Services). Free.

Which Degree 1977 (Haymarket Publications, annual). £15.

Some subject guides

Academic Courses in Great Britain relevant to the Teaching of English to speakers of other languages (British Council English Teaching Information Centre, annual). Free.

Agricultural Education: Full-time and Sandwich Courses serving England and Wales

(Department of Education and Science and Central Office of Information, annual). Free. Also *Opportunities in Agriculture* (Scottish Agricultural Colleges). Free.

Degree Course Guides, covering the main subjects studied at universities (Careers Research and Advisory Centre, Cambridge). Individual booklets, £1·00.

Degree Studies and the Accountancy Profession, Accounting Education Consultative Board. Free.

Dental Postgraduate Study (General Dental Council, 1974). Free.

Design Courses in Britain (Design Council, 1977). £1.

Entrance Requirements to Schools of Pharmacy (The Pharmaceutical Society of Great Britain, annual). Free.

A Guide to Degree Courses in English 1977–78, A. W. J. Lincoln (The English Association, 1976). £3·25.

Handbook for Degrees in Metallurgy/Materials Science (Institution of Metallurgists, London, 1975). Free.

History at the Universities, Polytechnics and Colleges, (R. P. Blows (Historical Association, 1977). £2·40.

Physics Courses in Higher Education (Institute of Physics, 1977). Free.

Postgraduate Courses in Business Studies, Management and Related Subjects at Universities and Business Schools in the United Kingdom (The Conference of University Management Schools, Cranfield Institute of Technology). £1.

Postgraduate Qualifications and Courses in Psychology (British Psychological Society, 1977). 40p.

Postgraduate Studentships in the Social Sciences (Social Science Research Council). Free. Awards quoted are solely for residents of Great Britain.

Programme of Long Courses for Qualified Teachers; course list no. 1 (Department of Education and Science annual). Free.

Research Fields in Physics in UK Universities and Polytechnics (Institute of Physics, 1976). £11 (UK).

Schedule of courses in translating, interpreting, practical linguistics and degree level courses in languages combined with scientific and technical subjects (The Institute of Linguists, 1977). 25p.

Summary of Postgraduate Diplomas and Courses in Medicine (Council for Postgraduate Medical Education in England and Wales, annual). 1977 edition, £2·50.

Scholarships and grants

Awards for Commonwealth University Staff (Association of Commonwealth Universities, biennial). 1978–80 edition, £2·75. Also supplementary Information Paper, *Some Awards open to Academic Staff of Foreign (non-Commonwealth) Universities and tenable at UK Universities*, £1·50. (see also page 57).

Financial Aid for First Degree Study at Commonwealth Universities (Association of Commonwealth Universities, 1977). 85p (see also page 57).

Grants Register, R.Turner, editor (St James Press, London, biennial). 1977–79 edition, £9.

Scholarships Guide for Commonwealth Postgraduate Students (Association of Commonwealth Universities, biennial). 1977–79 edition, £3·75. Also supplementary Information Paper, *Some Awards open to Graduates of Foreign (non-Commonwealth) Universities and tenable at UK Universities*, £1 (see also page 57).

Study Abroad (Unesco, Paris, biennial). £4·35. An international handbook of fellowships, scholarships, grants etc.

ADDRESSES OF UNIVERSITY INSTITUTIONS

Correspondence should be addressed to 'The Registrar' in each case, unless otherwise stated. (The addresses of certain institutions which are affiliated to or associated with universities (as distinct from being constituent colleges of a university), or have teachers recognised by a university, appear on pages 270–281).

Detailed information about each university is contained in the annual Commonwealth Universities Yearbook (see page 265).

University of Aberdeen, Aberdeen, Scotland AB9 1FX (The Secretary)

University of Aston in Birmingham, Gosta Green, Birmingham B4 7ET

University of Bath, Claverton Down, Bath BA2 7AY (The Secretary and Registrar)

The Queen's University of Belfast, Belfast, Northern Ireland BT7 1NN (The Secretary; *correspondence about admission to* Admissions Officer)

University of Birmingham, PO Box 363, Edgbaston, Birmingham B15 2TT

University of Bradford, Bradford BD7 1DP

University of Bristol, Senate House, Tyndall Avenue, Bristol BS8 1TH

Brunel University, Uxbridge, Middlesex UB8 3PH (The Academic Registrar)

University of Cambridge, University Registry, The Old Schools, Cambridge CB2 1TN (The Registrary)

The City University, St John Street, London EC1V 4PB (The Academic Registrar)

Cranfield Institute of Technology, Cranfield, Bedford MK43 0AL
National College of Agricultural Engineering (Cranfield Institute of Technology), Silsoe, Bedford MK45 4DT

University of Dundee, Dundee, Scotland DD1 4HN (The Secretary)

University of Durham, Old Shire Hall, Durham DH1 3HP (The Registrar and Secretary)

University of East Anglia, Norwich NR4 7TJ (The Registrar and Secretary)

University of Edinburgh, Old College, South Bridge, Edinburgh, Scotland EH8 9YL (The Secretary)

University of Essex, Wivenhoe Park, Colchester CO4 3SQ

University of Exeter, Exeter EX4 4QJ (The Academic Registrar and Secretary)

University of Glasgow, Glasgow, Scotland G12 8QQ (The Secretary and Registrar)

Heriot-Watt University, Chambers Street, Edinburgh, Scotland EH1 1HX (The Secretary)

University of Hull, Hull HU6 7RX

University of Keele, Keele, Staffordshire ST5 5BG

University of Kent at Canterbury, The Registry, The University, Canterbury CT2 7NZ

University of Lancaster, University House, Lancaster LA1 4YW (The University Secretary)

University of Leeds, Leeds LS2 9JT

University of Leicester, Leicester LE1 7RH

University of Liverpool, PO Box 147, Liverpool L69 3BX

University of London, Senate House, Malet Street, London WC1E 7HU (The Academic Registrar)
(For Schools and Institutions, see below)

Loughborough University of Technology, Loughborough LE11 3TU (The Academic Registrar)

University of Manchester, Manchester M13 9PL

*University of Manchester Institute of Science and Technology (UMIST), Manchester M60 1QD

University of Newcastle upon Tyne, Newcastle upon Tyne NE1 7RU

University of Nottingham, Nottingham NG7 2RD

*The Institute constitutes the Faculty of Technology in the University of Manchester.

The Open University, Walton Hall, Milton Keynes MK7 6AA (The Secretary)

University of Oxford, University Offices, Wellington Square, Oxford OX1 2JD

University of Reading, Whiteknights, Reading RG6 2AH

Royal College of Art, Kensington Gore, London SW7 2EU

University of St Andrews, College Gate, St Andrews, Scotland KY16 9AJ (The Secretary and Registrar)

University of Salford, Salford M5 4WT

University of Sheffield, Sheffield S10 2TN

University of Southampton, Highfield, Southampton SO9 5NH (The Secretary and Registrar; *correspondence about courses and admission to* The Academic Registrar)

University of Stirling, Stirling, Scotland FK9 4LA

University of Strathclyde, Royal College, 204 George Street, Glasgow, Scotland G1 1XW (*correspondence about courses and admission to* The Admissions Office (undergraduate) *or* The Postgraduate Office)

University of Surrey, Guildford, Surrey GU2 5XH (The Academic Registrar)

University of Sussex, Falmer, Brighton BN1 9RH (The Registrar and Secretary); correspondence about courses and admission to: *BA, BSc* – The Admissions Officer, Sussex House, BN1 9RH; *Arts (graduate)* – The Graduate Admissions Office, Graduate School in Arts and Social Studies, Arts Building, BN1 9QN; *Science (graduate)* – The Science Office, Sussex House, BN1 9RH; *BEd and Education (graduate)* – The Secretary of Education, Education Development Building, BN1 9RG)

The New University of Ulster, Coleraine, County Londonderry, Northern Ireland BT52 1SA

University of Wales, University Registry, Cathays Park, Cardiff CF1 3NS
University College of Wales, Aberystwyth, Dyfed SY23 2AX
University College of North Wales, Bangor, Gwynedd LL57 2DG (The Secretary and Registrar)
University College, Cardiff, PO Box 78, Cardiff CF1 1XL (The Vice-Principal (Administration) and Registrar)
University College of Swansea, Singleton Park, Swansea, West Glamorgan SA2 8PP (The Registrar/Secretary)
University of Wales Institute of Science and Technology (UWIST), Cardiff CF1 3NU (The Academic Registrar)
Welsh National School of Medicine, Heath Park, Cardiff CF4 4XN
St David's University College, Lampeter, Dyfed SA48 7ED (The Academic Registrar)

University of Warwick, Coventry CV4 7AL (The Academic Registrar)

University of York, Heslington, York YO1 5DD

APPENDIX
Schools and institutions of University of London.
Correspondence should be addressed to 'The Secretary' in each case, unless otherwise stated.

University institutes
Courtauld Institute of Art, 20 Portman Square, London W1H 0BE (The Registrar and Secretary)

Institute of Advanced Legal Studies, 17 Russell Square, London WC1B 5DR

Institute of Archaeology, 31–34 Gordon Square, London WC1H 0PY

Institute of Classical Studies, 31–34 Gordon Square, London WC1H 0PY

Institute of Commonwealth Studies, 27 Russell Square, London WC1B 5DS (The Assistant Secretary)

Institute of Education, Bedford Way, London WC1H 0AL

Institute of Germanic Studies, 29 Russell Square, London WC1B 5DP (The Deputy Director)

Institute of Historical Research, University of London, Senate House, London WC1E 7HU (The Secretary and Librarian)

Institute of Latin American Studies, 31 Tavistock Square, London WC1H 9HA

British Institute in Paris, 9–11 rue de Constantine, 75007 – Paris, France (London Secretary: University of London, Senate House, London WC1E 7HU)

School of Slavonic and East European Studies, University of London, Senate House, London WC1E 7HU (The Secretary–Registrar)

Institute of United States Studies, 31 Tavistock Square, London WC1H 9EZ

Warburg Institute, Woburn Square, London WC1H 0AB

Non-medical schools
Bedford College, Inner Circle, Regent's Park, London NW1 4NS (The Registrar)

Birkbeck College, Malet Street, London WC1E 7HX

Chelsea College, Manresa Road, London SW3 6LX (The Academic Registrar)

Imperial College of Science and Technology, London SW7 2AZ (The Registrar)

King's College, Strand, London WC2R 2LS (The Registrar)

London School of Economics and Political Science, Houghton Street, Aldwych, London WC2A 2AE (*for undergraduate courses*, The Registrar; *for graduate courses*, The Secretary of the Graduate School)

Queen Elizabeth College, 61–67 Campden Hill Road, London W8 7AH

Queen Mary College, Mile End Road, London E1 4NS (The Registrar and Secretary)

Royal Holloway College, Egham Hill, Egham, Surrey TW20 0EX (The Registrar)

Royal Veterinary College, Royal College Street, Camden Town, London NW1 0TU (The Secretary and Bursar)

School of Oriental and African Studies, Malet Street, London WC1E 7HP (The Registrar)

School of Pharmacy, 29–39 Brunswick Square, London WC1N 1AX (The Dean)

*University College, Gower Street, London WC1E 6BT (The Registrar)

Westfield College, Kidderpore Avenue, Hampstead, London NW3 7ST (The Registrar)

Wye College, Wye, Ashford, Kent TN25 5AH (The Secretary; *correspondence about courses and admission to* The Registrar)

Theological colleges
Heythrop College, 11–13 Cavendish Square, London W1M 0AN

King's College: Theological Department, Strand, London WC2R 2LS (The Dean)

General medical and dental schools
Charing Cross Hospital Medical School, The Reynolds Building, St Dunstan's Road, London W6 8RP

Guy's Hospital Medical School, London Bridge, London SE1 9RT

King's College Hospital Medical School, Denmark Hill, London SE5 8RX

London Hospital Medical College, Turner Street, London E1 2AD

Middlesex Hospital Medical School, Mortimer Street, London W1P 7PN

Royal Dental Hospital of London, School of Dental Surgery, 32 Leicester Square, London WC2H 7LJ (The School Secretary)

Royal Free Hospital School of Medicine, 8 Hunter Street, Brunswick Square, London WC1N 1BP

St Bartholomew's Hospital Medical College, West Smithfield, London EC1A 7BE

St George's Hospital Medical School, Cranmer Terrace, Tooting, London SW17 0RE

St Mary's Hospital Medical School, Norfolk Place, Paddington, London W2 1PG

St Thomas's Hospital Medical School, Lambeth Palace Road, London SE1 7EH

†University College Hospital Medical School, University Street, London WC1E 6JJ

Westminster Medical School, Horseferry Road, Westminster, London SW1P 2AR

Postgraduate medical schools
British Postgraduate Medical Federation, 33 Millman Street, London WC1N 3EJ

Institutes of the Federation:
Institute of Basic Medical Sciences, Royal College of Surgeons of England, Lincoln's Inn Fields, London WC2A 3PN
Institute of Cancer Research, Royal Cancer Hospital, 34 Sumner Place, London SW7 3NU
Cardiothoracic Institute, Brompton Hospital, London SW3 6HP (Fulham Road Branch) and 2 Beaumont Street, London W1N 1RB (Beaumont Street Branch)
Institute of Child Health, 30 Guilford Street, London WC1N 1EH
Institute of Dental Surgery, Eastman Dental Hospital, Gray's Inn Road, London WC1X 8LD
Institute of Dermatology, St John's Hospital for Diseases of the Skin, Lisle Street, Leicester Square, London WC2H 7BJ
Institute of Laryngology and Otology, Royal National Throat, Nose and Ear Hospital, Gray's Inn Road, London WC1X 8EE

Institute of Neurology, National Hospital for Nervous Diseases, Queen Square, London WC1N 3BG
Institute of Obstetrics and Gynaecology, Chelsea Hospital for Women, Dovehouse Street, London SW3 6LT
Institute of Ophthalmology, Judd Street, London WC1H 9QS
Institute of Orthopaedics, Royal National Orthopaedic Hospital, Great Portland Street, London W1N 6AD
Institute of Psychiatry, De Crespigny Park, Denmark Hill, London SE5 8AF
Institute of Urology, 172 Shaftesbury Avenue, London WC2H 8JE

London School of Hygiene and Tropical Medicine, Keppel Street (Gower Street), London WC1E 7HT

Royal Postgraduate Medical School, Hammersmith Hospital, Ducane Road, London W12 0HS

The names and addresses of the public educational institutions at which the University recognises certain teachers giving courses leading to internal degrees or diplomas of the University are included in the lists on pages 270–280.

* Pre-clinical medical courses held at University College.
† Clinical courses only are held at the University College Hospital Medical School.

ADDRESSES OF POLYTECHNICS

City of Birmingham Polytechnic, Academic Registry, Aston Street Annex, Birmingham B4 7DX

Brighton Polytechnic, Grand Parade, Brighton BN2 2JY

Bristol Polytechnic, Coldharbour Lane, Bristol BS16 1QY

Polytechnic of Central London, 309 Regent Street, London W1R 8AL

City of London Polytechnic, 117–119 Houndsditch, London EC3A 7BU

Hatfield Polytechnic, PO Box 109 College Lane, Hatfield, Hertfordshire AL10 9AB

Huddersfield Polytechnic, Queensgate, Huddersfield HD1 3DH

Kingston Polytechnic, Penrhyn Road, Kingston upon Thames KT1 2EE

Lanchester Polytechnic, Priory Street, Coventry CV1 5FB

Leeds Polytechnic, Calverley Street, Leeds LS1 3HE

Leicester Polytechnic, PO Box 143, Leicester LE1 9BH

Liverpool Polytechnic, 1 Rumford Place, Liverpool L3 9RH

Manchester Polytechnic, All Saints, Manchester M15 6BM

Middlesex Polytechnic, Bounds Green Road, London N11 2NQ

Newcastle upon Tyne Polytechnic, Ellison Building, Ellison Place, Newcastle upon Tyne NE1 8ST

North East London Polytechnic, Livingstone House, Livingstone Road, London E15 2LJ

Polytechnic of North London, Holloway Road, London N7 8DB

North Staffordshire Polytechnic, College Road, Stoke-on-Trent ST4 2DE

Oxford Polytechnic, Headington, Oxford OX3 0BP

Plymouth Polytechnic, Drake Circus, Plymouth PL4 8AA

Portsmouth Polytechnic, Alexandra House, Museum Road, Portsmouth PO1 2QQ

Preston Polytechnic, Corporation Street, Preston PR1 2TQ

Sheffield City Polytechnic, Pond Street, Sheffield S1 1WB

Polytechnic of The South Bank, Borough Road, London SE1 0AA

Sunderland Polytechnic, Chester Road, Sunderland SR1 3SD

Teesside Polytechnic, Borough Road, Middlesbrough, Cleveland TS1 3BA

Thames Polytechnic, Wellington Street, Woolwich, London SE18 6PF

Trent Polytechnic, Burton Street, Nottingham NG1 4BU

Ulster College, The Northern Ireland Polytechnic, Jordanstown, Newtownabbey, Co Antrim BT37 0QB

The Polytechnic of Wales, Pontypridd, Mid Glamorgan CF37 1DL

Wolverhampton Polytechnic, Wulfruna Street, Wolverhampton WV1 1LY

ADDRESSES OF COLLEGES OF TECHNOLOGY, ART, COMMERCE, ETC

Aberdeen College of Commerce, Holburn Street, Aberdeen AB9 2YT

Administrative Staff College, Greenlands, Henley-on-Thames, Oxfordshire RG9 3AU

College of Air Training, Hamble, Southampton SO3 5NA

Architectural Association School of Architecture, 34–36 Bedford Square, London WC1B 3ES

Askham Bryan College of Agriculture and Horticulture, Askam Bryan, York YO2 3PR

Ayr Technical College, Dam Park, Ayr

Barking College of Technology, Dagenham Road, Romford RM7 0XU

Barnsley College of Technology, Church Street, Barnsley, South Yorkshire S70 2AN

Bath Academy of Art, Corsham, Wiltshire SN13 0DB

Belfast College of Technology, College Square East, Belfast BT1 6DJ

Bell College of Technology, Almada Street, Hamilton

Benesh Institute of Choreology, 4 Margravine Gardens, Barons Court, London W6 8RH

Bingley College, Bingley, West Yorkshire BD16 4AR

Birkenhead College of Technology, Borough Road, Birkenhead L42 9QD

Birmingham College of Food and Domestic Arts, Summer Row, Birmingham B3 1JB

Birmingham School of Speech Training and Dramatic Art, 45 Church Road, Edgbaston, Birmingham B15 3SW

Bishop Grosseteste College, Lincoln, Lincolnshire LN1 3DY

Blackburn College of Technology and Design, Fieldon Street, Blackburn BB2 1LH

Blackpool College of Technology and Art, Ashfield Road, Bispham, Blackpool FY2 0HB

Bolton Institute of Technology, Deane Road, Bolton BL3 5AB

Bournemouth and Poole College of Art, Royal London House, Lansdowne, Bournemouth, Dorset BH1 3JJ

Bradford College, Great Horton Road, Bradford, West Yorkshire BD7 1AY

Brighton Technical College, Pelham Street, Brighton BN1 4FA

Bristol Old Vic Theatre School, 2 Downside Road, Clifton, Bristol BS8 2XF

Buckinghamshire College of Higher Education, Queen Alexandra Road, High Wycombe HP11 2JZ

Byam Shaw School of Drawing and Painting Ltd, 70 Campden Street, London W8 7EN

Cambourne School of Mines, Trevenson, Pool, Redruth, Cornwall TR15 3SE

Cambridgeshire College of Arts and Technology, Collier Row, Cambridge CB1 2AJ

Canterbury College of Art, New Dover Road, Canterbury, Kent CT1 3AN

Canterbury College of Technology, New Dover Road, Canterbury, Kent CT1 3AJ

Carlisle Technical College, Victoria Place, Carlisle CA1 1HS

Cassio College, Langley Road, Watford WD1 3RH

Cauldon College of Further Education, Stoke Road, Shelton, Stoke on Trent, ST4 2DG

Central School of Art and Design, Southampton Row, London WC1B 4AP

Central School of Speech and Drama, Embassy Theatre, Eton Avenue, London NW3 3HY

Chelmer Institute of Higher Education, Victoria Road South, Chelmsford, Essex CM1 1LL

Chelsea College of Aeronautical and Automobile Engineering, Shoreham Airport, Shoreham-By-Sea, Sussex BN4 5FJ

Chelsea School of Art, Manresa Road, London SW3 6LS

Chelsea School of Chiropody, 18 Stamford Street, London NW8 8EN

Cheltenham General Hospital, Sandford Road, Cheltenham, Gloucestershire GL53 7AN

Chesterfield College of Technology, Infirmary Road, Chesterfield, Derbyshire S41 7NG

Chichester College of Further Education, Westgate Fields, Chichester, West Sussex PO19 1SB

Christ Church College, Canterbury, Kent CT1 1QU

City of Leeds College of Music, Cookridge Street, Leeds LS2 8BH

City of Liverpool College of Higher Education, Liverpool Road, Prescot, Merseyside L34 1NP

City of Manchester College of Higher Education, Hathersage Road, Manchester M13 0JA

Colchester Institute of Higher Education, Sheepen Road, Colchester, Essex CO3 3LL

College For The Distributive Trades, 30 Leicester Square, London WC2H 7LE

College of Speech Therapists, Harold Poster House, 6 Lechmere Road, London NW2 5BU

Colquitt Technical College, Colquitt Street, Liverpool L1 4DB

Co-operative College, Stanford Hall, Loughborough, Leicestershire LE12 5QR

Cordwainers Technical College, Mare Street, Hackney, London E8 3RE

Cornwall Technical College, Redruth, Cornwall TR15 3RD

Coventry Technical College, Butts, Coventry CV1 3GD

Crawley College of Technology, College Road, Crawley, Sussex RH10 1NR

Crewe and Alsager College of Higher Education, Alsager, Cheshire ST7 2HL

Croydon College of Design and Technology, Fairfield, Croydon CR9 1DX

Darlington College of Technology, Cleveland Avenue, Darlington, Co Durham DL3 7BB

Dartington College of Arts, Totnes, Devon TQ9 6ES

Derby Lonsdale College of Higher Education, Uttoxeter New Road, Derby DE3 3JE

Derby School of Occupational Therapy, Highfield, 403 Burton Road, Derby DE3 6AN

Doncaster Metropolitan Institute of Higher Education, Waterdale, Doncaster DN1 3EX

Dorset Institute of Higher Education, Wallisdown Road, Wallisdown, Poole, Dorset BH12 5BB

Dorset House School of Occupational Therapy, 58 London Road, Headington, Oxford OX3 7PE

Drama Centre London Ltd, 176 Prince of Wales Road, Chalk Farm, London NW5 3PT

Duncan of Jordanstone College of Art, Perth Road, Dundee DD1 4HT

Dundee College of Commerce, 30 Constitution Road, Dundee DD3 6TB

Dundee College of Education, Gardyne Road, Broughty Ferry, Dundee DD5 1NY

Dundee College of Technology, Bell Street, Dundee DD1 1HG

Dunfermline College of Physical Education, Cramond Road North, Edinburgh EH4 6JD

Ealing College of Higher Education, St Mary's Road, Ealing, London W5 5RF

Early Music Centre, 62 Princedale Road, London W11 4NL

East of Scotland College of Agriculture, West Mains Road, Edinburgh EH9 3JG

East Sussex College of Higher Education, Hillbrow, 1 Denton Road, Eastbourne, East Sussex BN20 7SR

Edge Hill College of Higher Education, St Helens Road, Ormskirk, Lancashire L39 4QP

Edinburgh College of Art, Lauriston Place, Edinburgh EH3 9DF

Exeter College of Art and Design, Earl Richards Road North, Exeter EX2 6AS

F L Calder College of Education, Dowsefield Lane, Liverpool L18 3JJ

Falkirk College of Technology, Grangemouth Road, Falkirk FK2 9AD

Falmouth School of Art, 27 Woodlane, Falmouth, Cornwall TR11 4RA

Farnborough College of Technology, Boundary Road, Farnborough, Hampshire GU14 6SB

Foresthill College, Westburn Road, Aberdeen AB9 2XS

Gateshead Technical College, Durham Road, Gateshead, Tyne and Wear NE9 5BN

Garnett College, Downshire House, Roehampton Lane, London SW15 4HR

Glasgow Central College of Commerce, 300 Cathedral Street, Glasgow G1 2TA

Glasgow College of Building and Printing, 60 North Hanover Street, Glasgow G1 2BP

Glasgow College of Food Technology, 230 Cathedral Street, Glasgow G1 2TG

Glasgow College of Technology, Cowcaddens Road, Glasgow G4 QBA

Glasgow Eye Infirmary, 3 Sandyford Place, Glasgow G3 7NB

Glasgow School of Art, 167 Renfrew Street, Glasgow G3 6RQ

Glasgow School of Occupational Therapy, 29 Sherbrooke Avenue, Glasgow G41 4ER

Gloucestershire College of Art and Design, Pittville, Cheltenham GL52 3JG

Goldsmiths College, New Cross, London SE14 6NW

Guildford County College of Technology, Stoke Park, Guildford, Surrey

Guildford School of Acting and Drama Dance Education, Bellairs Centre, Millbrook, Guildford, Surrey

Guildhall School of Music and Drama, Barbican, London EC2Y 8DT

Gwent College of Higher Education, Clarence Place, Newport, Gwent NPT 0UW

Halton College of Further Education, Kingsway, Widnes, Cheshire WA8 7QQ

Hammersmith and West London College, South Park Branch, Hugon Road, London SW6 3ES

Harlow Technical College, College Gate, The High, Harlow CM20 1LT

Harper Adams Agricultural College, Newport, Salop TF10 8NB

Harrow College of Technology and Art, Northwick Park, Harrow HA1 3TP

Henley College of Further Education, Henley Road, Bell Green, Coventry CV2 1ED

Hertfordshire College of Art and Design, Hatfield Road, St Albans, Hertfordshire AL1 3RS

Hertfordshire College of Building, St Peter's Road, St Albans, Hertfordshire AL1 3RX

Hertfordshire College of Higher Education, Wall Hall, Aldenham, Watford, Hertfordshire

Highbury Technical College, Cosham, Portsmouth PO6 2SA

Hull College of Higher Education, Queens Gardens, Hull HU1 3DH

Ilkley College, Wells Road, Ilkley, Yorkshire LS29 9RD

Inverness Technical College, Longman Road, Inverness

Ipswich Civic College, Rope Walk, Ipswich

Jew's College London, 11 Montagu Place, London W1H 8RH

Jordanhill College of Education, Southbrae Drive, Glasgow G13 1PP

Kent College for the Careers Service, College Road, Hextable, Swanley, Kent BR8 7RN

Kidderminster College of Further Education, Hoo Road, Kidderminster, Hereford and Worcester DY10 1LX

King Alfred's College, Winchester SO22 4NR

Kingston College of Further Education, Kingston Hall Road, Kingston-upon-Thames KT1 2AQ

Kirkcaldy Technical College, St Brydedale Avenue, Kirkcaldy KY1 1EX

La Sainte Union College of Higher Education, The Avenue, Southampton SO9 5HB

Lancashire College of Agriculture, Myerscough Hall, Bilsborrow, Preston PR3 0RY

Lincoln College of Technology, Cathedral Street, Lincoln LN2 5HQ

Liverpool College of Occupational Therapy, Victoria Road, Huyton, Liverpool L36 5SB

Llandrillo Technical College, Llandudno Road, Rhos on Sea, Colwyn Bay, Clwyd LL28 4HX

London Bible College, Green Lane, Northwood, Middlesex HA6 2UW

London College of Fashion, 20 John Prince's Street, London W1M 9HE

London College of Furniture, 41 Commercial Road, London E1 1LA

London College of Music, Great Marlborough Street, London W1V 2AS

London College of Printing, Elephant and Castle, London SE1 6SB

London Graduate School of Business Studies, Sussex Place, Regents Park, London NW1 4SA

London International Film School, 24 Shelton Street, London WC2H 9HP

London School of Occupational Therapy, 55 Eton Avenue, London NW3 3ET

Londonderry College of Technology, Strand Road, Londonderry BT48 7BY

Loughborough College of Art and Design, Radmoor, Loughborough LE11 3BT

Loughry College of Agriculture and Food Technology, Cookstown, Co Tyrone BT80 9AA

Luton College of Higher Education, Park Square, Luton, Bedfordshire LU1 3JU

Mabel Fletcher College, Sandown Road, Liverpool L15 4JB

Maidstone College of Art, Oakwood Park, Oakwood Road, Maidstone, Kent ME16 8AG

Manchester Business School, Booth Street West, Manchester M15 6PB

Manchester Royal Eye Hospital, Oxford Road, Manchester M13 9RD

Matthew Boulton Technical College, Sherlock Street, Birmingham B5 7DB

Medway and Maidstone College of Technology, Maidstone Road, Horsted, Chatham, Kent ME5 9UQ

Middleton St George College of Education, Near Darlington, County Durham DL2 1RQ

Midland Orthoptic Training School, Orthoptic Department, Birmingham and Midland Eye Hospital, Church Street, Birmingham B3 2NS

Mountview Theatre School, 104 Crouch Hill, London N8 9EA

Napier College of Commerce and Technology, Colinton Road, Edinburgh EH10 5DT

National Audio-Visual Aids Centre, 254-256 Belsize Road, London NW6 4BT

National Film School, Beaconsfield Film Studios, Station Road, Beaconsfield, Buckinghamshire HP9 1LG

National Hospitals College of Speech Sciences, 59 Portland Place, London W1N 3AJ

Nene College, Moulton Park, Northampton NN2 7AL

New College Durham, Framwellgate Moor Centre, Durham DH1 5ES

Newark Technical College, Chauntry Park, Newark, Nottinghamshire NG24 1PB

Newcastle Upon Tyne College of Arts and Technology, Maple Terrace, Newcastle Upon Tyne NE4 7SA

Norfolk College of Arts and Technology, Tennyson Avenue, King's Lynn PE30 2QW

North East Surrey College of Technology, Reigate Road, Ewell, Epsom, Surrey KT17 3DS

North East Wales Institute of Higher Education, Kelsterton College, Connah's Quay, Deeside, Clwyd, North Wales CH5 4BR

North Gloucestershire College of Technology, The Park, Cheltenham GL50 2RR

North Hertfordshire College, Cambridge Road, Hitchin, Hertfordshire SG4 0JD

North London School of Physiotherapy for the Visually Handicapped, Archway Wing, Whittington Hospital, Highgate Hill, London N19

North of Scotland College of Agriculture, 581 King Street, Aberdeen AB9 1UD

North Worcestershire College, School Drive, Stratford Road, Bromsgrove, Worcestershire B60 1PQ

Northern College of Speech and Drama, Thorn Bank, Werneth Hall Road, Werneth, Oldham OL8 1QZ

Norwich City College, Ipswich Road, Norwich NR2 2LJ

Norwich School of Art, St George Street, Norwich NR3 1BB

Oldham College of Technology, Rochdale Road, Oldham, Lancashire OL9 6AA

Oxford Air Training School, Oxford Airport, Kidlington, Oxford OX5 1RA

Padgate College of Higher Education, Fearnhead, Warrington, Cheshire WA2 0DB

Paisley College of Technology, High Street, Paisley, Renfrewshire PA1 2BE

Perth Technical College, Brahan Estate, Crieff Road, Perth PH1 2NX

Queen's College, 1 Park Drive, Glasgow G3 6LP

Queen Margaret College, Clerwood Terrace, Edinburgh EH12 8TS

Radbrook College, Radbrook, Shrewsbury SY3 9BL

Rambert School of Ballet, Mercury Theatre, Ladbroke Road, London W11 3NG

Redditch College of Further Education, Peakman Street, Redditch, Worcester B98 8DW

Reigate School of Art, Blackborough Road, Reigate, Surrey RH2 7DE

Richmond Upon Thames College, Egerton Road, Twickenham TW2 7SJ

Robert Gordon's Institute of Technology, Schoolhill, Aberdeen AB9 1FR

Roehampton Institute of Higher Education, Grove House, Roehampton Lane, London SW15 5PJ

Rose Bruford College of Speech and Drama, Lamorbey Park, Sidcup, Kent DA15 9DF

Royal Academy of Dancing, 48 Vicarage Crescent, London SW11 3LT

Royal Academy of Dramatic Art, 62–64 Gower Street, London WC1E 6ED

Royal Academy of Music, Marylebone Road, London NW1 5HT

Royal Agricultural College, Cirencester, Gloucester GL7 6JS

Royal College of Music, Prince Consort Road, South Kensington, London SW7 2BS

Royal College of Nursing, Henrietta Place, Cavendish Square, London W1M 0AB

Royal Military College of Science, Shrivenham, Swindon, Wiltshire SN6 8LA

Royal National College for the Blind, Albrighton Hall, Broad Oak, Near Shrewsbury SY4 3AQ

Royal Northern College of Music, 124 Oxford Road, Manchester M13 9RD

Royal Scottish Academy of Music and Drama, St George's Place, Glasgow G2 1BS

St Andrew's School of Occupational Therapy, St Andrew's Hospital, Northampton NN1 5DG

St Helens College of Technology, St Helens, Merseyside WA10 1PZ

College of St Hild and St Bede, University of Durham, Durham DH1 1SZ

St Katharine's College, Stand Park Road, Liverpool L16 9JD

College of St Mark and St John, Plymouth, Devon

St Martin's School of Art, 107 Charing Cross Road, London WC2H 0DU

St Mary's College, The Park, Cheltenham, Gloucestershire GL50 2RH

St Paul's College, Cheltenham, Gloucestershire GL50 4AZ

Salford College of Technology, Frederick Road, Salford, Lancashire M6 6PU

Salisbury College of Technology, Southampton Road, Salisbury, Wiltshire SP1 2LW

School for the Study of Disorders of Human Communication, 86 Blackfriars Road, London SE1 8HA

Scottish College of Textiles, Galashiels, Selkirkshire TD1 3HF

Seale-Hayne Agricultural College, Newton Abbot, Devon TQ12 6NQ

Shuttleworth Agricultural College, Biggleswade, Bedfordshire SG18 9DX

Slough College of Higher Education, Wellington Street, Slough SL1 1YG

South Devon Technical College, Torquay, Devon TQ2 5BY

South East London College, Lewisham Way, London SE4 1UT

South Glamorgan Area Health Authority (Teaching), Area Training Service, Carville, The Avenue, Llandaff, Cardiff CF5 2LP

South Glamorgan Institute of Higher Education, Wester Avenue, Llandaff, Cardiff CF5 2YB

South London College, Knights Hill, London SE27 0TX

South West London College, Tooting Broadway, London SW17 0TQ

Southall College of Technology, Beaconsfield Road, Southall, Middlesex UB1 1DP

Southampton College of Art, East Park Terrace, Southampton SO9 4WU

Southampton College of Technology, East Park Terrace, Southampton SO9 4WW

Southampton School of Navigation, Warsash, Southampton SO3 6Z1

Stevenage College, Monkswood Way, Stevenage, Hertfordshire SC1 1LA

Stockport College of Technology, Wellington Road, South Stockport SK1 3UQ

Swindon College, North Star Avenue, Swindon, Wiltshire SN1 1PT

Thomas Danby College, Czar Street, Leeds LS11 9PR

Thomson Foundation Television College, Kirkhill House, Newton Mearns, Glasgow G77 5RH

Thurrock Technical College, Woodview, Grays, Essex RM16 4YR

Trinity College of Music, 11–13 Mandeville Place, London W1M 6AQ

College of Librarianship Wales, Llanbadarn Fawr, Aberystwyth, Dyfed SY23 3AS

Waltham Forest College, Forest Road, London E17 4JB

Warley College of Technology, Crocketts Lane, Smethwick, Warley, West Midlands B66 3BU

Watford College, Water Lane, Watford, Hertfordshire WD1 3EZ

Webber Douglas Academy of Dramatic Art, 30–36 Clareville Street, London SW7 5AW

Welsh School of Occupational Therapy, Combined Training Institute, University Hospital of Wales, Heath Park, Cardiff CF4 4XW

West Glamorgan Institute of Higher Education, Mount Pleasant, Swansea SA1 6ED

West Glamorgan Institute of Higher Education, School of Art, Alexandra Road, Swansea SA1 5AS

West London Institute of Higher Education, Lancaster House, Borough Road, Isleworth, Middlesex TW7 5DU

West Midlands College of Higher Education, Gorway, Walsall, Staffordshire

West of Scotland Agricultural College, Auchincruive, Ayr KA6 5HW

West Surrey College of Art and Design, Falkner Road, The Hart, Farnham, Surrey GU9 7DS

West Sussex Institute of Higher Education, Upper Bognor Road, Bognor Regis, Sussex PO21 1HR

Westhill College, Selly Oak, Birmingham B29 6LL

Westminster College, Vincent Square, London SW1P 2PD

Wigan College of Technology, Parsons Walk, Wigan WN1 1RR

Willesden College of Technology, Denzil Road, London NW10 2XD

Wimbledon School of Art, Merton Hall Road, Wimbledon SW19 3QA

Winchester School of Art, Park Avenue, Winchester SO23 8DL

Worcester College of Higher Education, Henwick Grove, Worcester WR2 6AJ

Writtle Agricultural College, Writtle, Near Chelmsford CM1 3RR

ADDRESSES OF COLLEGES OF EDUCATION AND POLYTECHNIC DEPARTMENTS/FACULTIES OF EDUCATION

†England and Wales

Most colleges offer certificate courses and accept men and women applicants unless otherwise stated.

Key to symbols:

d34	=	BEd degree courses (3 and 4 denote 3 or 4 yrs)
h	=	DipHE courses
C	=	certificate courses
G	=	1 yr graduate courses
(CE)	=	Church of England
(RC)	=	Roman Catholic
(D)	=	colleges which provide non-residential day courses for local students

d3		G	**Avery Hill C**, Bexley Road, London SE9 2PQ
d34 h	C	G	**Bath CHE**, Newton Park, Bath BA2 9BN
d3			**Bedford CHE**, Lansdowne Road, Bedford MK40 2BZ
d34 h	C	G	**Bingley C**, Bingley, Yorkshire BD16 4AR
			Birmingham P:
d34	C		Anstey Dept of Physical Education, 625 Chester Road, Sutton Coldfield, West Midlands B73 5HZ (women only)
	C		Bordesley Dept of Teacher Education and Training, Camphill, Birmingham B11 1AR (D)
d34		G	Edgebaston Dept of Teacher Education, Westbourne Road, Edgbaston, Birmingham B15 3TN
d34 h	C		**Bishop Grosseteste C**, Lincoln, Lincolnshire LN1 3DY (CE)
d3 h		G	**Bradford C**, Great Horton Road, Bradford BD7 1AY
d34	C	G	**Bretton Hall C**, West Bretton, Wakefield, West Yorkshire WF4 4LG
d34 h	C	G	**Brighton P**, Faculty of Education Studies, Falmer, Brighton, Sussex BN1 9PH
d34	C	G	**Bristol P**, Faculty of Education, Redland Hill, Bristol BS6 6UZ
d3 h			**Buckinghamshire CHE**, Newland Park, Chalfont St Giles, Bucks HP8 4AD
d34 h		G	**Bulmershe CHE**, Bulmershe Court, Earley, Reading RG6 1HY
d34 h	C		**Chelmer IHE**, Sawyer Hill Lane, Brentwood, Essex CM15 9BT
d34	C		**Cardiff S of Home Economics**, UC, Cardiff, Llantrisant Road, Llandaff, Cardiff CF5 2YT
d34 h			**Charlotte Mason CE**, Ambleside, Cumbria LA22 9BB
d34		G	**Chester C**, Cheyney Road, Chester CH1 4BJ (CE)
d34 h	C	G	**Christ Church C**, North Holmes Road, Canterbury CT1 1QU (CE)
d34 h	C	G	**City of Liverpool CHE**, Liverpool Road, Prescot, Merseyside L34 1NP
d34 h	C	G	**City of Manchester CHE**, Hathersage Road, Manchester M13 0JA
d34	C	G	**College of All Saints**, London N17 8HR (CE)
d34 h		G	**Coventry CE**, Kirby Corner Road, Canley, Coventry CV4 8EE
d34 h		G	**Crewe and Alsager CHE**, Crewe CW1 1DU, or Alsager ST7 2HL
d34 h	C	G	**De La Salle C**, Hopwood Hall, Middleton, Manchester M24 3XH (RC)
d34 h	C	G	**Derby Lonsdale CHE**, Mickleover, Derby DE3 5GX
d34	C	G	**Doncaster Metropolitan IHE**, Dept of Teacher Education, High Melton, Doncaster DN5 7SZ

†England and Wales address list adapted from the list given in the information booklet *Summary of Teacher Training Courses* issued by the Central Register and Clearing House Ltd in which the procedure for entry to these institutions is described. Obtainable from Lund Humphries, The County Press, Drummond Road, Bradford BD8 8DH.

d34   C G **Dorset IHE**, Cranford Avenue, Weymouth, Dorset DT4 7LQ

d34   C G **East Sussex CHE**, Milnthorpe Court, Meads Road, Eastbourne BW20 7QD (physical education only) (women only)

d34 h C   **Eaton Hall CE**, East Retford, Nottinghamshire DN22 0PR

d34 h C G **Edge Hill CHE**, Ormskirk, Lancashire L39 4QP

d34   C   **F. L. Calder CE**, Dowsefield Lane, Liverpool L18 3JJ

d34   C G **Gloucestershire IHE:**
St Mary's C, The Park, Cheltenham, Gloucestershire GL50 2RH (CE) (women only)
St Paul's C, Swindon Road, Cheltenham, Gloucestershire GL50 4AZ (CE) (men only)

d34   C G **Goldsmiths' C**, Lewisham Way, New Cross, London SE14 6NW

d34 h C   **Gwent CHE**, College Crescent, Caerleon, Newport, Gwent NP6 1XJ

d34   C G **Hertfordshire CHE**, Wall Hall, Aldenham, Watford WD2 8AT

d4   G **Homerton C**, Cambridge CB2 2PH

d34   C   **Huddersfield P**, Dept of Education, Queensgate, Huddersfield HD1 3DH (D)

d34   C G **Hull CHE**, Faculty of Teacher Education and Applied Social Studies, Cottingham Road, Hull HU6 7RT

d34   **I. M. Marsh C of Physical Education**, Barkhill Road, Liverpool L17 6BD (women only)

d34 h C   **Ilkley C**, Wells Road, Ilkley, Yorkshire LS29 9RD

d34   C   **Kesteven CE**, Kesteven College, Stoke Rochford, Grantham, Lincolnshire

d34   C G **Keswick Hall CE**, Norwich NR4 6TL (CE)

d34   G **King Alfred's CHE**, Sparkford Road, Winchester SO22 4NR

d34   C G **Kingston P**, Gipsy Hill Centre, Division of Educational Studies, Kenry House, Kingston Hill, Kingston-upon-Thames, Surrey KT2 7LB

d34   C G **La Sainte Union CHE**, The Avenue, Southampton SO9 5MB (RC)

d34   C G **Leeds P**, S of Education, Beckett Park, Leeds LS6 3QS

d34   C G **Leicester P**, Scraptoft Campus, Leicester LE1 9SU

d34   C G **Liverpool IHE:**
Christ's C, Woolton Road, Liverpool L16 8ND (RC)
St Katherine's C, Stand Park Road, Liverpool L16 9JD (CE)
Notre Dame C, Mount Pleasant, Liverpool L3 5SP (RC)

d34 h C G **Madeley CE**, Madeley, nr Crewe, CW3 9HY

d34   C G **Manchester P**, Dept of Education, Chester Street, Manchester M1 5GD

d34   G **Manchester P**, Didsbury Faculty, Wilmslow Road, Manchester M20 8RR

d34   C G **Matlock CE**, Matlock, Derbyshire DE4 3FW

d34   **Middlesex P**, Resource Centre for Performing Arts, Trent Park, Cockfosters, nr Barnet, Hertfordshire EN4 0PT

d34 h C   **Nene C**, Moulton Park, Northampton NN2 7AL

d34   G **New College**, Darlington Road, Durham DH1 4SY

d34   C G **Newcastle upon Tyne P**, Faculty of Education and Librarianship, Northern Counties Precinct, Coach Lane, Newcastle upon Tyne NE7 7XA

d34 h C   **Newman C**, Genners Lane, Bartley Green, Birmingham B32 3NT (RC)

d34 h C   **Nonington C of Physical Education**, Nonington, Dover, Kent CT15 4HH

d34   C G **Normal CE**, Bangor, North Wales LL58 2DE

d3   G **North East London P**, Barking Precinct, Longbridge Road, Dagenham, Essex RM8 2AS (D)

d34 h   **North East Wales IHE**, Catrefle College, Cefn Road, Wrexham, Clwyd LL13 9NL

d34   C   **P of North London**, Prince of Wales Road, Kentish Town, London NW5 3LB (D)

d34 h C   **North Riding CE**, Filey Road, Scarborough, North Yorkshire YO11 3AZ

d34 h C G **North Worcestershire C**, Burcot Lane, Bromsgrove, Worcestershire B60 1PQ

d4   C   **Northumberland CHE**, Ponteland, Newcastle upon Tyne NE20 0AB

d34 h   G **Oxford P**, Faculty of Educational Studies, Headington, Oxford OX3 0BP

d34 h C G **Padgate CHE**, Fearnhead, Warrington, Cheshire WA2 0DB

d34 h C G **Philippa Fawcett and Furzedown CE**, Leigham Court Road, London SW16 2QD d34   G   **Portsmouth P**, Faculty of Educational Studies, Alexandra House, Museum Road, Portsmouth PO1 2QQ

d34 h C G   **Preston P**, S of Education and Humanities, Beck Road, Poulton-le-Fylde, Blackpool FY6 7AN

d34 h C G   **Ripon and York St John CHE**, The College, Lord Mayor's Walk, York YO3 7EX

d34 h C G   **Roehampton IHE:**
                Digby Stuart C, Roehampton Lane, London SW15 5PH (RC)
                Froebel Institute C, Grove House, Roehampton Lane, London SW15 5PJ
                Southlands C, Wimbledon Parkside, London SW19 5NN
                Whitelands C, West Hill, London SW15 3SN (CE)

d34   C G   **Rolle C**, Exmouth, Devon EX8 2AT (joint courses with Dartington C Arts)

d34   G   **C of St Hild and St Bede**, Durham DH1 1SZ (CE)

d34   C G   **C of St Mark and St John**, Derriford Road, Plymouth PL6 8BH (CE)

d34 h   G   **St Martin's CE**, Bowerham, Lancaster LA1 3JD (CE)

d34   C G   **St Mary's C**, Fenham, Newcastle upon Tyne NE4 9YH (RC)

d34 h C G   **St Mary's C**, Strawberry Hill, Twickenham, Middlesex TW1 4SX

d34   G   **Sheffield City P**, 36 Collegiate Crescent, Sheffield S10 2BP

d34   **Shoreditch C**, Cooper's Hill, Englefield Green, Egham, Surrey TW20 0JZ

d3   **Sidney Webb S of Education**, P of Central London, 9–12 Barrett Street, London W1M 6DE (D)

d34   G   **P of the South Bank**, Manor House, 58 Clapham Common Northside, London SW4 9RZ (G Home Economics only)

d34   C G   **South Glamorgan IHE**, Cyncoed, Cardiff CF2 6XD

d34 h C G   **Stockwell CE**, The Old Palace, Rochester Avenue, Bromley, Kent BR1 3DH

d34   C   **Sunderland P**, Faculty of Education, Ryhope Road, Sunderland, Tyne and Wear SR2 7EE

d34   C   **Teesside CE**, Flatts Lane, Normanby, Middlesbrough, Cleveland TS6 0QS (D)

d34 h C   **Thomas Huxley C**, Woodlands, Avenue, London W3 9DP (D)

d34 h C G   **Trent P**, Dept of Education, Clifton Hall, Clifton, Nottingham NG11 8NT

d34   G   **Trinity and All Saints' C**, Brownberrie Lane, Horsforth, Leeds LS18 5HD (RC)

d34 h C G   **Trinity C**, Carmarthen, Dyfed, South Wales SA31 3EP

d4   C   **Ulster C, Northern Ireland P**, Jordanstown, Newtonabbey, Co Antrim BT37 0QB

d3   h C   **P of Wales**, Faculty of Education, Buttrills Road, Barry CF6 6SE

d34 h C   **West Glamorgan IHE**, Townhill Road, Cockett, Swansea SA2 0UT

d34 h C G   **West London IHE**, Gordon House, 300 St Margaret's Road, Twickenham, Middlesex TW1 1PT

d34   G   **West Midlands CHE**, Conway, Walsall, West Midlands WS1 3BD

d34   C G   **West Sussex IHE**, College Lane, Chichester PO19 4PE

d34 h   **Westhill CE**, Hamilton Building, Weoley Park Road, Selly Oak, Birmingham B29 6LL

d4   G   **Westminster C**, North Hinksey, Oxford OX2 9AT

d34 h C   **Wolverhampton P**, Faculty of Education, Castlenew, Dudley, West Midlands DY1 4HR

d34   G   **Worcester CHE**, Henwick Grove, Worcester WR2 6AJ

Northern Ireland
The following colleges offer 3-yr teacher training courses, BEd and postgraduate courses:

Belfast   St Joseph's CE, Trench House, Belfast BT11 9GA
               St Mary's CE, Falls Road, Belfast BT12 6FE (women only)
               Stranmillis College, Stranmillis Road, Belfast BT9 5DY

Londonderry A 1-yr course for teachers of commercial, subjects is offered at Londonderry CT, Strand Road, Londonderry, BT48 7BY.

The Faculty of Education of the Northern Ireland P (see page 38) provides training for specialist teachers at certificate and degree level.

Scotland
3- and/or 4-yr teacher training courses; 4-yr BEd courses; and 1-yr postgraduate training courses (unless otherwise indicated) available at:

Aberdeen   Aberdeen CE, Hilton Place, Aberdeen AB9 1FA

Ayr   Craigie CE, Ayr KA8 0SR

Dundee   Dundee CE, Park Place, Dundee DD1 4HP

Edinburgh   Craiglockhart CE, Colinton Road, Edinburgh EH14 1DJ (no BEd course)
Dunfermline CPE, Cramond Road North, Edinburgh EH4 6JD (women only; no 1-yr postgraduate course)
Moray House CE, Holyrood Road, Edinburgh EH8 8AQ

Falkirk   Callendar Park CE, Falkirk, Stirlingshire FK1 1YS (also diploma, 3 yrs)

Glasgow   Jordanhill CE, Southbrae Drive, Glasgow G13 1PP
Notre Dame CE, Bearsden, Glasgow G61 4GA

Hamilton   Hamilton CE, Bothwell Road, Hamilton, Lanarkshire ML3 0BD

ADDRESSES OF RESIDENTIAL COLLEGES OF ADULT EDUCATION

Long-term colleges   The colleges listed below provide 1-yr and, where indicated, 2-yr courses in the subjects stated. Students entering the colleges are normally between 20 and 40 years of age. No formal educational qualifications are required: admission is by essay, interview, etc. Fees vary considerably but the tuition fee is likely to be about £200 a year and the cost of residence about £500 per year. Details must be obtained from the individual colleges.

Coleg Harlech, Harlech, Gwynedd, North Wales LL46 2PU   Courses in Economics, English and Welsh Literature and Welsh Language, Industrial Relations, Politics, History, Philosophy and Sociology and for University of Wales Diploma in General Studies (2 yrs). Residential Summer schools.

Co-operative College, Stanford Hall, Lough-borough, Leicestershire LE12 5QR   Courses in Economic, Political and Social Studies for Diploma awarded by the University of Nottingham (2 yrs); courses in Co-operative Management ranging from short seminars to 5-month courses of professional education; and courses in Co-operative Development Overseas of 3 to 9 months including Diploma of Loughborough University of Technology.

Fircroft College, Selly Oak, Birmingham B29 6LH Courses in Economics, English Language and Literature, Government, History, Industrial Relations, Law, Philosophy, Politics, Psychology, Sociology.

Hillcroft College, Surbiton, Surrey KT6 6DF Courses in Economics, English Language and Literature, History of Art, History of Western Civilisation, Mathematics, Political Ideas, Psychology, Social History, Social Policy, Sociology and for the CNAA Certificate (2 yrs). (Women only).

Newbattle Abbey College, Newbattle Road, Lothian, Scotland EH22 3LL Courses in Economics, English Literature, Government, History, Logic, Philosophy, Political Theory, Sociology, Trade Union Studies, Diploma in Liberal Studies (2 yrs). Easter and summer courses.

Plater College (Catholic Workers' College), Oxford OX3 0DT Courses in the social sciences with special reference to the social implications of Christianity: University of Oxford Special Diplomas in Social Studies and in Public and Social Administration; College Diploma in Theology and Sociology (2 yrs). Residential summer schools.

Ruskin College, Oxford OX1 2HE Courses, mainly for students from the trade union movement and its associates, in Development Studies, Economics, English, Industrial Relations, Modern History, Modern Languages, Political Theory and Institutions, Sociology, and for the University of Oxford Special Diploma in Social Studies and a Diploma in Applied Social Studies (2 yrs). Special scholarships for students from overseas.

Woodbrooke College, 1046 Bristol Road, Selly Oak, Birmingham B29 6LJ Courses in Quakerism, Bible Study, Modern Religious Thought, and International and Social Questions, also in preparation for lay Christian service in Britain and overseas. Bursaries available for members of the Society of Friends and others closely connected with the Society.

Short-term colleges Note: For a general description of the courses provided by these colleges see pages 39–40.

Alston Hall, Longridge, Preston PR3 3BP
Ashridge Management College, Berkhamsted, Hertfordshire HP4 1NS
Avoncroft College, Stoke Prior, nr Bromsgrove, Worcestershire B60 4JS
Beamish Hall Residential College for Adult Education, Stanley, Co Durham DH9 0RG
Belstead House, via Sprites Lane, nr Ipswich, Suffolk IP8 3NA
Brant Broughton House, Brant Broughton, Lincoln LN5 0SL
Braziers Adult College, Ipsden, Oxford OX9 6AN
Burton Manor, Burton, Neston, Wirral, Cheshire L64 5SJ

Burwell House, Burwell, Cambridge CB5 0BA
Coleg y Fro (YMCA College), Rhoose, South Glamorgan CF6 9ZS
Debden House, Debden Green, Loughton, Essex
Denman College, Marcham, nr Abingdon, Oxfordshire OX13 6NW (normally restricted to Women's Institute members)
Devon Centre for Further Education, Dartington College of Arts, Totnes, Devon TQ9 6EH
Dillington House, Ilminster, Somerset TA19 9DT
Dyffryn House, St Nicholas, nr Cardiff CF5 6SU
Easthampstead Park, Easthampstead Park Educational Centre, Wokingham, Berkshire RG11 3DF
Grantley Hall, Ripon, North Yorkshire HG4 3GT
Hawkwood College, Stroud, Gloucestershire GL6 7QW
The Hill Residential College, Pen-y-pound, Abergavenny, Gwent NP7 7RP
Holly Royde College, 58–62 Palatine Road, West Didsbury, Manchester M20 9JP
Horncastle Residential Centre, Mareham Road, Horncastle, Lincolnshire LN9 6BW
Kingsgate College, Convent Road, Broadstairs, Kent CT10 3PX
Knuston Hall, Irchester, Wellingborough, Northamptonshire NN9 7EU
Lancashire College of Adult Education, Southport Road, Chorley PR7 1NB
Maryland College for Adult Education, Woburn, Milton Keynes MK17 9JD
Missenden Abbey, Great Missenden, Buckinghamshire HP16 0BD
Moor Park College, Farnham, Surrey GU10 1QR
The Old Rectory, Fittleworth, Pulborough, Sussex RH20 1HU
Pendley Manor, Tring, Hertfordshire HP23 5QZ
Pendrell Hall, Codsall Wood, Wolverhampton WV8 1QP
Pyke House, Battle, Sussex TN33 0AN
Rewley House, Wellington Square, Oxford OX1 2JA
Roffey Park Management College, Horsham, Sussex RH12 4TD
Ruislip College, Duck's Hill Road, Northwood, Middlesex HA6 2SU
Spode House, Hawkesyard Priory, Rugeley, Staffordshire WS15 1PT
Stafford House, Hassocks, Sussex BN6 8QJ
Theobalds Park College, Waltham Cross, Hertfordshire
Urchfont Manor, nr Devizes, Wiltshire SN10 4RG
Wansfell College, Theydon Bois, Epping, Essex CM16 7LF
Wedgwood Memorial College, Barlaston, Stoke-on-Trent, Staffordshire ST12 9DG
West Dean College, West Dean, Chichester, Sussex PO18 0QZ
Westham Adult Residential College, Barford, Warwick CV35 8DP
Wrea Head College, Scalby, nr Scarborough, North Yorkshire YO13 0PB

ADDRESSES OF NATIONAL AND PROFESSIONAL BODIES

England and Wales
Art and Design Admissions Registry, 16 Albion Place, Maidstone, Kent ME14 5DE
Association of Certified Accountants, 29 Lincoln's Inn Fields, London WC2
Association of Dispensing Opticians, 22 Nottingham Place, London W1M 4AT
Association of Medical Secretaries, Tavistock House South, Tavistock Square, London WC1H 9LN

Association of Professions for the Mentally Handicapped, 126 Albert Street, London NW1 7NF
Baptist Union of Great Britain and Ireland, The Baptist Church House, 4 Southampton Row, London WC1B 4AB
British Association of Occupational Therapists, 20 Rede Place, Bayswater, London W2 4TU
British Association of Social Workers, 16 Kent Street, Birmingham B5 6RD

British Broadcasting Corporation (BBC), Broadcasting House, Portland Place, London W1A 2AA

British Computer Society, 29 Portland Place, London W1N 4AP

British Dietetic Association, 305 Daimler House, Paradise Street, Birmingham B1 2BJ

British Examining Board in Occupational Hygiene, Medical Department, Associated Octel Ltd, Ellesmere Port, Wirral, Merseyside L65 4HF

British Institute of Management, Management House, Parker Street, London WC2B 5PT

British Institute of Surgical Technicians, 21 Tothill Street, London SW1H 9LL

British Optical Association, 65 Brook Street, London W1Y 2DT

British Orthopaedic Association, 47 Lincoln's Inn Fields, London WC2A 3PN

British Orthoptic Society, Tavistock House North, Tavistock Square, London WC1H 9JB

British Postgraduate Medical Federation, 33 Millman Street, London WC1N 3EJ

British Psychological Society, St Andrews House, 48 Princess Road East, Leicester LE1 7DR

British School of Osteopathy, 16 Buckingham Gate, London SW1E 6LB

British Theatre Association, 9–10 Fitzroy Square, London W1P 6AE

British Thoracic and Tuberculosis Association, 30 Britten Street, London SW3 6NN

Careers Service Training Committee of the Local Government Training Board, 8 The Arndale Centre, Luton LU1 2TS

Central Council for Education and Training in Social Work, Central Office, Derbyshire House, St Chad's Street, London WC1H 8AE

Central Midwives Board for England and Wales, 39 Harrington Gardens, London SW7 4JY

Chartered Institute of Public Finance and Accountancy, 1 Buckingham Place, London SW1E 6HS

Chartered Institute of Transport, 80 Portland Place, London W1N 4DP

Chartered Institution of Building Services, 49 Cadogan Square, London SW1X 0JB

Chartered Insurance Institute, The Hall, 20 Aldermanbury, London EC2V 7HY

Chartered Land Agents Society, 29 Lincoln's Inn Fields, London WC2A 3ED

Chartered Society of Physiotherapy, 14 Bedford Row, London WC1R 4ED

Church of England Advisory Council for the Church's Ministry, Church House, Westminster, London SW1P 3NZ

City and Guilds of London Institute, 76 Portland Place, London W1N 4AA

Civil Aviation Authority, Shell Mex House, Strand, London WC2R 0DP

Clearing House for Postgraduate Courses in Art Education, The Manor House, Heather, Leicestershire LE6 1QP

Clothing Institute, Albert Road, London NW4

College of Radiographers, 14 Upper Wimpole Street, London W1M 8BN

College of Speech Therapists, Harold Poster House, 6 Lechmere Road, London NW2 5BU

Committee of Directors of Polytechnics, 204 Albany Street, Regent's Park, London NW1 4AA

Conjoint Board of the Royal College of Physicians of London and the Royal College of Surgeons of England, Examination Hall, 8 Queen Square, London WC1N 3AR

Council for Educational Technology in the United Kingdom, 3 Devonshire Street, London W1N 2BA

Council for the Education and Training of Health Visitors, Clifton House, Euston Road, London NW1 2RS

Council for National Academic Awards, 344–354 Gray's Inn Road, London WC1X 8BP

Council for Professions Supplementary to Medicine, York House, Westminster Bridge Road, London SE1 7UH

Council of Engineering Institutions, 2 Little Smith Street, London SW1P 3DL

Constituent Members:

Royal Aeronautical Society, 4 Hamilton Place, London W1V 0BQ

Institution of Chemical Engineers, 165–171 Railway Terrace, Rugby CV21 3HQ

Institution of Civil Engineers, 1–7 Great George Street, London SW1P 3AA

Institution of Electrical Engineers, Savoy Place, London WC2 0BL

Institution of Electronic and Radio Engineers, 8–9 Bedford Square, London WC1B 3RG

Institute of Fuel, 18 Devonshire Street, Portland Place, London W1N 2AU

Institution of Gas Engineers, 17 Grosvenor Crescent, London SW1X 7ES

Institute of Marine Engineers, 76 Mark Lane, London EC3R 7JN

Institution of Mechanical Engineers, 1 Birdcage Walk, London SW1H 9JJ

Institution of Metallurgists, Northway House, High Road, London N20 9LW

Institution of Mining Engineers, Hobart House, Grosvenor Place, London SW1X 7AE

Institution of Mining and Metallurgy, 44 Portland Place, London W1N 4BR

Institution of Municipal Engineers, 25 Eccleston Square, London SW1V 1NX

Royal Institution of Naval Architects, 10 Upper Belgrave Street, London SW1X 8BQ

Institution of Production Engineers, Rochester House, 66 Little Ealing Lane, Northfields, London W5 4XX

Institution of Structural Engineers, 11 Upper Belgrave Street, London SW1X 8BH

Affiliate Members:

Institution of Highway Engineers, 3 Lygon Place, London SW1W 0JS

Institution of Nuclear Engineers, 1 Penerley Road, London SE6 2LQ

Council of Legal Education, 4 Gray's Inn Place, London WC1R 5DU

Department of Education and Science, Elizabeth House, 39 York Road, London SE1 7PH

Department of Health and Social Security, Alexander Fleming House, London SE1 6BY

English National Opera, (Theatre Design course) Camperdown House, Half Moon Passage, Aldgate, London E1

Faculty of Radiologists, c/o Royal College of Surgeons, Lincoln's Inn Fields, London WC2A 3PN

General Medical Council, Overseas Registration Division, 25 Gosfield Street, London W1P 8BP

General Nursing Council for England and Wales, 23 Portland Place, London W1A 1BA

General Optical Council, 41 Harley Street, London W1N 2DJ

HM Stationery Office, Atlantic House, Holborn, London WC1V 6HA

Hotel Catering and Institutional Management Association, 191 Trinity Road, London SW17 7HN

Incorporated Association of Architects and Surveyors, 24 Half Moon Street, London W1Y 8BT

Incorporated Law Society of Northern Ireland, Royal Courts of Justice, Belfast BT1 3JZ

Incorporated Society of Valuers and Auctioneers, 3 Cadogan Gate, London SW1X 0AS

Industrial Society, 48 Bryanston Square, London W1H 8AH

Institute of Administrative Management, 205 High Street, Beckenham, Kent BR3 1BA

Institute of Bankers, 10 Lombard Street, London EC3V 9AS

Institute of Biology, 41 Queen's Gate, London SW7 5HU

Institute of Brewing, 33 Clarges Street, London W1Y 8EE

Institute of Building, Englemere, Kings Ride, Ascot, Berkshire SL5 8BJ

Institute of Chartered Accountants in England and Wales, Chartered Accountants Hall, Moorgate Place, London EC2P 2BJ

Institute of Chartered Secretaries and Administrators, 16 Park Crescent, London W1N 4AH

Institute of Choreology, Highdown Tower, Littlehampton Road, Worthing, Sussex BN12 6PF

Institute of Cost and Management Accountants, 63 Portland Place, London W1N 4AB

Institute of Health Service Administrators, 75 Portland Place, London W1N 4AN

Institute of Information Scientists, 657 High Road, Tottenham, London N17 8AA

Institute of Landscape Arthitects, 12 Carlton House Terrace, London SW1Y 5AH

Institute of Linguists, 24a Highbury Grove, London N5 2EA

Institute of Marketing, Moor Hall, Cookham, Maidenhead, Berkshire SL6 9QH

Institute of Mathematics and its Application, Maitland House, Warrior Square, Southend-on-Sea SS1 2JY

Institute of Medical Laboratory Sciences, 12 Queen Anne Street, London W1M 0AU

Institute of Metal Finishing, 178 Goswell Road, London EC1V 7DU

Institute of Personnel Management, Central House, Upper Woburn Place, London WC1H 0HX

Institute of Physics, 47 Belgrave Square, London SW1X 8QX

Institute of Quantity Surveyors, 98 Gloucester Place, London W1H 4AT

Institute of Science Technology, 345 Gray's Inn Road, London WC1 8PX

Institute of Statisticians, 36 Churchgate Street, Bury St Edmunds, Suffolk IP33 1RD

Institution of Agricultural Engineers, West End Road, Silsoe, Bedfordshire MK45 4DU

Institution of Corrosion Science and Technology, 14 Belgrave Square, London SW1X 8PS

International Hospital Federation, 24 Nutford Place, London W1H 6AN

Joint Board of Clinical Nursing Studies, Adam House, 1 Fitzroy Square, London W1P 6DS

Law Society, 113 Chancery Lane, London WC2A 1PL

Library Association, 7 Ridgmount Street, London WC1E 7AE

Local Government Training Centre, 8 The Arndale Centre, Luton LU1 2TS

Methodist Church, Candidates' Secretary, Division of Ministries, 1 Central Buildings, Matthew Parker Street, London SW1H 9NH

Ministry of Overseas Development, Eland House, Stag Place, London SW1E 5DH

National Advice Centre, Council for Postgraduate Medical Education, 7 Marylebone Road, Park Crescent, London NW1 5HA

National Association of Teachers in Further and Higher Education, Hamilton House, Mabledon Place, London WC1H 9BH

National College of Rubber Technology, Polytechnic of North London, Holloway Road, London N7 8DB

National Committee for Audio-Visual Aids in Education, 33 Queen Anne Street, London W1M 0AL

National Council for the Training of Journalists, Harp House, 179 High Street, Epping, Essex CM16 4BG

National Institute of Adult Education, 35 Queen Anne Street, London W1M 0BL

Ophthalmic Nursing Board, 162 City Road, London EC1V 2PD

Pharmaceutical Society of Great Britain, 1 Lambeth High Street, London SE1 7JN

Plastics and Rubber Institute, 11 Hobart Place, London SW1W 0HL

Queen's Nursing Institute, 57 Lower Belgrave Street, London SW1W 0LR

Regional Advisory Council for Technological Education, London and Home Counties, Tavistock House, Tavistock Square, London WC1H 9LR

Royal College of General Practitioners, 14 Princes Gate, Hyde Park, London SW7 1PU

Royal College of Midwives, 15 Mansfield Street, London W1M 0BE

Royal College of Nursing of the United Kingdom, 1a Henrietta Place, Cavendish Square, London W1M 0AB

Royal College of Obstetricians and Gynaecologists, 27 Sussex Place, Regent's Park, London NW1 4RG

Royal College of Organists, Kensington Gore, London SW7 2QS

Royal College of Pathologists, 2 Carlton House Terrace, London SW1Y 5AF

Royal College of Physicians of London, St Andrews Place, Regent's Park, London NW1 4LE

Royal College of Psychiatrists, 17 Belgrave Square, London SW1W 0BU

Royal College of Radiologists, 28 Portland Place, London W1N 4DE

Royal College of Surgeons of England, Lincoln's Inn Fields, London WC2A 3PN

Royal College of Veterinary Surgeons, 32 Belgrave Square, London SW1 8QP

Royal Institute of British Architects, 66 Portland Place, London W1N 4AD

Royal Institute of Chemistry, 30 Russell Square, London WC1B 5DT

Royal Institute of Public Administration, Hamilton House, Mabledon Place, London WC1H 9BP

Royal Institute of Public Health and Hygiene, 28 Portland Place, London W1N 4DE

Royal Institution of Chartered Surveyors, 12 Great George Street, Parliament Square, London SW1P 3AD

Royal National Institute for the Blind, 224 Great Portland Street, London W1N 6AA

Royal National Institute for the Deaf, 105 Gower Street, London WC1E 6AH

Royal Society of Arts, 18 Adam Street, Adelphi, London WC2N 6AJ

Royal Society of Health, 13 Grosvenor Place, London SW1X 7EN

Royal Town Planning Institute, 26 Portland Place, London W1N 4BE

Society of Apothecaries of London, Apothecaries Hall, Blackfriars Lane, London EC4V 6EJ

Society of Chiropodists, 8 Wimpole Street, London W1M 8BX

Society of Dyers and Colourists, 82 Gratton Road, Bradford BD1 2JB

Southern and Western Regional Association for the Blind, 32 Old Queen Street, London SW1H 9HB
Textile Institute, 10 Blackfriars Street, Manchester M3 5DR
Thomson Foundation, 16 Stratford Place, London W1A 4YG
United Reformed Church, Ministerial Training Committee, 86 Tavistock Place, London WC1H 9RT
Universities Central Council on Admissions, PO Box 28, Cheltenham GL50 1HY
Worshipful Company of Spectacle Makers, Apothecaries Hall, Blackfriars Lane, London EC4V 6EL

Scotland
Central Midwives Board for Scotland, 24 Dublin Street, Edinburgh EH1 3PU
Church of Scotland Offices, Department of Education, 121 George Street, Edinburgh EH2 4YN
Committee of Principals and Directors of Central Institutions, Robert Gordon's Institute of Technology, Schoolhill, Aberdeen AB9 1FR
Faculty of Advocates, 11 Parliament Square, Edinburgh EH1 1RF
General Nursing Council for Scotland, 5 Darnaway Street, Edinburgh EH3 6DP
General Teaching Council for Scotland, 5 Royal Terrace, Edinburgh EH7 5AF
Institute of Chartered Accountants of Scotland, 27 Queen Street, Edinburgh EH2 1LA
Law Society of Scotland, 26 Drumsheugh Gardens, Edinburgh EH3 7YR

Royal College of Physicians, Edinburgh, 9 Queen Street, Edinburgh EH2 1JQ
Royal College of Physicians and Surgeons, Glasgow, 242 St Vincent Street, Glasgow G2 5RJ
Royal College of Surgeons of Edinburgh, 18 Nicolson Street, Edinburgh EH8 9DW
Scottish Association of Opticians, 116 Blythswood Street, Glasgow G2 4JQ
Scottish Conjoint Board, 18 Nicolson Street, Edinburgh EH8 9DW
Scottish Education Department, St Andrew's House, Edinburgh EH1 3DB
Scottish Post Graduate Medical Federation, 8 Queen Street, Edinburgh EH2 1JE
Scottish Technical Education Council, 38 Queen Street, Glasgow G1 3DY

Ireland
Northern Ireland Council for Nurses and Midwives, 216 Belmont Road, Belfast BT4 2AT
Department of Education, Rathgael House, Balloo Road, Bangor, Co Down BT19 2QS
Honourable Society of the Inn of Court of Northern Ireland, Royal Courts of Justice, Belfast BT1 3JF
Incorporated Law Society of Northern Ireland, Royal Courts of Justice, Belfast BT1 3JZ
Institute of Chartered Accountants in Ireland, 7 Fitzwilliam Place, Dublin 2
Pharmaceutical Society of Northern Ireland, 73 University Street, Belfast BT7 1HL

BRITISH COUNCIL OFFICES OVERSEAS

(including Cultural Attachés' offices in countries where the British Council has no separate office)

Afghanistan
855/2 Shehabuddin Wat, Kabul (PO Box 453, Kabul)

Algeria
6 Avenue Souidani Boudjemaa, Algiers

Argentina
Marcelo T de Alvear 590–4°, Buenos Aires

Australia
Edgecliff Centre, 203–233 New South Head Road, Edgecliff (Sydney), NSW 2027

Austria
Schenkenstrasse 4, A-1010 Vienna

Bahrain
Al Mathaf Square, Manama (PO Box 452, Manama)

Bangladesh
5–7 Fuller Road, Ramna, Dacca 2 (PO Box 161, Ramna, Dacca 2)

Belgium and Luxembourg
Avenue Galilée-Galileilaan 5 (Boîte 10), 1030 Brussels

Botswana
Queens Road, Gaborone (PO Box 439, Gaborone)

Brazil
CRN 708/9–B13 Nos 1/3 (Caixa Postal 14–2336, 70.000 Brasilia DF)
Rua Otavio Corrêa 30, Rio de Janeiro 20.000 (Caixa Postal 2237–ZC–00, 20.000 Rio de Janeiro)
c/o Sociedade Brasileira de Cultura Inglesa, Rua General Carneiro 679, 80000 Curitiba (Pr) (Caixa Postal 505, 80.000 Curitiba (Pr))
Rua Nicaragua 112, Espinheiro, 50.000 Recife PE, Pernambuco (Caixa Postal 870, 50.000 Recife, Pernambuco)
c/o Sociedade Grasileira de Cultura Inglesa, Avenida Higienopolis 449, 01000 São Paulo SP (Caixa Postal 1604, 01000 São Paulo SP)

Cameroon
Les Galeries,
Rue de l'Intendence, Yaoundé (BP 818, Yaoundé)

Canada
c/o British High Commission,
80 Elgin Street, Ottawa K2P OK8

Chile
Eliodoro Yañez 832, Casilla 154–D, Santiago

Colombia
Calle 11 No 5–16, Bogotá 1 (Apartado Aeréo 4682 Bogotá 1)

Cyprus
3 Museum Street, Nicosia (PO Box 1995, Nicosia)

Czechoslovakia
Cultural Section,
Jungmannova 30, Prague 1
(British Embassy, c/o FCO (Prague)
King Charles Street, London SW1A 2AH)

Denmark
British Embassy,
Møntergade 1, 1116 Copenhagen K

Egypt
192 Sharia el Nil, Agouza, Cairo
(British Embassy, c/o FCO (Cairo),
King Charles Street, London SW1A 2AH)

Ethiopia
Artistic Building,
Adua Avenue, Addis Ababa
(PO Box 1043, Addis Ababa)

Finland
Eteläesplanadi 22A, 00130 Helsinki 13/06

France
9 Rue de Constantine, 75005 Paris

Federal Republic of Germany
Hahnenstrasse 6, 5 Cologne-1
Hardenbergstrasse 20, 1 Berlin-12
Harvestehuder Weg 8a, 2 Hamburg 13
Giselastrasse 10/1, 8 Munich 40

Ghana
Liberia Road, Accra (PO Box 771, Accra)
Claude Street, Kumasi (PO Box 1996, Kumasi)

Greece
17 Philikis Etairias, Kolonaki Square, Athens 138
(PO Box 488, Athens 138)
49 Proxenon Coromila Street, Salonica

Hong Kong
Easey Commercial Building (20th Floor),
253–261 Hennessy Road, Wan-Chai, Hong Kong

Hungary
British Embassy,
Harmincad Utca 6, Budapest 1051 (British Embassy, c/o FCO (Budapest), King Charles Street, London SW1A 2AH)

India
British High Commission, British Council Division,
21 Jor Bagh, New Delhi 110003
British High Commission, British Council Division,
French Bank Building, Hamji Street, Bombay 400001
British High Commission, British Council Division,
5 Shakespeare Sarani, Calcutta 700016
British High Commission, British Council Division,
150–A Anna Salai, Madras 600002

Indonesia
Jalan Imam Bonjol 57–59, Jakarta
Jalan Merdeka 43, Bandung (PO Box 5, Bandung)

Iran
Kh Ferdowsi 58 and 38, Teheran
(PO Box 1589, Teheran)
Kh Chaharbagh Bala 171, Isfahan
(PO Box 28, Isfahan)
Kh Kouhsangi 34, Meshed
(PO Box 13, Meshed)
Kh Zand 275, Shiraz
(PO Box 65, Shiraz)
Keyanian House,
Kuche Ahrab 148, 5th Quarter, Tabriz (PO Box 5, Tabriz)
Kh Aref 13, Amaniyeh, Ahwaz
(PO Box 896, Ahwaz)

Iraq
7/2/9 Wazariya, Baghdad (PO Box 298, Baghdad)

Israel
140 Hayarkon Street, Tel Aviv
(PO Box 3302, Tel Aviv)

Italy
Palazzo del Drago,
Via delle Quattro Fontane 20, 00184 Rome
British Institute,
Via Manzoni 38, 20121 Milan
British Institute,
Riviera di Chiaia 185, 80121 Naples

Japan
Iwanami Jimbo Cho Building,
1 Jimbo-cho 2-chome, Kanda, Chiyoda-ku, Tokyo 101
(c/o British Embassy, No 1 Ichiban-cho, Chiyoda-ku, Tokyo 102)
77 Kitashirakawa, Nishimachi, Sakyo-ku, Kyoto 606

Jordan
Amman Centre,
Jebel Amman, Amman (PO Box 634, Amman)

Kenya
Kenya Cultural Centre,
Harry Thuku Road, Nairobi
(PO Box 40751, Nairobi)
Oginga Odinga Road, Kisumu
(PO Box 454, Kisumu)
City House,
Nyerere Avenue, Mombasa
(PO Box 90590, Mombasa)

Korea
c/o British Embassy,
No 4 Jung-dong, Sudaemoon-Ku, Seoul 120

Kuwait
Al Arabi Street, Al Mansouriyah, Safat, Kuwait
(PO Box Safat 345, Kuwait)

Lebanon
Beit Fawzi Azar, Sharia Sidani, Sharia Sadat, Ras-Beirut, Beirut
(c/o British Embassy, Avenue de Paris, Ras-Beirut)

Lesotho
Hobson's Square, Maseru (PO Box 429, Maseru)

Malawi
Taurus House, Capital City, Lilongwe (PO Box 30222, Lilongwe 3)
Victoria Avenue, Blantyre (PO Box 456, Blantyre)

Malaysia
Jalan Bukit Aman, Kuala Lumpur 10–01
(PO Box 539, Kuala Lumpur 01–02, Peninsular Malaysia)
Wing-Onn Life Building, 1st Floor, 1 Chester Street, Kota Kinabalu, Sabah, East Malaysia
(PO Box 746, Sabah)
Bangunan Ang Cheng Ho, Jalan Tuangku Abdul Rahman, Kuching, Sarawak, East Malaysia (PO Box 615, Kuching, Sarawak)

Malta GC
Pjazza Indipendenza, Valletta

Mauritius
Royal Road, Rose Hill (PO Box 111, Rose Hill)

Mexico
Maestro Antonio Caso 127, Mexico 4 DF
(Apartado Postal 30–588, Mexico 4 DF)

Morocco
22 Avenue Moulay Youssef, Rabat (BP 427, Rabat)

Nepal
Kanti Path, Kathmandu
(PO Box 640, Kathmandu)

Netherlands
Keizersgracht 343, Amsterdam C

New Zealand
c/o British High Commission, Reserve Bank Building,

2 The Terrace, Wellington 1
(c/o British High Commission, PO Box 1812,
Wellington 1)

Nigeria
Western House,
8–10 Broad Street, Lagos
(PO Box 3702, Lagos)
36 Ogui Road, Enugu (PO Box 330, Enugu)
Dugbe, Ibadan (PMB 5103, Ibadan)
Hospital Road, Kaduna (PO Box 81, Kaduna)
Kofar Nasarawa, Kano City (PMB 3003, Kano)

Norway
Fridtjof Nansens Plass 5, Oslo 1

Oman
Mutrah, Oman (PO Box 1090, Muscat, Oman)

Pakistan
23, 87th Street, G 6/3, Islamabad (PO Box
1135, Islamabad)
50 Abdullah Haroon Road, Karachi 0409 (PKO
Box 146, Karachi 0409)
32 Mozang Road, Lahore (PO Box 88, Lahore)

Peru
Edificio Pacifico Washington, Piso 11, Natalio
Sánchez 125 (Cuadra 6, Av Arequipa) Lima 1
(Apartado 11114, Santa Beatriz, Lima)

Poland
Al Jerozolimskie 59, 00–697 Warsaw (British
Embassy c/o FCO (Warsaw) King Charles
Street, London SW1A 2AH)

Portugal
Rua de Luis Fernandes 3, Lisbon 2
Associaçião Luso-Britanica do Porto, Rua do
Breyner 155, Oporto
British Institute,
Rua Alexandre Herculano 34, Coimbra

Qatar
PO Box 2992, Doha, Qatar

Romania
British Embassy,
24 Strata Jules Michelet, Bucharest
(British Embassy, c/o FCO (Bucharest),
King Charles Street, London SW1A 2AH)

Saudi Arabia
Sharia Sitteen, Malaz, Riyadh
(PO Box 2701, Riyadh)
Jeddah (PO Box 3424, Jeddah)

Senegal
38 Boulevard de la République, Dakar
(c/o British Embassy, BP 6025, Dakar)

Sierra Leone
Tower Hill, Freetown (PO Box 124, Freetown)

Singapore
310 Cathay Building, Mount Sophia, Singapore
9

South Africa
c/o British Embassy,
170 Pine Street, Arcadia, Pretoria 0083
91 Parliament Street, Cape Town 8001

Soviet Union
British Embassy, Cultural Section,
Ulitsa Morisa Tereza 14, Moscow V-79
(c/o FCO (Moscow), King Charles Street,
London SW1A 2AH)

Spain
Calle Almagro 5, Madrid 4
British Institute,
Calle Amigo 83, Barcelona 6

Sri Lanka
British High Commission,
190 Galle Road, Colombo 3 (PO Box 753,
Colombo)

Sudan
45 Sharia Gama'a Khartoum (c/o British
Embassy, FCO (Khartoum), King Charles
Street, London SW1A 2AH)

Sweden
c/o British Embassy,
Skarpøgatan 6-8, S-115-27 Stockholm

Syria
c/o British Embassy,
Quarter Malki, 11 Mohammad Kurd Ali Street,
Imm. Kotob, Damascas

Tanzania
Independence Avenue, Dar es Salaam (PO Box
9100, Dar es Salaam)

Thailand
428 Rama 1 Road, Siam Square 2, Bangkok 5
(c/o British Embassy, Ploenchit Road,
Bangkok)

Tunisia
c/o British Embassy,
5 Place de la Victoire, Tunis

Turkey
Dr Mediha Eldem Sokak 32, Yenisehir, Ankara Y10
c/o The British Consulate-General,
Pera House, Tepebasi, Beyoglu, Istanbul (PK 436 Beyoglu, Instanbul)

United Arab Emirates
British Council Centre,
Nr Rashid Hospital, al Kamara, Dubai (PO Box 1636, Dubai)

United States
British Embassy,
3100 Massachusetts Avenue NW, Washington DC 20008

Venezuela
c/o British Embassy,
Edificio La Estancia Piso 12, Avenida La

Estancia No 10, Ciudad Comercial Tamanaco, Caracas (Apartado 1246, Caracas 101)

Yemen Arab Republic
Sheikh Sinan Abu Luhum Building, PO Box 2157, Sana'a

Yugoslavia
Generala Zdanova 34, 11000 Belgrade (Post Fah 248, Belgrade) Ilica 12/1, 41001 Zagreb

Zaire
c/o British Embassy, Kinshasa

Zambia
Heroes Place, Cairo Road, Lusaka (PO Box 3571, Lusaka)

BRITISH COUNCIL OFFICES AND CENTRE IN BRITAIN

Headquarters
10 Spring Gardens, London SW1A 2BN

Overseas Students Centre
11 Portland Place, London W1N 4EJ

England

Birmingham
Scottish Amicable House, 1 Cornwall Street, Birmingham B3 2RR

Brighton
69 Ship Street, Brighton BN1 1AE

Bristol
7 Priory Road, Tyndall's Park, Bristol BS8 1UA

Cambridge
Norwich Union Building, 10 Downing Street, Cambridge CB2 3DS

Canterbury
31 Oaten Hill, Canterbury CT1 3HZ

Exeter
New North Road, Exeter EX4 4JY

Hull
138 Cottingham Road, Hull HU6 7RY

Leeds
1 St Mark's Avenue, Leeds LS2 9BJ

Leicester
259 London Road, Leicester LE2 3BE

Liverpool
Bluecoat Chambers, School Lane, Liverpool L1 3BX

Manchester
139 Barlow Moor Road, West Didsbury, Manchester M20 8PS

Newcastle upon Tyne
89/91 Jesmond Road, Newcastle upon Tyne NE2 1PF

Nottingham
8 Sherwood Rise, Nottingham NG7 6JF

Oxford
1 Beaumont Place, Oxford OX1 2PJ

Reading
22 Queens Road, Reading RG1 4AJ

Sheffield
Beechfield House, 25 Broomhall Road, Sheffield S10 2DT

Southampton
60 The Avenue, Southampton SO9 1PG

Stratford upon Avon
Hall's Croft, Old Town, Stratford upon Avon CV37 6BG

Northern Ireland

Belfast
1 Chlorine Gardens, Belfast BT9 5DJ

Scotland

Aberdeen
Provost Ross's House, Shiprow, Aberdeen AB1 2BY

Dundee
40 Perth Road, Dundee DD1 4LN

Edinburgh
3 Bruntsfield Crescent, Edinburgh EH10 4HD

Glasgow
6 Belmont Crescent, Glasgow G12 8ES

Wales

Cardiff
46 Caroline Street, Cardiff CF1 1PT

Swansea
21 St Helen's Road, Swansea SA1 3DU

OVERSEAS STUDENTS OFFICES IN LONDON

Arab Republic of Egypt
The Cultural Affairs Office, ARE Embassy, 4 Chesterfield Gardens, London W1Y 8BR

Bahamas
Bahamas High Commission, 39 Pall Mall, London SW1Y 5JG

Bahrain
Bahrain State Embassy, 98 Gloucester Road, London SW7 4AU

Bangladesh
Education Officer, Bangladesh High Commission, 28 Queens Gate, London SW7 5JA

Barbados
Barbados High Commission, 6 Upper Belgrave Street, London SW1 8AZ

Belgium
Cultural Attaché, Belgian Embassy, 103 Eaton Square, London SW1W 9AB

Belize, Bermuda, British Solomon Islands, Falkland Islands, Gibraltar, St Helena, Virgin Islands, Western Pacific Islands
These countries have no Student Office in London and applications should be sent through the British Council, Technical Cooperation Training Department, 10 Spring Gardens, London SW1A 2BN

Botswana
Botswana High Commission, 162 Buckingham Palace Road, London SW1

Brunei
Brunei Government Agency, Students Unit, 153–156 Grand Buildings, Trafalgar Square, London WC2R 0AU

Bulgaria
The Cultural Attaché, Embassy of the People's Republic of Bulgaria, 12 Queens Gate Gardens, London SW7 5NA

Burma
The Cultural Attaché, Embassy of the Union of Burma, 19a Charles Street, London W1X 8ER

Cameroon
The Cultural Attaché, Cameroon Embassy, 84 Holland Park, London W11 3SB

Colombia
The Cultural Attaché, Colombian Embassy, Flat 3A, 3 Hans Crescent, London SW1

Cyprus
Student Liaison Officer, Cyprus High Commission, 93 Park Street, London W1Y 4ET

Denmark
Cultural Attaché, Royal Danish Embassy,
29 Pont Street, London SW1X 0BA

Eastern Caribbean
(Antigua, Dominica, Grenada, Montserrat, St
Kitts-Nevis-Anguilla, St Lucia, St Vincent):
The Students' Officer, Eastern Caribbean
Commission,
King's House, 10 Haymarket, London SW1
4DA

Ethiopia
Cultural Attaché, Ethiopian Embassy,
17 Princes Gate, London SW7 1PZ

Fiji
Education Officer, Fiji High Commission, 34
Hyde Park Gate, London SW7

The Gambia
The Gambia High Commission,
60 Ennismore Gardens, London SW7 1NH

Ghana
The Director, Education Unit, Ghana High
Commission, 38 Queens Gate, London SW7
5HT

Greece
Cultural Attaché, Greek Embassy,
1A Holland Park, London W11 3TP

Guyana
Student Officer, Guyana High Commission,
3 Palace Court, Bayswater Road, London W2
4LP

Honduras
Honduras Embassy,
48 George Street, London W1H 5RF

Hong Kong
Student Adviser, Hong Kong Government
Office,
6 Grafton Street, London W1X 3LB

Iceland
The Counsellor, Icelandic Embassy,
1 Eaton Terrace, London SW1W 8EY

India
The Student Welfare Officer, High
Commission of India, India House,
Aldwych, London WC2B 4MA

Indonesia
Cultural Attaché, Indonesian Embassy,
38 Grosvenor Square, London W1X 9AD

Iran
The Counsellor (Student Affairs), Embassy of
Iran, 14 Kensington Square, London W8
Consulate-General of Iran,
7 Booth Street, Manchester M2 4AB

Iraq
Cultural Attaché, Embassy of the Republic of
Iraq,
22 Queens Gate, London SW7 5JG

Israel
Cultural Department, Embassy of Israel,
2 Palace Green, London W8 4QB

Italy
Education Officer, Italian Institute,
39 Belgrave Square, London SW1X 8NX

Jamaica
The First Secretary, Students Office, High
Commission for Jamaica,
48 Grosvenor Street, London W1X 9FH

Japan
The Cultural Attaché, Embassy of Japan,
46 Grosvenor Street, London W1X 0BA

Jordan
The Third Secretary, Royal Jordanian
Embassy,
6 Upper Phillimore Gardens, London W8 7HB

Kenya
Assistant Education Attaché, Kenya High
Commission,
45 Portland Place, London W1N 4AS

Korea
Cultural Attaché, Korean Embassy,
4 Palace Gate, London W8 5NF

Kuwait
Cultural Attaché, Embassy of the State of
Kuwait,
40 Devonshire Street, London W1N 2AX

Lebanon
Cultural Attaché, Lebanese Embassy,
21 Kensington Palace Gardens, London W8
4QM

Lesotho
Lesotho High Commission,
16a St James's Street, London SW1A 1EU

Liberia
Student Adviser and Educational Attaché,
Embassy of Liberia,
21 Princes Gate, London SW7 1QB

Libya
Cultural Attaché, Libyan Embassy,
58 Princes Gate, London SW7 2PW

Luxembourg
First Secretary, Luxembourg Embassy,
27 Wilton Crescent, London SW1X 8SD

Malawi
Education Attaché, Malawi High Commission,
47 Great Cumberland Place, London W1H
8DB

Malaysia
Education Adviser, Malaysian Students'
Department,
44 Bryanston Square, London W1H 8AJ

Malta
Students' Liaison Officer, Malta High
Commission,
24 Haymarket, London SW1Y 5DJ

Mauritius
Education Attaché, Students Unit, Mauritius
High Commission,
32/33 Elvaston Place, London SW7

Mexico
Embassy of Mexico,
8 Halkin Street, London SW1X 7DW

Morocco
Cultural Attaché, Royal Moroccan Embassy,
49 Queens Gate Gardens, London SW7 5NE

Netherlands
First Secretary, Cultural Affairs, Royal
Netherlands Embassy,
38 Hyde Park Gate, London SW7 5DP

Nigeria
Education Section, Nigeria High Commission,
178–202 Great Portland Street, London W1
6BQ

Norway
Cultural Attaché, Royal Norwegian Embassy,
25 Belgrave Square, London SW1X 8QD

Pakistan
Education Adviser, Embassy of Pakistan,
Education Division, 35 Lowndes Square,
London SW1X 9JN

Philippines
Cultural Attaché, Philippine Embassy,
9a Palace Green, London W8 4QE

Qatar
Embassy of Qatar,
10 Reeves Mews, London W1Y 3PB

Saudi Arabia
Saudi Arabian Cultural Office,
23 Park Square East, London NW1 4LH

Sierra Leone
Education Attaché, Sierra Leone High
Commission,
33 Portland Place, London W1N 3AG

Singapore
Students' Department, Singapore High
Commission,
5 Chesham Street, London SW1 HN0

Somalia
First Secretary, Somali Embassy,
60 Portland Rise, London W1N 3DJ

Sri Lanka
Sri Lanka High Commission,
13 Hyde Park Gardens, London W2 2LX

Sudan
Cultural Attaché, Sudan Embassy,
3 Cleveland Row, St James's, London SW1A
1JB

Tanzania
The Director of Students, Tanzania High
Commission, 46 Hertford Street, London W1Y
7PF

Thailand
The Cultural Adviser, The Royal Thai
Embassy,
30 Queens Gate, London SW7 5JB

Trinidad and Tobago
Student Welfare Officer, High Commission for
Trinidad and Tobago,
42 Belgrave Square, London SW1X 8NT

Turkey
The Cultural Attaché, The Turkish Embassy,
43 Belgrave Square, London SW1X 8PA

Yemen
Cultural Attaché, Embassy of the People's
Democratic Republic of Yemen,
57 Cromwell Road, London SW7 2ED

Yugoslavia
The Cultural Attaché, Yugoslav Embassy,
5 Lexham Gardens, London W8 5JJ

Zambia
The Education Officer, Zambia High
Commission,
7–11 Cavendish Place, London W1N 0HB

EXAMINING BODIES FOR THE GENERAL CERTIFICATE OF EDUCATION

The bodies in England and Wales listed below conduct examinations for the General Certificate of Education. In Northern Ireland, the Northern Ireland Schools Examinations Council, Beechill House, 42 Beechill Road, Belfast BT8 4RS, conducts similar examinations (for a GCE). In Scotland, the Scottish Certificate of Education Examination Board, Ironmills Road, Dalkeith, Midlothian EH22 1BR, conducts examinations for the Scottish Certificate of Education.

It should be particularly noted that *only* the four bodies indicated by an asterisk (*) regularly conduct GCE examinations which can be taken *outside* the United Kingdom. The GCE examination of the University of Cambridge Local Examinations Syndicate can be taken overseas only at schools approved by the Syndicate (but see also note ‡ on page 296); and that of the Oxford Delegacy of Local Examinations only by pupils of a school at which a centre for the Oxford Local Examinations has been approved or by candidates normally resident in Malta. The GCE examinations of The Associated Examining Board and of the University of London are open to schools and private candidates overseas provided that the appropriate Overseas Authority makes application to the board or university for the recognition of a centre and is willing to accept responsibility for the local arrangements; in a Commonwealth or dependent country the authority is the government Education Department and in a foreign country Her Majesty's representative (or, in the case of The Associated Examining Board, a responsible educational establishment, e.g. universities, colleges or schools); a school wishing to enter candidates must first apply to the board/university through the Overseas Authority for recognition as a centre.

Of the other four bodies, the Southern Universities' Joint Board would be prepared to examine candidates in overseas centres, if requested to do so by a Ministry of Education or other responsible authority and subject to arrangements for the conduct of the examinations being approved by the Board. The remaining three bodies *may* very occasionally examine a candidate overseas, but only where there are exceptional circumstances.

The Scottish Certificate of Education examination may also be taken overseas, but only at a centre recognised as a Presenting Authority. The Northern Ireland GCE may only be taken overseas if special permission is obtained from the Secretary of the Schools Examinations Council.

To find out whether it is possible for him to take an examination in his own country, a student living outside the United Kingdom should enquire at the local office of the British Council (for a list, see pages 287–291), or, in the case of dependent territories, at the local Department of Education.

*The Associated Examining Board,
Wellington House, Station Road, Aldershot, Hampshire GU11 1BQ

*‡University of Cambridge Local Examinations Syndicate,
17 Harvey Road, Cambridge CB1 2EU

*University Entrance and School Examinations Council,
University of London, Senate House, London WC1E 7HU

Joint Matriculation Board of the Universities of Manchester, Liverpool, Leeds, Sheffield and Birmingham,
Manchester M15 6EU

*Oxford Delegacy of Local Examinations,
Ewert Place, Summertown, Oxford OX2 7BZ

Oxford and Cambridge Schools Examination Board,
Elsfield Way, Oxford OX2 8EP, or
10 Trumpington Street, Cambridge CB2 1QB

§Southern Universities' Joint Board for School Examinations,
Cotham Road, Bristol BS6 6DD
Welsh Joint Education Committee,
245 Western Avenue, Cardiff CF5 2YX
‡Also holds examinations at overseas centres by means of which university entrance requirements can be satisfied, namely: joint examinations for School Certificate and GCE and for Higher School Certificate and GCE, and (in collaboration with the responsible local authorities) for the Indian School Certificate, the Malaysia Certificate of Education and the Singapore–Cambridge GCE. (For foreign students an examination is also held, in association with the British Council, for the Certificate of Proficiency in English which is accepted by certain universities as evidence of the holder's knowledge of English. See also pages 45 and 49.)
§This is *not* a matriculating body and enquiries about admission to the universities of Bath, Bristol, Exeter, Reading, Southampton and Surrey should be sent direct to the Registrars of these universities.

ABBREVIATIONS USED IN THIS BOOK

ALUT	Associateship of Loughborough U of Technology
ARC	Agricultural Research Council
BA	Bachelor of Arts
BAO	Bachelor of Obstetrics
BArch	Bachelor of Architecture
BCh	Bachelor of Surgery
BCL	Bachelor of Civil Law
BCom	Bachelor of Commerce
BD	Bachelor of Divinity
BDS	Bachelor of Dental Surgery
BEd	Bachelor of Education
BEng	Bachelor of Engineering
BH	Bachelor of Humanities
BLib	Bachelor of Librarianship
BLing	Bachelor of Linguistics
BLitt	Bachelor of Letters
BLS	Bachelor of Library and Information Studies
BM	Bachelor of Medicine
BMedSc/BMedSci	Bachelor of Medical Science
BMus	Bachelor of Music
BPharm	Bachelor of Pharmacy
BPhil	Bachelor of Philosophy
BS	Bachelor of Surgery
BSc	Bachelor of Science
BSocSc/BSSc	Bachelor of Social Science
BTech	Bachelor of Technology
BTh	Bachelor of Theology
BVetMed	Bachelor of Veterinary Medicine
BVMS/BVM&S	Bachelor of Veterinary Medicine and Surgery
BVSc	Bachelor of Veterinary Science

CAg/AgC	College of Agriculture
CArt	College of Art
C Art and T	College of Art and Technology
CC	College of Commerce
CC and T	College of Commerce and Technology
CDS	College of Domestic Science
CE	College of Education
CEI	Council of Engineering Institutions
CFE	College of Further Education
ChB	Bachelor of Surgery
CHE	College of Higher Education
ChM	Master of Surgery
CNAA	Council for National Academic Awards
CPE	College of Physical Education
C Science	College of Science
CT	College of Technology
DChD	Doctor of Dental Surgery
DCL	Doctor of Civil Law
DD	Doctor of Divinity
DDS	Doctor of Dental Surgery
DDSc	Doctor of Dental Science
DEng	Doctor of Engineering
DIC	Diploma of Imperial College
DipHE	Diploma of Higher Education
DIS	Diploma in Industrial Studies
DLitt	Doctor of Letters
DM	Doctor of Medicine
DMS	Diploma in Management Studies
DMus	Doctor of Music
DPhil	Doctor of Philosophy
DPS	Diploma in Professional Studies
DSc	Doctor of Science
GCE	General Certificate of Education
A-level	Advanced level
O-level	Ordinary level
HNC	Higher National Certificate
HND	Higher National Diploma
ICWA	Institute of Cost and Works Accountants
IFE	Institute of Further Education
IHE	Institute of Higher Education
IMA	Institutional Management Association
IT	Institute of Technology
LLB	Bachelor of Laws
LLD	Doctor of Laws
LLM	Master of Laws
MA	Master of Arts
MAdmin	Master of Administrative Studies

MAO	Master of Obstetrics
MArch	Master of Architecture
MB	Bachelor of Medicine
MBA	Master of (or in) Business Administration
MBSc	Master in Business Science
MCh	Master of Surgery
MCIT	Membership of Cranfield Institute of Technology
MCom	Master of Commerce
MD	Doctor of Medicine
MDes	Master of Design
MDS	Master of Dental Surgery
MEd	Master of (or in) Education
MEng	Master of Engineering
MFA	Master of (or in) Fine Art
MLib	Master of Librarianship
MLitt	Master of Letters
MLS	Master of Library Studies
MMedSci	Master of Medical Science
MPharm	Master of Pharmacy
MPhil	Master of Philosophy
MS	Master of Surgery
MSc	Master of Science
MSocSc	Master of Social Science
MSW	Master of (or in) Social Work
MTech	Master of Technology
MTh/MTheol	Master of Theology
MVS	Master of Veterinary Surgery
MVSc	Master of Veterinary Science
ONC	Ordinary National Certificate
OND	Ordinary National Diploma
P	Polytechnic
PhD	Doctor of Philosophy
RIBA	Royal Institute of British Architects
RIC	Royal Institute of Chemistry
RICS	Royal Institution of Chartered Surveyors
RSM	Royal Schools of Music
S	Sandwich
S Art	School of Art
SCE	Scottish Certificate of Education
SRC	Science Research Council
SRN	State Registered Nurse
TEC HD	Technical Education Council Higher Diploma
TC	Technical College
UCCA	Universities Central Council on Admissions
VetMB	Bachelor of Veterinary Medicine

INDEX to pages 10–65 (introductory sections of the book)

Note: Only the more important references are indicated and references to individual universities etc, except the Open University, are not included.

INDEX to Directory of Subjects

The page numbers refer to the beginning of each section